Quantitative Methods in Practice

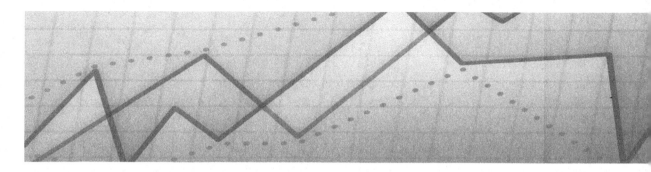

Quantitative Methods in Practice

READINGS FROM **PS**

EDITED BY DAVID A. ROCHEFORT

NORTHEASTERN UNIVERSITY

CQ PRESS

A Division of Congressional Quarterly Inc.

CQ Press
1255 22nd Street, NW, Suite 400
Washington, DC 20037

Phone: 202-729-1900; toll-free, 1-866-427-7737 (1-866-4CQ-PRESS)

Web: www.cqpress.com

Text credits can be found on page 266.

Cover design: McGaughy Design

♾ The paper used in this publication exceeds the requirements of the American National Standard for Information Sciences—Permanence of Paper for Printed Library Materials, ANSI Z39.48-1992.

Printed and bound in the United States of America

09 08 07 06 05   1 2 3 4 5

Library of Congress Cataloging-in-Publication Data

Quantitative methods in practice : readings from PS / edited by David A. Rochefort.
    p. cm.
  Includes bibliographical references.
  ISBN 1-933116-53-6 (alk. paper)
  1. Political science—Methodology. 2. Political science—Research. I. Rochefort, David
A. II. Title.

  JA71.5.Q36 2005
  320.072—dc22

                                      2005028634

Contents

Preface

Statistics is an applied discipline best learned through the analysis of real data gathered to answer real research questions. A typical statistics text, however, contains only brief illustrations of concepts and formulas in practice, leaving students and instructors to look elsewhere for an integrated perspective on quantitative methodology within the overall process of empirical inquiry. To fill this gap, for many years I have relied on handouts and packets of readings linking the techniques introduced in class with published research. This approach worked well, as far as it went, but neither my students nor I had the benefit of a single volume that combined readings with appropriate editorial commentary and discussion questions. *Quantitative Methods in Practice: Readings from* PS is intended to serve as that type of resource.

Among the varied items in my reading packets, the most useful studies were those taken from *PS: Political Science & Politics*. The association that produces the journal describes it this way:

> *PS* is the journal of record for the American Political Science Association. The journal provides coverage of the broad range of observations and information about the discipline. Its coverage has evolved since its introduction in 1968 to include critical analyses of contemporary political phenomena by authors working within their own subfields aimed at the informed, general reader. (American Political Science Association 2005)

For the purposes of my teaching, *PS* has proved to be a reliable source of high-quality, concise research studies relating theory and methods in a fashion suitable for a student audience. The articles span the diverse specialties of political science, while the format eschews jargon, ornate writing, and excessively "heavy" methodological and statistical presentations. The result is a virtual handbook for the examination of empirical practice in our discipline, pitched exactly at the right level of sophistication for students in undergraduate and graduate programs who are being introduced to political science research methodology for the first time. Given the appeal of *PS* as a source of material for the kind of volume I wanted to prepare, I was both delighted and grateful to receive permission from the American Political Science Association, and its publisher, Cambridge University Press, to base this book entirely on selections from *PS*.

The format of this book, which is explained at greater length in the introduction, is straightforward. A sequence of twenty readings has been compiled to display quantitative techniques of increasing complexity, ranging from simple descriptive statistics to multiple regression analysis. While not all relevant topics are dealt with in depth, the coverage is representative of the broad range of basic quantitative techniques currently in use by political science researchers. Each reading is supplemented by two features to spark students' interest and assist them in absorbing the content:

1. A brief overview highlights the subject matter and methodological approach of the research study, including its use of specific statistical measures.
2. A question set directs students to examine the study with respect to four overarching concerns: the need for the research; the way the study was carried out; the findings of the research; and the meaning, or implications, of the findings.

Although this book concentrates on the use of quantitative techniques, these editorial features also call attention to issues of research design, measurement, and data collection to help students put statistical applications into context. Working within this general framework, instructors and students will, of course, decide which elements of the readings merit special emphasis, depending on their own purposes and interests. For the convenience of the reader, a guide to the research methods and statis-

tical procedures contained in this volume as a whole can be found in the topical guide that follows this preface (pp. x–xi).

As part of the design for this book, I also sought brief afterwords from the authors of the original *PS* articles. The idea was to give these authors an opportunity to update their research findings where appropriate and to comment on the methodological choices and challenges they faced in their work. Nearly all of the authors agreed to my request enthusiastically. For the time they took to make these additional contributions, which enhance this book's value as an educational tool, I am indebted to these scholars.

The staff of CQ Press has been terrific to work with. I first put my inchoate ideas for this book before James Headley when he was visiting my campus. His supportive reaction helped me to overcome any initial uncertainties about the potential utility of a book like this for teachers and students in the field. Similarly, the encouragement I received from Brendan McCarthy and, most recently, Amanda Bednarz has been motivating. The talents of project editor Jennifer Campi, one of the best copy editors I have encountered in more than two decades of academic publishing, improved the clarity and grace of my contributions to this book. Finally, Charisse Kiino, acquisitions editor at CQ Press, played the pivotal role in shepherding this book through the approval process, in securing needed permissions, and in setting tough but realistic deadlines for my work. Her interest in the quality and timely production of this book was palpable at every stage.

The most intense period of writing and editing for this book happened to fall in the summer months of 2005, when my children, Alex, Hope, and Nathan, were on summer break from elementary and middle school. Alas, the project did limit my availability in sundry ways during this period, and I want to thank my children, along with my wife, Eileen, for their forbearance.

Teaching statistics is not supposed to be great fun, but I have always found it to be so. The course Quantitative Techniques became a standard part of my teaching load when I first arrived at Northeastern University in 1982.

By this time, I have lost count of the hundreds and hundreds of undergraduate and graduate students I have introduced to this subject. Of one thing I am certain, however, and that is the fact that my involvement with this course has made me a much better teacher, not only in quantitative techniques but also in my other courses. Teaching statistics has helped me to bring precision to my explanations, to engage my students actively, and to find ways of enlivening difficult subject matter. These are all good habits for any teacher to acquire. My students, for their part, have taught me much through their questioning intelligence, their openness, and their perseverance. It is to these students—past, present, and future—that I dedicate this book.

—*David A. Rochefort*

Reference

American Political Science Association. 2005. "PS Submission Guidelines." www.apsanet.org/content_4979.cfm.

Topical Guide

	1 • Undergraduate Research Methods Training	2 • When Osama Became Saddam	3 • Domestic Obstacles to International Affairs	4 • The Real Invisible Hand	5 • Interviewing Political Elites	6 • The Size of the Anti-Nazi Opposition in Germany	7 • The End of the Cold War	8 • Traditional Versus Technology-Aided Instruction	9 • How Americans Responded	10 • "The Most Liberal Senator"?
RESEARCH METHODS										
Survey Research	X						X		X	
Questionnaire Design	X	X			X				X	
Interviewing					X	X				
Sampling					X					
Panel Studies							X		X	
Original Data Collection	X	X			X	X	X	X	X	
Secondary Data Analysis		X	X	X						X
Experimental Design								X		
Combining Quantitative and Qualitative Data			X		X	X				
QUANTITATIVE TECHNIQUES										
Percentage Analysis	X	X	X		X	X	X		X	X
Graphs and Charts		X	X	X					X	X
Measures of Central Tendency and Dispersion				X				X	X	
Index Construction									X	
Confidence Intervals										X
Probability										X
Difference of Means								X	X	
Cross Tabulation	X					X	X			
Cross Tabulation with Controls										
Analysis of Variance										
Regression and/or Correlation							X			
Multiple Regression										
Logit/Probit Analysis, Logistic Regression										
Game Theory										

	11 • Political Views from Below	12 • Untangled Web	13 • Tuning In, Tuning Out	14 • Choosing Canada?	15 • Forecasting Presidential Nominations	16 • Monica Lewinsky's Contribution	17 • Zog for Albania, Edward for Estonia	18 • Mixing and Matching	19 • Moral Issues and Voter Decision Making	20 • Cooperation Through Threats
RESEARCH METHODS										
Survey Research	X			X					X	
Questionnaire Design	X								X	
Interviewing										
Sampling	X								X	
Panel Studies										
Original Data Collection	X	X		X		X		X	X	
Secondary Data Analysis			X	X	X	X	X		X	
Experimental Design										
Combining Quantitative and Qualitative Data										X
QUANTITATIVE TECHNIQUES										
Percentage Analysis	X	X	X	X	X	X			X	
Graphs and Charts	X		X	X			X		X	
Measures of Central Tendency and Dispersion								X		
Index Construction	X									
Confidence Intervals										
Probability									X	
Difference of Means										
Cross Tabulation	X	X						X		
Cross Tabulation with Controls		X								
Analysis of Variance	X									
Regression and/or Correlation			X							
Multiple Regression			X	X	X	X	X	X	X	
Logit/Probit Analysis, Logistic Regression			X	X				X	X	
Game Theory										X

From Knowledge to Practice in Quantitative Research

The British writer H. G. Wells, who is undergoing a resurgence of popularity following the 2005 movie *War of the Worlds,* maintained that "Statistical thinking will one day be as necessary a qualification for efficient citizenship as the ability to read and write" (quoted in Watson and Callingham 2003, 5–6). This is a splendid thought that, unfortunately, seems to be the minority sentiment. Negative quotations about statistics easily outnumber the positive quotations. Or have the negative statements just become more repeated and well known over time? This is an intriguing quantitative research question in and of itself as we ponder a sampling of familiar witticisms:

> There are three kinds of lies: lies, damned lies and statistics.
>
> —Benjamin Disraeli, as quoted by
> (and sometimes attributed to) Samuel Clemens

> There are two kinds of statistics, the kind you look up and the kind you make up.
>
> —Rex Stout

> Numbers are like people; torture them enough and they'll tell you anything.
> —Anonymous

> Figures don't lie, but liars figure.
>
> —Samuel Clemens

> Statistics are like lampposts; they are good to lean on but they don't shed much light.
>
> —Robert Storm-Petersen

Political science students have their own expressions of fear and loathing for "sadistics." Faced with required coursework in quantitative methods, many bob and weave deftly, putting it off until the end of their academic programs. By this time, however, much of the course's value as an integrated part of their training has been lost.

The purpose of this book is to provide a tool that can help political science students improve their mastery of—and comfort level with—quantitative research methods. To claim that students have the wrong impression of this formidable subject, that it really is a snap after all, would neither be true nor very credible. Statistics is a complex topic that can take years of study to achieve proficiency at the most advanced levels. Yet students enrolling in their first quantitative techniques course are able to acquire a foundation of competency rapidly, particularly if they begin by recognizing the proper connections between theory and practice, between calculations and reasoning, and between numbers and words. This book, used as a resource to supplement classroom instruction and a conventional statistics textbook, should go a long way toward reinforcing these vital connections.

Knowledge of a subject's evolution is helpful in orienting the beginning student, but few statistics texts devote much space to this topic. Accordingly, in the next two sections of this introduction, I provide a brief history of statistics and a discussion of the place of quantitative analysis within political science. Then I explain how learning to use statistics involves a hierarchy of skills, and I discuss the benefits that are gained by developing quantitative competency. I conclude the introduction with an explanation of the format used in this book for organizing readings with commentary and questions.

A Brief History of Statistics

Statistics is concerned with the description and analysis of numerical data. The most elementary statistical task is enumeration, or the simple counting of people, events, and other measurable phenomena. The practice of enumeration dates back to ancient times and remains crucial today, both in the maintenance of public records and in the beginning stages of many types of research. Although the earliest uses of statistics occurred thousands of years ago, statistics did not emerge as an organized branch of study and professional practice until the late 1600s. Statistics and government were closely linked in the early development of the field and that relationship has continued over time. Today statistics and related quantitative methods are indispensable tools for organizing and assessing empirical data in scientific and social scientific fields. Within the realm of public affairs, use of statistical evidence has also become commonplace as a means of supporting positions in political debate.

The keeping of statistics dates back to the ancient world in 2000 B.C., when the Babylonians started to maintain detailed tax records on clay tablets (Cohen 2005, chap. 1). Even earlier than this, around 3500 B.C., there is evidence the Egyptians tracked the prisoners and animals they had captured in battle. The Bible makes reference to official population counts, or censuses. The birth of Jesus in Bethlehem occurred in connection with what Cohen (2005, 29) calls "perhaps the most frequently cited census ever taken," as Joseph and Mary journeyed homeward in order to be registered by the Roman authorities.

Although census-taking for tax purposes was useful to governments at different times throughout history, the collection and analysis of a broader range of numerical information in the "promotion of sound, well-informed state policy" did not take place until the seventeenth century (Porter 1986, 18). In England, government officials began to use statistical data to gain insight into the operation of the economy, status of the military, and population mortality trends, which facilitated social monitoring and policymaking. The first example of a statistical analysis was a study by John Graunt in 1662 that tabulated mortality in London by sex and cause of death; Graunt also produced an estimate of the size of the city's population. Building on Graunt's work, Sir William Petty put forward the concept of "political arithmetic" in works published in the 1680s and 1690s to describe public administration and lawmaking based on numerical records pertaining to demography, natural resources, and the economic sectors of manufacturing and agriculture (Cohen 2005, 51–58; Porter 1986, 18–20).

In the New World, learned individuals like Benjamin Franklin and Thomas Jefferson were aware of this school of thought and were enthusiastic about applying numbers to political questions (Cohen 2005, chap. 4). Franklin took an avid interest in numerical measurement in the areas of trade and demographics. He used his quantitative understanding of population growth to argue for a policy of territorial expansion in North America, a view that ultimately contributed to his support for political independence (Houston 2003, 32). Franklin also advocated for inoculation of the population against smallpox, compiling data in the 1750s to demonstrate the safety and effectiveness of this preventive practice. After the Revolutionary War had been won and America's new political system was being implemented, Jefferson struggled with developing an equitable formula for apportionment of representation in Congress among the states. It was on the basis of Jefferson's astute numerical critique that President George Washington vetoed Congress's first proposed method for accomplishing this task. According to Cohen (2005, 94), "Franklin and Jefferson brought their fascination with numbers into the creation of the new republic." The use of numbers "as instruments of policy was becoming clear even to people who were not geniuses."

In the late 1700s and early 1800s, as the practice of "statecraft" grew more advanced, many countries instituted national censuses and adopted systematic methods of gathering public health and vital statistics (Cohen 2005, chaps. 5 and 6). By the mid-1800s, societies of professional statisticians had formed on the national and international levels. Adolphe Quetelet, a Belgian who is considered to be "the founder of quantitative social science" (Cohen 2005, 126), documented regularities in criminal behavior while raising new questions about the social determinants of crime. Quetelet applied principles of probability in his work together with an exploration of the concept of averages ("l'homme moyen"). He emphasized the importance of looking at the mean in conjunction with the dispersion of individual observations about the mean, a simple but valuable insight that can prevent errors of interpretation when comparing summary statistics for different groups (Stigler 1999, 63).

As social statisticians refined and extended their methods, some critics voiced concern (Cohen 2005, chap. 8). In the early 1800s, philosopher Thomas Carlyle accused the British government of misusing statistics to block social policies that could benefit the workingman. Like Carlyle, author Charles Dickens worried about the alienating effect of a statistical, rather than individualistic, perspective on social life. But, as Kruskal (1968, 218) has pointed out, the humanistic criticism of statistics often boils down to an objection to "*poor* statistical method, not of statistics per se" (italics in original). Reformers in Europe and the United States continued to amass statistics as a way to attract official attention for neglected problems and groups in society.

Numbers had largely achieved their "triumph" in society by the dawn of the twentieth century, at which point new computing machines began to greatly expand the amount and kinds of data that could be analyzed (Cohen 2005, 178–180). Growing use of statistics in government, business, journalism, medicine, and other professional and scientific fields consolidated this triumph. And an increasingly sophisticated research orientation in the social sciences went far toward establishing quantitative techniques as tools of analysis and advocacy.

Quantitative Methodology in Political Science

In an essay first published in 1923, Charles Merriam, who became president of the American Political Science Association (APSA) in 1924, assessed the latest advances in methods within his discipline (Merriam 1993). He called attention to the "tendency toward observation, survey, measurement" as a defining development in the contemporary study of political process. A major long-term impetus in this movement was the census and the "great masses of material" it produced for the observer and the analyst (139). Merriam also noted the increased borrowing of research concepts and techniques by political science from economics, psychology, and sociology, disciplines that were rapidly adopting standardized methods of observation and measurement. From Merriam's standpoint, political science was plainly in a transition marked by an eclectic, somewhat conflicting, combination of old and new methods. He wrote that "Even the most dogmatic [scholars] lapsed into statistics at times, and the most statistically inclined developed philosophical attitudes somewhat inconsistent with the general position of the statistician" (137).

The balance between historical and descriptive approaches and social scientific analysis in political science did not shift decisively toward the latter until the behavioral revolution of the post–World War II era. Dahl (1993) identifies six main forces as responsible for this transformation:

- Merriam's leadership as president of the APSA and chair of the Department of Political Science at the University of Chicago
- the influence of European scholars, some of them refugees to the United States during the 1930s, who favored a sociological approach to the study of politics
- World War II, which presented American political scientists with a new set of practical political and administrative problems for analysis
- the role of the Social Science Research Council— an independent nonprofit organization created in 1923 by the leaders of the APSA, the American Sociological Society, and other academic professional associations to promote interdisciplinary social science research on public issues—which identified the need for "the development of theory and improvement in methods" in studies on the political process
- the impact of survey research methods, which facilitated the study of the behavior and characteristics of individual voters
- the financial support of private foundations for interdisciplinary and behavioral research projects in political science

Under the influence of all these factors, Dahl writes, advocates of the behavioral approach increasingly came to represent the "establishment" in political science by the late 1950s.

The behavioral approach was not merely a reaction against traditional styles of legal, historical, and institutional analysis. It also embodied a faith in the scholarly insights that would be gained by embracing a "scientific empiricism" (Dahl 1993, 250). This concept required the formulation of theories and hypotheses subject to testing with data according to standardized procedures. Within such a framework, the proper use of statistics was paramount. One early advocate of the behavioral school, David Truman, stressed that the "political behavior orientation . . . aims at being quantitative wherever possible" (Dahl 1993, 257). In time, the influence of behavioralism could be detected across a spectrum of research interests within political science, resulting in seminal works on voting, public opinion, and comparative political culture, to name but a few areas of study (Almond 1996).

The use of specific statistical techniques has also evolved over the years (Beck 2000). In the 1950s and early 1960s, the primary quantitative method in political science was analysis of contingency tables or cross tabulations. Path analysis came into vogue by the late 1960s. And in the 1970s, multiple regression emerged as the dominant mode of analysis, a position it has retained to the present time. All of these methods are illustrated in the readings collected in this book. Increased maturity in the conduct of empirical research has also led political scientists to a greater concern with methodological issues that cut across quantitative and qualitative work. Although this volume concentrates mainly on quantitative analysis, the readings also emphasize the importance of sound methods of study design and data collection.

Today there are many indicators of the prominence of quantitative analysis within political science. Beck (2000) notes the development of a "cadre" of people within the discipline specializing in methodology, in addition to the emergence of academic political science journals having this focus. Within the work published in political science journals generally, quantitative approaches are also prevalent. Bennett, Barth, and Rutherford (2003) surveyed the methods used in articles published in a group of seven multimethod political science journals in the United States between 1975 and 2000. After classifying each article's methodology as formal modeling, statistics, or case studies, they found use of statistics to be the dominant approach. This finding was consistent over time and, as of 2000, true for all subfields of American politics, international relations, and comparative politics, although to a greater or lesser extent depending on the particular subfield. Since the use of statistics "can be combined with either formal models or case studies" (377), their centrality in contemporary political science research is unquestionable.

Yet it would be misleading to suggest the quantitative trend is universal within political science. Schwartz-Shea (2003) recently examined the requirements of fifty-seven political science doctoral programs in the United States. Among these programs, 18 percent did not have a quantitative/statistics methods requirement, while 16 percent offered students a choice between learning statistics or a language. Thies and Hogan (2005)—in the first reading of this book—studied the undergraduate curriculum in a sample of 303 political science departments and determined that only 64 percent had a required course in research design or methodology. An unexpected finding was that political science departments offering the doctoral degree were *less* likely than other departments to have such a requirement for undergraduates.

As this overview makes clear, students beginning their study of quantitative political science are joining a long intellectual tradition. There is a dual heritage rooted in the history of statistics as well as the movement to make political science more scientific. But, like most revolutions, the behavioral revolution in political science is incomplete, even as the discipline moves on to a variety of "postbehavioral" research topics and approaches (Goodin and Klingermann 1996). Not all political scientists today make use of, or are at ease interpreting, quantitative analysis, nor do all political science students receive training in these skills. Although the observation is much less true now than a generation ago, developing quantitative competency is still a way of entering a disciplinary vanguard of sorts in political science—or at least this is a notion I like to suggest to my students to encourage them in their work. Unlike fifty or sixty years ago, however, the challenge today is not to establish the relevance of quantitative techniques within political science, but rather to master quantitative methodology as one of several forms of rigorous empirical research. The readings in this book should help students recognize the circumstances best suited for this particular method of inquiry.

What Is Involved in Learning Quantitative Methods?

Why do political science students sometimes feel intimidated by the prospect of studying statistics? In my experience, political science majors arrive at college eager to learn about and debate public affairs, but without much exposure to empirical political research. Despite the behavioral revolution, the teaching of government at the high school level still is likely to be characterized by an emphasis on civics, or institutional history and description, rather than social scientific investigation. Given this preparation, students may be surprised to encounter a "math" course as part of their college political science curriculum.

Yet the identification of statistics with mathematics is a misperception. First, statistics does involve counting and calculation, but it is an applied subject that mostly avoids the difficult abstract concepts and derivations associated with mainstream mathematics. In fact, the type of thinking used in statistics and mathematics is sufficiently different that some statistics educators argue the two are distinct disciplines (Garfield 2003). Second, the calculations involved in statistics are straightforward, generally requiring no more than middle school math skills; even a relatively complicated formula, such as the correlation coefficient, can be broken down into a string of simple multiplications, divisions, additions, and subtractions. Third, although certain statistical procedures require elaborate mathematical manipulations, specialized computer programs are available to do the work.

The primary difficulties faced by political science students learning quantitative methodology are those of reasoning and interpretation, not arithmetic (Garfield 2003). It is easy to work out a numerical formula accurately without applying it correctly. Similarly, when a computer has generated error-free output, the challenge lies in programming the right procedure for the situation and then making sense of the statistical plethora received. Effective use of statistics requires a variety of (mostly nonmathematical) skills that lead to intelligent conclusions about data. But the context is always what makes the numbers meaningful (Moore and McCabe 2006, xv). The trick is recognizing the set of individual skills needed for this style of analysis and combining them successfully.

This perspective is consistent with a hierarchical concept of statistical learning. Watson and Callingham (2003, 20) observe that "Statistical literacy is not just knowing curriculum-based formulas and definitions but integrating these with an understanding of the increasingly sophisticated and often subtle settings within which statistical questions arise." Based on exploratory research with more than three thousand elementary and high school students in Australia, these authors propose six levels of skill needed for competency in statistics. The sequence begins with basic counting and calculating tasks, progresses to descriptive measures and probability, and culminates in analyses that involve more demanding calculations and complex research contexts. In the same way, Garfield (2003) writes about the stages of statistical learning in terms of an expanding ability to reason correctly about data, statistical measures, and uncertainty while recognizing how to avoid the most common pitfalls of faulty statistical reasoning.

These multilayered constructs from statistics education research are a good departure point for considering the learning objectives of the introductory quantitative methods course in political science. Although the sequencing of objectives listed in Figure 1 has an idiosyncratic element, reflecting my own syllabus and pedagogical approach, most course offerings in this area will be quite similar. The foundation of the pyramid is an understanding of the concept of variables and different levels of measurement. Next, students should become sensitive to observing how data are distributed while learning how to describe these distributions both statistically and graphically. This work provides the footing for probability and the branch of statistics concerned with making inferences from samples to populations. With these tools, including an understanding of the logic of hypothesis testing, the significance and strength of two-variable relationships can be examined. Finally, students are ready to be introduced to the multivariate model, including the process of statistical control, with a focus on the versatile technique of multiple regression.

So far, I have described only the structured topics appearing in a typical social science statistics text. Three other, less structured progressions must also take place as the student absorbs this hierarchical content. First is the ability to *verbalize* the use of statistics (Makar and Confrey 2005). This means communicating the purpose, process, and findings of statistical analysis in succinct language. At first, students will only be able to approach formulas mechanically, closely following the steps outlined in their book or in class. Over time, this imitative behavior should give way to a greater sense of independence and ownership, marked by the capability for describing data distributions and relationships and explaining the basis of statistical judgments. Success is achieved in the development of this skill when the same verbalizations can pass muster, allowing for appropriate nuance, with both those well versed and those untrained in political science quantitative methodology.

Next is the ability to *critique* the use of statistics. A key sign of methodological competency is that students become confident in assessing the way others employ quantitative techniques. At first, this skill is practiced in the classroom setting, on a peer level with other students; eventually, it should encompass published scholarship in the discipline. The kind of critical faculty I have in mind is concerned with all parts of research production, from the initial selection and measurement of variables to the interpretation of findings. It is also very important, as

Figure 1 • Learning Objectives for Political Science Quantitative Methods

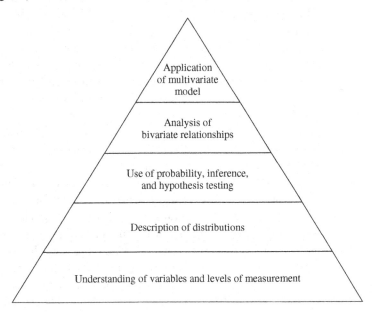

part of this critical skill, for students to situate statistical analysis in an overall process of research design and data collection. Students should become comfortable with the distinction between quantitative and qualitative work. This means they must be able to evaluate when one type of methodology will be superior for dealing with an actual research problem and when the two methodologies can be used in conjunction.

If it is true that "those who can, do," then the final progression in learning statistics must be the ability to *apply* quantitative analysis within one's own research. Such work begins modestly, with the exercises and assigned projects of the quantitative course. Ideally, students will proceed to recognize opportunities for integrating statistics into their paper writing in other political science courses. The last hurdle is carrying out original quantitative research, whether through a directed study, a senior thesis, or as part of a collaboration with a faculty member. As in so many other subjects, nothing can replace firsthand experience in developing an appreciation for the fine details,

the interrelationship of multiple skills and tasks, and the analytical power of quantitative research.

This book provides a good view of quantitative research in practice via a broad collection of published political science research. The methods illustrated in the book progress from simple to intermediate to advanced so that readings are available to reinforce the complete hierarchy of statistical content shown in Figure 1. At the same time, by carefully exploring these professional research products from the earliest stages of their statistical learning, students can accelerate acquisition of the communication, critical, and application capacities that define the competent quantitative analyst.

On the Benefits of Quantitative Competency

At this point, students may be thankful for a direct answer to the question, "How do I benefit from this quantitative competency, in practical terms?" Becoming part of a vibrant disciplinary tradition may have little appeal for political science majors with their sights set on law school or other professional fields that do not involve original political research. The answer for these students is that there are still concrete benefits to be gained.

Statistical Literacy

The term *statistical literacy* was introduced in the previous section to describe the achievement of competency in understanding and using statistics. Statistical literacy is a component of the broader concept of *numeracy,* which refers to a basic ability to work with numbers, parallel to the idea of literacy as a basic ability to read and to write (Watson and Callingham 2003). Statistical literacy is a pivotal skill because of its role in supporting effective learning in various academic subjects, as well as its utility in negotiating everyday life. Much of the information that members of society consume on a daily basis is statistical in nature, or can be critically scrutinized with the benefit of a statistical orientation. Through such books as *Innumeracy* (1988) and *A Mathematician Reads the Newspaper* (1995), mathematician John Allen Paulos has done more than any other writer to highlight the common misperceptions that result from popular ignorance of math and statistics. Paulos and like-minded authors (Shaffner 1999; Tal 2001) convincingly demonstrate the relevance of statistical thinking for interpreting a broad segment of the news, factual claims, and generalized observations that one encounters from the media and other sources. Knowledge of statistics also improves personal judgment in myriad situations involving assessment of risk and probability, among them decisions concerning financial investments, health care options, and purchases of consumer goods (Andersen and Harsell 2005). Not least, as H. G. Wells suggested, statistical literacy informs good citizenship by giving the public tools for appraising the conflicting information that inevitably arises in the rhetoric of politics and government (Watson and Callingham 2003).

Marketability

Political science students find they become much more marketable when they have quantitative skills. It's a pattern I've witnessed repeatedly. A background in statistics and research methods can open doors, whether it is in the selection of assistants by faculty members, the screening of applicants for internships, or the hiring of graduates for full-time employment. Even a basic ability to help with data preparation can distinguish a student who is "job ready" from one who is an unknown quantity from an employer's perspective. (Pardon the statistical pun.) And, rather than find themselves limited to low-level data processing, many students entering an organization on this basis eventually acquire larger responsibilities, after having proven their reliability and initiative. How many department heads in organizations began their careers as research analysts? The question as posed here is rhetorical, but I wish the numbers were available because it's a transition I've observed firsthand. Research by Andersen and Harsell (2005, 17) supports the idea that training in quantitative methods benefits students as members of the workforce: "Looked at quite instrumentally, such skills are particularly useful in the present economy, where post-college employment is increasingly competitive and numerous reports suggest that employers place high value on computing and analytical skills in prospective employees."

Professional Advantage

An understanding of statistics can offer valuable advantage to students in almost any professional field they choose to enter. Business? Statistics are essential in tracking product sales, income and expenses, resource management, and more. Public administration? Effective managers in the public sector are savvy about the diverse ways statistics can be used to measure activity and support decision making for planning, regulation, and service delivery. Law? It is only necessary to consult such books as *Statistics for Lawyers* (Finkelstein and Levin 2001) and *Statistical Science in the Courtroom* (Gastwirth 2000) to appreciate the immense role statistics has come to play in the operation of the legal system. Statistical analysis is a way of presenting, as well as evaluating, evidence. Statistical questions have been crucial in legal contests dealing with issues as diverse as employment discrimination, the death penalty, school finance, voting rights, and medical liability. A lawyer need not produce the complicated statistical studies that inform judgments in these matters. However, familiarity with quantitative logic and methods is necessary to make this research information intelligible.

A Guide to this Book

A last word is needed to explain the format of this book.

The twenty reading selections that follow touch upon a variety of topics in American government and politics, public administration, international affairs, and comparative politics. Three of these readings are concerned with curriculum and teaching issues in political science. Each reading selection includes three elements: a brief editorial commentary; the research article as originally published by the APSA journal *PS*; and discussion questions. Most include an afterword written by the author of the reading for the students using this book.

The opening commentary highlights each reading's content and methodology. By identifying elements of special interest, it serves to connect this book with the syllabus or textbook in a typical course on quantitative methods. (The chart on pp. x–xi also indicates at a glance how particular quantitative topics are distributed among the twenty reading selections.)

The discussion questions following the readings have been grouped under four headings. Each question category directs attention to a different ingredient in the mix of items that go into fashioning a political science quantitative research narrative.

Why Was This Research Needed?

An author needs to explain why his or her research was needed. This justification, which comes at or near the beginning of a research report, is concerned with scholarship on a topic, the need for information about a public issue, or both. Questions under this heading ask students to assess the effectiveness with which authors put their research into context through the use of literature reviews, descriptions of current events, and other means. Students are also asked to evaluate whether the

objectives of a project and its potential research contributions are clearly articulated.

How Was the Topic Studied?

The next step in the presentation of a research project is a description of study methods. Questions under this heading ask students to take note of sources of data and the fit between a study's methods and objectives. The relationship between a study's methodology and the approaches in previous research on the same subject is important, because differences of this type can account for divergent findings. Other basic but fundamental questions in understanding how a study was carried out include "What are the variables of interest?" and "How were the variables measured?"

What Are the Findings?

A core aspect of statistical competency is being able to understand a study's findings in relation to the author's stated research questions or hypotheses. Questions under this heading require students to examine, in detail, the use of particular quantitative procedures and to explain their suitability for analyzing data at designated levels of measurement. Students are asked to notice how authors present their findings with graphs and tables (or to suggest ways that such display formats could have conveyed findings more effectively than they were originally). One of the most useful challenges to put before students who have read a complex quantitative study is simply to ask them to summarize the findings concisely and in their own words.

What Do the Results Mean?

Questions under this last heading explore the broad implications of study findings, applying them to disciplinary, political, or social contexts. Students are also asked to explain how they would build upon published research with original studies of their own.

Finally, in the afterwords at the end of the reading selections, the authors write about the theoretical and methodological aspects of their work that they consider most important. It is a refreshing kind of communication, direct from scholar to student, in which professional political scientists discuss the motivations behind their research, the things they would have done differently in their projects if they had the chance, and their follow-up investigations. In a book filled with formal presentation of numbers and concepts, this section is more personal, marked at times by the kind of advice a novice researcher might hope to receive from a valued mentor. ■

References

Almond, Gabriel A. 1996. "Political Science: The History of the Discipline." In *A New Handbook of Political Science*, ed. Robert E. Goodin and Hans-Dieter Klingermann, 50–96. New York: Oxford University Press.

Andersen, Kristi, and Dana Michael Harsell. 2005. "Assessing the Impact of a Quantitative Skills Course for Undergraduates." *Journal of Political Science Education* 1 (January–April): 17–27.

Beck, Nathaniel L. 2000. "Political Methodology: A Welcoming Discipline." *Journal of the American Statistical Association* 95 (June): 651–654.

Bennett, Andrew, Aharon Barth, and Kenneth R. Rutherford. 2003. "Do We Preach What We Practice? A Survey of Methods in Political Science Journals and Curricula." *PS: Political Science & Politics* 36 (July): 373–386.

Cohen, I. Bernard. 2005. *The Triumph of Numbers: How Counting Shaped Modern Life*. New York: W. W. Norton.

Dahl, Robert A. 1993. "The Behavioral Approach in Political Science: Epitaph for a Monument to a Successful Protest." In *Discipline and History: Political Science in the United States*, ed. James Farr and Raymond Seidelman, 249–265. Ann Arbor: The University of Michigan Press.

Finkelstein, Michael, and Bruce Levin. 2001. *Statistics for Lawyers*. 2nd ed. New York: Springer.

Garfield, Joan B. 2003. "Assessing Statistical Reasoning." *Statistics Education Research Journal* 2 (May): 22–38.

Gastwirth, Joseph L., ed. 2000. *Statistical Science in the Courtroom*. New York: Springer.

Goodin, Robert E., and Hans-Dieter Klingermann. 1996. "Political Science: The Discipline." In *A New Handbook of Political Science*, ed. Robert E. Goodin and Hans-Dieter Klingermann, 3–49. New York: Oxford University Press.

Houston, Alan. 2003. *Population Politics: Benjamin Franklin and the Peopling of North America*. Working Paper 88, Center for Comparative Immigration Studies Seminar, University of California, San Diego.

Kruskal, William H. 1968. "Statistics: The Field." In *International Encyclopedia of the Social Sciences*, vol. 15, ed. David Sills, 206–224. New York: The Macmillan Company and the Free Press.

Makar, Katie, and Jere Confrey. 2005. "'Variation-Talk': Articulating Meaning in Statistics." *Statistics Education Research Journal* 4 (May): 27–54.

Merriam, Charles E. 1993. "Recent Advances in Political Methods." *In Discipline and History: Political Science in the United States*, ed. James Farr and Raymond Seidelman, 129–146. Ann Arbor: University of Michigan Press.

Moore, David S., and George P. McCabe. 2006. *Introduction to the Practice of Statistics*. 5th ed. New York: W. H. Freeman.

Paulos, John Allen. 1988. *Innumeracy: Mathematical Illiteracy and Its Consequences*. New York: Hill and Wang.

———. 1995. *A Mathematician Reads the Newspaper*. New York: Basic Books.

Porter, Theodore M. 1986. *The Rise of Statistical Thinking, 1820–1900*. Princeton: Princeton University Press.

Schwartz-Shea, Peregrine. 2003. "Is This the Curriculum We Want? Doctoral Requirements and Offerings in Methods and Methodology." *PS: Political Science & Politics* 36 (July): 379–386.

Shaffner, George. 1999. *The Arithmetic of Life*. New York: Ballantine Books.

Stigler, Stephen M. 1999. *Statistics on the Table: The History of Statistical Concepts and Methods*. Cambridge: Harvard University Press.

Tal, Joseph. 2001. *Reading Between the Numbers: Statistical Thinking in Everyday Life*. New York: McGraw-Hill.

Thies, Cameron G., and Robert E. Hogan. 2005. "The State of Undergraduate Research Methods Training in Political Science." *PS: Political Science & Politics* 38 (April): 293–297.

Watson, Jane, and Rosemary Callingham. 2003. "Statistical Literacy: A Complex Hierarchical Construct." *Statistics Education Research Journal* 2 (November): 3–23.

1

The State of Undergraduate Research Methods Training in Political Science

Cameron G. Thies and Robert E. Hogan

Political science, like other social sciences such as sociology and economics, is a research-based discipline. What this signifies is that advancement of knowledge—rather than simple recording of events or articulation of opinion—is the primary goal of the field. The means of producing this knowledge is empirical research, or the collection and analysis of data derived from political experience. Research of this kind broadens description of the political world, heightening our awareness of its people, ideas, and institutional processes. It also deepens our understanding of the connections between political variables by guiding the establishment of theories with verified explanatory power.

What better way to begin the readings in this volume than with a research study investigating the teaching of research methods in political science departments? All political science students conduct research. Any writing assignment that requires you to make even the briefest foray to the library (or the Internet) for information includes a research component. The question of interest in the following reading is whether undergraduate students are being taught the skills necessary to carry out original political science research systematically and in depth by means of courses devoted to that purpose. Does your own academic institution require such a course for undergraduate political science students? You may be surprised to see how much variability exists in course requirements of this type.

Cameron G. Thies and Robert E. Hogan attempt to answer a straightforward question using a research approach that is not complex. In this way, their study provides a suitable starting point for our examination of the organization and presentation of data within the practice of empirical research.

D ebates over methodology have long occupied a prominent role in political science and its various empirical subfields. Recently, these debates and occasional dialogues seem to have intensified. The Perestroika movement within APSA protested the perceived hegemony of rational choice and quantitative methods in journal publications and graduate training (Kasza 2001). Renewed attention has focused on the types of methodologies employed by studies published in the discipline's leading journals (Garand and Giles 2003; Bennett, Barth, and Rutherford 2003; Braumoeller 2003). The kinds of concerns over methodological diversity that motivate these studies also inform discussions about graduate training (Alvarez 1992; Dyer 1992; Schwartz-Shea 2003; Morrow 2003; Smith 2003).

Advocates of particular methodological approaches have even developed institutes designed to train graduate students and faculty members in methods that are thought to be under-represented in graduate curricula. The Consortium for Qualitative Research Methods (CQRM) offers an annual Training Institute at Arizona State University, as does the Institution for Social and Policy Studies at Yale University on field experiments. Both were preceded by the Inter-University Consortium for Political and Social Research's (ICPSR) summer program at the University of Michigan, launched as a result of the impact of the behavioral revolution on the social sciences. Methodologies associated with rational choice have also had their institutes, such as the now defunct Hoover Institution Summer Program in World Politics and the recently launched Empirical Implications of Theoretical Models (EITM) Summer Institutes. Qualitative Methods has now followed Political Methodology's lead to become the second APSA organized section specifically devoted to advancing methodology. Clearly, a great deal of intellectual effort is spent on ascertaining the relative status and merit of methodologies in the discipline and on attempting to alter the extent of their use through graduate training.

However, absent from this activity is any apparent concern for the impact of methodological debates on undergraduate education. There has always been discussion about the appropriate ways to teach undergraduate methods courses (Rodgers and Manrique 1992; McBride 1994, 1996), with *The Political Methodologist* serving as a reliable resource for advice about content and teaching strategies (Adams 2001; Clawson, Hoffman, and McCann 2001; Hojnacki 2001; Janda 2001; Lewis-Beck 2001; Stone 2001; Poggione 2001). There are also discussions of the use of the scientific method in substantive courses (Hewitt 2001; Segal 2002; Bennett 2002) and, to a lesser extent, essays explaining particular methods designed for undergraduate consumption (Odell 2001; Thies 2002). However, the high level of attention focused on the desirability of teaching different methods in graduate training and their presence in the discipline's journals has rarely been directed at our undergraduate programs.

Kim Quaile Hill's (2002) reflective essay "lamenting" the state of science education is an exception to the silence on undergraduate methods training. His essay reasons why the scientific method should be taught to political science undergraduates, and argues that undergraduates should learn what science is, how it compares to other forms of knowledge generation, what questions it can and cannot answer, and its procedures of inquiry. He also suggests that students become familiar with the state of theoretical and empirical knowledge in political science, the evolution of the scientific study of politics, the creative aspects of the research process, and how political science can be applied to the real world. We too believe that these are laudable goals for undergraduate education in political science. As Wahlke (1991, 48–49) notes in his report concerning the activities of APSA's Task Force on the Political Science Major, a liberal education requires a mastery of inquiry, including abstract, logical thinking and critical analysis, the understanding of numerical data, and science. Wahlke (1991, 51) reports that the Task Force recommends "that every political science major gain familiarity with the different assumptions, methods, and analytical approaches used by political scientists and by cognate disciplines (e.g., economics, history, psychology, law, and others)." In a recent *Chronicle of Higher Education* survey, 84% of respondents thought it was "important" or "very important" for colleges to teach students how to "discover more about the world through research" (Selingo 2003). An understanding of the variety of methodologies employed to make sense of the social and political world would serve all of our students well as they pursue a liberal education and move on to professional careers.

However, as Hill (2002, 116) notes, very few political science departments require systematic training in methodology, and none comes close to approaching his aforementioned goals for a curriculum. However, Hill's evidence is anecdotal in this regard. His conclusions are based on published degree requirements in the top 20 political science departments, along with those in "selected" lower-ranked departments, a review of syllabi in APSA's *Course Syllabi Collection,* conversations with "leading" political scientists, and the recollections of first-year graduate students in his home department concerning their own undergraduate training. While Hill's informal methodology matches our own intuition about the status of undergraduate training in research methods, we decided to undertake a more rigorous, systematic survey of the discipline.

Data and Methods

Data for this analysis come from a survey of departments identified by APSA as offering some type of undergraduate curriculum in political science. There are approximately 1,226 such programs, which APSA breaks down into categories based upon the highest degree offered: Ph.D., M.A., and B.A. programs in political science, B.A. programs in Social Science, and B.A. Combined programs (e.g., political science and history or geography). The survey was administered in late June and early July 2003, to 717 departments that had an email address listed in APSA's *Directory of Political Science Faculty: 2002–2004* (2002). After sending an initial email along with a follow-up message a few weeks later, we received 303 completed surveys for a response rate of 42.3%.

Recent discussions of email survey research suggest a wide variation in response rates. As Sills and Song (2002, 25) note, reported response rates vary between 0 and 70% across the literature in the social sciences. In a direct comparison between email, web, and postal mail, Smee and Brennan (2000) find that email had the

Table 1
Response Rates by Degree Program

Highest Degree	Sent	Responded	Response Rate
B.A. Combined Programs	113	45	39.8%
B.A. Social Science	61	19	31.1
B.A. Political Science	308	130	42.2
M.A. Political Science	115	47	40.9
Ph.D. Political Science	120	62	51.7
Overall	717	303	42.3

lowest response rate at 12.7% compared to 50% for postal mail and 61% percent for web-based questionnaires. Schaefer and Dillman (1998) found no significant difference between postal and email response rates, which in their study both came in at around 58%. As is the case with postal mail surveys, the characteristics of the sample and the subject of the study probably have significant effects on response rates. A recent APSA (2000) departmental survey using postal mail achieved a 41% response rate. Therefore, we believe that 42.3% is a respectable response rate given our choice of media, our potential respondents, and the subject of the study. The response rates are broken down by degree program in Table 1.

In addition to the general problem of response rates, the data produced by our current sample may not adequately represent the entire population of cases. Stanton (1998) and Couper (2000) point out that there are two categories of mismatches between the sample and the population to consider regarding representativeness. The first category is the proportion of the target population that can be reached via email. This should not pose a problem on its own as we can reach 58% of departments via email. However, the second category, differences in key characteristics between the proportion of the target population reached via email versus those who cannot be reached, may pose a problem for our study. There may be significant differences between the 509 departments that do not publish an email address with APSA and the 717 that do. The 509 non-email departments are likely to be very small in terms of faculty members, may

Table 2
Representativeness of the Sample Compared to the Universe by Degree Program

Highest Degree	Percent of Total Institutions Listed in APSA Directory	Percentage of Total Emails Sent	Percentage of Total Received
B.A. Combined Programs	22.3%	15.8%	14.9%
B.A. Social Science	17.6	8.5	6.3
B.A. Political Science	37.9	43.0	42.9
M.A. Political Science	12.0	16.0	15.5
Ph.D. Political Science	10.1	16.7	20.5
Overall	100%	100%	100%
N =	1,226	717	303

be more likely to be part of combined programs, and the lack of Internet savvy may reflect an underlying predisposition against the teaching of social science. Table 2 suggests that the B.A. Combined and B.A. Social Science programs are less likely to have email addresses. Our current sample more closely represents B.A., M.A., and Ph.D. programs in political science.

In order to avoid the problem of response inconsistency induced by technical issues regarding Internet-based surveys (Stanton 1998; Couper 2000), we included the text of the survey in the body of the email and asked respondents to simply "reply with history." We considered more complicated Internet survey techniques, but decided on a basic format that nearly all Internet users could access. The survey instrument itself is relatively short (see Appendix) and asked mostly for descriptive information about required courses on research design and research methods.

Findings

Table 3 reports the findings from the first question on the survey instrument regarding the presence of a required undergraduate course in research design or methodology. We are immediately struck by an interesting paradox: those institutions which have at their core the goal of producing original research and graduate students capable of such re-

search are also the least likely to require any training in research methods at the undergraduate level. Only 46.8% of Ph.D.-granting institutions require such training for undergraduates. That number rises to the highest percentage when one considers M.A.-granting institutions, of which 78.7% require a methods course of their undergraduates. B.A. programs in political science fall in between, with 60.8% having a methods requirement. Most interesting are the B.A. Combined and Social Science programs, which have methods requirement rates near that of the M.A. institutions at 77.8% and 73.7%, respectively.

What are we to make of these findings? First, it is clear that while Ph.D. institutions are in the business of producing knowledge, they are not necessarily in the business of teaching undergraduates their trade. This reinforces Hill's (2002) anecdotal findings and his general belief

Table 3
Percentage of Departments Having an Undergraduate Methods Requirement

Highest Degree	Percent	N =
B.A. Combined Programs	77.8	45
B.A. Social Science	73.7	19
B.A. Political Science	60.8	130
M.A. Political Science	78.7	47
Ph.D. Political Science	46.8	62
Overall	64.0	303

Table 4
Percentage of Departments Having an Undergraduate Research Design or Methods Course Requirement by Faculty Size and Students per Faculty Member

Faculty Size/Students Per Faculty Member	Percent	N =
Fewer than 10 Faculty	67.4	144
10 or More Faculty	61.0	159
Fewer than 750 Students per Faculty Member	58.9	163
750 or More Students per Faculty Member	70.0	140

that research methodology is not uniformly taught across the discipline. However, we were startled to see how much more likely M.A.- and B.A.-granting institutions were to require a methods course. It appears that institutions that focus on the goals of a liberal arts education may be more likely to see research methodology as a useful addition to the undergraduate curriculum. The differences between requirements in a B.A. in Political Science versus a Combined or Social Science program are stark as well. Interdisciplinary programs are much more likely to emphasize the unifying factor of methodology than traditional B.A. programs in political science. Hill's (2002) lament about social science teaching is particularly appropriate for political science B.A. programs. Finally, M.A. programmatic goals to prepare students for admission to Ph.D.-granting institutions may spill over into their undergraduate course requirements as indicated by their higher rate of methods course requirement.

Second, we thought that the decision to require an undergraduate research methods course might be a resource issue. We augmented our survey data with descriptive data from APSA on faculty size and the faculty to student ratio at each college or university for a quick comparison. Surprisingly, by either measure, schools with less faculty resources are more likely to require a research methods course, as reported in Table 4. Clearly, this is a resource issue, but not one of scarcity. Smaller programs (the B.A. and M.A. programs) are willing to devote faculty to teaching required research methods courses while larger programs (Ph.D. programs) are not. This may explain why much of the debate in the literature over research methodology coursework in political science is

confined to graduate courses (e.g., Burns 1990; Dyer 1992; Bennett, Barth, and Rutherford 2003; Schwartz-Shea 2003). It may be the case that faculty at research universities are concerned with what they teach their graduate students, not with what those students' backgrounds may have been at their undergraduate institutions, nor what their own undergraduates are learning about methodology.

We were also curious about the timing of the decision to adopt a required undergraduate methods course among departments that have such a requirement. Table 5 reports the results from question 3 of the survey. The majority of departments that have a required course adopted it at least a decade ago. For those departments that do not currently have a required methods course, we asked in question 2 of the survey whether they had any plans to adopt one. Table 6 indicates that the vast majority of those who do not have a requirement have no plans to adopt one in the near future. About one-quarter of respondents reported some general discussion about a future methods course, with only a little over 5% saying that specific plans were underway to require an undergraduate methods course.

Conclusion

The results of this survey are quite provocative given the current state of methodological debate in political science. We discuss at length in our journals, at our meetings, and among colleagues the state of graduate methods training in the discipline. Such debates revolve around what types of methodological training are most appropriate—not *whether* it is important. By contrast, little discussion is found in our journals about undergraduate methods training. What discussion one finds suggests that little if any such training exists. The results of this survey demonstrate that such a conclusion is unwarranted.

Table 5
Among Departments with a Research Design or Methods Course Requirement: How Many Years Ago Was It Adopted?

Highest Degree Offered	Less than 5	5 to 10	11 to 20	More than 20	Do Not Know	N =
B.A. Combined Programs	11.8	17.6	41.2	23.5	5.9	34
B.A. Social Science	21.4	35.7	14.3	28.6	0.0	14
B.A. Political Science	15.4	16.7	26.9	32.1	9.0	78
M.A. Political Science	10.8	16.2	40.5	21.6	10.8	37
Ph.D. Political Science	13.7	31.0	31.0	24.1	0.0	29
Overall	14.1	20.3	31.8	27.1	6.8	192

Table 6
Department Plans to Adopt a Required Methods Course if None in Place at This Time

Highest Degree	No Plans	General Talk	Specific Plans	N =
B.A. Combined Programs	66.7%	22.2%	11.1%	9
B.A. Social Science	60.0	40.0	0.0	5
B.A. Political Science	63.1	30.4	6.5	46
M.A. Political Science	50.0	40.0	10.0	10
Ph.D. Political Science	75.8	21.2	3.0	33
Overall	66.0	28.2	5.8	103

Undergraduates at Ph.D. institutions are the least likely to be required to take a course in methodology. Perhaps this accounts for Hill's skepticism about the state of science education in political science. The institutions that research faculty inhabit, and are most familiar with, are the least likely to educate their undergraduates in social science methodology. Yet, almost half of Ph.D.-granting institutions in our sample have some undergraduate methodology requirement. The numbers improve as one moves to B.A. programs in political science, yet a student is far more likely to receive required training in methodology at an M.A.-granting institution in political science, or in a Combined or Social Science B.A. program. Future study will be needed to determine why these differences exist. One possible explanation for the relative deficiency of methods training at research institutions is that the faculty already incorporates methodological issues into all of their political science classes, making a separate course unnecessary. Whatever the cause, the fact remains that method-

ological training is occurring, just not as frequently in the places that we have looked for it.

As a result, we believe that there is some room for optimism that political science undergraduates are receiving useful training in social science methodology. What is clear is that our knowledge generating departments must also begin to consider the importance of teaching undergraduates the methods of producing knowledge at their own institutions. This may require a reallocation of teaching resources in some cases, away from substantive coverage in all possible areas to giving students the ability to learn about the world on their own. If our colleagues at B.A. and M.A. institutions with limited faculty resources think it is important enough to require methodology in such high percentages, then perhaps it is time for Ph.D. institutions to reconsider their role in undergraduate education too. ■

References

Adams, Greg. 2001. "Teaching Undergraduate Methods." *Political Methodologist* 10 (fall): 2–4.

Alvarez, R. Michael, ed. 1992. "Methods Training: Student Perspectives." *Political Methodologist* 5 (spring): 2–9.

American Political Science Association. 2000. *APSA Survey of Political Science Departments: A Report for the 1999–2000 Academic Year.* Washington, D.C.: American Political Science Association.

———. 2002. *Directory of Political Science Faculty: 2002–2004,* 1st Edition. Washington, D.C.: American Political Science Association.

Bennett, Andrew, Aharon Barth, and Kenneth R. Rutherford. 2003. "Do We Preach What We Practice? A Survey of Methods in Political Science Journals and Curricula." *PS: Political Science and Politics* 36 (July): 373–378.

Bennett, D. Scott. 2002. "Teaching the Scientific Study of International Relations to Undergraduates." *PS: Political Science and Politics* 35 (March): 127–131.

Braumoeller, Bear F. 2003. "Perspectives on Pluralism." *PS: Political Science and Politics* 36 (July): 387–389.

Burns, Nancy Elizabeth. 1990. "Methodology in Graduate Political Science Programs." *Political Methodologist* 3 (winter): 9–10.

Clawson, Rosalee, Aaron Hoffman, and James A. McCann. 2001. "If We Only Knew Then What We Know Now: A Few Reflections on Teaching Undergraduate Quantitative Methods Courses." *Political Methodologist* 10 (fall): 4–5.

Couper, M. P. 2000. "Web Surveys: A Review of Issues and Approaches." *Public Opinion Quarterly* 64:464–494.

Dyer, James A. 1992. "A Survey of Political Science Research Methods Courses." *Political Methodologist* 5 (spring): 17–19.

Garand, James C., and Micheal W. Giles. 2003. "Journals in the Discipline: A Report on a New Survey of American Political Scientists." *PS: Political Science and Politics* 36 (April): 293–308.

Hewitt, J. Joseph. 2001. "Engaging International Data in the Classroom: Using the *ICB Interactive Data Library* to Teach Conflict and Crisis Analysis." *International Studies Perspectives* 2 (November): 371–383.

Hill, Kim Quaile. 2002. "The Lamentable State of Science Education in Political Science." *PS: Political Science and Politics* 35 (March): 113–116.

Hojnacki, Marie. 2001. "Teaching Undergraduates About the Quantitative Study of Politics." *Political Methodologist* 10 (fall): 5–6.

Janda, Kenneth. 2001. "Teaching Research Methods: The Best Job in the Department." *Political Methodologist* 10 (fall): 6–7.

Kasza, Gregory. 2001. "Perestroika: For an Ecumenical Science of Politics." *PS: Political Science and Politics* 34 (September): 597–599.

Lewis-Beck, Michael S. 2001. "Teaching Undergraduate Methods: Overcoming 'Stat' Anxiety." *Political Methodologist* 10 (fall): 7–9.

McBride, Allan. 1994. "Teaching Research Methods Using Appropriate Technology." *PS: Political Science and Politics* 27 (September): 553–557.

———. 1996. "Creating a Critical Thinking Learning Environment: Teaching Statistics to Social Science Undergraduates." *PS: Political Science and Politics* 29 (September): 517–521.

Morrow, James D. 2003. "Diversity through Specialization." *PS: Political Science and Politics* 36 (July): 391–393.

Odell, John S. 2001. "Case Study Methods and International Political Economy." *International Studies Perspectives* 2 (May): 161–176.

Poggione, Sarah. 2001. "Teaching Undergraduate Methods for the First Time." *Political Methodologist* 10 (fall): 10–11.

Rodgers, Pamela, and Cecilia Manrique. 1992. "The Dilemma of Teaching Political Science Research Methods: How Much Computers? How Much Statistics? How Much Methods?" *PS: Political Science and Politics* 25 (June): 234–237.

Schaefer, David R., and Don A. Dillman. 1998. "Development of a Standard E-mail Methodology: Results of an Experiment." *Public Opinion Quarterly* 62 (autumn): 378–397.

Schwartz-Shea, Peregrine. 2003. "Is This the Curriculum We Want? Doctoral Requirements and Offerings in Methods and Methodology." *PS: Political Science and Politics* 36 (July): 379–386.

Segal, Jeffrey. 2002. "Teaching the Scientific Study of Law and Courts to Undergraduates." *PS: Political Science and Politics* 35 (March): 117–119.

Selingo, Jeffrey. 2003. "What Americans Think About Higher Education." *Chronicle of Higher Education* (May 2): A10-A16.

Sills, Stephen J., and Chunyan Song. 2002. "Innovations in Survey Research: An Application of Web-Based Surveys." *Social Science Computer Review* 20 (spring): 22–29.

Smee, Alan, and Mike Brennan. 2000. "Electronic Surveys: A Comparison of E-mail, Web and Mail." ANZMAC 2000: Visionary Marketing for the 21st Century: Facing the Challenge, 1201–1204.

Smith, Rogers M. 2003. "Progress and Poverty in Political Science." *PS: Political Science and Politics* 36 (July): 395–396.

Stanton, J. M. 1998. "An Empirical Assessment of Data Collection Using the Internet." *Personnel Psychology* 51:709–726.

Stone, Peter. 2001. "Making the World Safe for Methods." *Political Methodologist* 10 (fall): 9–10.

Thies, Cameron G. 2002. "A Pragmatic Guide to Qualitative Historical Analysis in the Study of International Relations." *International Studies Perspectives* 3 (November): 351–372.

Wahlke, John C. 1991. "Liberal Learning and the Political Science Major: A Report to the Profession." *PS: Political Science and Politics* 24 (March): 48–60.

Appendix
Survey Instrument

Dear Colleague,

We are conducting a nation-wide survey of Political Science Departments to determine how prevalent research methods and design courses are in undergraduate education. Would you kindly take a minute or so to answer a few questions concerning the use of these courses by your department? If you could simply answer the four questions within the text below and then reply to this e-mail, we would greatly appreciate it. Feel free to provide any additional information that would help us better understand this aspect of your undergraduate program.

Please note that your participation in this survey is completely voluntary. We would be happy to share the results with you once they have been tabulated. If you would like to receive these findings, please indicate so at the end of the survey. Thank you for your assistance, we look forward to receiving your response.

Sincerely,

Cameron Thies and Robert Hogan
Department of Political Science
Louisiana State University

1. Does your department <u>require</u> undergraduate students majoring in political science to take a course (or courses) on research design and/or research methods? (Please choose only one of the following)

   a. _____ Yes. **Please name the course (or courses) and briefly describe the content.**

   b. _____ No course such as this is required, but these topics are covered in another required course (e.g., *Introduction to Political Science*). **Please name the course (or courses) and briefly describe the content:**

   c. _____ No such course is required as part of the political science major.

2. IF YOU ANSWERED **NO** TO QUESTION #1, does your department have any plans to adopt such a requirement? (Please choose only one of the following)

   a. _____ No plans at this time.

   b. _____ No specific plans, but some general discussion about adopting such a requirement.

   c. _____ Yes, specific plans are underway. **When will this be implemented and what is the course to be adopted?**

3. IF YOU ANSWERED **YES** TO QUESTION #1, when was this course requirement adopted?

   a. _____ Less than 5 years ago.

   b. _____ 5 to 10 years ago.

   c. _____ 11 to 20 years ago.

   d. _____ More than 20 years ago.

   e. _____ Do not know.

4. IF YOU ANSWERED **YES** TO QUESTION #1, at what level is this course (or courses) taught?

   a. _____ Freshman-level

   b. _____ Sophomore-level

   c. _____ Junior-level

   d. _____ Senior-level

Thanks again for your assistance.

Why Was This Research Needed?

1. What kinds of methodological debates have developed in political science? How do these debates pertain to the scientific aspect of political science?
2. Summarize the arguments in favor of rigorous methodological training for undergraduate political science students.
3. The authors write that existing evidence concerning the status of undergraduate political science methods training is "anecdotal." What do they mean? How is their research designed to gather information that is more reliable than anecdotes?

How Was the Topic Studied?

1. How did the authors select the sample for their study? In general, what are the advantages and disadvantages of e-mail surveys?
2. What does the "representativeness" of a sample mean? Based on the response rate data in Tables 1 and 2, how representative is this sample? What sampling concerns (other than the response rate) are relevant to the representativeness of this study?
3. Evaluate the clarity of the survey instrument, or questionnaire, prepared by the authors. At what level of measurement are the data being collected?

What Are the Findings?

1. What paradox emerges when the data in Table 3 are examined?

2. How did the authors supplement the data from their survey to incorporate two additional independent variables for analyzing the diversity of methods course requirements? (See Table 4.) What second paradox is revealed at this stage?
3. Based on the data in Table 5, why is it accurate to say that most political science departments with a methods course requirement did not add that requirement during the past decade? What category of department is the exception to this pattern?
4. Based on the data in Table 6, what is the modal response of departments in this survey to the question about current plans to adopt a required methods course? Explain why the concept of the mode is applicable to data at this level of measurement.

What Do the Results Mean?

1. What possible explanation do the authors propose for the seemingly low level of commitment among doctoral institutions to undergraduate methods training? Describe follow-up research that you believe could assess the accuracy of this and other alternative explanations.
2. In education as in government, sometimes new research findings can help put an issue on the agenda. How might this research study bolster the arguments of those political scientists who want their departments to begin discussing the adoption of an undergraduate methods requirement?

3. How important do you feel it is to have a required methods course as part of the undergraduate political science curriculum? To what extent does such a course relate to the competencies you hope to gain through your political science training? What should be included in the course content, in your view?

Afterword from Cameron G. Thies and Robert E. Hogan

While it is often difficult to pinpoint exactly why one decides to pursue a particular research topic, this study developed out of a debate within our own department over a proposed undergraduate curriculum change. Several of our department faculty members favored creating a mandatory course covering research methods and design for all political science majors. However, other faculty members strenuously opposed this change. A key element in our deliberations over the proposed requirement was whether such a course was common among political science departments across the country. Many of us assumed that such courses were a staple of the undergraduate curriculum in research-intensive universities. However, the anecdotal evidence we gleaned from an examination of course requirements at a handful of universities suggested this assumption might be flawed. Once the debate over this issue ended in our department (the new course requirement proposal ultimately failed), we decided to undertake a systematic analysis of this question.

The findings from our survey were quite surprising to us—departments in research-intensive institutions were the ones *least likely* to require a research methods and design course for undergraduates. As our conclusion shows, we are uncertain about the explanation for this finding and clearly future research is warranted. One central question involves why some departments choose to have such a requirement while others do not. Are there other characteristics of departments that we did not examine that might explain these differences? Another important question involves the nature of the research methods and design classes that are being taught. The dichotomous indicator used in our study is a rather blunt tool for measuring the extent to which research methods and design topics are incorporated into the undergraduate curriculum. Closer examination may demonstrate that there is wide variation in how these courses are taught. More importantly, a detailed look at the overall curriculum in departments lacking these requirements may show that topics of method and design are indeed covered in their substantive courses, although not in a separate course. In other words, future research in this area will need to develop more refined measures to more fully understand these phenomena before any definitive conclusions can be reached.

When Osama Became Saddam: Origins and Consequences of the Change in America's Public Enemy #1

Scott L. Althaus and Devon M. Largio

The 9/11 Commission's final report, released in July 2004, included an unambiguous statement on the question of a link between Iraq and al Qaeda. The commission found no evidence of "a collaborative operational relationship between Osama bin Laden and Iraqi officials" (National Commission on Terrorist Attacks Upon the United States 2004, 66). Nor did the commission identify any signs of Iraq's involvement in the planning or implementation of the events of September 11, 2001. The commission's conclusions gave powerful impetus to critics of the Bush administration who claimed that the nation had been misled into war against Iraq, at least partly on the basis of a purported tie between Saddam Hussein and terrorism against the United States. The topic proved to be contentious throughout the 2004 presidential campaign. At one tense moment in the vice presidential debate between John Edwards and Richard Cheney, Edwards proclaimed:

> *Mr. Vice President, there is no connection between the attacks of September 11th and Saddam Hussein. The 9/11 Commission has said it. Your own secretary of state has said it. And you've gone around the country suggesting that there is some connection. There is not.*
>
> *And in fact the CIA is now about to report that the connection between al Qaeda and Saddam Hussein is tenuous at best.*
>
> *And, in fact, the secretary of defense said yesterday that he knows of no hard evidence of the connection.*
>
> *We need to be straight with the American people. (FDCH E-Media 2004)*

Later in the debate, Vice President Cheney responded to these charges: "The senator has got his facts wrong. I have not suggested there's a connection between Iraq and 9/11, but there's clearly an established Iraqi track record with terror."

Despite the commission's findings, a substantial proportion of Americans have continued to say that Iraq played a role in the attacks of September 11. In February 2005, 64 percent of respondents agreed with the poll statement that "Saddam Hussein had strong links with Al Qaeda," while 47 percent agreed that "Saddam Hussein helped plan and support the

*hijackers who attacked the U.S. on September 11, 2001"
(Harris Interactive 2005). What accounts for this public
perception? Is it a result of the Bush administration's public communications strategy? According to Scott L. Althaus
and Devon M. Largio, the answer is much more complicated than this. They point to both the nature of media
coverage and the process of measuring public opinion as
factors that need to be explored.*

*Althaus and Largio use two main techniques in dis-
secting their research question: the tracking of different
indicators over a span of time and a critical comparison of the content of polling questions. Both methods
are useful in providing insight into the meaning of
public opinion information and other kinds of survey
research data.*

References

FDCH E-Media. 2004. "Transcript: Vice Presidential
Debate." *Washington Post* online, October 5. www.
washingtonpost.com/wp-srv/politics/debatereferee/
debate_1005.html.

Harris Interactive. 2005. "Iraq, 9/11, Al Qaeda and Weapons of
Mass Destruction: What the Public Believes Now, According to Latest Harris Poll." *Harris Poll,* no. 14, February 18.
www.harrisinteractive.com/harris_poll/index.asp?PID=544.

National Commission on Terrorist Attacks Upon the United
States. 2004. *The 9/11 Commission Report.* Washington:
U.S. Government Printing Office. www.gpoaccess.gov/911.

In the days following the 9/11 terrorist attacks, Osama
bin Laden quickly became America's leading enemy. But
as the Bush administration prepared its case for war
against Iraq in the first half of 2002, officials began to
avoid mentioning Osama bin Laden's name in public. At
the same time, administration officials increasingly linked
Saddam Hussein with the threat of terrorism in an effort
to build public support for war. By the first anniversary
of the 9/11 attacks it appeared that this public relations
effort had produced results beyond all expectations: several polls released around the time of the anniversary
revealed that majorities of Americans believed Saddam
Hussein was personally responsible for 9/11.

This was a completely unsubstantiated belief, and
not even the Bush administration was willing to suggest
such a direct connection. But it was a powerful rationale for going to war among those who held it. According to Gallup polls conducted on the eve of war in mid-
March of 2003, between a quarter and a third of those
believing Hussein was responsible for the 9/11 attacks
cited this belief as the main reason why they would support invading Iraq.

How did the American public come to hold this misperception about Saddam Hussein? The popular view
suggests that it was a byproduct of the information campaign waged by the Bush administration in making its
case for war. However, we show that this popular view is
wrong. By charting the changing levels of public attention given to Osama bin Laden and Saddam Hussein in
American news coverage and in President Bush's public
statements, our analysis provides a clear perspective on
the timing and impact of the administration's communication efforts. By also systematically examining the
full range of survey findings that appear to reveal widespread misperceptions about the link between Iraq and
the 9/11 attacks, we show that mistaken beliefs about
Saddam Hussein's culpability were less a product of the
Bush administration's public relations campaign than of
the 9/11 attacks themselves. Moreover, the apparently
high levels of public misperception are in part an artifact
of the wording and format of poll questions put to the
American public.

When Osama Became Saddam

To identify trends in news coverage given to Osama bin
Laden and Saddam Hussein, we used the Nexis/Lexis
news database to identify stories mentioning these names
as well as stories mentioning the phrase "War on Terror"
or "War on Terrorism." We confine our present analysis
to stories distributed by the Associated Press wire service,
but a parallel analysis of *New York Times* coverage finds
essentially the same patterns.[1] During the period from
July 2001 to August 2003, a total of 17,531 Associated
Press stories used the phrase "War on Terrorism" or
"War on Terror"; 29,979 mentioned Osama bin Laden;

Figure 1 • Mentions of Osama bin Laden, Saddam Hussein, and the War on Terrorism in Associated Press Stories, July 2001–August 2003

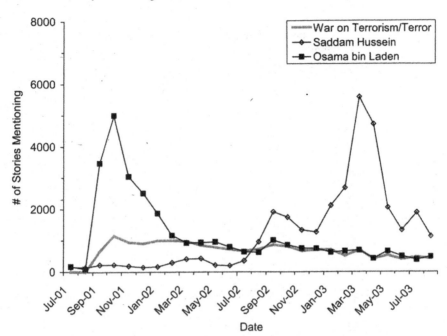

and 31,907 mentioned Saddam Hussein.[2] Figure 1 shows the changing frequency with which these terms appeared in Associated Press reports over time.

Osama bin Laden had been mentioned in nearly 300 stories during the two months prior to 9/11 before becoming the focus of public attention in September and especially October of 2001. But news attention to bin Laden began to wane in November, and as bin Laden's trail grew cold after the fall of the Taliban government, the amount of coverage mentioning his name continued to decline rapidly. By March of 2002 he was mentioned in fewer than 1,000 articles per month, a level that stabilized but which would continue gradually to decline over the next year and a half.

Likewise, Saddam Hussein had also been mentioned in nearly 300 stories over the two months before the attacks, but even following the attacks his name came up in just 200 to 400 stories per month through July of 2002. In August his coverage more than doubled to 956 stories,

making him for the first time more widely covered than Osama bin Laden. News attention to Hussein doubled again in September to 1,919 stories as the Bush administration began pressing Congress to authorize the use of military force against Iraq. But it was not until March of 2003, with the start of the war against Iraq, that Saddam Hussein was mentioned in more stories per month than Osama bin Laden ever was in the aftermath of 9/11.

Thus, long before the war against Iraq actually commenced, and while Osama bin Laden was still on the run, news coverage came to focus squarely on Saddam Hussein and the situation in Iraq. What caused this shift in public attention?

Prompting by the Bush Administration

The Bush administration began preparing the American public for a war with Iraq soon after the 9/11 attacks—

Figure 2 • Mentions of Osama bin Laden, Saddam Hussein, and the War on Terrorism in Public Statements by President George W. Bush, July 2001–August 2003

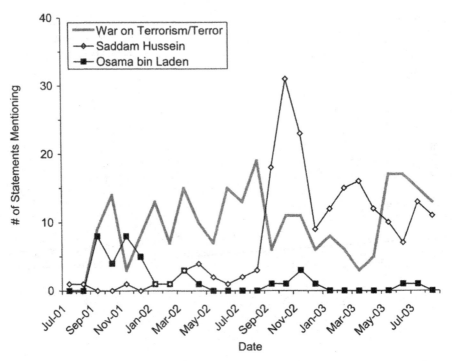

by late 2001 the Bush administration strategy was openly discussed as "Afghanistan first"—but the shift in media attention from Osama to Saddam was not merely due to the administration's initiative. As a complete accounting of this transformation is beyond the scope of this brief article, we encourage the interested reader to examine a detailed 200-page study of this case conducted by Devon Largio (available at http://www.pol.uiuc. edu/news/largio. htm). Here we will merely examine a small part of this larger story: the rhetorical shift from Osama to Saddam that occurred in the public statements of President Bush. For this analysis, we keyword-searched the public statements of the president[3] for the same terms that were examined in Associated Press coverage.

As shown in Figure 2, President Bush frequently discussed Osama bin Laden in his public statements between September and December of 2001, during the active phase of Operation Enduring Freedom in Afghanistan. In contrast, during this period he mentioned Saddam Hussein by name only once, in November. In January and February of 2002, Saddam and Osama were each mentioned once, but following President Bush's State of the Union speech in which Iraq was named as part of the "Axis of Evil," his public references to Saddam Hussein became more frequent. Beginning in April, references to Saddam Hussein outnumbered mentions of Osama bin Laden. By this time, bin Laden had largely disappeared from the president's rhetorical field: between May of 2002 and August of 2003, President Bush mentioned bin Laden by name on only eight occasions, while referring to Saddam Hussein in 185 public statements.

If April of 2002 marks the turn in presidential emphasis from Osama to Saddam, it is notable that the news trends in Figure 1 show no parallel shift until several months later. And when the Associated Press began mentioning Saddam more than Osama in August of 2002, this shift occurred before President Bush began his campaign for congressional authorization of force against Iraq in September of 2002. Beginning in that month, and continuing in every month until after the overthrow of the Iraqi regime in mid-2003, President Bush personalized his push against Iraq by naming Hussein more frequently than he had ever mentioned bin Laden. Presidential references to Hussein jumped from three in August of 2002 to 18 in September and 31 in October, the month of the congressional vote to authorize military action.

In short, Osama was the primary target in presidential rhetoric during the fall of 2001, but beginning in April of 2002, Saddam became the president's main rhetorical adversary. Yet there is an additional pattern in these trends that is especially revealing of the administration's public relations strategy. Figure 1 shows that journalistic use of the term "War on Terrorism" peaked in October of 2001 before declining steadily thereafter. The president's use of the term follows a very different pattern.

In Figure 2, the president's use of the term "War on Terrorism" first surfaces in the month of the 9/11 attacks, peaks in October, and then falls off in November. But following the collapse of the Taliban in December of 2001, President Bush begins using the term "War on Terrorism" with increasing frequency. President Bush's use of the term is particularly notable during June, July, and August of 2002, when this phrase is mentioned by the president between 13 and 19 times per month, the most intense and sustained use of the phrase in presidential rhetoric since it was first coined after the 9/11 attacks. Suddenly, in September of 2002, President Bush nearly stops using the term "War on Terrorism" and starts naming Hussein almost daily. Indeed, "War on Terrorism" declines steadily as a stock phrase in presidential rhetoric—its low point is March of 2003, the month in which the Iraqi invasion began. It is only resurrected in May of 2003 and for four months thereafter, when it had become clear that an active campaign of insurrection and resistance was occurring against the American occupation in Iraq.

This unusual pattern in the president's speeches—rising attention to the war on terror *following* the Afghan

campaign coupled with a sudden focus on Saddam Hussein while Osama bin Laden is pushed rhetorically out of sight—becomes especially notable in light of a discovery trumpeted in the American media around this same time. In mid-August and September of 2002, a series of polls conducted by different survey organizations found that majorities of Americans believed Saddam Hussein was personally responsible for the 9/11 attacks. As journalists publicly marveled at the degree of misinformation revealed in these results—not even the Bush administration was asserting such a direct connection—the seemingly obvious implication was that political leaders had somehow deceived the American public.

Was the Public Duped?

Had the switch in administration rhetoric from bin Laden to Hussein, along with linking Saddam Hussein to the War on Terror, misled Americans into supporting a military campaign against Iraq? At first glance, the evidence in support of this conclusion seems compelling: American beliefs about Hussein's culpability surfaced only after the Bush administration shifted its attentions from Osama to Saddam and began discussing Saddam in connection with the War on Terrorism. Moreover, the only poll result bearing on Saddam's culpability that received public attention in the immediate aftermath of the attacks seemed to confirm that few Americans saw a direct connection between Hussein and 9/11. Appearing in a *New York Times* article two weeks after 9/11,[4] the CBS/*New York Times* poll found that 45% of Americans laid sole blame for the attacks on Osama bin Laden, another 21% blamed Osama bin Laden and others, but only 2% said that Saddam Hussein was solely responsible, and another 6% said Hussein and bin Laden were jointly responsible.

However, this popular reading of the sequence of events is mistaken. While the Bush administration clearly aimed to link Saddam Hussein to Osama bin Laden and the War on Terrorism, our analysis of all available survey data reveals that the American public needed no convincing on this point. While it appeared from publicly

Figure 3 • Percentage of Americans Holding Saddam Hussein Responsible for the 9/11 Attacks, Sept. 2001–May 2004

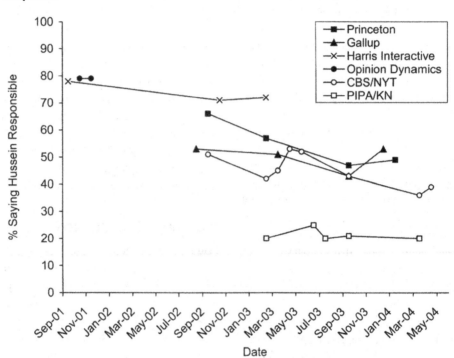

reported surveys that Americans initially blamed Osama and only later blamed Saddam, our analysis shows that Americans were willing to blame Saddam immediately after 9/11 when survey respondents were presented with that possibility. Indeed, rather than seeing a sudden spike in Saddam's culpability around the first anniversary of the 9/11 attacks, our analysis shows a steady decline in the percentage of Americans willing to blame Saddam, a percentage that has been dropping ever since the first days following 9/11.

Using the iPOLL database maintained by the Roper Center for Public Opinion Research, we found every publicly available survey question that asked Americans whether Saddam Hussein might be responsible for the 9/11 attacks. Six survey organizations asked relevant questions that were repeated at least once; the trends from these questions are shown in Figure 3 (the wording of questions posed by these organizations is given in Table 1).

The earliest polls were conducted two days after the 9/11 attacks by Harris Interactive and in October and November by Opinion Dynamics. Using similar questions, both organizations found that nearly 8 in 10 Americans believed Saddam Hussein was responsible for the terrorist attacks. By late 2002 and early 2003, belief in Hussein's responsibility had dropped to around 71% in the Harris polls, but as shown in Figure 3, other surveys using differently worded questions were registering lower levels of misperception. In early February of 2003, Princeton Survey Research Associates found that 57% of Americans believed Hussein "helped the terrorists in the September 11th attacks," but CBS/*New York Times* found that only 42% of Americans thought Hussein "was personally involved in the September 11th attacks." The first PIPA poll on misperceptions, the only poll that allowed respondents to choose among differing levels of culpability, was also conducted during this time. Using

Table 1
Survey Questions about Saddam Hussein's Responsibility for 9/11

CBS/*New York Times*	"Do you think Saddam Hussein was personally involved in the September 11th (2001) terrorist attacks (against the World Trade Center and the Pentagon), or not?"
Gallup	"Do you think Saddam Hussein was personally involved in the September 11th (2001) terrorist attacks (against the World Trade Center and the Pentagon), or not?"
Harris Interactive	"How likely is it that Saddam Hussein [is/was] personally involved in [Tuesday's/the] terrorist attacks (on the World Trade Center and the Pentagon September 11, 2001)? Would you say that it is very likely, somewhat likely, not very likely, or not at all likely?" *(Figure 3 combines very and somewhat likely)*
Opinion Dynamics	"How likely is it that Iraqi leader Saddam Hussein was involved in the September 11 (2001) terrorist attacks (on the World Trade Center and the Pentagon)? Very likely, somewhat likely, not very likely, or not at all likely?" (*Figure 3 combines very and somewhat likely*)
Princeton Survey Research Associates	10/02 and 2/03: "And what's your opinion, based on what you've heard or read: do you believe Saddam Hussein helped the terrorists in the September 11th (2001) attacks (on the World Trade Center and the Pentagon), or don't you think he was involved?"
	9/03 and 1/04: "Do you think Saddam Hussein's regime in Iraq was directly involved in planning, financing, or carrying out the terrorist attacks (on the World Trade Center and the Pentagon) on September 11th, 2001, or not?"
Program on International Policy Attitudes/Knowledge Networks	"Please select what you think is the best description of the relationship between the Iraqi government under Saddam Hussein and the terrorist group al-Qaeda: (1) There was no connection at all; (2) A few al Qaeda individuals visited Iraq or had contact with Iraqi officials; (3) Iraq gave substantial support to al Qaeda, but was not involved in the September 11th attacks; (4) Iraq was directly involved in carrying out the September 11th attacks. (*Figure 3 shows % saying that Iraq was directly involved in the 9/11 attacks*)

this more sensitive question format, PIPA found that only 20% believed "Iraq was directly involved in carrying out the September 11th attacks." Another 36% believed that "Iraq gave substantial support to al Qaeda, but was not involved in the September 11th attacks"; 29% agreed that "a few al Qaeda individuals visited Iraq or had contact with Iraqi officials"; and the remaining 7% believed "there was no connection at all" between Iraq and al Qaeda.

When seemingly minor differences in question wording lead to such large disparities in survey results—the early February PIPA poll shows 8 in 10 Americans believing Saddam had no direct involvement, while the early February Harris polls shows 7 in 10 Americans believing Saddam was personally behind the attacks—survey researchers typically presume that the public's views are ill-formed and uncrystallized. However, the story in this case is more complicated and nuanced. Our interpretation of the available data suggests most Americans were inclined to believe that Saddam was behind the attacks *when explicitly presented with this possibility in forced-choice*

questions that required respondents to choose from a list of possible answers. But few spontaneously volunteered such a connection when presented with open-ended questions asking who they thought was responsible.

Open-ended questions that recorded the unprompted, verbatim answers given by survey respondents consistently revealed that Americans were more likely to blame Osama bin Laden for the terrorist strikes. The late September, 2001 CBS/*New York Times* poll that found only 8% believed Saddam Hussein might have had something to do with the attacks was using an open-ended question. Similar results were found with other open-ended questions in the early polls. Three days after the 9/11 attacks, Wirthlin Worldwide asked respondents "Who do you think is more responsible for the recent terrorist attacks on the New York World Trade Center and the Pentagon?" Without prompting, 57% named Osama bin Laden and only 3% named Saddam Hussein. However, when asked who "is the second most responsible," 27% spontaneously mentioned Saddam Hussein. This suggests that in the immediate aftermath of 9/11, Americans primarily blamed bin Laden but were already willing to believe Hussein was involved. This pattern becomes even clearer in a Harris Interactive poll conducted two days after the 9/11 attacks. In an open-ended question which asked "If Congress were to declare war, who do you think it should declare war against or aren't you sure?" 61% said they were not sure. But 25% named either Afghanistan, the Taliban, or Osama bin Laden; while only 6% mentioned Iraq or Saddam Hussein. Yet when presented with a forced-choice question later in the same poll, fully 78% said that it was very or somewhat likely that "Saddam Hussein is personally involved in Tuesday's terrorist attacks."

A few other early forced-choice questions that were never repeated reinforce the conclusion that Americans were predisposed to blame Saddam Hussein for the attacks. A Gallup poll on September 21, 2001 found that if the U.S. took military action to retaliate, 68% of Americans believed that "removing Saddam Hussein from power in Iraq" would be a very important goal, and another 22% said it would be a somewhat important goal. Likewise, during the first week of October 2001, Techno Metrica Institute of Polling and Politics presented Americans with a list of "different things that the United States could do in its fight against terrorism." When asked "How important is removing Saddam Hussein from power?" fully 62% said it was "extremely important," and another 24% indicated that it was somewhat important.

Although the popular impression is that public misperceptions of Saddam Hussein's role in 9/11 must have grown in the year following the attacks, our analysis shows a general decline in the belief that Saddam was responsible. Most of the trends in Figure 3 tend to diminish over time. The main exceptions are the PIPA trend, which is low and stable, and the spike in culpability registered in the CBS/NYT trend around the start of the 2003 Iraq war. It appears that rather than becoming duped, as the popular account has it, the American public has gradually grown more critical of the idea that Hussein had a hand in 9/11.

Why wasn't this noticed before? Our scan through the Nexis/Lexis news database suggests that the early polls received almost no public attention. Indeed, the only relevant survey data reported in national newspapers and wire service reports was the open-ended CBS/*New York Times* question asked in late September of 2001. This lack of attention to the early polls is certainly understandable given the flood of coverage on the aftermath of the 9/11 attacks and the start of the Afghanistan campaign. But the lack of public attention to these early data made the levels of misperception "discovered" in the weeks surrounding the first anniversary of 9/11 seem a new and startling development. This was compounded by the finding that no open-ended versions of the "who's responsible" question were asked after late September of 2001. Since open-ended questions registered the lowest levels of culpability for Saddam Hussein, the universal switch to forced-choice formats in the spate of polls that suddenly appeared in the weeks surrounding the first anniversary of the 9/11 attacks seems to have overstated the degree to which Americans laid the blame for 9/11 at the feet of Saddam Hussein.

Conclusion

The shift from Osama to Saddam occurred in media coverage during August of 2002, but began four months earlier in the public statements of President George Bush. As Osama bin Laden faded in news coverage and all but disappeared in President Bush's public statements, clear efforts were made by the Bush administration to replace Osama bin Laden as America's foremost enemy by linking Saddam Hussein to the War on Terror.

Yet the American public needed no convincing on the possibility that Hussein was involved in 9/11. In polls taken in the days immediately following the 9/11 attacks, open-ended questions showed that Americans were not spontaneously blaming Iraq for the attacks. But forced-choice questions showed that as many as 8 in 10 Americans thought that Hussein was probably behind them. When explicitly presented with the possibility in the immediate aftermath of the 9/11 attacks, Americans by wide margins were already prepared to believe that Saddam was to blame long before the administration began building popular support for the war.

The American public's apparently widespread belief that Saddam Hussein was responsible for the 9/11 terror attacks was no feat of misdirection by the Bush administration. Instead, the Bush administration inherited and played into a favorable climate of public opinion, which may have greatly facilitated its task of building public support for war against Iraq. The mistaken belief that Saddam Hussein was responsible for the 9/11 attacks was already widespread among Americans long before President Bush began publicly linking Saddam Hussein with the War on Terrorism. Indeed, nearly seven months before the 9/11 attacks, an Opinion Dynamics poll in late February of 2001 found that 73% of Americans said it was very or somewhat likely that "Saddam Hussein will organize terrorist attacks on United States [sic] targets to retaliate for the air strikes" that had recently been conducted in Iraq by American and British air forces.

Our analysis of surveys about the mistaken belief that Hussein was responsible for 9/11 also suggests that the degree of misperception was overstated in many polls. This was partly due to the universal switch to forced-choice survey questions after September 2001, which exaggerated the degree to which Americans saw a connection between Hussein and the 9/11 attacks. The other reason was that most questions only permitted respondents to assess the likelihood that Hussein was involved in 9/11, rather than allowing them to choose from a range of alternative options featuring different degrees of involvement. The only survey to have done this, conducted by the Program on International Policy Attitudes and Knowledge Networks, found that fewer than a quarter of Americans saw a direct tie between Hussein and the terror attacks in New York and Washington, D.C.

News coverage and presidential rhetoric may have replaced Osama with Saddam over time, but Saddam was on the short list of most likely suspects from the beginning for most Americans. Rather than showing a gullible public blindly accepting the rationales offered by an administration bent on war, our analysis reveals a self-correcting public that has grown ever more doubtful of Hussein's culpability since the 9/11 attacks. ∎

Notes

1. We also searched for the term "Iraq," which produced similar results as "Saddam Hussein." For details on the "Iraq" patterns as well as the *New York Times* analysis, see Devon Largio (2004), *Uncovering the Rationales for the War on Iraq,* available at http://www.pol.uiuc.edu/news/largio.htm.

2. Interestingly, only 2,299 AP stories included references to both bin Laden and Hussein.

3. These are available at www.whitehouse.gov, but we used the collection of "Speeches and Public Statements" maintained by Project Vote Smart at www.vote-smart.org because of its superior keyword search engine.

4. Richard L. Berke and Janet Elder, "A Nation Challenged: The Poll; Poll Finds Support for War and Fear on Economy." *New York Times,* Late Edition, A2 (September 25, 2001).

Why Was This Research Needed?

1. How did the Bush administration encourage the public to refocus its attention from Osama bin Laden to Saddam Hussein starting in early 2002?
2. How is this topic of research relevant to debates about the start of the war in Iraq? How is it relevant to the study of public opinion in general?

How Was the Topic Studied?

1. What is the database for this study? What screening criteria did Althaus and Largio use to identify relevant stories from this source?
2. What type of graph is represented in Figures 1–3? When is it appropriate to use this graphing technique? Explain your answer in terms of the kinds of variables that are combined in this visual format.

What Are the Findings?

1. What are the main news coverage trends that appear in Figure 1?
2. How does the information in Figure 2 document the changing rhetorical emphasis of the Bush administration between July 2001 and August 2003?
3. Why is a comparison of the trends in Figures 1 and 2 pivotal to the analysis in this study? What discrepancy does this comparison bring to light?
4. In addition to the count of mentions of Osama bin Laden and Saddam Hussein, how does including a third variable—mentions of the "War on Terrorism/Terror"—contribute to the analysis in this study?
5. The authors draw on the results of several public opinion surveys, including some not widely reported by the media, to dispel the idea that the Bush administration succeeded in linking Saddam Hussein to the war on terrorism in the minds of the public. Summarize the logic of their analysis.
6. What does the review of survey data about Saddam Hussein's responsibility for September 11 reveal about the sensitivity of public opinion measurements to small changes in the wording of questions? Give an example. Explain the distinction between open-ended and forced-choice question formats.

What Do the Results Mean?

1. The authors end their article on a note of optimism, saying their research found the American public to be not so much "gullible" as "self-correcting" in its view of Saddam Hussein's culpability for September 11. Does this study prompt you to feel more optimistic or pessimistic regarding the American public's understanding of international affairs? Explain.
2. One way to view the "War on Terrorism/Terror" theme in this study is as a general plot line, while mentions of Osama bin Laden and Saddam Hussein refer to leading characters inserted into the plot. What kinds of additional data gathering and analysis might you undertake to delve more deeply into the interaction between plot line and characters during the period under examination? Can you think of ways this same plot-and-character framework might be used to study media coverage and political rhetoric for other kinds of political issues?
3. Based on the information in this study, what kinds of critical questions should you have in mind when presented with news reports about public views on political issues?

Afterword from Scott Althaus

Sometimes light can be shed on important research questions by simply counting the number of times keywords appear in news coverage or political speeches. The greatest risks in such an undertaking are the tendencies to overgeneralize from the patterns in a particular news outlet, and to oversimplify the measurement of concepts in the news by counting only keywords with the most obvious relevance to the topic of interest. This project attempted to minimize these risks by analyzing news coverage in the most widely used wire service in the United States, and by focusing narrowly on counting the instances of proper names (Osama bin Laden and Saddam Hussein) and a particular phrase ("War on Terrorism/Terror"). By tailoring the research in this way, we as authors—one of whom was an undergraduate student completing her senior honors thesis—were able to demonstrate using simple graphs that the public's misperceptions about Saddam Hussein's involvement in the September 11 attacks were not simply a product of the Bush administration's information campaign to justify the invasion of Iraq.

A quantitative analysis like this one obviously scratches only the surface of a complicated set of relationships. A fuller and more nuanced treatment of this topic was given in Devon Largio's senior thesis project, which documented the evolving set of rationales used by the Bush administration to make the case for war against Iraq. Her thesis became the object of national and international media attention during the 2004 presidential campaign, and it was even quoted by Democratic presidential candidate John Kerry. This goes to show that research by undergraduate students, if carefully done and focused on questions of broad importance, can have a substantial impact on politics in the United States.

Domestic Obstacles to International Affairs: The State Department Under Fire at Home

Steven W. Hook

The January 2005 nomination of Condoleezza Rice to serve as secretary of state was widely regarded as one of the most notable appointments of President Bush's second term. Rice had served as national security adviser for the previous four years, but this position would put her at the head of a major cabinet department under the media spotlight in the United States and abroad. After a contentious confirmation process in the Senate, which challenged the nominee to defend the administration's policy in Iraq, Rice won approval by a broad margin (Deans 2005). Since that time, her tenure in office has been marked by a series of highly visible trips abroad to meet with top foreign leaders. Observers detect a more aggressive and outspoken style in Rice's management of the U.S. diplomatic establishment compared with that of her predecessor (Weisman 2005).

When viewed through the lens of State Department history, the promotion received by Secretary Rice may actually be a mixed blessing. There is often a distinction between image and reality in the configuration of power among Washington's elite. In fact, as Steven W. Hook explains in the following reading, the State Department generally has had to struggle to achieve effective influence, both in its dealings with Congress and even within the executive branch. Ironically, in modern times the foreign policy insider with closest access to the president has been the national security adviser, the position resigned by Rice. To make her job switch worthwhile, the new secretary will have to draw on her existing relationship with the president while finding ways to battle her department's perennial problems of underfunding and political distrust.

In this reading, Hook supplements his qualitative discussion of the historical status of the State Department with a detailed compilation of budgetary data that illustrates the department's often unsuccessful competition for federal resources. He pays special attention to funding for foreign aid, the single largest part of the U.S. international affairs budget and one of its most controversial items. Students should note how the author integrates various statistics into his political analysis, how he displays quantitative information in graphic form, and how he chooses his measurements when seeking to place these State Department data into a meaningful comparative context.

References

Deans, Bob. 2005. "Rice Confirmed, Starts Job Today." *Atlanta Journal-Constitution,* January 27, 1A.

Weisman, Steven R. 2005. "Secretary Rice, the New Globetrotter." *New York Times,* February 7, 6.

O ne of the most peculiar aspects of the U.S. foreign-policy process is the low regard in which the non-military institutions of foreign affairs are held by the rest of the federal government.[1] Distrust of the State Department and its diplomatic *milieu* is deeply embedded in U.S. political culture, never far beneath the surface in Congress, the White House, and other agencies of the executive branch. As a result, the State Department is routinely neglected in each of its primary areas of responsibility: the development and articulation of foreign policy; the conduct of private and public diplomacy; and the transfer of foreign assistance. The State Department's marginalized status, codified and institutionalized with the passage of the National Security Act of 1947, persists in the administration of President George W. Bush. The costs of this bureaucratic neglect are difficult to gauge. They can be detected, however, in the mixed signals coming from the myriad government agencies regarding U.S. foreign policy, in the problems experienced by the foreign service in recruiting and retaining personnel, and in the failure of many aid programs to achieve their stated goals. Widely publicized accounts of the State Department's interagency disputes and lack of clout undermine the credibility of foreign service officers (FSOs) as they engage daily with foreign governments and private citizens.

These FSOs and international civil servants receive daily reminders of their second-tier status in the form of cramped working conditions, modest pay, chronic personnel shortages, and faulty communications systems. A study by the Overseas Presence Advisory Panel (1999) found U.S. embassies, consulates, and specialized missions to be "near a state of crisis." The panel reported "shockingly shabby and antiquated building conditions" in overseas missions, which were increasingly staffed by personnel from other U.S. agencies.[2] Despite new funding to improve security after the August 1998 bombings of the U.S. embassies in Kenya and Tanzania, the panel reported that U.S. employees in these facilities still faced "an unacceptable risk from terrorist attacks and other threats." A central recommendation of the panel—that staffing levels at foreign posts be "rightsized" to reflect shifting workloads and requirements—encountered a series of obstacles and resource limitations that hindered progress for more than two years (U.S. General Accounting Office 2001a). Computer networks in the State Department have not kept pace with the technological advances that enhance productivity in the private sector and other government agencies. The panel found computers in these offices to be "grossly inefficient," with few employees having desktop Internet access.[3]

The State Department has long confronted a skeptical and sometimes hostile Congress, especially during budget deliberations. Legislators complain about management problems in the department, its lack of clearly defined goals, poor coordination, and, most recently, its lack of responsiveness to terrorist threats before and after the September 2001 attacks on the United States. Perceptions of elitism in the department remain firmly embedded in the minds of many legislators, along with concerns that FSOs suffer from "clientitis," or a subjective bias favoring the countries in which they are stationed over U.S. self-interests. Congress reserves its strongest criticism for the foreign aid programs supervised by the State Department, which account for most of the international-affairs budget.

Given the State Department's lack of a formidable domestic constituency, members of Congress air these grievances without fear of alienating voters or powerful interest groups. Indeed, such denouncements may provide political, or even electoral, benefits by framing legislators as defenders of citizens' interests at home against the wasteful practices of rootless bureaucrats. Such posturing, however, obscures the differences between legitimate and superfluous problems. The common legislative remedy—punitive and indiscriminate spending cuts and restrictions—deprives the State Department of adequate funding for programs with proven track records, or for new initiatives. As membership on congressional committees involved in foreign affairs becomes less attractive than domestic committee assignments, and as ideologically driven policy "mavericks" dominate these committees and sub-committees, the prospects for effective congressional oversight diminish further (Binder 1996).

This article explores the U.S. government's estranged relationship with its foreign service. The first section reviews the origins and evolution of this relationship, which has been fraught with tension throughout its history.

The second and third sections examine trends in the State Department and Foreign Operations budgets, respectively, the primary non-defense spending categories in the area of international affairs. I conclude with a review of findings and an assessment of future prospects.

Strengthening the non-defense agencies of U.S. foreign policy need not be equated with a "softer" or more idealistic approach to global relations, nor one that subordinates U.S. self-interests to transnational concerns. An empowered, properly equipped foreign service enables policy makers to communicate coherently and persuasively with their counterparts overseas. Adequate resources permit FSOs to coordinate their efforts with the Pentagon, intelligence agencies, and the foreign-economic bureaucracy. An effective campaign of public diplomacy generates mass support for U.S. principles and goals that is increasingly central to the foreign-policy calculations of elected leaders. And carefully targeted economic support for developing countries, used in conjunction with funds from other donors and with the technical expertise of non-governmental organizations, enhances the prospects for economic growth and democratic development overseas, both of which serve the long-term interests of the United States.

State's Long Uphill Battle

The U.S. government's disregard for its own foreign service is hardly a recent phenomenon. Early leaders dismissed the practice of diplomacy as a collusive game played by monarchs, priests, and feudal despots. Thomas Jefferson, the first secretary of state, dismissed eighteenth-century diplomacy as "the pest of the peace of the world, as the workshop in which nearly all the wars of Europe are manufactured" (Rubin 1985, 3). Members of Congress expressed a cultural disdain for diplomats, whose background, interests, and lifestyles were unlike those of the general public. In the popular imagination, the nation's early foreign-policy achievements, particularly the rapid pace of continental expansion and economic growth, resulted from the government's *rejection* rather than embrace of diplomacy. George Washington's geopolitical objective to exploit the "detached and distant" position of the United States, reaffirmed in 1821 by Secretary of State John Quincy Adams and two years later in the Monroe Doctrine, established the pretext for this minimalist approach to statecraft. The State Department's stature in Congress was so dubious that Rep. Benjamin Stanton of Ohio declared in 1858 that he knew of "no area of public service that is more emphatically useless than the diplomatic service—none in the world."

The U.S. government did not create a full-scale foreign service until 1924, long after the United States emerged as a major world power. Even then, Congress strictly limited State Department budgets and closely scrutinized the diplomatic corps. The budget cutbacks of the Great Depression, which took place after the United States effectively withdrew from great-power politics, weighed more heavily on international affairs than domestic programs. Ironically, the largest expansion of the State Department, which occurred after World War II, coincided with the dilution of its role in the policy process. The creation of the National Security Council (NSC) in 1947 effectively produced two foreign ministries, with the White House-based NSC having greater access to the president and more impact on strategic and crisis decision making. All this complicated the tasks of the secretary of state, who was forced to contend not only with foreign governments but also with rival power centers in the executive branch.

Henry Kissinger epitomized the transformed balance of domestic foreign-policy power by overshadowing, then taking over the State Department as national security adviser in the Nixon and Ford administrations. Jimmy Carter's pledge to revive State failed as Zbigniew Brzezinski, his national security adviser, dominated the policy process during the Iranian hostage crisis and revived superpower tensions. For his part, Ronald Reagan left Secretary of State George Schultz out of the loop in many critical areas of foreign policy—a blessing for Schultz in the Iran-*Contra* scandal. An exception to this pattern involved George H. W. Bush, who granted Secretary of State James A. Baker III broad authority to manage U.S. foreign policy. Baker, however, did little to enhance the overall stature of the State Department or to secure larger budgets for international affairs after the Cold War.

Secretaries of State Warren Christopher and Madeleine Albright never gained the traction they needed to implement the Clinton administration's grand strategy of "engagement and enlargement," which itself originated in the NSC. After taking office, deficit reduction and health-care reform preoccupied Clinton, who refused to expend his political capital or considerable marketing skills on a campaign to gain popular support for the new paradigm. The failure of the U.S. military intervention in Somalia late in 1993 weakened the already soft public support for humanitarian intervention and peacekeeping. After the Republican Party gained control of both houses of Congress in November 1994, the legislature's frontal attack on the State Department paralyzed the international-affairs bureaucracy. The foreign service and aid budget endured deep funding cuts despite the opening of new embassies in the former Soviet Union, a broader and more complex diplomatic agenda, and the unprecedented capacity of the United States at its "unipolar moment" to shape the international system. Sen. Jesse Helms, the new chairman of the Senate Foreign Relations Committee, called for a "new" State Department that would eliminate the U.S. Agency for International Development (USAID), the U.S. Information Agency (USIA), and the U.S. Arms Control and Disarmament Agency (ACDA). In an unprecedented move, he indefinitely recessed the committee until his demands were met.[4]

The ordeal of Colin Powell in his first two years as George W. Bush's secretary of state personified the State Department's continuing plight. It was expected when Bush took office that Powell, with his exceptional credentials and public approval, would play a pivotal role in both foreign and defense policy. Writing in the *New York Times* after the election, columnist Thomas Friedman (2000, A35) expressed concern that Powell "so towered over the president-elect . . . that it was impossible to imagine Mr. Bush ever challenging or overruling Mr. Powell on any issue." Yet halfway through Bush's term, Vice President Dick Cheney, National Security Adviser Condoleezza Rice, and Secretary of Defense Donald Rumsfeld carried more weight than Powell in most policy deliberations. George Tenet, the director of central intelligence, personally conducted diplomatic negotiations in the Middle East while presidential adviser Karl Rove participated in foreign-policy discussions despite his limited background in the area. Lower-level appointees such as Deputy Secretary of Defense Paul Wolfowitz strongly influenced the president, whose adoption of a more antagonistic and unilateral foreign policy preceded the terrorist attacks of September 2001. By this time, Powell had such a low profile in the administration that *Time* magazine asked on its cover, "Where Have you Gone, Colin Powell?" (McGeary 2001).

With little direct input from State, the administration in 2002 revived a national-security strategy based on U.S. primacy and "preempting" foreign challengers that Wolfowitz initially drafted in the first Bush administration (Lemann 2002). The president's determination in 2002 to overthrow the Iraqi government despite opposition among U.S. allies, moderate Arab states, and the United Nations further isolated the State Department. Powell, "who once envisioned himself as arbiter of the Bush foreign policy, (was) relegated to cleaning up the diplomatic imbroglios that the hard-liners leave behind" (Hirsh 2002, 26). Powell also seemed out of step with other State Department appointees such as John Bolton, the undersecretary of state for arms control and international security, who spent much of 2001 and 2002 blocking, weakening, or withdrawing from international agreements rather than pursuing them.[5]

Figure 1 • Distribution of Federal Spending: Fiscal Year 2001

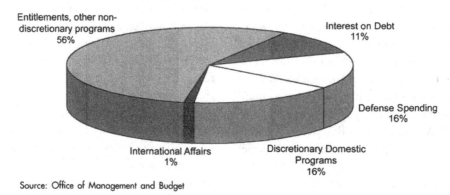

Source: Office of Management and Budget

The State Department's Ends-Means Gap

A tangible sign of the State Department's problems at home is the difficulty it faces in gaining budget support from Congress and the White House. Spending by the U.S. government has special significance in the area of foreign policy. "If budget levels are thought to affect the behavior of potential foreign threats, budget totals then become an instrument of foreign policy" (Wildavsky and Caiden 1997, 232). In this respect, the U.S. government's financial commitments to the various institutions of foreign policy, on an absolute level and relative to other spending programs, is a tangible expression of the government's priorities and future intentions. Shifts in foreign-policy spending over time also send important signals abroad.

More than any other federal agency, the State Department suffers from a chronic gap between its stated goals, or ends, and the means by which these goals are pursued. This ends-means gap is perhaps inevitable given the ambitious, wide-ranging goals identified in the department's mission statements and annual reports. Its 2000 strategic plan claimed a "vital role" for the State Department in pursuing a full range of U.S. national interests and strategic goals, which included:

- preventing regional conflicts from threatening U.S. interests;

- increasing global economic growth and expanding U.S. exports while lessening disparities of wealth within and among countries;
- protecting the safety and security of American citizens abroad;
- reducing the entry of illegal drugs into the United States;
- promoting democratic reforms in formerly autocratic countries;
- securing a sustainable global environment;
- reducing the rate of global population growth; and
- strengthening international health capabilities.[6]

The U.S. government's spending on foreign policy occurs entirely within its discretionary budget authority, which comprises about one-third of the federal budget. The defense budget, which totaled about $350 billion in Fiscal Year 2002 and is expected to surpass $400 billion in FY2005, consumes by far the largest volume of discretionary spending, a level about equal to that of all domestic agencies combined (see Figure 1). Of particular interest in this analysis is the budget for international affairs (IA), which includes the costs of operating the State Department and other non-defense agencies, foreign assistance programs, and contributions to multilateral organizations. Taken together, these expenses amounted to $22.8 billion in FY2001 and $24 billion in FY2002 (U.S. Department of State 2002). The Bush administration requested

Figure 2 • Federal Outlays Spent on International Affairs, Fiscal Years 1964–2001: Percentage of Total Spending

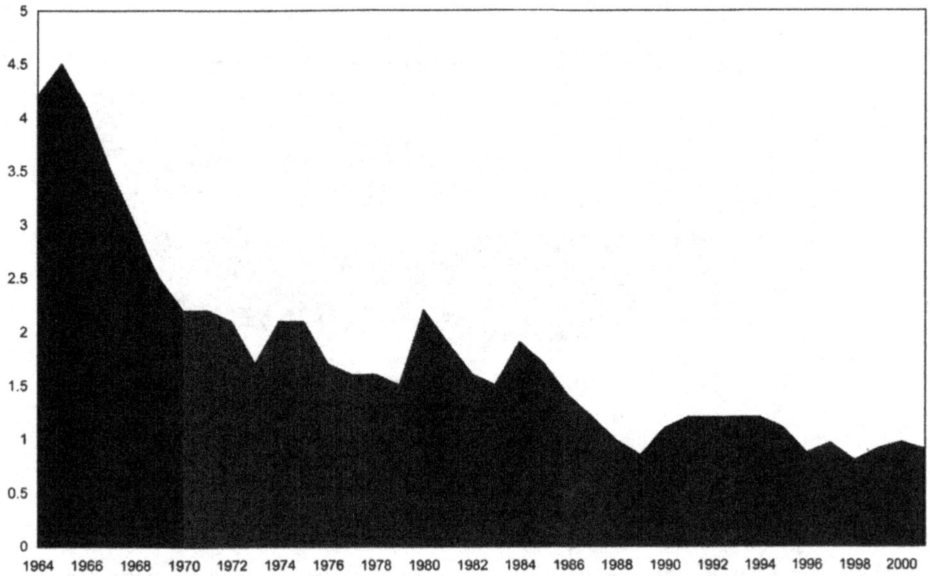

Source: Office of Management and Budget

$25.4 billion for international affairs in FY2003, largely to fund improved embassy security and higher levels of security assistance related to the war on terrorism.

The gap between the State Department's ends and means widened along with the global roles and responsibilities of the United States after World War II. Other demands on government resources, primarily defense, entitlement programs, and interest payments on the national debt, claimed a growing share of the federal budget. As a percentage of all federal outlays, post-World War II spending on IA declined steadily from its peak of nearly 17% in 1947 to less than 1 percent in 2001 (see Figure 2). As a percentage of the U.S. defense budget, IA expenditures fell from their peak level of 50% in 1948 to an average of 6% in the 1990s. Higher budgets for IA in the mid-1980s, primarily to provide security assistance to Central American states and base-rights countries such as the Philippines, were followed by sharp reductions in spending. The budget cuts accelerated in the aftermath of the Cold War, totaling nearly 21% in the three fiscal years

from 1994 through 1996. Measured in constant dollars, the $19.1 billion in IA budget authority in FY1997 was the lowest in more than 20 years and just over half the 1985 peak of $36.1 billion (Nowels 2000, 6). Additional funding in FY1998 and FY1999 covered overdue payments to the UN, enhanced embassy security, and emergency humanitarian assistance. Another increase in IA budget authority followed the September 2001 terrorist attacks, including a $2.2 billion supplemental appropriation in FY2002. These increases after FY1997 still left the IA spending levels lower than post-World War II averages when calculated in constant dollars or as a percentage of the federal budget.

Spending on the day-to-day conduct and administration of foreign affairs claims about one-third of the IA budget (see Figure 3). Outlays in this category include the operational costs of the State Department headquarters and foreign service, public-information campaigns, exchange and democratization programs, and assessed U.S. contributions to international organizations and

Figure 3 • Distribution of International Affairs Budget, Fiscal Year 2001

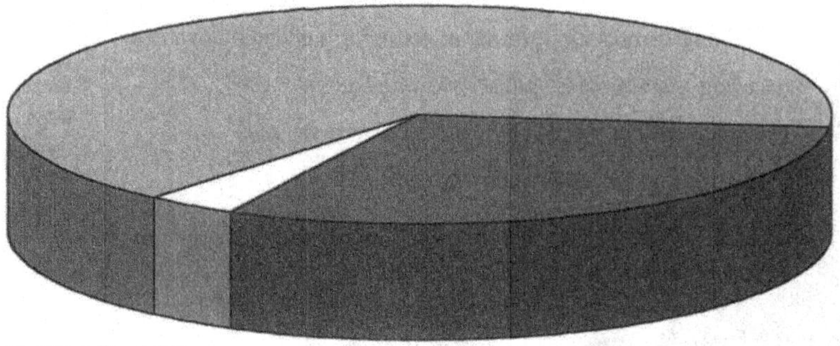

Foreign Operations
65%

Agriculture-Food Aid
4%

State Department Programs
31%

Source: Department of State

peacekeeping. After rising in the 1980s and early 1990s to a peak of $7 billion in FY1994, these budget levels dropped by more than 20% in real terms over the next four years (Nowels 2000, 19). A sharp increase in embassy-security spending in 1999 contributed to a one-year spike in overall spending, but congressional support declined again until the terrorist attacks in 2001. Powell has received broad increases in his operational budget, and a recruitment drive is under way to hire 1,400 FSOs and civil servants by 2004. But the return of federal deficits, which forced deep cuts at State in the 1980s and 1990s, may limit this expansion in personnel.[7]

Funding Foreign Aid

Doubts about the State Department are mild in contrast to the contempt many legislators and executive-branch agencies have for U.S. foreign aid. By far the largest part of the IA budget, spending on Foreign Operations includes bilateral and multilateral aid programs, disaster relief, support for refugees, debt relief, and voluntary payments to international organizations. The United States also provides security assistance with this budget, particularly to recipients in the Middle East.[8]

In the view of its advocates, foreign aid reflects the generosity, compassion, and best intentions of the U.S. government and its people. Others defend aid on utilitarian grounds. They argue that aid serves U.S. self-interests by securing allies, promoting stable and democratic governments, fostering export markets, and subsidizing domestic farmers and manufacturers through the tying of aid. Critics charge that aid flows are wasted on bloated bureaucracies, reward corrupt dictators, and serve as an agent of U.S. hegemony. To many opponents of aid, the U.S. government can better advance international development by encouraging private investment rather than providing government assistance (see Hook 1995).[9]

The United States provided the largest volumes of economic and military assistance during the Cold War, transferring $390 billion in aid to more than 120 foreign governments (USAID 1996, 4). As a percentage of U.S. economic output, the level of foreign aid spending steadily dropped throughout this period and after the Cold War (see Figure 4). Japan replaced the United States as the world's leading aid donor in 1989 and continues to maintain this distinction despite a prolonged recession. In real terms, U.S. spending declined from a peak of $33 billion in FY1985 to less than $14 billion in FY1997 (Now-

Figure 4 • Foreign Assistance as a Percentage of U.S. GDP, Fiscal Years 1946–2001

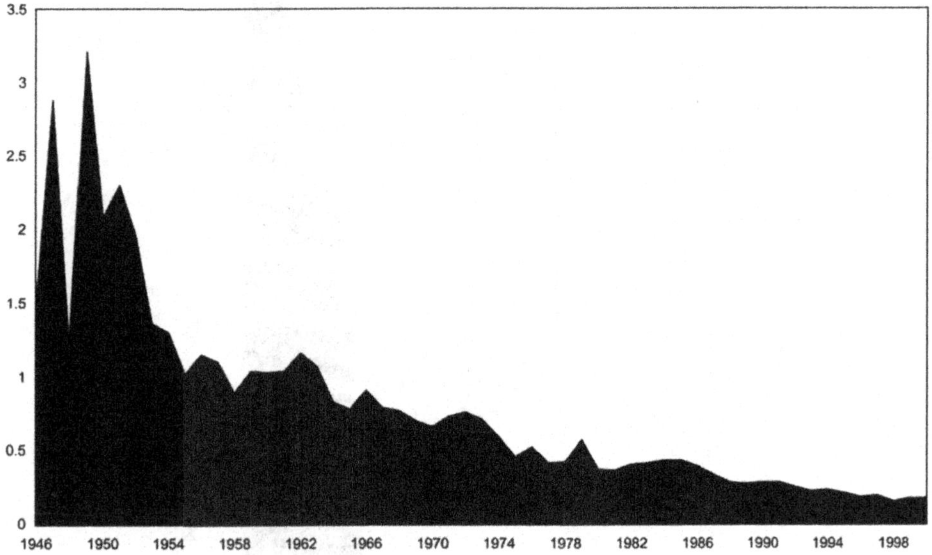

Source: Congressional Research Service

els 2002, 5). Cutbacks in the late-1980s resulted from the Gramm-Rudman deficit-reduction program. Additional cuts followed the end of the Cold War, which removed the rationales of several security-aid programs. As noted above, the Republican Party's capture of both houses of Congress in November 1994 led to even deeper reductions in the aid budget, which Helms likened to a "rat hole" of government waste.

The poisoned political climate surrounding aid prompted the Foreign Operations authorization committees in Congress to stop "authorizing" aid expenditures in the late 1990s and to surrender this responsibility to the appropriations committees. With the exception of large bilateral aid packages to Israel and Egypt, a by-product of the Camp David accords, U.S. aid fell to negligible levels in absolute as well as relative terms by the turn of the century (Tarnoff and Nowels 2001, 23–24). The level of aid as a percentage of U.S. gross domestic product in 2000 was the lowest level of support among members of the Organization for Economic Cooperation and Development (see Figure 5). Members of Congress frequently cite low levels of public support for foreign aid in supporting these cutbacks. In doing so, they fuel a public misperception that the volume of aid spending is much larger than it actually is.[10]

The politicization of U.S. foreign aid further undermines the credibility of the State Department. Among his first acts after taking office in 2001, President Bush reinstated the Mexico City policy, first adopted by Reagan in 1984 but later suspended by Clinton, that prevents the transfer of U.S. aid to family-planning agencies in developing states that offer abortion counseling or services. Bush's action, though praised by conservative interest groups at home, further isolated the United States among other members of the OECD and recipient states. In July 2002, Bush suspended $34 million in U.S. commitments to the UN Population Fund on the grounds that China, a beneficiary of the program, was engaged in forced abortions. The suspension deprived the agency of U.S. funds for other developing countries and hindered its work in less controversial areas, such as maternal and child health care, cancer screening, and HIV prevention.

Figure 5 • Development Aid as a Percentage of GDP, Fiscal Year 2000

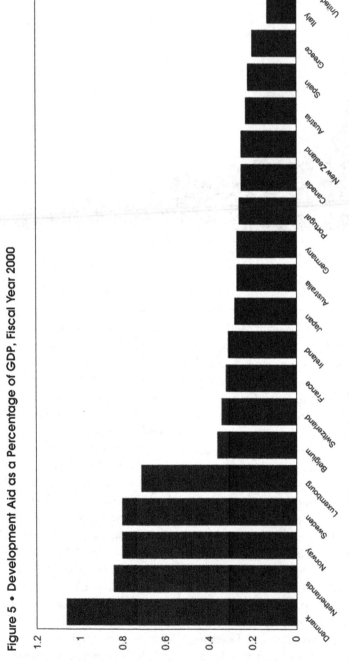

Source: Organization for Economic Cooperation and Development

President Clinton, it should be noted, also manipulated the foreign aid budget to gain political support among domestic interest groups.

The Foreign Operations budget rebounded after the terrorist attacks of September 2001, reaching $16.8 billion in FY2002. The White House and Congress approved additional funds for "front-line" states in the war on terrorism, including Afghanistan, Pakistan, and their neighbors in central Asia. In March 2002, Bush pledged a $5 billion increase in aid spending from FY2004 through FY2006 that would reward developing countries that institute political and economic reforms. This general pattern suggests that even a skeptical president and Congress can find effective uses for U.S. foreign aid. But most of the proposed increases have yet to be appropriated, and foreign aid is among the first spending programs Congress curtails in times of fiscal austerity. There is also a danger that renewed interest in security versus development assistance will bring a return to the Cold War days when the United States supported dozens of autocratic regimes in return for their support in containing communism.

Conclusion

Questions regarding the fiscal solvency of the State Department must ultimately be placed in the context of ongoing U.S. foreign relations. No amount of funding could overcome the diplomatic ruptures that occurred between the United States and much of the world in the Bush administration's first two years. Its approach to foreign policy, best described as *assertive unilateralism,* alienated global opinion at the very time the United States needed the support of foreign governments, international organizations, and mass publics in the war on terrorism. A year after the terrorist attacks, U.S. bilateral relations were strained, for a variety of disconnected and overlapping reasons, with most member states of NATO and the European Union, Russia, China, Japan, and Mexico. Meanwhile, the government's turn away from the multilateral regimes it helped create in the half-century after World War II produced resentment and ill-will

toward Washington that will be difficult to overcome in the near term.

As noted earlier, this dysfunctional behavior is hardly unique to the current period but instead has deep roots in the history and political culture of the United States. The disregard for diplomacy in general, and the State Department in particular, reflects a societal ambivalence regarding foreign affairs that extends beyond immediate questions of grand strategy, spheres of influence, and the scope of military interventions. An embedded sense of national exceptionalism, combined with an equally pervasive belief that the United States has the necessary resources to go it alone, are persistent if paradoxical elements of the nation's "style" of foreign policy (Hook and Spanier 2000). Fundamental doubts also persist regarding the most appropriate and effective *sources* of international influence. To many in and out of government, the United States is best served when its values and interests are expressed by citizens and groups in the normal course of their international interactions. In this view, these purveyors of "soft-power" are the most potent agents of U.S. foreign policy. Diplomats and aid programs simply consume public resources and get in the way. When the United States faces a direct security threat, a favorable outcome can be assured through the use of overwhelming military force.

Such a perspective continues to resonate deeply within the legislative and executive branches of the U.S. government. Yet, for all the benefits that may be derived from the soft-power projection of civil society, a clear and singular statement of national purpose is essential. Military policy, trade relations, and other substantive aspects of foreign policy must flow deductively from such a statement, which can only originate within the federal government. Historical experience suggests that this cannot be accomplished in the absence of a national consensus that is achieved through open and vigorous debate. Nor can the United States achieve its primary foreign-policy goals without first gaining the support of its allies, which must be thoroughly consulted and not simply notified of pending U.S. actions.

Unlike much of the NSC staff, the State Department's diplomatic corps is directly engaged with governments and private citizens abroad. Members of the foreign service are uniquely situated to convey the interests of the United States to foreign governments and to relay information to senior decision makers regarding the likely outcomes of specific policy initiatives. In this respect, "clientitis" is overstated by critics of the State Department. More often than not, the malady refers to the discomfort officials in the White House and Congress experience when they receive information from the field that conditions are more complex than suspected and are, for this reason, less amenable to the immediate realization of U.S. objectives. The perception of FSOs as unduly averse to risks or bold departures in foreign relations is similarly exaggerated. Among their primary duties is to translate the proclaimed national interests of the United States to the ever-changing realities of world politics. Such a task requires a degree of political and ideological detachment that can, if properly managed, serve as an asset to foreign-policy makers. As Theodore Sorensen (1987–88, 238), special counsel to President Kennedy, observed with respect to the State Department:

> The caution, continuity, and constant consultations for which the department is chided reflect in large part the reality of a dangerous world that does not change merely because we change presidents. The department's institutional memory, in-depth planning and orderly procedures can protect an eager president from his errors as well as his enemies. The experienced eye and pragmatic perspective of career specialists … are needed to balance White House pressures for quick and dramatic solutions that conform with campaign slogans or popular sentiment.

Its potential attributes notwithstanding, the diminished role of the State Department is now a permanent fixture of the U.S. foreign-policy process. The locus of decision making in military as well as foreign economic policy is increasingly centered in the White House. The NSC will continue to take the lead in coordinating policy, and the national security adviser will remain the president's primary source of strategic guidance and crisis management. The State Department has effectively conceded this primacy to the NSC, focusing instead on the day-to-day conduct of diplomatic relations and the administration of non-military programs. These are not trivial duties, however. And they are impossible to carry out effectively when those responsible for international affairs are under attack at home. ∎

Notes

1. The author would like to acknowledge the research assistance of James Bralski and David Rothstein in preparing this article.

2. More than two dozen federal agencies are currently engaged in foreign affairs alongside the State Department at more than 250 U.S. facilities abroad. These agencies include, among others, the departments of Agriculture, Commerce, Defense, Energy, Justice, Labor, Treasury, and Veterans Affairs; the Environmental Protection Agency, the Federal Bureau of Investigation, and the National Science Foundation. Personnel from various intelligence agencies are also stationed at these posts.

3. No centralized system of managing the department's information services existed until October 1998. Since then, a fully integrated system connecting the domestic and foreign offices to each other, and to other government agencies and databases, has yet to be deployed (Dizard 2001; U.S. General Accounting Office 2001b).

4. Helms effectively held much of U.S. foreign policy hostage by the end of 1995, including nearly 400 foreign-service promotions, 30 ambassadorial nominations, more than a dozen treaties and international agreements, and many daily functions of the State Department. The Clinton Administration, which endorsed the downsizing of the foreign-affairs bureaucracy in its own internal reports, agreed to abolish ACDA and USIA as independent agencies and fold them into the State Department. Congress reluctantly retained USAID's independent status but brought its director under the direct authority of the secretary of state.

5. These agreements included the Anti-Ballistic Missile Treaty with Russia; global bans on land mines, biological weapons, and nuclear testing; and curbs in the trafficking of small arms. The one agreement Bolton successfully negotiated, the Treaty of Moscow that called for deep cuts in U.S. and Russian long-range nuclear weapons, was most distinctive for

its lack of details, binding obligations, interim deadlines, and enforcement mechanisms.

6. See <www.state.gov/m/rm/rls/dosstrat/> for the full text of the 2000 Strategic Plan.

7. According to recent OMB projections, the State Department's budget authority is expected to grow by less than 10% between FY2003 and FY2007, from $9.1 billion to $10 billion.

8. The primary recipients of U.S. assistance in FY2002 included Israel ($2.8 billion), Egypt ($2 billion), Pakistan ($921 million), Afghanistan ($420 million), Colombia ($382 million), and Jordan ($230 million).

9. While the United States is the largest source of funding for the World Bank and International Monetary Fund, these multilateral agencies provide concessional loans rather than grants to recipients and are thus not considered in most foreign aid spending totals.

10. Respondents in public-opinion surveys consistently estimate that the U.S. government spends 15–20% of the federal budget on foreign aid, in contrast to the less than 1% actually spent. In the same surveys, the median level of *preferred* spending is between 5 and 10% (Kull and Destler 1999, 124; see also Rielly 1999).

References

Binder, Sarah A. 1996. "The Disappearing Political Center: Congress and the Incredible Shrinking Middle." *Brookings Review* 14 (Fall): 36–39.

Dizard, Wilson, Jr. 2001. *Digital Diplomacy: U.S. Foreign Policy in the Information Age.* Westport, CT: Praeger.

Friedman, Thomas L. 2000. "The Powell Perplex." *The New York Times* (December 19): A35.

Hirsh, Michael. 2002. "Bush and the World." *Foreign Affairs* 81 (September-October): 18–43.

Hook, Steven W. 1995. *National Interest and Foreign Aid.* Boulder: Lynne Rienner Publishers.

Hook, Steven W., and John Spanier. 2000. *American Foreign Policy Since World War II.* Washington, D.C.: CQ Press.

Kull, Steven, and I. M. Destler. 1999. *Misreading the Public: The Myth of a New Isolationism.* Washington, D.C.: Brookings Institution.

Lemann, Nicholas. 2002. "The Next World Order." *The New Yorker* (April 1): 42–48.

McGeary, Johanna. 2001. "Odd Man Out." *Time,* September 10, 24–32.

Nowels, Larry. 2002. "Appropriations for FY2003: Foreign Operations, Export Financing, and Related Programs." Congressional Research Service, July 17.

Nowels, Larry. 2000. "International Affairs Budget Trends, FY1980–FY2000." Congressional Research Service, September 29.

Office of Management and Budget. 2002. *Budget of the United States Government, 2002.* Washington, D.C.: Executive Office of the President of the United States.

Overseas Presence Advisory Panel. 1999. "America's Overseas Presence in the 21st Century." Washington, D.C.: U.S. Department of State.

Rielly, John E. 1999. *American Public Opinion and U.S. Foreign Policy, 1999.* Chicago: Chicago Council on Foreign Relations.

Rubin, Barry. 1985. *Secrets of State: The State Department and the Struggle over U.S. Foreign Policy.* New York: Oxford University Press.

Sorensen, Theodore. 1987–88. "The President and the Secretary of State." *Foreign Affairs* 66 (Winter): 231–248.

Tarnoff, Curt, and Larry Nowels. 2001. "Foreign Aid: An Introductory Overview of U.S. Programs and Policy." Congressional Research Service, January 16.

U.S. Agency for International Development. 1996. *U.S. Overseas Loans and Grants and Assistance from International Organizations.* Washington, D.C.: USAID.

U.S. Department of State. 2002. *Budget Tables, FY2003 International Affairs Summary.* www.state.gov/m/rm/rls/iab/2003/7807.htm.

U.S. General Accounting Office. 2001a. "Overseas Presence: More Work Needed on Embassy Rightsizing." Washington, D.C.: GAO.

U.S. General Accounting Office. 2001b. "Information Technology: State Department Led Overseas Modernization Program Faces Management Challenges." Washington, D.C.: GAO.

Wildavsky, Aaron, and Naomi Caiden. 1997. *The New Politics of the Budgetary Process.* 3rd ed. New York: Longman.

Why Was This Research Needed?

1. Hook writes that the State Department possesses a "marginalized status" within the U.S. government and American political culture. What does he mean? What consequences does this low standing have?

2. What mileposts in State Department history does the author cite to support his argument? What is the special importance of the National Security Act of 1947?

3. Which brief passage from the introductory part of this reading identifies Hook's purpose in conducting this research?

How Was the Topic Studied?

1. What is Hook's primary source of data for this reading? If you were to update this research, where would you obtain the budget data for years since fiscal year 2001?

2. What is the distinction between "absolute" and "relative" measurements of program spending? What different types of relative measurements are presented in this reading?

3. What is the difference between spending growth measured in "real" versus "constant" dollars? How would a constant dollar adjustment be calculated?

4. How many different types of graphs appear in this reading? Based on these examples, explain for what types of data and circumstances each type of graph is appropriate.

What Are the Findings?

1. What is the spending level for international affairs with respect to overall federal spending in 2001? How has this statistic changed over time? How could you reorganize the data in Figure 2 according to successive presidential administrations? Would your reorganization add any useful information to the interpretation of yearly funding changes?

2. What does the breakdown of the international affairs budget in Figure 3 contribute to the author's discussion in this reading?

3. Figure 5 compares development aid from the United States with similar statistics from other Organization for Economic Cooperation and Development countries. If the graph depicted aid in dollars per capita, rather than as a percentage of gross domestic product, do you think the United States would fare better or worse in this international comparison? Which measure is more appropriate for this analysis?

What Do the Results Mean?

1. On p. 26, Hook writes: "More than any other federal agency, the State Department suffers from a chronic gap between its stated goals, or ends, and the means by which these goals are pursued." Do you feel the research presented in this reading has proven this point? Why or why not?

2. If you were a member of the congressional committee responsible for the State Department's budget, how might you use the same (or different) statistical data to counter the argument in this reading?

3. According to information in this reading, the public tends to believe the United States spends more on foreign aid than it actually does. If you were to use data from a follow-up survey to calculate respondents' perceptions of foreign aid spending as a percentage of actual spending, what would be the level of measurement of this new variable? Formulate two research hypotheses—one featuring this measure as an independent variable and another with this measure as a dependent variable—that could help explain public views of the State Department.

4. In his conclusion, Hook writes:

The disregard for diplomacy in general, and the State Department in particular, reflects a societal ambivalence regarding foreign affairs that extends beyond immediate questions of grand strategy, spheres of influence, and the scope of military interventions. An embedded sense of national exceptionalism, combined with an equally pervasive belief that the United States has the necessary resources to go it alone, are persistent if paradoxical elements of the nation's "style" of foreign policy.

What questions would you include in your follow-up survey (see question 3, above) to prove or disprove various aspects of this statement?

Afterword from Steven W. Hook

Researchers of foreign aid from the United States and other governments must confront a variety of methodological questions. Although this is a data-rich environment, with the volume of aid transfers and other variables easily quantifiable, several judgments must be made in the construction of data sets. Researchers must consider precisely which types of assistance—economic or security, and what specific types of each—will be the object of study. They must also build in appropriate time lags between aid appropriations, expenditures, and whatever outcomes may be anticipated or tested by aid donors and researchers, respectively. Other questions relate to the use of absolute aid volumes versus aid as a percentage of donor gross national product or overall government spending, and aid levels relative to recipient population or GNP. When considering living standards in recipient states, per capita rather than aggregate GNP is commonly used. Cross-national aid studies inevitably confront questions regarding currency valuations and appropriation schedules. Finally, aid output is often viewed as only one measure of donor performance; aid "quality" is also measured by multilateral versus bilateral transfers, economic versus security aid, grants versus loans, and the distribution of aid to the poorest states and societies. Cross-national data regarding aid commitments are best obtained from the OECD's Development Assistance Committee (DAC), which provides ample statistics on aid quality as well as quantity.

The United States today maintains its status as the world's largest donor of development aid, although it also remains the greatest aid "miser" in terms of aid as a percentage of donor GNP. As in the past, the U.S. government calls attention to other economic contributions—to the World Bank and International Monetary Fund; in the form of security assistance, or more indirectly through U.S. military spending; and through unmatched levels of trade and foreign direct investment. In recent years the Bush administration created the Millennium Challenge Corporation (MCC), based upon a "business model" that requires competitive bids from prospective recipients, as an institutional source of aid alongside the Agency for International Development (AID). Although the MCC was launched with great fanfare early in President Bush's first term, aid transfers through MCC have thus far been modest. The same can be said for aid volumes stemming from the administration's program to fight AIDS in Africa. Iraq has become by far the largest recipient of U.S. economic aid, and security assistance levels have also increased as a result of the war on terrorism.

The Real Invisible Hand: Presidential Appointees in the Administration of George W. Bush

G. Calvin Mackenzie

Making political appointments is one of the president's most significant powers. Presidents use these appointments to bring new talent into government and to gain control of the top levels of the federal bureaucracy (Fesler and Kettl 2005, chap. 8). Appointees are expected to be the eyes and ears of the administration as well as staunch advocates of its public policies. Should they fail at, or reject, this role, it is understood they will be removed from their position.

Who are political appointees? The members of the president's cabinet and the ambassador corps are likely to be the first groups to come to mind. In fact, thousands of jobs must be filled below these elevated ranks, from deputy secretaries to personal assistants. As the president's powers have expanded, the number of political appointments has increased. It is also common to think of the political appointments process as taking place during the transition from one presidential administration to another, with confirmations occurring in the early days of a presidency. True, much publicity is given to the high-profile positions filled in this period. Yet, as G. Calvin Mackenzie discusses in the following reading, delays can leave many posts unstaffed long after a new administration has settled into office. How bad has this situation become over recent years? What is the Bush administration's record in completing its process of political appointments? For Mackenzie, these are questions best addressed by means of data collection and analysis.

The main quantitative techniques of interest in this reading are the use of graphs and measures of central tendency. With these elementary statistical tools, the author is able to document with clarity why reforms should be considered in the appointments process.

Reference

Fesler, James W., and Donald F. Kettl. 2005. *The Politics of the Administrative Process.* 3rd ed. Washington, D.C.: CQ Press.

It was to be the single most visible decision of George W. Bush's first year in office, inspiring even a rare prime-time televised address to announce and explain to the American people his decision on government support for stem cell research. For weeks, the White House press office told of the President's wide-ranging search for advice: the meetings with ethicists and scientists, with interest group representatives, and with dozens of ordinary citizens.

But Bush's wide search for advice did not include consultations with the director of the White House Office of Science and Technology Policy—the president's chief science adviser—nor with the Director of the National Institutes of Health, the government's leader in health research.

The simple reason why George W. Bush did not consult with his appointees in those positions is that there were none. President Bush was making decisions that affected the health and concerned the moral values of millions of Americans without the support of scores of important players in his administration.

In fact, many of the 500 top positions in the executive branch that required Senate confirmation were not filled in the first nine months of his term in office. Figure 1 shows the month-by-month progress through September 2001 (the deadline for this article).

Many of those who voted for George W. Bush wanted decisive action on the new education approaches he had promised. But until the end of May, his Education Secretary Rod Paige was the only confirmed appointee at work in that department. Around the government, the story was much the same: No one but the secretary confirmed at Energy until May 24; no one but the secretary confirmed at Interior until June 29; on September 1, eight of the 14 cabinet departments had no confirmed chief financial officer; when terrorists struck a brutal blow to the country on September 11, there was no confirmed U.N. Ambassador, no commissioner of customs, no director of the U.S. Marshals, no undersecretaries for the Army or Air Force.

In 1993, the Clinton transition had broken every record for the slowest ever. But the most recent transition will come very close, perhaps even surpass—if that's the right word—the painfully slow pace of its predecessor.

These are not measures of human failure, of the inability of new presidents and their aides to master the task of staffing an administration. There are some breakdowns and false starts in every transition, of course. But the starker reality is that the presidential appointments process has become a monster that quickly overwhelms any new administration's capacity to tame it. The problem is systemic, and it grows with each new election.

Embedded in all mainstream theories of democracy is the notion that elections are critically important navigational devices. They point political leaders in certain directions and away from others. They supply new leaders determined to pursue the goals that citizens choose with their votes. Democratic citizens rely on the assumption that, once chosen, elected leaders will do as they are bid.

But in a complex democracy, that can occur only when elected leaders have teams of experts and administrators in place to help them refine policy options, build support for their initiatives among the people and the legislature, and then implement them. Nowhere in all of democratic theory is there a provision for a lag of six months or nine months or a year between the time the people speak and the essential administrative appointees are in place to act on their instructions.

And yet that, consistently, has been the practice in America over the past decade.

Historical Perspective

Experienced observers of presidential transitions found little surprising in the difficulty George W. Bush confronted in his efforts to staff the first new presidential administration of the twenty-first century. Despite the days of uncertainty following the vote in November, Governor Bush pushed forward with the essentials of transition planning. Clay Johnson, an old friend of the new president and an experienced hand in helping Bush staff his administration in Austin, had begun to plan for this personnel recruitment and selection task long before it began. He knew the magnitude of the task and the pitfalls he would encounter.[1] But knowing what lies ahead only takes away some of the surprise when you get there. It doesn't guarantee easy negotiation of the obstacles.

Figure 1 • Pace of Completed Appointments in Top 500 Positions in Executive Branch, 2001

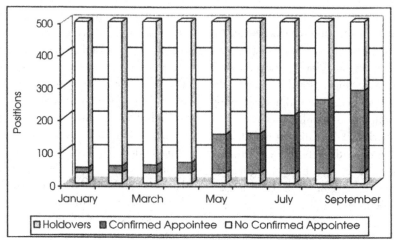

Source: Prepared by the author from data calculated from offical sources by Michael Hafken of the Presidential Appointee Initiative of the Brookings Institution.

The modern appointments process is a morass of forms and questionnaires, of background checks and investigations, of redundancy and complexity. Every nominee is subjected to a scrutiny so thorough, so invasive, so tediously picayune, that some nominees spend almost as much time getting through the appointments process as they do in office.

It hasn't always been so. For most of the twentieth century, the appointments process flowed smoothly through the routines of government. A vacancy occurred, a suitable candidate was identified (often by the managers of the president's political party), a few questions were asked to ensure that the candidate was in agreement with most of the president's program, the nomination was announced, and a quick review and confirmation by the Senate soon followed.

That description fit the appointments process as recently as the late 1960s. One useful measure of the pace of the appointments process is the length of time that passes between inauguration and confirmation for the average appointee in an administration. The average for the Kennedy administration was 2.38 months.[2] Nixon in the late 1960s was only slightly slower, 3.39 months. Even Carter, a near total stranger to Washington, managed to get his appointees in place in an average of 4.55 months.

But then real changes began to occur as law and process caught up with the post-Watergate cynicism about public servants. The Ethics in Government Act of 1978 was the major monument to those concerns. But it was amended and its interpretation expanded often in subsequent years to seek to prevent every form of misbehavior the mind could imagine.

Nowhere in all of democratic theory is there a provision for a lag of six months or nine months or a year between the time the people speak and the essential administrative appointees are in place to act on their instructions.

By the time of the Reagan transition, a noticeable change had appeared in the appointments process, and it is clearly revealed in our measure. The average Reagan

Figure 2 • Number of Bush Nominees Announced, Nominated, and Confirmed by Month, 2001

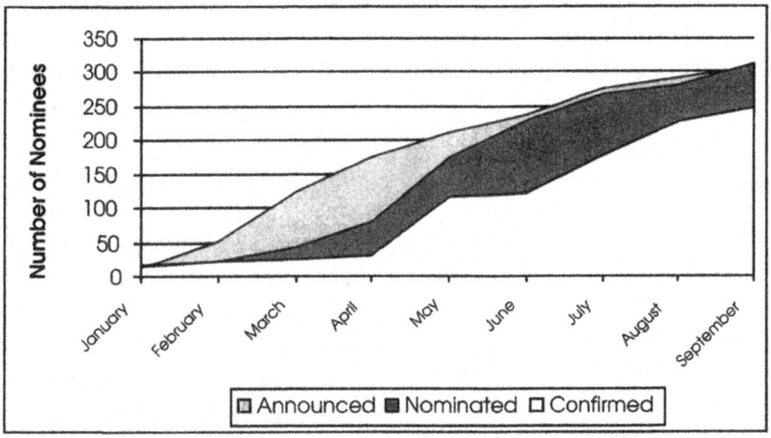

Source: Prepared by the author from data calculated from offical sources by Michael Hafken of the Presidential Appointee Initiative of The Brookings Institution.

appointee was confirmed in 5.3 months, more than twice as long as the average Kennedy appointee 20 years earlier. By the end of the 1980s, the modern appointments process was fully in place. Confirmation for the appointees of the first President Bush took 8.13 months on average, and for President Clinton four years later, 8.53 months. While it is too soon to calculate the average for the second President Bush, there seems now every likelihood that this will be the slowest transition in American history. Figure 2 indicates the progress of the Bush administration through September 30, 2001.

It's the Process, Stupid

What explains the very long time that it has taken to staff the new Bush administration in 2001? Not a lack of diligence or concern on the part of the new president. He was calling for changes in the appointments process months before his election. Not the people to whom President Bush delegated the task of managing the process. They worked as hard and with as much competence as any presidential personnel advisers ever had. The answer is the process itself. Staffing a new administration in the twenty-first century has become a task too large, burdened by procedures too dense and resistance too potent.

Too Many Appointees

Without any blueprint or defining theory, the number of positions filled by presidential appointees has grown steadily over recent decades, expanding outward with the creation of new departments and agencies, expanding downward as positions once filled by senior civil servants have been converted to political appointments. President Bush had nearly 3,300 positions subject to his appointment, more than any president could hope to fill in a timely fashion even with an appointments process far more efficient than the one under which we currently labor. In 2001, thoughtful members of Congress have begun to call for a substantial reduction in the number of presidential appointments, perhaps as many as a third of the current total.

Some people oppose this reduction, arguing that it will undercut the president's ability to control and lead the government.[3] Others argue that every one of the positions currently filled by appointment is critical to good management.

Perhaps. But there is a heavy and unmet burden of proof on those who make this argument. It's called the facts. We have never succeeded in developing an appointments process that could adequately meet the staffing burden this many positions imposes. As a consequence, it now takes nearly a quarter of a presidential term to get an administration staffed. It is hard to sustain the case for so many appointed positions when it is so long and arduous a task to fill them.

Too Thick a Process

The Bush appointees in 2001 were expected to complete forms and questionnaires that asked more than 200 questions.[4] The IRS reviewed their taxes. Law enforcement authorities across the country were solicited for any relevant files. The FBI conducted a complete full-field investigation on them. They were subject to intensive questioning by the Office of Presidential Personnel, by vetters, and by the White House Counsel.

The Office of Government Ethics and lawyers in the White House and at the agency where they would serve scrutinized every detail of their personal finances, often requiring that they divest assets or alter their portfolios to avoid potential conflicts of interest. Their policy views, their public record, and all of their writings and public statements were combed for any material that might undermine their nomination or embarrass the president. When they were done with all of this, if they ever were, then they endured largely duplicative inquiries and investigations at the hands of Senate committee staffs.

That it may take many months to accomplish all of this, especially at the outset of a new administration when all the systems are in overload, is no surprise—except to those unfortunate nominees who are unfamiliar with the appointment process when they enter it, and as the months pass are shocked to discover just how hard it has become to serve one's country.[5]

Too Fragmented a Senate

The Senate has an important role in the appointments process and the framers of the Constitution were astute in recognizing that personnel evaluations often must rely on personal judgments. In substantial part, that is why the appointments process, as they invented it, was so uncluttered with rules, constraints, standards, and specifications.

But the framers could not have envisioned the impacts of a long period of divided government. The intensifying partisanship of contemporary legislative-executive conflict has invaded the appointments process and altered it substantially. For most of our history, the dominant Senate view was that the president was entitled to staff his administration with persons of his own choosing, that the Senate would object to the president's choices only when there was overwhelming necessity. That view prevails now only rhetorically.

In practice, the modern Senate regards itself as a co-equal participant in the appointments process. And individual senators have come to regard the appointments process as fertile ground for their own efforts to shape the ideology of the administration, to fight for their own policy initiatives, to settle old scores, and to second guess administrative decisions.

The most effective device at their disposal is the "hold," an arcane Senate tradition that allows an individual senator to place a hold on a nomination for whatever reasons and for however long he or she may choose. During the time a hold is in place, the nomination is dead in the water.

Holds reached epidemic proportions in the final years of the Clinton presidency. Some observers assumed that this was simply a consequence of bad relations between a Democratic president and a Republican-controlled Senate, that things would change when one party controlled both houses.

But the habits of divided government die hard, and even in the few months before Senator Jim Jeffords undercut the Republican majority in the Senate, holds were being imposed by senators of both parties. For example, Jesse Helms, the Senate's leading holder, had no reservations about putting a five-month hold on Kenneth Dam, Bush's nominee for deputy Treasury secretary.

The practice of holds, combined with the much more thorough investigations that Senate committees conduct of nominees, the growing burden of scheduling hearings for nominees to so many positions, and the benefits of delay that come to those who dislike a nominee or the nominee's policy views have changed the Senate's role from that of ultimate quality check on nominees to a

Figure 3 • Average and Median Number of Days between Senate Receipt of Nomination and Confirmation of Executive Branch Appointees, 1989–1999

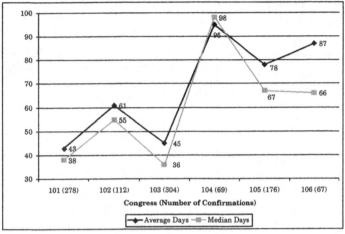

Source: Constructed from data in Loomis 2001 (165).

place where nominations often go and disappear for months at a time, as Figure 3 indicates.

Conclusion

It was business as usual for the Bush administration in 2001, but it's a lousy business. Staffing the highest levels of government has become a nightmare for contemporary presidents. And for friends of democracy who believe that those who win elections ought to be able to govern, the deep flaws in the presidential appointments process are more than arcane matters of public management. They are central concerns that pose serious questions about what democracy can be and what it has become in America at the beginning of the twenty-first century. ∎

Notes

1. Clay Johnson, interview, White House Interview Project, 23 February 2001.

2. Calculations for this and the presidential averages reported in subsequent paragraphs were done by the author from data reported in *Congressional Quarterly Almanacs* for 1961, 1969, 1981, and 1989. The average for the Clinton administration was calculated from reports prepared by Rogelio Garcia for the Congressional Research Service.

3. Robert Moranto and Robert Moffit, "Keep 'Em Coming: In Defense of Political Appointees," *Washington Times*, 2 May 2001.

4. See Terry Sullivan's (2001) detailed analysis of these forms.

5. The confirmation process for judicial appointments has similarly lengthened over the past decade. See Binder 2001.

References

Binder, Sarah. 2001. "Lessons Learned from Judicial Appointments." In *Innocent Until Nominated: The Breakdown of the Presidential Appointments Process,* ed. G. Calvin Mackenzie. Washington, DC: Brookings.

Loomis, Burdett. 2001. "The Senate: An Obstacle Course?" In *Innocent Until Nominated: The Breakdown of the Presidential Appointments Process,* ed. G. Calvin Mackenzie. Washington, DC: Brookings.

Presidential Appointee Initiative. Washington, DC: The Brookings Institution. <www.appointee.brookings.edu>.

Sullivan, Terry. 2001. "Repetitiveness, Redundancy, and Reform: Rationalizing the Inquiry of Presidential Appointees." In *Innocent Until Nominated: The Breakdown of the Presidential Appointments Process,* ed. G. Calvin Mackenzie. Washington, DC: Brookings.

Why Was This Research Needed?

1. In what ways does a slow appointments process undermine the practice of American democracy, according to Mackenzie?
2. When did the appointments process begin to slow down in recent decades and for what reasons?
3. How does the author intend to use his research to contribute to a better understanding of the appointments process?

How Was the Topic Studied?

1. What sources of published data does the author rely on in this study?
2. Which aspects of this study would you characterize as primarily descriptive? Which aspects are analytical?
3. What are the variables examined in this research? Classify them in terms of nominal, ordinal, and interval scales.
4. What kinds of graphs are presented in the reading? Explain how both the format of the data and the narrative objective determined the author's selection of different graphing techniques in Figures 1, 2, and 3. How else might the author have organized these data?

What Are the Findings?

1. How does Mackenzie measure the "pace of the appointments process"? By how much has the appointments process slowed down over the past four decades?

2. Based on Figure 2, by what date had all of President Bush's nominees been announced? Based on the data in this graph, would you say the Bush administration was prompt in nominating its political appointees after taking office? Explain.
3. Figure 3 presents two measures of central tendency: the mathematical average, or mean, and the median. How are these measures calculated? Would identification of the mode have contributed additional information about confirmation delays? Explain.
4. What does it signify when the mean and median of a distribution differ? What insight into the appointments process can we gain by noting the changing relationship between the mean and median over the different Congresses examined in Figure 3? What is an outlier, and how might it be useful to check for outliers in this data set?

What Do the Results Mean?

1. Mackenzie cites both political and procedural factors to explain the slowing down of the political appointments process. Explain how you would begin to assess the contribution of each type of factor, either by further analysis of the data presented here or the collection of new data.
2. Certain members of Congress have called for reductions in the number of political appointees. Would you favor this solution? What other possible reforms of the appointments process can you suggest?

Afterword from G. Calvin Mackenzie

I conducted research on presidential appointments for more than thirty years. Although I constantly sought new information sources and research strategies, I always depended heavily on two old staples of the research trade. One is tracking and counting. With enough presidential appointments over enough years, one begins to see patterns. Sometimes those patterns reveal change—as in the time it takes to staff new administrations—and sometimes they reveal consistency. When I first published data on the changing length of presidential personnel transitions, my findings were widely reported—not because the techniques were especially sophisticated but rather because no one had previously undertaken the painstaking task of tracking and counting the time it took to fill appointed positions at the outset of new administrations.

The second technique on which I've relied heavily is interviewing. I'm often asked to review manuscripts on presidential appointments for scholarly journals. In those manuscripts I find assessments of why presidents chose a particular person for a position or what appointment strategies a president was following. Yet far too often those assessments are based on pure speculation. Why not just ask the people around a president why a particular appointment was made or what strategies governed their appointment decisions? I've interviewed nearly all the presidential personnel directors of the past half-century. They've been wonderfully forthcoming in describing their task, their approaches, their successes, and their failures. A substantial portion of what I've learned about this complex process has come from my discussions with the people who have had to manage it.

I "retired" from writing about presidential appointments after the Bush transition of 2000–2002. My research has moved on to other subjects. But the presidential appointment process remains a vital and highly charged component of contemporary American government. I hope others will find it as interesting and challenging a topic as I did for several decades. And I hope that they'll keep counting and tracking—and talking to the people about whose activities they are writing.

Interviewing Political Elites: Lessons from Russia

Sharon Werning Rivera, Polina M. Kozyreva, and Eduard G. Sarovskii

As the readings in this volume demonstrate, the range of quantitative techniques available to the political science analyst is extensive, and there are many issues involved in selecting and interpreting the correct measure for a given circumstance. Yet sound statistical applications do not guarantee high-quality research products. Calculations come late in the overall research sequence, after the research strategy has already been developed and executed. Whether data are meaningful and sufficient to the purposes of a study is a direct function of how they have been collected.

Although numerous books present information on research methodology—the alternative procedures and expected outcomes of different approaches—no single text can anticipate all the contingencies that arise in the field. Therefore it is important that scholars with a variety of research experiences share their hard-won wisdom, explaining the adaptations they have found necessary in settings that are ill suited to conventional data gathering. In short, there is a politics (and an anthropology) of research that must be understood if projects are to be implemented effectively.

The following reading by Sharon Werning Rivera and her two colleagues at the Russian Academy of Sciences, Polina M. Kozyreva and Eduard G. Sarovskii, was part of a PS *symposium on political science interview methods. This selection concerns the methodology of survey research with political elites. Survey research is a familiar technique in political science; its many components—including sample selection, instrument design, and interviewing—have been thoroughly documented by specialists, often in a manner that encourages a kind of rigorous standardization. For Rivera and her coauthors, context is everything. They argue that a nation's political environment should be factored into the survey research process, and they address questions that could arise in conducting a study such as theirs. How do you deal with respondents whose past political experiences have made them suspicious of strangers asking questions? How do you conduct sampling when no listing of people in your target population has been published? How do you overcome barriers of communication when navigating a disorganized bureaucracy?*

Ultimately, this reading presents a number of practical suggestions for those carrying out population-based research under a defined set of political-environmental conditions. Students should take note of the authors' overarching perspective that links the beginning, middle, and ending stages of the research process.

The past decade has opened up unprecedented opportunities for scholars of post-communist countries. Throughout much of Eastern Europe and the former Soviet Union, scholars can now engage policymakers and other elites directly through interviews—probing their decision calculi and obtaining unpublished information and data. Yet there are gaps in the scholarly literature that would prepare researchers for interviewing highly placed individuals in these countries.

This is largely because most of the related literature discusses techniques for interviewing elites in advanced industrial democracies (e.g., Aberbach, Chesney, and Rockman 1975; Dexter 1970; Peabody et al. 1990). While informative and to some extent applicable, there are significantly fewer works that address obstacles confronted by those working in the post-communist world. Even experience gained in other countries undergoing transitions from authoritarian rule may not be entirely applicable, since the post-communist countries arguably exhibit a number of unique features that set them apart from other instances of authoritarian breakdown (Bunce 1998; Terry 1993). The experience of communist rule and its sudden collapse produced, in varying degrees, a disorganized and often disoriented civil society, poorly-institutionalized political parties, weak and financially strapped states, only partially reconstructed security agencies, and in some regions, suspicion of the West. All of these features can pose unique problems for the elite researcher, examples of which include difficulties in constructing sampling frames due to incomplete information; problems in locating respondents who may work without receptionists or answering machines; a general apprehension towards foreigners and/or interviews; an aversion to advance scheduling; and suspicions aroused by standard demographic questions.

There is now a wealth of English-language studies spanning a range of post-communist countries that rely extensively on elite interviews and/or surveys (e.g., Fish 1995; Hahn 1993; Higley and Lengyel 2000; Jacob, Ostrowski, and Teune 1993; Lane 1995; Lukin 2000; McFaul 2001; Miller, Hesli, and Reisinger 1997; Miller, White, and Heywood 1998; Remington 2001; Rohrschneider 1999; Sperling 1999; Steen 1997; Stoner-Weiss 1997; Szelényi and Szelényi 1995; Yoder 1999; Zimmerman 2002). However, there are few methodological tools to guide scholars of post-communist countries who either lack the resources to commission surveys by in-country experts or desire to conduct in-depth personal interviews.

Such concerns motivated us to write this article. We offer a few suggestions on interviewing elites in Russia;[1] our advice should also be applicable to other post-communist countries and possibly to other states that exhibit higher levels of political instability than do advanced industrial countries. We base our conclusions on a series of 133 in-depth interviews with top-level bureaucrats and parliamentary deputies which we conducted (in Russian) in Moscow and two regions of the Russian Federation (Nizhnii Novgorod and Tatarstan) in 1996, and which will be replicated in the Putin era.[2]

Selecting an Appropriate Sample Design

The selection of an appropriate sample design is a key decision that affects the type of conclusions that one can draw later during data analysis. In considering various ways of drawing a sample of Russia's national political elite, we initially believed that probability sampling would be impossible. We reasoned that although a sampling frame could be constructed without much difficulty, the polarized political context and general suspicion of foreigners would frustrate our efforts to arrange interviews with the individuals selected for the sample. Hence, we considered nonprobability sampling techniques that tend to rely more heavily on personal contacts and introductions, such as a referral (or snowball) sample.

Yet due to the limitations that nonprobability sampling would impose on our ability to generalize from our sample to the population of Russian national political elites,[3] we chose to employ probability sampling.[4] We used a stratified random sample design, in which the strata were defined by institutional affiliation. The political elite was defined by positional criteria, consisting of parliamentary deputies from the lower house of the national legislature and top-level bureaucrats working in federal ministries. Although Russia's "national political elite" arguably encompasses more sectors than just these two, we narrowed our scope in order to be comparable to the Aberbach, Putnam, and Rockman (1981) study of bureaucratic and parliamentary elites in seven advanced industrial nations. Using their criteria for defining our survey populations, our bureaucrats directed departments, divisions, or bureaus in federal ministries; were situated in the nation's capital; and occupied positions roughly one to two rungs below the minister.[5] The parliamentarians were members of the lower house of Russia's national legislature, the State Duma. Analogous samples were drawn in each of the two provincial capitals as well.[6]

For the national-level sample, a sampling frame was readily available for only the parliamentary deputies and consisted of a published list of the 450 deputies elected in the December 1995 parliamentary elections. Constructing a sampling frame for the federal bureaucrats was considerably more problematic, although as Aberbach and Rockman (2002) point out, this is a challenge not restricted to the Russian experience. Over the past decade, government directories of all sorts have proliferated in Russia, but we did not find one that was entirely comprehensive and up-to-date. Consequently, we compiled our own list of ministry department heads (379 in all), using a variety of published directories to draft a preliminary list. We then personally contacted all of the ministries and cajoled them to verify and update the information. (Vestiges of Soviet-era secrecy still live on in Russia's federal bureaucracy: ministerial information centers were often quite reluctant to divulge information on their organizational structures, personnel, or contact numbers—especially to anyone speaking Russian with a foreign accent.) Within each stratum, a random sample of individuals was selected to represent the stratum.

From there it often took 15 to 20 phone calls to arrange a single interview, whereas a 1959 survey of U.S. members of Congress averaged 3.3 callbacks per respondent (Robinson 1960, 129). Yet sheer persistence paid off. Response rates mirrored and in some cases surpassed rates achieved in other elite studies in a variety of contexts.[7] As Table 1 shows, we interviewed 81.8% of the national parliamentary deputies in our sample, 74.5% of the federal bureaucrats, and between 60.9% and 86.7% of the four regional samples. Moreover, most of the nonresponses were not outright refusals to grant an interview. Most failures to interview respondents stemmed from a problem endemic to all elite interviewing—the extraordinarily busy lives of the respondents. (Respondents were particularly busy at this

Table 1
Reasons for Nonresponse

	Interviews Completed n (%)	Refusals n (%)	Unavailable n (%)	Total Sample Size n (%)
Duma deputies	45 (81.8)	2 (3.6)	8 (14.6)	55 (100.0)
Federal bureaucrats	38 (74.5)	4 (7.8)	9 (17.7)	51 (100.0)
N. Novgorod deputies	11 (73.3)	1 (6.7)	3 (20.0)	15 (100.0)
N. Novgorod bureaucrats	14 (60.9)	0 (0.0)	9 (39.1)	23 (100.0)
Tatarstan deputies	13 (86.7)	1 (6.7)	1 (6.7)	15 (100.1)
Tatarstan bureaucrats	12 (80.0)	0 (0.0)	3 (20.0)	15 (100.0)

Note: Response rates are calculated based on the number of eligible elements in each sample. In total, there were only four blanks (all in the federal bureaucratic sample), since four ministerial departments were no longer in existence. In Nizhnii Novgorod, there was one substitution made for a deputy who refused an interview, and in two cases, deputy department heads were interviewed because the department heads were unavailable. Percentages may not sum to 100.0% due to rounding.

time because the 1996 presidential campaign was in full swing.) This type of nonresponse was coded as unavailable, meaning either that contact could not be made with the respondent or that a convenient time for the interview could never be arranged.

Although a great deal of persistence was necessary to convince respondents to grant us interviews, accessibility was greater than anticipated overall.[8] Thus, although there are circumstances in which nonprobability sampling is the preferred option, probability sampling is a viable option for many countries outside of the developed world. The key to its success is perseverance in locating respondents and convincing them to grant interviews.

Gaining Access to Respondents

Some of the factors impeding access to highly placed officials in Russia are undoubtedly similar to those faced by elite interviewers in any context. However, those working in post-communist societies confront additional problems in securing interviews. First, the simple process of locating respondents and agreeing on a time for an interview is complicated by the fluidity of the political environment and the newness of various political institutions. For example, deputies in the Russian Duma often worked without receptionists and/or answering machines. Second, some respondents may be less familiar with the interview process than elites in advanced industrial democracies. This no doubt contributed to the greater apprehension about the interviews that we observed among the civil servants than among the parliamentary deputies, a finding also reported by Denitch (1972, 155) in the former Yugoslavia.

Third, respondents in more politically unstable environments may be a good deal more suspicious about the goals and purposes of the research project. As noted earlier, our project coincided with the highly politicized, polarized environment of the 1996 presidential elections, leading several respondents to suspect that the survey was merely a cover for their political opponents to acquire potentially damaging information. Several expressed concern that "someone wanted to learn about their views"—whether it be the Yeltsin administration, their political competitors,

state security agencies, or foreigners. For instance, in answering the demographic questions, one regional deputy (D-115) remarked that it seemed as if the information was being collected for the "organs" [of state security].[9] Deputies from the Communist Party of the Russian Federation (CPRF) were particularly guarded since a listening device reportedly had been found in their offices during the presidential campaign.[10]

Hence, the process of gaining access to respondents in Russia and then winning their confidence requires some special attention. We present a few suggestions for surmounting potential roadblocks in post-communist and other countries in transition.

Have an Institutional Affiliation

All the interviews in our project were conducted under the auspices of the Institute of Sociology of the Russian Academy of Sciences, with the interviewing responsibilities in Moscow divided between the American (Rivera) and the Russian (Sarovskii). Interviewers were affiliated with either the Institute of Sociology or another institute of the Academy of Sciences, and the questionnaire itself mentioned the institute's sponsorship and listed a contact name and phone number. Despite the interviewers mentioning the goals of the interview and the sponsoring organization when introducing themselves, respondents often asked additional questions about who was sponsoring the research. The fact that the study was being undertaken in association with an authoritative, well-established institution seemed to assure respondents that the research was genuinely intended for academic purposes.[11] In a study of Yugoslav opinion leaders conducted in 1968, the role of having appropriate "legitimizers" is also clear (Denitch 1972, 153).[12] In China, however, interpersonal connections and relationships were found to be more crucial than official channels in obtaining access (Hsu 2000, Ch. 3).

Reassure the Respondent That There Are No Right Answers

Another problem we encountered in securing interviews was that some respondents apparently equated the interview situation with an examination. Some expressed concern that they would not be able to answer our questions; this was particularly true for bureaucrats, who said they could answer questions about the work of their ministries but not about more general themes. One Duma deputy was unconcerned about the confidentiality of the information, but rather wanted reassurance that the interviewer would not ridicule him (D-026). During the interview itself, some respondents became perceptibly guarded and tense, and when answering, they seemed to be searching for words that would demonstrate a certain level of competence and erudition.

Throughout the entire process, we tried to reassure respondents that there were no correct answers to our questions. We also stressed that they were members of a highly select group of individuals, whose task it was to make key decisions in the realm of public policy. As a result, any answers they could provide in and of themselves would constitute very valuable information for us. Such reassurances seemed to alleviate certain insecurities and anxieties felt by some respondents in this regard.

One potential pitfall is the tendency for the interviewer to be overly deferential and concerned with establishing rapport, thereby losing the ability to control the direction and scope of the interview (Ostrander 1993).

Establish an Appropriate Identity for the Interviewer

One of the issues that must be resolved by each researcher is how to present oneself to the respondents in the study. Some researchers believe that "in the typical interview there exists a hierarchical relation, with the respondent being in the subordinate position." Accordingly, feminist researchers have suggested that a way of responding to these inequalities and minimizing status differences is for interviewers to "show their human side and answer questions and express feelings" (Fontana and Frey 2000, 658).

Yet to preserve our structured interview format, we chose to address these potential inequalities by emphasizing the status and rights of the respondents. For instance, when respondents were deciding whether to grant us interviews, we would remind them that since we were only the "requesting party," they always had the last word. This reassured them that they had the upper hand in the interview and could refuse to answer any question if they so chose.

At the same time, elite researchers emphasize the need for balance when establishing the researcher's identity. One potential pitfall is the tendency for the interviewer to be overly deferential and concerned with establishing rapport, thereby losing the ability to control the direction and scope of the interview (Ostrander 1993). As a counterweight, some recommend conveying to respondents that you've "done your homework" on them so that the extent of preparation for the interview causes respondents to take you seriously (Richards 1996, 202–203; Zuckerman 1972, 164–66). However, we concur with the views expressed by Denitch (1972, 154), whose interviewers in the Yugoslav context gave no indication that they knew anything about the backgrounds of the respondents. Revealing knowledge about the interviewees, he contends, might raise too many doubts about anonymity.

Another helpful factor was that the occupational status of the interviewers—by and large professional researchers—was roughly equivalent to many of the respondents. This appeared to foster mutual understanding and convince respondents that their answers and comments would be understood. In much the same way, Alan Aldridge (1993) notes that emphasizing the congruence between his occupational status as an academic and that of his respondents facilitated access, rapport, and high-quality responses. Occupational status seemed to outweigh potential problems created by gender. Despite 95.2% of the Moscow-based respondents being male, this was not a significant obstacle for the female (American) interviewer in any discernible way.[13]

Request Interviews in Person When Possible

In most elite projects (and indeed, in other projects described in this symposium), initial contact is made via an introductory letter explaining the goals of the project.

This is usually followed by a phone call to set a date and time for the interview. Outside of the developed world, however, this approach is of less utility for a variety of reasons, both technical and cultural. Technical barriers to advance scheduling of interviews can include an undependable mail service, unreliable reception and delivery of mail in offices, and incomplete—or in some cases—nonexistent directories and phone books. Cultural barriers involve—at least in the Russian case and also in China—a penchant for day-to-day scheduling without much advance notice. As a matter of fact, when requesting an appointment for the following week, respondents frequently told us that it was too far in advance to plan and requested that we call back on the day that we wished to speak with them. Other interviewers working with Russian elites also found that introductory letters were of limited use and that it was necessary to approach potential interviewees by telephone (White et al. 1996, 310).[14] Thus, rather than using an introductory letter, we simply phoned respondents directly with our requests.

Once we were granted a pass to a ministerial building or the parliament for one interview, it proved useful simply to appear unannounced at the offices of other respondents on our sample list who were located in the same institution. In most cases, a request made in person increased the likelihood that the target respondent would agree to an interview.

Developing a Questionnaire

The methodological costs and benefits of open-ended queries versus closed-ended questions have been discussed in the literature (Aberbach, Chesney, and Rockman 1975; Schuman and Presser 1981, 79–112), and we will not repeat them here. Like several other authors in this symposium, we wish to highlight the importance of open-ended questions for elite interviewing. In our experience, Russian elites strongly resisted the imposition of categories or choices on their reasoning processes. One Duma deputy remarked that "sociologists aren't inclined to understand that it's impossible to answer some questions in the way that they've instructed us to. They are not inclined to

make a notation to the effect that a certain answer is not precisely as stated but is rather slightly different" (D-013).

Yet we did not use open-ended questions exclusively; rather, we used a combination of open-ended and closed-ended questions (refined through pretesting and back-translation), presented in alternating fashion. The first five questions were very general open-ended queries, followed by a couple of closed-ended questions, and so on in a similar fashion. This sequencing had several advantages. First, once the introductory open-ended questions had been covered, it was easy to elicit answers to the more formulaic questions. We had demonstrated respect for the complexity of their views through the open-ended questions and thus had "earned" the right to ask questions posed exclusively from our frame of reference. Also, the closed-ended questions probably allowed respondents to recover a bit from the more demanding open-ended question format. Second, since political elites can expound on their responses at great length, especially in the early stages of an interview, we tried to channel such tendencies toward subjects on which we desired elaboration. Third, although the interview was fully structured, the frequency and format of the open-ended questions (with scripted probes written into the interview protocol) gave it a more semi-structured feel.[15]

The oral interview also included a series of background questions, which we anticipated would be perceived by some as threatening since they included not only standard demographic questions such as age, education, and place of birth, but also questions dealing with past and present political activities, travel abroad, business dealings, and the like. By contrast, elite interviewers working in Austria and France several decades ago encountered an entirely different situation. According to them, asking personal and biographical questions at the beginning of the interview "served to relax respondents and involve them in the interview" (Hunt, Crane, and Wahlke 1964, 68). In the Russian context, however, these types of questions can raise suspicions, and thus we heeded the following advice—to put threatening behavioral questions "near the end of the interview so that the interviewer has a chance to establish good rapport with the respondent" (Sudman and Bradburn 1974, 143). In an attempt to minimize response effects, we asked the background questions after all of the substantive questions and also phrased them in the most general and non-threatening way. For example, when questioning elites about their residence abroad, we formulated the question as follows: "Did you ever happen to live abroad (not including the Commonwealth of Independent States and the Baltics) for a period of three months or more?" By phrasing the question in this way, we tried to: (1) draw attention away from their reason for living abroad, and (2) downplay their having been in a position to live abroad during the Soviet era, as this was a right granted only with Communist Party approval. This was important because in the post-communist era, some respondents may be reluctant to disclose the extent of their previous involvement with the Party.

Another means of putting respondents at ease during the interviews was to assure them that their identities would remain confidential, be presented only in aggregate or anonymous form, and be used only in academic research. Several other phrases also proved helpful in coaxing answers out of reluctant respondents: asking them to say "something—if only a few words" in response to a question; telling them that there are as many different opinions as there are people (*Skol'ko lyudei, stol'ko mnenii*); and reminding them—if they objected to a question—that they had the last word in deciding whether to answer it.

After completing the oral part of the interview (which was conducted in Russian and, in the vast majority of cases, tape recorded), we asked all respondents to fill out a short, self-administered written questionnaire consisting primarily of closed-ended value questions. Again, building on the rapport that had developed over the course of the interview, most respondents completed this questionnaire on the spot, in the presence of the interviewer. Occasionally, time constraints required that questionnaires be left with respondents; in those cases, we usually expended substantial efforts on retrieving them. In the end, only 7.5% of all 133 respondents (from Moscow and the two regions) failed to complete the self-administered written questionnaires.

One additional issue that affected our use of both open-ended and closed-ended questions was the challenge of translating certain concepts into Russian. For example, the phrase "authoritarian rule" can be translated literally as *avtoritarnaya vlast'*. Alternatively, a more commonly used phrase, "strong hand" (*zhestkaya ruka*), can be used, although the latter phrase has a weaker connotation and its meaning is subject to a wider variety of interpretations. In such cases, the American researcher deferred to the judgment of native Russian speakers, aiming above all to capture the spirit of the phrase or concept. Several pretests with "debriefings" by native Russian speakers as to how they understood problematic concepts were also helpful, as was back-translation of the questionnaire into English by a native English speaker fluent in Russian. In cases where conceptual problems arose with the meanings of standard closed-ended questions that had been used previously by other researchers, we retained the original Russian-language wording. We regarded the ability to conduct reliable comparisons with prior findings as more important than linguistic clarity. ∎

Notes

The authors gratefully acknowledge the financial support of a Rackham Graduate School-Russian Academy of Sciences' Institute of Sociology Collaboration Grant provided by the University of Michigan. Rivera thanks Cornell University's Institute for European Studies for a Mellon-Sawyer Postdoctoral Fellowship in Democratization that facilitated the writing of this article. For helpful comments and suggestions, we thank Carolyn Hsu, Steve Heeringa, David Rivera, and Aseema Sinha.

1. For insights on conducting surveys of the mass public in the post-communist region, see Gibson 1994; Swafford 1992.

2. For details on the interviews, sample, and methodology, see Rivera 1998, 2000.

3. As Judd, Smith, and Kidder (1991, 133) succinctly state, "Probability sampling is the only approach that makes possible representative sampling plans. It makes it possible for the investigators to estimate the extent to which the findings based on their sample are likely to differ from what they would have found by studying the population."

4. We recognize that nonprobability sampling may be the most appropriate vehicle for certain projects where acces-

sibility is much more problematic (e.g., interviewing economic or business elites, as in McDowell 1998) or where the sample size is very small. Nonprobability sampling also has the advantage of convenience and cost effectiveness, which may outweigh the researcher's desire to be able to "specify the chances that the sample findings do not differ by more than a certain amount from the true population values"—a feature of probability sampling (Judd, Smith, and Kidder 1991, 134–136). See also Kalton 1983, 90–93.

5. Following Aberbach, Putnam, and Rockman (1981, 27), we excluded (1) the Ministries of Defense and Internal Affairs (though we included the Ministry of Foreign Affairs) and (2) departments that "performed obvious staff functions." In the Russian case, first deputy ministers and deputy ministers were considered to constitute one level.

6. We are grateful to Yurii Gapeenkov and his team, Liliya Sagitova, and Guzel Stolarova for their help in the regions.

7. Robert D. Putnam (1973, 15) reports response rates of 85% for British MPs and 78% for Italian parliamentarians. See also Aberbach, Putnam, and Rockman 1981, 26; Hoffmann-Lange, 1987, 36; McDonough 1981, 253; Verba et al. 1987, 280–81.

8. In both the Yugoslav and American contexts (Denitch 1972, 146; Ostrander 1993, 9; Zuckerman 1972, 161), researchers imply that the difficulties of gaining access to certain elites have been overstated.

9. These numbers identify the interviewees in the study. "D" denotes deputies and "G" stands for government bureaucrats.

10. Interviews conducted in non-election years should meet less politically charged suspicion. Moreover, if Michael McFaul (1997) is correct that the 1996 presidential race was the last "revolutionary," highly ideological, and polarized election in which the principal divide was between pro-reform and anti-reform groups, even interviews conducted during election campaigns in Russia should be less problematic in the future. On the other hand, a certain measure of secrecy on the part of the CPRF has extended beyond the 1996 elections. Deputies will not say in advance where plenary sessions of the party's Central Committee will be held. As one deputy, Yurii Chunkov, explains: "We want to keep the location secret as long as possible so they won't tape us. They listen to everything. One hour after a conversation, the transcript is on the desk of whoever needs to see it" (Bohlen 1998, 1).

11. In the context of this single study, it is difficult to measure precisely what difference such an affiliation made in terms of access and information supplied to the interviewers. For reflections on the impact of sponsorship by an elite interviewer working in London, see McDowell (1998, 2136).

12. This is also an important factor in Zuckerman's access to Nobel laureates in science (Zuckerman 1972, 162–63). For more on sponsorship, see Dexter 1970, 50–55, and Javeline 1996.

13. In a series of interviews with high-status employees of merchant banks in London, McDowell (1998, 2140–41) expresses a similar viewpoint. To her surprise, most of her male interviewees "seemed to feel surprisingly free to be open with [her]," even when discussing gender relations and respondents' attitudes toward their women colleagues. Similarly, in a study of local elites in Scotland and France, Sabot (1999, 334) concludes that gender "becomes secondary to other positional factors," such as nationality. However, in other contexts (e.g., rural areas in India), interviews conducted by a person of another gender can be problematic in many respects.

14. However, one study of elites in Russia sent prospective respondents an interview schedule and accompanying letter that described the goals and character of the research, achieving a response rate of 70% (Mikul'skii et al. 1995, 35–36).

15. We should note one drawback to this approach. Some elites, especially civil servants, found the lack of specificity inherent in the opening battery of questions disconcerting. They felt that the questions were too general and wide ranging.

References

Aberbach, Joel D., James D. Chesney, and Bert A. Rockman. 1975. "Exploring Elite Political Attitudes: Some Methodological Lessons." *Political Methodology* 2:1–27.

Aberbach, Joel D., Robert D. Putnam, and Bert A. Rockman. 1981. *Bureaucrats and Politicians in Western Democracies.* Cambridge: Harvard University Press.

Aberbach, Joel D., and Bert A. Rockman. 2002. "Conducting and Coding Elite Interviews." *PS: Political Science and Politics* 35:673–76.

Aldridge, Alan. 1993. "Negotiating Status: Social Scientists and Anglican Clergy." *Journal of Contemporary Ethnography* 22:97–112.

Bohlen, Celestine, "Communists Risking Perks and Power in Yeltsin Battle," *New York Times,* 24 April 1998, sec. A.

Bunce, Valerie, 1998. "Regional Differences in Democratization: The East Versus the South." *Post-Soviet Affairs* 14:187–211.

Denitch, Bogdan, 1972. "Elite Interviewing and Social Structure: An Example from Yugoslavia." *Public Opinion Quarterly* 36:143–58.

Dexter, Lewis Anthony. 1970. *Elite and Specialized Interviewing.* Evanston, IL: Northwestern University Press.

Fish, M. Steven. 1995. *Democracy from Scratch: Opposition and Regime in the New Russian Revolution.* Princeton: Princeton University Press.

Fontana, Andrea, and James H. Frey. 2000. "The Interview: From Structured Questions to Negotiated Text." In *Handbook of Qualitative Research,* 2nd ed., eds. Norman K. Denzin and Yvonna S. Lincoln. Thousand Oaks, CA: Sage Publications, 645–72.

Gibson, James L. 1994. "Survey Research in the Past and Future USSR: Reflections on the Methodology of Mass Opinion Surveys." In *Research in Micropolitics: New Directions in Political Psychology,* Vol. 4, eds. Michael X. Delli Carpini, Leonie Huddy, and Robert Y. Shapiro. Greenwich, CT: JAI Press.

Hahn, Jeffrey. 1993. "Attitudes Toward Reform Among Provincial Russian Politicians." *Post-Soviet Affairs* 9:66–85.

Higley, John, and György Lengyel, eds. 2000. *Elites after State Socialism: Theories and Analysis.* New York: Rowman and Littlefield.

Hoffmann-Lange, Ursula. 1987. "Surveying National Elites in the Federal Republic of Germany." In *Research Methods for Elite Studies,* eds. George Moyser and Margaret Wagstaffe. Boston: Allen & Unwin.

Hsu, Carolyn. 2000. "Creating Market Socialism: Narratives and Emerging Economic Institutions in the People's Republic of China." Ph.D. diss. University of California, San Diego.

Hunt, William H., Wilder W. Crane, and John C. Wahlke. 1964. "Interviewing Political Elites in Cross-cultural Comparative Research." *American Journal of Sociology* 70:59–68.

Jacob, Betty M., Krzysztof Ostrowski, and Henry Teune, eds. 1993. *Democracy and Local Governance: Ten Empirical Studies.* Honolulu, HI: Matsunaga Institute for Peace.

Javeline, Debra, 1996. "Effects of the American Sponsor on Survey Responses in Russia, Ukraine, and Central Asia." Presented at the Annual Meeting of the American Association for the Advancement of Slavic Studies.

Judd, Charles M., Eliot R. Smith, and Louise H. Kidder. 1991. *Research Methods in Social Relations.* 6th ed. Philadelphia: Harcourt Brace Jovanovich College Publishers.

Kalton, Graham. 1983. *Introduction to Survey Sampling.* Newbury Park, CA: Sage Publications.

Kullberg, Judith. 1994. "The Ideological Roots of Elite Political Conflict in Post-Soviet Russia." *Europe-Asia Studies* 46:929–53.

Lane, David. 1995. "Political Elites Under Gorbachev and Yeltsin in the Early Period of Transition: A Reputational and Analytical Study." In *Patterns in Post-Soviet Leadership,* eds. Timothy J. Colton and Robert C. Tucker. Boulder, CO: Westview Press, 29–47.

Lukin, Alexander. 2000. *The Political Culture of the Russian 'Democrats.'* New York: Oxford University Press.

McDonough, Peter. 1981. *Power and Ideology in Brazil.* Princeton: Princeton University Press.

McDowell, L. 1998. "Elites in the City of London: Some Methodological Considerations." *Environment and Planning A* 30:2133–46.

McFaul, Michael. 1997. *Russia's 1996 Presidential Election: The End of Polarized Politics.* Stanford: Hoover Institution Press.

McFaul, Michael. 2001. *Russia's Unfinished Revolution: Political Change from Gorbachev to Putin.* Ithaca: Cornell University Press.

Mikul'skii, K. I., et al. 1995. *Rossiiskaya elita: opyt sotsiologicheskogo analiza—Chast' 1. Kontseptsiya i metody issledovaniya* [The Russian elite: an attempt at a sociological analysis—part one. Conceptualization and research methods]. Moscow: Nauka.

Miller, Arthur H., Vicki L. Hesli, and William M. Reisinger. 1997. "Conceptions of Democracy Among Mass and Elite in Post-Soviet Societies." *British Journal of Political Science* 27:157–90.

Miller, William L., Stephen White, and Paul Heywood. 1998. *Values and Political Change in Postcommunist Europe.* New York: St. Martin's Press.

Ostrander, Susan A. 1993. "Surely You're Not in This Just to Be Helpful': Access, Rapport, and Interviews in Three Studies of Elites." *Journal of Contemporary Ethnography* 22:7–27.

Peabody, Robert L., et al. 1990. "Interviewing Political Elites." *PS: Political Science & Politics* 23:451–55.

Putnam, Robert D. 1973. *The Beliefs of Politicians: Ideology, Conflict, and Democracy in Britain and Italy.* New Haven: Yale University Press.

Remington, Thomas F. 2001. *The Russian Parliament: Institutional Evolution in a Transitional Regime, 1989–1999.* New Haven: Yale University Press.

Richards, David. 1996. "Elite Interviewing: Approaches and Pitfalls." *Politics* 16:199–204.

Rivera, Sharon Werning. 1998. "Communists as Democrats? Elite Political Culture in Post-Communist Russia." Ph.D. diss. University of Michigan.

Rivera, Sharon Werning. 2000. "Elites in Post-Communist Russia: A Changing of the Guard?" *Europe-Asia Studies* 52:413–32.

Robinson, James A. 1960. "Survey Interviewing among Members of Congress." *Public Opinion Quarterly* 24:127–38.

Rohrschneider, Robert. 1999. *Learning Democracy: Democratic and Economic Values in Unified Germany.* New York: Oxford University Press.

Sabot, Cladie Emmanuèle. 1999. "Dr. Jekyl, Mr H(i)de: The Contrasting Face of Elites at Interview." *Geoforum* 30:329–35.

Schuman, Howard, and Stanley Presser. 1981. *Questions and Answers in Attitude Surveys: Experiments on Question Form, Wording, and Context.* New York: Academic Press.

Sperling, Valerie. 1999. *Organizing Women in Contemporary Russia: Engendering Transition.* New York: Cambridge University Press.

Steen, Anton. 1997. *Between Past and Future: Elites, Democracy and the State in Post-Communist Countries—A Comparison of Estonia, Latvia, and Lithuania.* Brookfield: Ashgate.

Stoner-Weiss, Kathryn. 1997. *Local Heroes: The Political Economy of Russian Regional Governance.* Princeton: Princeton University Press.

Sudman, Seymour, and Norman M. Bradburn. 1974. *Response Effects in Surveys: A Review and Synthesis.* Chicago: Aldine Publishing.

Swafford, Michael. 1992. "Sociological Aspects of Survey Research in the Commonwealth of Independent States." *International Journal of Public Opinion Research* 4:346–57.

Szelényi, Iván, and Szonja Szelényi. 1995. "Circulation or Reproduction of Elites during the Postcommunist Transformation of Eastern Europe: Introduction." *Theory and Society* 24:615–38.

Terry, Sarah Meiklejohn. 1993. "Thinking about Post-Communist Transitions: How Different Are They?" *Slavic Review* 52:333–37.

Verba, Sidney, et al. 1987. *Elites and the Idea of Equality: A Comparison of Japan, Sweden, and the United States.* Cambridge: Harvard University Press.

White, Stephen, Olga Kryshtanovskaia, Igor Kukolev, Evan Mawdsley and Pavel Saldin. 1996. "Interviewing the Soviet Elite." *The Russian Review* 55:309–16.

Yoder, Jennifer A. 1999. *From East Germans to Germans? The New Post-communist Elites.* Durham, NC: Duke University Press.

Zimmermann, William. 2002. *The Russian People and Foreign Policy: Russian Elite and Mass Perspectives, 1993–2000.* Princeton: Princeton University Press.

Zuckerman, Harriet. 1972. "Interviewing an Ultra-Elite." *Public Opinion Quarterly* 36:159–75.

Why Was This Research Needed?

1. How has the end of the Communist era created new opportunities for political science researchers interested in the former Soviet bloc?

2. Why do researchers need to modify conventional methodologies when doing survey research in post-Communist countries?

3. What is "elite research"? Describe the kinds of theoretical questions in political science research for which elite research should be conducted as an adjunct or alternative to general public opinion research.

How Was the Topic Studied?

1. What was this study's target population? How do the authors operationalize the concept of Russia's current political elite? What was the sample size?

2. What is the distinction between probability sampling and nonprobability sampling? According to the authors, what trade-offs are involved when choosing between these two sampling designs?

3. What is a "stratified random sample"? Which variable was used to establish the strata in this sample? In general, why is stratification seen as a means of increasing the accuracy of a sample?

4. Describe the process of developing a sampling frame in survey research. What were the challenges of creating the sampling frame for this study? How might the value of a study be undermined by problems in the sampling frame?

What Are the Findings?

1. What steps were necessary to achieve a satisfactory response rate for the sample selected for this study? How could the authors have tried to confirm whether there was any bias in which elites did and did not participate in the interviews?
2. Describe the authors' four general tips on techniques for gaining interviews in unstable political environments. What are the common themes and concerns across these techniques?
3. Explain the distinction between open-ended and closed-ended questions in survey research. Why are open-ended questions often preferred in elite interviews? Why did the authors choose a combination of closed- and open-ended questions?
4. What do the authors conclude about the importance of question sequencing in conducting interviews?

5. In what ways can existing research studies on a topic influence the content and design of subsequent research?

What Do the Results Mean?

1. What claims do the authors make about the applicability of their findings to other settings?
2. In what ways can the process of conducting research in a new social setting help teach researchers about the local political environment, even before the research data have been analyzed?
3. Do you think the authors may have exaggerated the differences in the research environments of Russia and the United States? Are there certain topics, geographic locations, subcultures, or political circumstances in which the advice in this reading would be helpful to survey researchers in the United States?
4. What kinds of analyses can you envision for the next stage of a project like this based on the kinds of data collected? What would the independent and dependent variables be? By what means is it possible to make use of qualitative data—such as the responses to open-ended questions—in quantitative analysis?

Afterword from Sharon Werning Rivera

When embarking upon a new research project, it is tempting to rush immediately into data collection. Before going into the field, however, researchers should think carefully about the kind of data most suitable for answering their research questions, as well as the merits and drawbacks of various ways of collecting the data. Our article highlights the crucial role of the planning stage, since the possibilities for data analysis are greatly constrained by the quality and type of one's data. Once we had decided upon face-to-face elite interviews—a method that may not be appropriate for all research questions dealing with political elites (Lilleker 2003)—we then chose to select our respondents with a probability sampling design. Although this allowed us to generalize from our sample to the population of Russian national political elites, it came at a cost to us in terms of the time and effort involved in seeking to interview only those specific individuals on our sample list.

A second lesson to be drawn from our article is the need to adapt standard survey methodology to the specifics of the project. As Seligson (2005) argues in his overview of survey research in Latin America, the difficulties of conducting research in the developing world should not be used as an excuse for accepting the violation of basic norms of survey research. We found that standard protocols developed for mass surveys needed to be tailored to our elite population, and that other practices had to be adapted to the particularities of the local culture. In cross-national research, researchers must strike a fine balance between adhering to rigorous standards and being willing to change tactics if circumstances warrant it.

In retrospect, although we are still firm believers in the value of open-ended questions—especially in elite studies (for confirmation, see Pierce 2002)—these proved to be extremely time consuming to transcribe verbatim and often difficult to code and analyze. The extent to which such questions are used should be determined in large part by the resources that will be available for the post-interview phase of research. Since we have obtained a full range of possible responses to various open-ended questions of interest to us, we plan to close those questions for use in future surveys.

References

Lilleker, Darren G. 2003. "Interviewing the Political Elite: Navigating a Potential Minefield." *Politics* 23 (3): 207–214.

Pierce, Jason L. 2002. "Interviewing Australia's Senior Judiciary." *Australian Journal of Political Science* 37 (March): 131–142.

Seligson, Mitchell A. 2005. "Improving the Quality of Survey Research in Democratizing Countries." *PS: Political Science & Politics* 38 (January): 51–56.

The Size and Composition of the Anti-Nazi Opposition in Germany

Gabriel A. Almond, with Wolfgang Kraus

Gabriel Almond, the primary author of this reading, is considered one of the giants of twentieth-century American political science. When he died in 2002, Almond left a legacy of scholarship spanning nearly seventy years and encompassing a broad gamut of topics central to the evolution of the discipline—political sociology, public opinion, political psychology, political culture, religion and politics, leadership, and more (Eulau, Pye, and Verba 2003). Almond's greatest contributions were in the area of comparative politics, which he helped shape into a vibrant interdisciplinary field focusing on political development, values, and systemic performance rather than just the formal organization of governments. Almond's work was marked by an eclectic methodological orientation throughout his career. As Almond was equally comfortable planning interviews, digging through documentary sources, and carrying out statistical analysis, he became a compelling advocate for the complementary use of qualitative and quantitative approaches.

The reading that follows was originally prepared as a report to the U.S. Air Force by Almond and his coauthor following Germany's defeat in World War II. Almond's analysis, which returns us to a fateful juncture in U.S. history, is a significant artifact from the history of social science research. In the late 1940s, American political science was still a few years from the burst of productive energy and new methods and perspectives known as "the behavioral revolution" of the 1950s and 1960s. Yet Almond's involvement in the gathering of American intelligence during World War II attested to the growing stature of social scientists in American society. Almond's assignment, which was a retrospective assessment of the extent of anti-Nazi opposition inside Germany, was difficult because the research data were fragmentary, not easily accessible, and only partly relevant to the question at hand. It was up to the young scholar, using the tools of his trade, to piece together the puzzle as best he could.

Almond's final report is inconclusive, and his use of statistics seems rudimentary from the standpoint of contemporary political science. Still, one must appreciate the sophisticated understanding of the research problem that his work demonstrated, as well as the creative way in which he synthesized various forms of information to produce this analysis.

Reference

Eulau, H., L. Pye, and S. Verba. 2003. "Memorial Resolution: Gabriel Almond." *Stanford Report,* May 21. http://newsservice.stanford.edu/news/2003/may21/gabrielmem-521.html.

This document, titled "The Size and Composition of the Anti-Nazi Opposition in Germany," was found among the reports of the United States Strategic Bombing Survey (USSBS) of the U.S. Air Force in the National Archives. The finder was Professor Karl-Heinz Reuband of the Institute of the Social Sciences of the Heinrich Heine University of Dusseldorf, who was engaged in research on German attitudes during the Nazi period. The report was identified in handwriting, "Technical Report, G. Almond." There is an illegible set of letters and numbers, designating its location in the National Archives. Professor Reuband notified me of his find, and sent me a copy.

This report, written in a collaboration with my colleague Wolfgang Kraus, the details of which I have forgotten, was one of the supporting reports of the Morale Division of USSBS. The Morale Division was headed by Rensis Likert, later of University of Michigan Survey Research Center fame. The USSBS social science team included several of the social psychologists who would later staff the Institute of Social Sciences and the Survey Research Center of the University of Michigan—Rensis Likert, Angus Campbell, Daniel Katz, Dorwin Cartwright, as well as Otto Klineberg and Herbert Hyman of Columbia University. The major job of the Morale Division was to conduct an attitude survey on the effects of bombing on German morale using a questionnaire administered to a probability sample of Germans in the immediate aftermath of the war.

In the Morale Division I was given the assignment of planning and conducting a supplementary study on documentary sources, such as surviving records of German police and intelligence organizations and on interviews with captured and interned Gestapo and Sicherheitsdienst officials and surviving opposition leaders.

My section consisted of two six-men teams: one headed by me, and a second headed by Wolfgang Kraus, a political scientist knowledgeable about National Socialist Germany who was on leave from George Washington University. Each team had a jeep and weapons carrier, and consisted of two German-speaking GIs and one or two military personnel. My team went east, first to Leipzig and Halle—to territory that would end up in the Soviet Zone, but at the time recently American-captured and still American-occupied—and then north to the British Zone—to Hannover, Braunschweig, Hamburg, Bremen, and Luebeck. Kraus's team went first to Cologne and then south to the American Zone, working in Wiesbaden, Mainz, Darmstadt, Frankfurt, and Munich. From mid-May until mid-July, the two teams were in the field accumulating documents, interviewing in the internment camps, and interviewing opposition and concentration camp survivors. In mid-July we gathered in Bad Nauheim, at the headquarters of the Strategic Bombing Survey, and drafted the report. The report drew on our interviews and documentary materials. Some of the prose was written by Wolfgang Kraus, but I drafted and edited the final report. Wolfgang Kraus and I continued our collaboration when we returned to the States, ultimately producing two coauthored chapters on the German resistance in a book published in 1948.[1]

This is the text of our report.

Gabriel A. Almond

June 11, 1999

Data concerning the existence, size, and significance of an anti-Nazi opposition within Germany are forthcoming from two primary sources. The first source is the direct testimony of opposition leaders still surviving after the occupation; the second source consists of official German intelligence reports or interrogations of interned Gestapo and Sicherheitsdienst officials. The direct testimony of opposition leaders is, of course, subject to the qualification that it is to the interest of the leader and his group to represent the activities of his movement during the war years in the best possible light. Estimates of the size and scope of activities provided by such leaders may be viewed as more or less exaggerated. However the experience of Bombing Survey Field Teams also suggests that such estimates may in some cases be low rather than high because of the extreme secrecy in which such movements were forced to operate. For example, a number of Communist leaders knew in general terms that other Communist groups and cells were operating in their area, but because of the absence of any connection they were unable to estimate the size of the group. Throughout the opposition movement it was an elementary principle of safety, confirmed by repeated experience with Gestapo terror and torture, never to know more about the personnel and activities of the movement than was absolutely essential. In evaluating the information from this source it is also necessary to keep in mind that the best informants in a great many cases had been executed in the last wave of terror. Frequently the knowledge of the survivors was fragmentary; many of those who had occupied central points in the organization had fallen.

To some extent the lack of precise information from the side of the opposition groups themselves can be made good by official statistics and reports of the Nazi police agencies.[2] Here again the data are fragmentary because of the generally thorough execution of the order to destroy documents and records before the occupation. Even when such documents have been preserved official statistics of subversive and oppositional activity are subject to question. From the testimony of Gestapo officials it would appear to have been a frequent practice on the part of regional officials to "pad" their arrest statistics in order to show "progress." It is apparent, therefore, that in dealing with quantitative estimates from either the oppositional or the official Nazi side, some correction must be made for exaggeration.

Some idea of the extent of oppositional activity throughout Germany can be obtained from the statistics of arrests by the Gestapo for the first six months of 1944 [Table 1].

The statistics of arrests for political offences for the first three months of 1944 give a general picture of the frequency of such acts throughout the

Reich. However, acts of both Germans and foreign workers are grouped together. Even more confusion results from the fact that under "Reaction-Opposition" are included not only acts emanating from or tending toward the formation of right-wing groups, but the whole range of individual acts of opposition covered under "treachery" (*Heimtuckeangelegenheiten*). This category includes arrests of individuals for the spreading of rumors, making jokes about the regime, listening to the BBC, etc. [Table 2].

Data for April, May, and June give us a clearer picture of the extent and composition of opposition in this period. Arrests for what the Gestapo labelled "communist" activity among Germans ranged from around 400 to more than 500 per month; while arrests for Marxist (Social Democratic) activity were around 100 per month. "Reaction" (including "legitimism" and "liberalism") ranged between 300 and 350 for the same period. Figures for the last half of 1944 would undoubtedly have shown a large increase because of the wave of arrests among all oppositional circles after the July attempt on Hitler's life. The number of arrests in connection with this attempt has been estimated anywhere between 5,000 and 20,000.

For the three-month period from April to June 1944 the number of arrests for Communist activity among Germans alone was 1442, for Social Democratic activity 282, for "Middle" and "right wing" opposition 1014. Individual "acts of treachery" not definitely connected with organized oppositional activity amounted to 4,426. Recognizing the possible exaggerations in these figures it is nevertheless legitimate to conclude that the frequency of organized oppositional activity was probably several times the number of arrests.

Table 1

Consolidation of Statistics of Arrests from the Regional Offices of the Gestapo for January-March 1944

	January	February	March	Total
Communism/ Marxism	1340	1877	1283	4500
Reaction- Opposition	2079	2154	2322	6555

Table 2
Consolidation of Statistics of Arrests from the Regional Offices of the Gestapo for April-June 1944

	April		May		June		Total	
	German	Foreign	German	Foreign	German	Foreign	German	Foreign
Communism	391	882	523	1551	528	850	1442	3283
Marxism	90	24	107	7	85	15	282	46
Reaction-Opposition	294	235	321	246	399	324	1014	805
Treachery	937	628	1204	709	2285	913	4426	2250

This impression is confirmed by interviews with oppositional leaders in various parts of Germany. In Hamburg, a city with a strong left wing tradition, a large number of anti-Nazi groups were identified. In the beginning of 1945 an Antifaschistisches Deutsches Kampf Komittee was established. This group was supposed to have included 700 Communists, Social Democrats, and other left wing elements, 200 of whom were organized into armed *Hundertschaften* (hundreds). The group possessed stolen antiaircraft guns, machine guns, rifles, and pistols. A former leader of the Social Democratic Reichsbanner (the Socialist paramilitary organization) estimated that about 600 former Reichsbanner men continued to meet together in small groups of 3–4.

In the Hamburg shipyards and plants anti-Nazi cells operated throughout the period of the war. In the Deutsche Werft, the largest shipyard on the continent, there was a nucleus of 36 primarily Communist activists with a larger group of sympathizers. In the Blohm and Voss shipyard it was estimated that some 250–300 workers were organized into anti-Nazi groups. In Menck and Hambrock, manufacturers of construction implements, there was a nucleus of 12 activists and a larger group of sympathizers. In the Hamburger Oelwerke there was a consolidated Communist and Social Democratic group of about 25 in 1944.

In Bremen the Communists had about two hundred activists. This figure was reported both from Gestapo and Communist sources. The Sozialistische Arbeiterpartei, a group to the left of the Social Democrats, had some thirty to forty activists. The Social Democrats had

a few informal social groups. The aircraft plants Focke-Wulf and Weser Flugzeug A. G. had some thirty Communists. The shipyard Deschmag had around a hundred anti-fascists. In 1944 they formed a consolidated organization called "Kampf gegen Fascismus" (KGF). Immediately after the Allied occupation the KGF claimed a membership of over four thousand in Bremen, three-fourths from left wing groups, and the remainder from "middle of the road" elements.

The Social Democrats in Luebeck had a group of some 25–30 active members who met regularly and participated in political discussions during the early years of the war. By 1944 the SPD opposition numbered around two hundred, inclusive of foreign workers. In March of 1945 the activities of the group were discovered and most of the leaders were arrested. The Luebeck KPD in 1939 had 25–30 Germans organized in groups of three (*Dreiergruppen*). They had cells in the munitions plants, Deutsche Waffen and Munitionsfabrik and the Massenverpackung fuer Munition. In the last months before the occupation the KPD had an organized group of some 225 armed Germans and foreign workers. In March of 1945 the plan of this group to seize central points in Luebeck in order to prevent the town's defence was discovered and some 20 of the movement's leaders were arrested.

In Leipzig in 1943 a number of left wing groups formed a National Kommittee Freies Deutschland in response to Russian Radio propaganda. After the July 20, 1944 attempt on Hitler's life there were a large number of arrests, and in early 1945 some 53 leaders of the NKFD were executed. The membership of the NKFD immediately before the occupation is estimated at 300–400 members. Immediately after the occupation the group claimed a membership of several thousands. Halle numbered some 30 active Communists and Social Democrats. By 1943 it was claimed that among the police reservists there were 125 men ready to put themselves at the disposal of the opposition. Shortly before the occupation a consolidated Anti-Nationalsocialistische Bewegung was formed.

In the Ruhr and the Rheinland there is evidence of oppositional activity during the war years, but quantitative estimates from the side of the opposition itself are not available. The SPD and the KPD had small groups, but the former leaders of the Zentrum did not engage in organized opposition. The Gestapo reported more than 150 arrests in the Cologne area during the first six months of 1944; Dortmund reported 30.

In Frankfurt a/M the left claimed to have a hundred activists and sympathizers. Several of the industrial plants in the area had underground cells. In south Germany there is evidence of the existence of left wing groups in such towns as Munich, Kempten, and Tuebingen. An NKFD group was formed in Munich at the beginning of 1944.

Significance of Oppositional Activities for the Allied War Effort

Propaganda

During the years of the war, the major activity of the left wing oppositional groups was the spreading of propaganda. In the earlier years of the Nazi regime, the issuance of leaflets and even small newspapers was a commonplace. As the Nazi terror became more effective the issuance of leaflets became less frequent and the primary propaganda medium became *mundpropaganda,* the spread of information and slogans by word of mouth. This was done systematically. News heard from BBC the night before would be spread among the workers in the "breakfast pause," or at lunch time in the plants.

One of the most important contributions of the opposition for the air campaign of the Allies was the effort of many of the opposition organizations to counteract the Nazi *Luftterror* propaganda. In Leipzig the NKFD distributed a leaflet after the great raid of December 1943. The leaflet in part reads as follows:

The Nazi bosses are attempting to use this bombing attack as they are using the whole air war, as a means of directing the attention of the masses away from those who are truly guilty and strengthening their own piratical war effort. We anti-Fascists say to you:

1. The air war is a part of the whole war. Whoever is against the air war and its terrible effects, must be against the whole criminal war.

2. The air war was begun by Hitler and the German war criminals, just as the war in general was begun by them. Hitler wanted to "coventrize" the English cities, and to "erase" all of England. The Nazi press reported with sadistic satisfaction the destruction and suffering in England caused by the air attacks of the German air force. Therefore whoever is against the air war, must be against the man who started it, must be against Hitler.

3. The air war proves that Germany is conquerable. What do you think of Goering's false promises now, that no enemy airplanes would ever cross the German border? Just as you have been betrayed in this regard, so have the Nazis lied to you in all respects. We say to you: All Germany will lie in ruins, if we don't throw out these war criminals. The military power of the Allies is already so strong that the fate of Germany is settled. Therefore we say to you: Make an end of this hopeless war!

4. In every raid the Nazi leaders bring themselves to safety in plenty of time. They have their specially safe shelters. They have villas and country houses in Bavaria and the Tirol, where they can go in the event that their houses are damaged and continue their luxurious existence. They have their second layout of furniture and linens and everything else long in safety. Therefore remove these Nazi bosses.

5. The Nazis are consoling the people who have suffered from raids with the promise of revenge. With this promise of revenge the people are supposed to hope for victory. We say to you: that is also a lie. Even

if we should discover a weapon of revenge, this discovery will be turned against us and the air war against Germany will take on proportions which are unimaginable. Therefore we say to you: Don't believe in this swindle of Nazi revenge!

The Leipzig Anti-Fascists tell you what to do. When an air raid comes, first you must save your own life. Run to safety. In case of an air raid, leave the armament plants and take care of your families and dwellings. The whole war industry may be destroyed, but you must preserve your own lives. Don't permit the Nazi industrial bosses or the plant police to keep you in the factory. After a raid stay away from your job; excuse yourself by claiming the need of cleaning up debris, or poor transportation conditions. "Langsam arbeiten" leads to a quicker end of the war. Help one another when it is possible to save the lives, dwellings, and possessions of other workers. The life of the German worker is a thousand times more important than the armament plants of the Nazi criminals.

Fight with the Anti-Fascists against the Total War of Hitler for a Total Peace!

Similar leaflets were reported to have been distributed in such towns as Hamburg, Bremen, and Cologne, but copies were no longer available. Where there were no leaflets, similar arguments were advanced orally at the breakfast and lunch periods in plants, in queues before stores, even in shelters during the long period of anxious waiting.

Sabotage

Sabotage in its more dramatic forms was not frequent. There are some reports of sabotage of U-boats and other vessels by German Communists in the Hamburg and Bremen shipyards. The Gestapo in Hannover discovered frequent cases of sabotage in armament plants for which Russian workers were primarily responsible. But wherever there were left wing oppositional groups the slogan "Langsam Arbeiten" was spread. Oppositional activists in positions of administrative responsibility sometimes sabotaged on the job. A woman member of the NKFD in Leipzig who was in charge of female labor discipline

in the Reichstreuhaender der Arbeit (the agency in charge of foreign workers) administered the minimum penalty, and encouraged some of her colleagues to do the same. Foremen in the Deutsche Werft in Hamburg deliberately wasted steel, and slowed down U-boat production by delaying in the transmission of information as to changes in design.

Undermining of *Volkssturm* and Efforts to Prevent Last-Ditch Resistance

As the war neared an end and the German military manpower shortage became more and more apparent the Nazis attempted to ensure a last-ditch resistance through the calling up of the *Volkssturm* (the levy of older men and boys). There is evidence from a number of areas from opposition sources that anti-fascist groups attempted to infiltrate the *Volkssturm* and undermine its will to resist. Certainly, on the whole the poor record of the *Volkssturm* cannot be attributed to this oppositional sabotage. Even to Nazis the small numbers, lack of training, and inferior arms of the *Volkssturm* in contrast to the numbers and equipment of the attacking troops was apparent. This overwhelming physical and technical disproportion and the general hopelessness of resistance were undoubtedly the primary factors in the widespread demoralization of *Volkssturm* units. But wherever there were oppositional groups efforts were made to render the hopelessness of resistance clear through propaganda.

In a number of cases oppositional groups put pressure on the authorities to yield towns without fighting; in one or two cases armed uprisings were planned to yield areas without resistance.

The Leipzig NKFD issued a leaflet on April 14 exhorting the Germans not to defend the town.

The Nazi regime is about to collapse! American and English troops stand before our city. In order to avoid further bloodshed and destruction of the remnants of our residential and industrial areas, we must mobilize all the anti-fascist forces. The solution is: an end to the insane war of the Nazis. The hour of emancipation from Nazi slavery is at hand. Now it is necessary to act! What is to be done?

No resistance to the English and Americans!
Resistance means death and destruction!
Resisting soldiers should be disarmed.
Orders to report to the *Volkssturm* should be disobeyed!

On April 16 a leaflet in the form of an open letter addressed to the Oberburgermeister and Polizeipresident of Leipzig was distributed. The leaflet urged the hopelessness of any further resistance, and held the authorities responsible for any death and destruction resulting from resistance in Leipzig. "We are making you responsible for every sacrifice and all destruction resulting from resistance. . . . We demand surrender of our city without resistance in the interest of the population of Leipzig."

The Leipzig opposition leaders claim that in Lindenau, a Leipzig worker's neighborhood where the NKFD was strong, the *Volkssturm* revolted. They also claim that no resistance was offered the American troops in these workers' areas.

In Hamburg the *Antifa* planned an internal revolt in the event of a decision by Gauleiter Kaufmann to resist. Soldiers in the Hindenburg and Mackensen barracks are reported as having been prepared to mutiny. 5,000 copies of a leaflet were distributed in Blohm and Voss five weeks before the occupation urging the workers not to defend the town. Although the workers were threatened if they did not hand in the leaflets, only 47 of the total were given to the authorities. During the last weeks before the occupation a unit of 250 partly armed men was formed among the Blohm and Voss workers, and it was planned to use these units to seize key buildings in the town in the event of resistance in Hamburg. The anti-fascist organizations also sent delegations to Hamburg industrialists threatening violence if the town was defended. The industrialists were ordered to go to the Gauleiter at once and inform him that the Hamburg workers were taking up arms and would revolt unless the town were peacefully surrendered. The *Antifa* distributed leaflets among the *Volkssturm* and posted a public announcement in the *Gaensemarkt* (Goose Market) to the effect that the town was to be surrendered without resistance. The declaration was torn down by SS men, but not before its contents had become publicly known.

In Halle a/S the Anti-Nazional-Sozialistische Bewegung (ANB) issued two leaflets urging surrender without resistance. Both of the leaflets urged surrender in order to prevent the destruction of Halle by thousands of bombers. "People of Halle," read the first leaflet, "The hour of decision is at hand. The Americans stand before the gates of the city. Do not resist the approaching Americans, or else thousands of bombers . . . will lay your city in ashes, and will destroy you, your wives, and children. Do you wish to die in order to preserve the lives of the Party bosses for a few days?" The second leaflet again argued that Halle, which had suffered very little from raids, would be destroyed by bombs if resistance were offered. "One thing we must prevent: that our city like all other large German cities should be reduced to rubble, that our wives and children should be killed by the tens of thousands. This will certainly happen if Halle is uselessly defended. A great air raid by Allied bombers will be the immediate consequence."

Representatives of the ANB met the American forces on the outskirts of the city, told them the town was undefended and prevented any attack on the town. Within the city opposition leaders before the arrival of American troops seized the police and party headquarters and prevented looting and destruction of records.

In Luebeck in March of 1944 the Communist opposition issued a leaflet urging that the time for active opposition had come, that the war was lost because of the Allied conquests and the destruction of German industry by air attacks. The group had 225 armed men—Germans and foreign workers—and claim to have had an arsenal of eleven machine guns, 180 rifles, 300 pistols, explosives, and hand grenades. They had a detailed plan for the seizure of Luebeck, and a number of trucks were available to them. The plot was discovered on March 23, and the leaders were imprisoned.

In Munich the right wing Bavarian separatist group FreedomAction Bavaria organized an armed revolt on April 28, and broadcast from a radio station for a short period of time. The revolt was put down, but the effort stimulated other groups in the Munich area, and played a role in the surrender of the town.

The Effect of Air Raids on Opposition

The effects of strategic bombing on the extent and effectiveness of oppositional activity may be treated under three categories: 1) positive, 2) negative, 3) the effects of different types of bombing experience on oppositional activity.

The primary positive effects of strategic bombing in oppositional activity were: a) rendering the public more receptive to oppositional propaganda; b) increasing the size and the intensity of oppositional group activity; c) creating physical and administrative disorder which permitted greater freedom of action on the part of oppositional groups.

Receptivity to Oppositional Propaganda

The leaders of the NKFD in Leipzig testified that the great raid of December 4, 1943 was the "turning point" in German morale. The raids preceding this had been small and appeared to have been directed at random targets. These small RAF night raids had been grist for the Nazi propaganda mill. But the full significance of strategic bombing was brought home with the December 1943 raid. To the minds of the Leipzig population it signified the breakdown of German defense. From this point on, according to the NKFD leaders it was possible to reach increasingly larger elements among the public with propaganda concerning the hopelessness of the German war situation.

The Hamburg Communist and Social Democratic leaders similarly testified that it was easier to reach workers and bring them around to the oppositional point of view after air raids. The workers were more rebellious after raids. A Hamburg Social Democratic leader asserted that there was a process of radicalization as the air war was pressed home. The slogan among the workers was "Better an end with horror, than horror without end" (Besser eine Ende mit Schrecken, als Schrecken ohne Ende).

The Bremen opposition leaders claim that air raids did not result in increasing hatred of the Allies or of the opposition, but resulted in a widespread opposition to the war itself. In general the Bremen anti-fascist leadership felt that the population of the city became more receptive to oppositional propaganda as a consequence of the air raids.

Though the city of Halle suffered only minor damage through raids, the threat of bombing was always present. Nearby town and industrial concentrations were heavily raided, and Halle was on the route of the air fleets bound for Berlin. In the judgment of Halle opposition leaders the onset of the great raids on Germany in 1942 and 1943 was the first tangible military evidence that Germany had lost the war. Persons previously unapproachable were more receptive to oppositional talk. Criticism of the regime was expressed more openly. The great raids over Germany made it possible for the opposition to come more into the open. It was possible to speak to people in street cars and on the streets. The opposition tried to direct reactions to news of the destructive effects of raids into anti-Nazi channels by spreading such slogans as "Je schwerer der Krieg auf uns lastet, umso schneller kommt der Krieg zu Ende" (The heavier the war weighs on us, the more quickly will the war come to an end).

Increases in the Size and Intensity of Oppositional Activity

Evidence from both the side of the Gestapo and the opposition indicates an increase in the number, size, and intensity of activity of oppositional groups beginning in 1943. These developments, however, cannot be attributed in any specific way to the air war. Encouragement to the opposition resulted from the general shift in the war situation, of which the air war was only a part. No evidence is available which shows any connection between personal bombing experience and recruitment to active opposition, although such experience may have been an important motivating factor.

Physical and Administrative Disorder

One of the important consequences of air raids for oppositional activity was the creation of physical and administrative confusion and disorder. The most dramatic evidence of this aid to oppositional activity was found in Hamburg. According to German army authorities there existed in Hamburg during 1944 and until the end of the war an enterprise to hide and maintain army deserters. Neither the Military Police nor the Gestapo was able to break it up. Leading Hamburg Anti-Fascists claimed that they had been able to hide up to thirty deserters at a time, in the air raid ruins in the city. Some were hidden for as long as a year and more. Identity papers were forged and jobs were found for the deserters. The antifascists undertook a campaign of encouraging soldiers on furlough in Hamburg to desert. They would then hide and feed them until it was possible safely to return the deserters to civilian life with false papers.

A Gestapo official from Hannover testified that Russian workers sometimes engaged in sabotage during air raids. The plant police went into the shelters leaving the plant unprotected. In a Hannover tank factory Russian workers took advantage of this opportunity by cutting power transmission belts, sabotaging guns and tanks. Claims were made by the Leipzig left wing leaders that oppositionists wanted by the Gestapo would be given out as air raid casualties, and were enabled to commence new existences under false papers.

The freedom of action of oppositional groups was also increased through air raids as a consequence of the disruption of the police apparatus. Gestapo headquarters were sometimes hit, and valuable card files were destroyed. The network of undercover agents engaged in the observation of oppositional activities was frequently disrupted.

The Breakdown of Oppositional Communications

Just as the network of intelligence, communications and control of the Nazis was frequently disturbed and sometimes even shattered by air raids, so also did the activities of some oppositional groups suffer from the same disturbances. This was particularly true of groups which strove to maintain more than local connections. The testimony of a member of the Wehrmacht opposition is good evidence of this negative consequence of air raids. This particular Wehrmacht officer was functioning as a liaison man (*Verbindungsmann*) for the Anti-Nazi officer circle. After the onset of larger raids he found it increasingly difficult to maintain contact between the various local oppositional Wehrmacht groups. He would often arrive in cities only to find that the address to which he had been directed was that of a bombed out house. Frequently in the disorder and confusion in bombed cities he would be unable

to locate and reestablish the ties thus disrupted by bombing. In Hannover a Communist informant similarly complained that it was difficult to reestablish contacts even within Hannover itself after severe raids. He pointed out that while the public was more receptive to oppositional propaganda, contacts were disrupted and people had less time to devote to carrying on oppositional activity. This disruption of oppositional contacts in Hannover was also reported from the side of the Social Democrats.

A leader of the Zentrum Party in Cologne pointed out that it became increasingly difficult to call together small meetings of oppositional people in a social way because of the continual threat of air raids. The fear of raids was so great that people were unwilling to go far from their shelters.

While oppositional communications suffered as a consequence of air raids, its importance should not be overestimated. By the time of the outbreak of the war oppositional activity had already been atomized by Nazi espionage and terror. Oppositional organization was primarily local. The main activity of organized resistance was propaganda, and the main coordinating medium was Allied radio. The continuation of these activities was not dependent upon an elaborate system of communications. Connections within the town itself could in most cases be reestablished after a raid without much difficulty.

Physical Exhaustion and Reduction of Working

Just as Gestapo officials admitted that the increasing tempo and severity of air raids wore them down physically and psychologically and reduced the amount of time and energy available for their work, so also did the effectiveness of oppositional activity decrease from the same causes. Evidence with regard to these air raid consequences came from many areas in Germany but were particularly stressed in reports from Cologne and Hannover, two cities among the most heavily bombed in Germany in proportion to population and area.

A leader of the Zentrum in Cologne claimed that the air raids had been so severe that all elements of the population lacked the will and energy to engage in any activity save that related to the immediate needs of finding shelter, food, and safety. Leaders of the KPD and SPD in Hannover pointed out that much of the time of the oppositional groups was taken up in locating comrades after raids, in helping the bombed-out to find places to stay, clothing, furniture, and the like. They also stressed the physiological exhaustion which followed after air raids, and the incapacity of people to think of anything save the danger of the moment.

Types of Bombing and Oppositional Activity

A number of interesting connections between differences in bombing experience and oppositional activity were observed. The bombing of workers' quarters through raids on industrial areas and area raids created difficult problems of explanation for the oppositional leadership everywhere. The special severity of the bombing of Cologne, a Catholic city never fertile soil for Nazism, appears to have created hostility toward the Allies. The question on all sides was "Why should Cologne, a city in which the Nazis had one of their weakest footholds, suffer the most severe and most continuous bombing of all?"

Two members of the Austrian resistance movement who had been eyewitnesses of the raid on Vienna of February 28, 1945, and who had been able to escape to neutral territory, protested against this area raid.[3] They claimed that the earlier raids on industrial installations had been understood and appreciated by the Austrian resistance groups, but the "carpet raids" since September of 1944 had created hostility toward the Allies among the resistance groups. The informants stated that the destructive and aimless character of the raids had embittered the population, and caused them to make unfavorable comparisons of Allied bombing policy with that of Russia. They also claimed that this type of air warfare

contributed to a favorable reaction on the part of the Austrian population to the Nazi *Luftterror* propaganda.

With regard to the important question of the effects of differences in the severity and continuity of bombing upon oppositional activity the data on the whole is fragmentary and inadequate. Some of the sharper contrasts may be made by comparing the experience of Hamburg, Luebeck, and Cologne [Table 3].

It is of interest that the city of Luebeck received a bomb load of only 5,000 tons, and a large proportion of that in the single RAF area raid in 1942. By the testimony of Luebeck opposition leaders the primary effect of this area raid was to arouse hostility against the Allies. The question raised on all sides was, "Why should Luebeck, an anti-Nazi town of little importance industrially, have been the recipient of this first great area raid?" Parts of the older and historically most valuable and picturesque areas of the town were destroyed. In addition there was no follow up after the 1942 raid and the town was able to recover rapidly. In the judgment of opposition leaders the specific air raid experience of Luebeck, if anything, hindered oppositional activity. Certainly the immediate consequence of the 1942 raid was to increase the hostility of the population against the Allies.

The contrast between Cologne and Hamburg with regard to the extent and effectiveness of oppositional activity has already been indicated. In Hamburg there was an aggressive left wing tradition and comparatively large groups of activists. In Cologne the evidence suggests a relatively small amount of left wing and Zentrist activity. Both political tradition and bombing experience contributed to these patterns. Hamburg historically was a left wing town. The most aggressive groups in general under the Nazis were the left wing groups. Cologne, on

Table 3
Bombing Experience of Hamburg, Leubeck, and Cologne

	Pop. 1939	Total Tonnage	Percent Night	Percent Area	Percent High Explosives
Luebeck	185,000	5,000	49	49	67
Hamburg	1,711,000	41,300	52	65	82
Cologne	772,000	47,000	63	67	76

the other hand, was a town in which the Catholic Party, the Zentrm, dominated. In proportion to area and population Cologne received approximately twice as heavy a bomb load as Hamburg. The Hamburg oppositional groups according to their own testimony were able to retain their aggressiveness, and utilize the opportunities presented by air raids. The Cologne informants report that although raids resulted in an increase in war-weariness and susceptibility to oppositional propaganda, the severity of the raids was so great as to result in a general breakdown of all activity including that of the oppositional groups. Unfortunately data on other towns is not adequate to confirm and elaborate this probable relationship between the seventy and continuity of bombing experience and the degree and effectiveness of oppositional activity. ■

Notes

1. Gabriel A. Almond (Ed.), *The Struggle for Democracy in Germany,* Chapel Hill, University of North Carolina Press, 1948, Chapters 2 and 3.

2. The only Gestapo statistics which survived had been acquired by the OSS, and were from the *Meldungen Aus Dem Reich,* for the first six months of 1944. The *Meldungen* were the central reports of the Sicherheitsdienst, Himmler's top intelligence organization, and to have gotten them was a great coup for the OSS. I got access to these reports through the coincidence that the OSS was anxious to get copies of USSBS interviews with opposition leaders which I had in my possession. Alex George, now my professional colleague at Stanford, and then a young GI working for the OSS, trailed my team "through the underbrush" so to speak, and we struck a deal—the OSS *Meldungen* for my interviews. I suppose that these reports had been gotten by the OSS through an agent. I never saw anything more than the reports for the first six months of 1944; it may be that this is all that the OSS had. All government departments were under strict orders to destroy documents as the Allied armies neared. We encountered charred records in some of the Gestapo headquarters that we investigated. The copies that I received from the OSS had been "sanitized." Anything identifying how they had been acquired, or from which unit of the Gestapo they had come, had been eliminated.

3. This particular report came from an OSS document (#F 1583).

Why Was This Research Needed?

1. When and under what auspices did this study take place?
2. Why do you think gathering information on the German anti-Nazi movement was important after World War II?
3. What difficulties did Almond and Kraus encounter in gauging the size of the anti-Nazi opposition?

How Was the Topic Studied?

1. What official data sources did the authors use to estimate the extent of oppositional activity? What were the limitations of these sources? What does the information provided in note 2 reveal about the role bureaucratic turf played in shaping the database for this study?
2. How and why do the authors combine quantitative data with qualitative information in their analysis?
3. How do the authors attempt to link Allied bombing with levels of oppositional activity? How would you state their working hypotheses about this linkage in formal terms?

What Are The Findings?

1. What are the main trends that emerge from the arrest data in Table 1?
2. In what ways do the data in Table 2 provide additional useful information about wartime arrest patterns? How could you use percentages to make this table even easier to read?

3. If you were to present the information in Tables 1 and 2 in graphic rather than tabular form, which type of chart would you use and why? Please explain the specific design approach that would make it possible to depict all of the information available—type of arrest by time period and nationality—in a single image.

4. How did this research help define important variables concerning the effects of strategic bombing, even if precise measurement of outcomes was not possible? According to the authors' narrative concerning bombing effects, what kinds of local-level variables intervened in the relationship between amount and type of attacks, on the one hand, and anti-Nazi opposition, on the other? How would you diagram a multivariate model of these described relationships?

What Do the Results Mean?

1. Considering the overall synthesis of information presented by the authors, how would you characterize the quality of the "intelligence" gained by this research?

2. What are your observations about the style of writing in this report? Which conventions of typical political science writing were modified or omitted due to the intended audience? What are the advantages and disadvantages of the authors' approach?

3. Do you believe this study provided sufficient information to make specific recommendations to military authorities about the future use of bombing as a tool in generating internal opposition against an enemy during war? Explain.

4. What are your suggestions for a follow-up study on this topic that would be more sophisticated in its methods? If you had the necessary resources, how would you attempt to overcome some of the data limitations of the original project? What additional quantitative techniques might you incorporate in your analysis?

7

The End of the Cold War, Attitude Change, and the Politics of Defense Spending

Bruce Russett, Thomas Hartley, and Shoon Murray

Events in the political world have dual dimensions of meaning that are based in factual reality and in social perception. As historical reality, certain facts about the cold war are clear. The struggle dates back to 1947 when the alliance of the Soviet Union, the United States, and Great Britain, having emerged victorious from World War II, dissolved into a fierce competition between East and West to shape the political and economic future of Europe (Harvey 2004; Encyclopaedia Britannica Online *2005). Among the most significant cold war occurrences was the erection of the Berlin Wall in 1961 to seal the border of East Germany, preventing population movement into the West via West Berlin. Abandonment of the wall in 1989 served as compelling evidence of unrest inside the Communist bloc; the collapse of the Soviet Union itself soon followed in 1991.*

Much more complex than this factual chronology is the socially constructed meaning of the cold war. Social constructs are created through a combination of information, beliefs, and acquired explanations as citizens try to make sense of their political environment. What dangers did the cold war represent for the United States? What priority did cold war issues merit within national security policymaking? How should we define U.S. interests abroad? Answers to such questions as these provided a solid base of public support for American foreign policy over a period of more than forty years. However, the sudden conclusion of the cold war challenged Americans to shift their views of the world. As Bruce Russett, Thomas Hartley, and Shoon Murray discuss in the following reading, because long-held values and beliefs resist change, the process of attitudinal reorientation offers a fascinating topic for empirical inquiry. This reading attempts to untangle the twisted threads of knowledge and ideology in foreign policy belief systems by reviewing a variety of research studies about public opinion and the end of the cold war. Central to the analysis is a tabulation of popular views over time. According to the authors, there are ample data to show the evolution, as well as the persistence, of public attitudes depending on the indicator chosen.

References

Encyclopaedia Britannica Online. 2005. "Cold War."
www.britannica.com (accessed May 29, 2005).
Harvey, R. 2004. *A Short History of Communism.* New York:
St. Martin's Press.

Throughout the Cold War, United States national security policy, and the public attitudes that supported
it, seemed anchored in the great ideology and power
rivalry with the Soviet Union. A basic component of that
policy, the ups and downs of American military spending,
was largely predictable by changes in the level of Soviet
military spending and by public preferences, as expressed
in opinion surveys, for increases or decreases in American
military spending. Public beliefs about the appropriate
level of military spending, moreover, appeared firmly
rooted in a larger set of foreign policy beliefs. Attitudes
toward the Soviet Union, toward the circumstances justifying the use of military force internationally, and toward cooperating with other countries were all part of a
stable and well-defined system of beliefs. In turn, foreign
policy attitudes frequently were predictable from a reasonably coherent set of attitudes toward domestic policy.

The end of the Cold War brought remarkable changes
in both policy and attitudes. The major anchoring point
for the rivalry—the Soviet Union itself—has ceased to
exist, and Russia no longer poses the same level or kind
of military threat. Rationales for U.S. military spending,
for the use of military force abroad, and for international
cooperation have likewise changed. But in some respects
they have not changed so greatly. These historic events
present us with an extraordinary opportunity to study
the structure of Americans' foreign policy beliefs and the
dynamics of attitude change. They also provide a chance
to speculate about how changed and stable attitudes may
affect national security policy.

Attitude Change and Stability

The end of the Cold War offers a rare opportunity to explore the identity and coherence of the basic organizing
principles around which people's foreign policy preferences form. For example, we can now test whether some
beliefs (such as people's images about the nature of the
Soviet Union) had served to organize or constrain other
beliefs; investigate the rationality of ordinary citizens (by
observing whether people adjusted their policy preferences to fit a changed international environment); and
explore how deeply foreign events—even occurrences as
dramatic as the demolition of the Berlin Wall or the disintegration of the Soviet Union—can affect people's
basic postures toward international affairs.

A few scholars took advantage of these research opportunities. For instance, Peffley and Hurwitz (1992) consider how Americans' opinions toward various national
security policies changed as a result of warmer relations
with Russia. In doing so, they assign to attitudes toward
the Soviet Union/Russia a key structuring role in a hierarchy of beliefs and policy preferences. They find (p. 454)
that ordinary citizens responded in a manner that was
"structured and systematic rather than random—largely
precipitated by revisions in respondents' images of the
Soviet Union." As people revised their beliefs about
the Soviet Union between 1987 and 1988, attitudes toward some specific policies—such as defense spending—
also moved in a dovish direction. But—not surprisingly
considering the timing of their surveys—they also (p. 453)
"uncovered evidence of impressive stability in respondents' images of the Soviet Union." Even their later survey predates the momentous events, beginning with the
demolition of the Berlin Wall in 1989, that finally ended
the Cold War.

Bartels (1993a) is less convinced that attitudes toward
the Soviet Union were so crucial. Using cross-sectional
data, he compares data collected prior to the end of the
Cold War with 1992 survey results. He finds (p. 13) that
"changing perceptions of the Soviet Union were necessary
but not sufficient to precipitate significant restructuring
of defense spending preferences" because "only the more
informed stratum of the general public has so far succeeded in grasping . . . the *implications* of the declining Soviet threat for U.S. defense policy." More specifically, the

relative magnitude of different determinants of defense spending (e.g., respondents' attitudes about Russia, stances toward isolationism, willingness to use military force, ideological orientations, and economic stake in the policy) remained fairly stable for the less-informed citizens when tested on separate surveys over time.

Only among well-informed citizens does Bartels find (p. 8) "very marked changes in the structure of defense spending preferences." For this group, the effects of ideology, isolationism, and attitudes about Russia were smaller in 1992 than before, and the estimated effect of willingness to use force—already the primary determinant of people's preferences toward defense spending—was larger. He interprets these results as evidence that only the well-informed citizenry had responded to changes in the international environment.

Questions remain about what are the key organizing elements of foreign policy belief systems, and what elements change. Murray (1993) offers the most direct individual-level data on how the attitudes of Americans—albeit opinion leaders—were affected by the end of the Cold War. She constructed a 1988–92 panel study with 660 elite respondents: people drawn from *Who's Who,* State Department officials, politicians, foreign policy experts, clergy, and media leaders (Murray 1992, 1993). She (1993) finds that opinion leaders—a select portion of the well-informed citizenry—indeed responded to issues directly related to the end of the Cold War. For instance, respondents changed their views about the foreign policy motivations of Russia. Table 1 shows the sea change in perceptions of Russian motivations between 1988 and 1992. Fully 80% of those who had agreed in 1988 that the Soviet Union was generally expansionist in its foreign policy goals *did not* think the same about Russia by

1992.[1] Opinion leaders also attributed much less importance to containing communism. As shown in Table 2, 78% of those who had thought containing communism was a "very important" goal in 1988 considered it only "somewhat important" or "not important at all" by 1992.

Likewise, by 1992 an overwhelming majority agreed that defense spending should be cut. Opinion leaders were asked in 1988 about "reducing the defense budget in order to increase the federal education budget": 67% had agreed with this statement. Sentiment for reducing the defense budget preceded the end of the Cold War. But that sentiment later swelled into a consensus. Respondents were asked in the second wave whether defense spending "should be increased, kept about the same, or decreased." Over 90% then wanted it cut back. Moreover, 80% of those who in 1988 were against reducing the defense budget changed their positions by 1992 (see Table 3).

At the same time, Murray (1993) finds continuity in opinion leaders' more general beliefs about how the United States should interact with other countries. Past research identifies two dimensions—militant internationalism and cooperative internationalism—as necessary if not sufficient to characterize Americans' foreign policy beliefs (Wittkopf 1990; Holsti and Rosenau 1990, 1993). Building on this research, Murray measures respondents' 1988 and 1992 stances toward the use of military instruments of power and toward U.S. involvement in cooperative ventures with other countries. She finds a high over-

Table 1

Turn-Over Table, Attitudes about the Expansionist Nature of the Soviet Union in 1988 and Russia in 1992, LOP, Column Percents

		TIME 1 Soviet Union Expansionist, 1988 [Columns]		
TIME 2 Russia Expansionist, 1992 [Rows]		Agree	Disagree	Total
	Agree	20%	7%	17%
	Disagree	80%	93%	83%
	Total	100%	100%	100%
	N	421	165	586

Table 2
Turn-Over Table, Attitudes about the Importance of Containing Communism, LOP, 1988 and 1992, Column Percents

		TIME 1 [Columns] 1988			
		Very	Somewhat	Not	Total
TIME 2 [Rows] 1992	Very	23%	3%	0%	9%
	Somewhat	55%	33%	6%	37%
	Not	23%	64%	94%	54%
	Total	100%	100%	100%	100%
	N	216	314	95	625

treat other countries did not change either.

Although American opinion leaders now agree in general that the end of the Cold War warrants a reduction in spending, ideological groups may continue to fight over how much is enough. Bartels finds people's willingness to use force to be the primary determinant of their preferences toward military spending. Murray, in turn, shows that willingness to use military force remained quite stable between 1988 and 1992. Equally important, at least among opinion leaders, it was constrained by ideology—encompassing a range of domestic and international attitudes—both during and after the Cold War.

time correlation between indices used to measure their positions on militant internationalism ($r = .72$) and a high over-time correlation between indices of cooperative internationalism ($r = .78$). The object of key American foreign policy positions changed, but general dimensions of policy orientation proved very resistant to change.

What does this tell us about the structure of opinion leaders' beliefs? Why would people's basic foreign policy postures remain stable despite profound changes in the international environment? Murray shows that respondents' foreign policy postures were constrained over time by their domestic ideological orientations.[2] The evidence is consistent with (though not proof of) the explanation that foreign policy postures and domestic ideological orientations are derived from the same source: that is, common core values. She posits that because respondents' core values were untouched by the Soviet collapse, their basic orientations about how to

Policy Change and Stability

Will policy makers respond to changes in the attitudes of Americans toward the Soviet Union and increased

Table 3
Turn-Over Table, Attitudes about Defense Spending, LOP, 1988 and 1992, Column Percents

		TIME 1 Reduce Spending, 1988 [Columns]		
		Agree	Disagree	Total
TIME 2 Defense Spending Policy, 1992 [Rows]	Increase	0%	4%	1%
	Keep Same	4%	16%	8%
	Decrease	96%	80%	91%
	Total	100%	100%	100%
	N	418	210	628

Percentages may not add to 100 due to rounding.

opposition to increased military spending? Research on the congruence between public opinion and policy in the area of defense spending, using different research designs and relying on a variety of assumptions, suggests that the answer is yes. There has been substantial congruence in the past, and it should also be possible after the end of the Cold War.

Most evidence indicates that changes in public opinion are followed, more often than not, by changes in policy. Majorities of opinion also tend to be associated with changes in policy (Monroe 1979; Page and Shapiro 1983). These conclusions come from a research design that compares opinion (or opinion change) with policy change over a few years. It has the advantage of allowing opinion-policy data from a variety of policy areas to be combined. Other research has focused specifically on defense spending, allowing us to estimate the magnitude of the effect of spending on policy and to discover whether opinion affects policy consistently over time. First, we know that the largest influence on U.S. defense spending decisions was Soviet military spending (Ward 1984; Ostrom and Marra 1986; Hartley and Russett 1992). In the absence of a Soviet threat, we would expect this influence to lessen dramatically, or be replaced by new threats. Other influences include the deficit—which will most likely continue to depress military spending. Perhaps some independent influence was attributable to recent Republican administrations, but this influence is unstable depending on which years are included in the analysis (Hartley and Russett 1992; Wlezien 1992). If an independent Reagan-Bush effect existed, it is now over.

Some factors not previously important may assume a bigger role with the end of the Cold War. In particular, economic performance has not played an important role in decisions on defense; this is not surprising since there is little evidence that defense spending has any influence on the national economy (Kinsella 1990). However, the effect of a dramatic reduction of defense spending on the national economy is somewhat uncertain, and large cuts may influence policy in a way that small ones could not.

Public opinion is the most substantively important influence on the budget that remains after the Cold War.

In the past it exerted a greater influence on U.S. military spending than did the deficit, and it is likely to continue to play at least as important a role with the decline in importance of the Soviet threat. Currently, public opinion points strongly towards a smaller military budget. If those attitudes—and their influence—remain constant, the military budget will decline dramatically.

Public opinion is the most substantively important influence on the budget that remains after the Cold War.

This expectation is bolstered by findings that public opinion has a consistent effect on policy over time (Hartley and Russett 1992; Higgs and Kilduff 1992; Wlezien 1992). That matters, since earlier research with a simple change model (in which specific polls are paired with specific instances of policy change) was susceptible to selection bias. It is possible that polls were taken in years when a policy was particularly salient, and that government is most responsive when a policy is most salient. Jacobs and Shapiro (1993), for example, point to one instance in which the responsiveness of a president changed over time. If policy responds to opinion over a large number of years, it is less likely that responsiveness is a rare event.

The finding that opinion consistently affects policy is important for a second reason. If the appearance of responsiveness is in fact manipulation by government elites, then manipulation cannot be the result merely of occasional efforts by elites to manipulate opinion. Instead, it has to be structurally embedded in the institutions responsible for governance and the transmission of news. Statistical analyses suggest that although public opinion may cause changes in military spending policy, the reverse is not true; changes in military spending are not systematically followed by changes in public opinion. Public opinion is predicted as well by its own past values as it is by past values of military spending (Freeman et al. 1989; Hartley and Russett 1992; Higgs and Kilduff 1992). There are other kinds of evidence of manipulation, however. One mechanism by which elites can influence opinion—televised messages of certain actors—does have an influence on changes in public opinion (Page, Shapiro and Dempsey 1987; Bartels 1993b). Research is underway to determine whether this effect is consistent over time and how large its impact is in relation to other influences on public opinion (Hartley 1994).

All this raises some important possible challenges for democratic theory. If basic foreign policy orientations toward cooperation and military action persist after a fundamental change in the international system, in what ways are public or elite beliefs rooted in "objective" reality? What if beliefs about appropriate levels of military spending change, but military spending itself proves resistant? ■

Notes

1. Respondents were asked in 1988 whether "the Soviet Union is generally expansionist rather than defensive in its foreign policy goals." Due to political changes, the 1992 question asked whether, "once their economic crisis stabilizes, Russia will become an expansionist military power."

2. This finding may be unique to elite samples. Although others (Russett 1970; Russett and Hanson 1975; Holsti and Rosenau 1988) found an association between foreign policy and domestic policy in leadership groups, Bartels (1993a) does not find that ideology predicts willingness to use force in a cross-sectional national sample.

References

Bartels, Larry M. 1993a. "The American Public's Defense Spending Preferences in the Post-Cold War Era." Paper presented at the Annual Meeting of the American Political Science Association, Washington, DC.

———. 1993b. "Messages Received: The Political Impact of Media Exposure." *American Political Science Review* 87:267–85.

Freeman, John R., T. Williams, and Tse-Min Lin. 1989. "Vector Autoregression and the Study of Politics." *American Journal of Political Science* 33:842–77.

Hartley, Thomas. 1994. *Public Opinion, Mass Media and Defense Spending.* Ph.D. Dissertation, Yale University, New Haven, CT.

Hartley, Thomas, and Bruce Russett. 1992. "Public Opinion and the Common Defense: Who Governs Military Spending in the United States?" *American Political Science Review* 86:905–15.

Higgs, Robert, and Anthony Kilduff. 1992. "Public Opinion: A Powerful Predictor of U.S. Defense Spending." *Defence Economics* 4:227–38.

Holsti, Ole R., and James N. Rosenau. 1988. "The Domestic and Foreign Policy Beliefs of American Leaders." *Journal of Conflict Resolution* 32:248–94.

———. 1990. "The Structure of Foreign Policy Attitudes among American Opinion Leaders." *Journal of Politics* 52:94–125.

———. 1993. "The Structure of Foreign Policy Beliefs Among American Opinion Leaders—after the Cold War." *Millennium: Journal of International Studies* 22: forthcoming.

Jacobs, Lawrence R., and Robert Y. Shapiro. 1993. "The Public Presidency, Private Polls and Policymaking: Lyndon Johnson." Paper presented at the Annual Meeting of the American Political Science Association, Washington, DC.

Kinsella, David. 1990. "Defence Spending and Economic Performance in the United States: A Causal Analysis." *Defence Economics* 1:295–309.

Monroe, Alan D. 1979. "Consistency Between Public Preferences and National Policy Decisions." *American Politics Quarterly* 7:3–19.

Murray, Shoon. 1992. "Turning an Elite Cross-sectional Survey into a Panel Study While Protecting Anonymity." *Journal of Conflict Resolution* 36:586–95.

———. 1993. *American Elites' Reaction to the End of the Cold War: A 1988–1992 Panel Study.* Ph.D. Dissertation, Yale University, New Haven, CT.

Ostrom, Charles, and Robin Marra. 1986. "U.S. Defense Spending and the Soviet Estimate." *American Political Science Review* 80:819–42.

Page, Benjamin, and Robert Shapiro. 1983. "Effects of Public Opinion on Policy." *American Political Science Review* 77:175–90.

Page, Benjamin, Robert Shapiro, and Glenn Dempsey. 1987. "What Moves Public Opinion?" *American Political Science Review* 81:23–43.

Peffley, Mark, and Jon Hurwitz. 1992. "International Events and Foreign Policy Beliefs: Public Response to Changing Soviet-U.S. Relations." *American Journal of Political Science* 36:431–61.

Russett, Bruce M. 1970. *What Price Vigilance? The Burdens of National Defense.* New Haven: Yale University Press.

Russett, Bruce M., and Elizabeth C. Hanson. 1975. *Interest and Ideology: The Foreign Policy Beliefs of American Businessmen.* New York: W. H. Freeman.

Ward, Michael D. 1984. "Differential Paths to Parity: A Study of the Contemporary Arms Race." *American Political Science Review* 78:297–317.

Wittkopf, Eugene R. 1990. *Faces of Internationalism: Public Opinion and American Foreign Policy.* Durham, NC: Duke University Press.

Wlezien, Christopher. 1992. "The Dynamics of Representation: The Case of Spending on Defense." Presented at the Annual Meeting of the American Political Science Association, Chicago, IL.

Why Was This Research Needed?

1. What kinds of beliefs affected popular support for U.S. foreign policy during the cold war?

2. For what reasons do the authors see the end of the cold war as "a rare opportunity" for research on public opinion and foreign policy?

3. What does the "rationality" of beliefs refer to in the study of public opinion? What is the concept of a "belief system"?

4. What are the main conclusions of previous research on American attitudes toward international affairs and the end of the cold war? What have past researchers written about the link between public opinion and foreign policy decisions like defense spending?

How Was the Topic Studied?

1. What is a "panel study"? Describe the methodology used in coauthor Shoon Murray's study (published in 1993) of cold war attitudes.

2. What key variables did Murray's study measure?

3. How did Murray's panel study seek to build upon earlier research on Americans' foreign policy beliefs?

What Are the Findings?

1. As demonstrated in Tables 1, 2, and 3, cross tabulation is a statistical technique for analyzing relationships between variables at what level of measurement?

2. In Table 1, what is the independent variable (X) and what is the dependent variable (Y)? How would you state the null hypothesis (H_0) and the research hypothesis (H_1)?

3. Percentages in Tables 1, 2, and 3 were calculated on the basis of columns. How is this done? Why is this procedure preferred for tables setting up the independent variable and dependent variable as they appear here?

4. What is striking for the authors about Table 1 is not the percentage differences across categories of the independent variable but their similarity. Why is this so?

5. How do the multicategory ordinal data in Table 2 permit a directional statement about the relationship between changes in X and Y? How would you formulate this statement?

6. The authors describe the nature of the relationship between X and Y in their discussion of Tables 1, 2, and 3, but they do not provide measures of significance or strength. What information would be gained if such measures had been calculated? Which measures of significance and strength should be used for these tabular data?

7. What information is provided by the correlation results discussed on page 81? For what types of data is correlation the appropriate method of analysis?

What Do the Results Mean?

1. What does this research indicate about the dynamic between "core values" and reactions to

current events in the public's attitudes regarding foreign policy issues?

2. What kind of research would you propose for evaluating the authors' suggestion that foreign policy and domestic ideology orientations stem from the same value source?

3. Why does an adequate explanation of defense spending decisions require a multivariate approach? What variables would you include in your model for defense spending by the current presidential administration?

4. Why is it difficult to sort out the relationship between defense spending and changes in public opinion over time? What kinds of evidence have scholars used to specify the nature of this causal link?

5. Does this study indicate a possibility that citizens can be manipulated by their leaders or political ideologues when it comes to foreign policy issues? If so, to what extent? Explain your answer.

Afterword from Bruce Russett

A major theme of this article is that fundamental attitudes toward foreign policy change slowly, among both elites and the general public. The differences between militant internationalism and cooperative internationalism correspond to the competing belief systems that characterize academic and policy discussions about foreign policy; namely, the competing schools of realism and liberal internationalism. Adherents of the first school more readily endorse the need for military superiority and a readiness to use force, whereas those of the second school are more likely to support arms control, foreign aid, and the United Nations. Moreover, those fundamental positions continue to correlate highly with the conservative-liberal ideological spectrum on domestic politics (Murray 1996; Murray, Cowden, and Russett 1999). This anchoring of specific foreign policy attitudes in wider belief systems explains why so many of the arguments and positions remain little changed even by dramatic events like the end of the cold war and the rise of terrorism.

Another theme is the effect of public opinion on foreign policy. But a focus on public opinion and world events as the major influences on policy is incomplete. One new work distinguishes between those foreign policy leaders who are veterans of military service and those without military experience. Feaver and Gelpi (2004) find that the veterans are less ready to use military force than are those who have always been civilians, but the veterans are also more resistant to civilian pressures to limit the use of military force once a campaign is undertaken. In another recent study, Jacobs and Page (2005) track public opinion, opinion among various groups of elite decision makers, and actual policy over three decades. They conclude that business leaders have the most impact on policy and, in contrast with our article, the influence of public opinion is small.

In any case, the public can exercise little influence without accurate and reliable information. For example, the public thought Saddam Hussein was supporting terrorist groups even before September 11, and many Americans were ideologically inclined to believe it afterward. The U.S. government used that perception to justify its invasion of Iraq even though evidence of such a link was lacking (Bloch-Elkon and Shapiro 2005; for further discussion of this issue, see Reading 2 by Scott L. Althaus and Devon M. Largio). So, evaluating the impact of public opinion on foreign policy—a key to understanding how democracy may work effectively—requires study of how public opinion is shaped by government leaders, policy elites, and the mass media.

References

Bloch-Elkon, Yaeli, and Robert Y. Shapiro. 2005. "Deep Suspicion: Iraq, Misperception, and Partisanship." *Public Opinion Pros*. June. www.publicopinionpros.com.

Feaver, Peter, and Christoper Gelpi. 2004. *Choosing Your Battles: American Civil-Military Relations and the Use of Force*. Princeton, N.J.: Princeton University Press.

Jacobs, Lawrence R., and Benjamin I. Page. 2005. "Who Influences U.S. Foreign Policy?" *American Political Science Review* 99:107–124.

Murray, Shoon Kathleen. 1996. *Anchors Against Change: American Opinion Leaders' Beliefs after the Cold War*. Ann Arbor: University of Michigan Press.

Murray, Shoon, Jonathan Cowden, and Bruce Russett. 1999. "The Convergence of American Elites' Domestic Beliefs with their Foreign Policy Beliefs." *International Interactions* 25:153–180.

8

Traditional Versus Technology-Aided Instruction: The Effects of Visual Stimulus in the Classroom

Donald L. Jordan and Peter M. Sanchez

Effective teaching is easy to recognize but difficult to define. We all know of individuals who are described as "born teachers." Yet inspiring teachers come in all shapes and sizes, and they possess many different philosophies, personalities, and styles. Teaching as an art form is a central theme of many current books on education. However, if good teaching is largely instinctive and intuitive, the successful teacher may be the last one able to explain the secrets of the craft. The traditional poem about the centipede is suggestive here: when asked to explain how it managed to walk, the creature reflected on its complicated motions, then collapsed in a tangled heap.

Without negating teaching's holistic, creative dimension, it is logical from an evaluation perspective to approach teaching as a set of techniques and course components that may or may not produce desired results in students. From the outset, it seems wise to acknowledge the complexity of the issue. Methods that work for one student population may not be as effective for another. There could also be variations across academic subjects. The only way to begin to sort out such possibilities is to analyze the classroom experience by developing appropriate measurements for both the input and output sides of the equation.

The following reading by Donald L. Jordan and Peter M. Sanchez offers an example of this type of careful empirical approach. The focus of their research is narrow and specific: will a standard American government course be enhanced by combining the use of video clips with customary instructional techniques? Students should note how the authors set up their study to isolate the impact of the video intervention. The fact that the findings of this research are open to different interpretations also illustrates how difficult it is to assess cause and effect, even in the context of a controlled experiment.

The extravagant claims of the vendors of multimedia applications have raised the expectations of teachers who are searching for ways to improve their classroom performance. These teachers frequently see multimedia resources as a natural way to present material to a generation of students weaned on hours of television.

Educators also assume that the students of today will learn and retain more through visual or computerized instruction, or that students, at a minimum, will enjoy their educational experience more if it is enhanced by visual stimulation. For example, it is logical to think that students who are learning about congressional politics will gain a better understanding if they can see the U.S. Congress at work.

One major pitfall in this technological approach, however, is the enormous cost of many multimedia applications, especially in times of tight budgetary constraints. Perhaps more importantly, some evidence suggests that the use of technology and other innovations in the classroom does not significantly improve student performance (Janda 1992; Spencer 1991; and Summers 1990–1991). Before educational institutions spend significant portions of their budgets on multimedia technology, they should consider the utility of such expenditures.

The Experiment: A Brief Description

We undertook this small, controlled experiment to see whether the use of short video clips in the classroom would enhance our students' ability to learn and retain information about some basic concepts in American government. We divided 117 freshmen into six sections in an introductory American government class at the United States Air Force Academy. As one might expect at a military academy, this population was fairly homogeneous.[1]

The students were placed into specific sections by an alphabetic process; the first student was placed into section one, the second into section two, and so on. Each instructor had three sections of approximately 19 students. For each instructor, two sections were designated "treatment" or "video" sections—a total of four sections and 79 students. Each instructor also had a section labeled "traditional," which would serve as control groups, with a total of 38 students.

Through this relatively random process,

we were fairly confident that the sections began with no significant differences in aptitude. This assumption was also supported by the results of an American government pretest administered to all incoming students the previous summer. The independent t-test results in Table 1 demonstrate that the pretest performance of the two groups— "traditional" and "video"—was indistinguishable.

In the video sections, many of the concepts in the course were presented through video clips.[2] The two instructors jointly planned each lesson to ensure that all video sections received the same video clips. These clips were then shown in all of the video sections. For example, when discussing judicial restraint, we showed a short video clip of Judge Robert Bork discussing this concept during the Senate Judiciary Committee's hearings to consider his ratification for the Supreme Court.

In the other sections we used a traditional method of classroom instruction to provide a control for the experiment. In these sections almost all teaching was accomplished through lectures and discussions. When films were used, they lasted the entire class period, or close to the entire period. In every case, the concepts highlighted in the video sections by the use of videos, were discussed in detail more traditionally in the control sections.

To determine the effects of the visual stimulus in the video sections, multiple-choice questions addressing the concepts augmented by video were constructed and incorporated into three examinations throughout the course. Thus, we tagged certain questions in the exams as "video" questions. Our working assumption/hypothesis was that if the video clips helped the students to better understand concepts, then they should on average score better on these questions than the students in the traditional sections. We expected that the video sections would have

Table 1
Pretest

Group	N	Mean Score	St Dev
traditional	38	68.6%	12.5
video	76	67.6	13.1
pooled variance	t = .369	DF = 112	Prob = .713

a higher mean than the traditional sections on all examinations, especially on those questions that we categorized as video questions.[3]

Results of the Experiment

The results on the first examination were striking. Table 2 shows that there was no difference in performance on test questions that had no video augmentation.

These results are very important to the experiment since they suggest that all students performed at the same level on questions that were not aided with video clips. If students in the video sections had done poorly on the nonvideo questions, then we would have to conclude that an emphasis on concepts supported by video clips hindered student learning on nonvideo-aided concepts. Or, we would conclude that the instructors placed so much emphasis on the video concepts that they short-changed the non-video concepts.[4]

At this point, though, the most exciting result was the difference in performance on those questions that tested concepts expanded upon with video. Table 3 demonstrates that the students in the video sections on average scored 9.3 percentage points higher than the students in the two traditional sections, with a significance level of 99.8%. Despite our determination to remain objective and even skeptical about the potential effectiveness of the use of video, the statistically significant difference of almost ten percentage points agitated both researchers.

Our initial enthusiasm was quickly sobered by the results of the second exam. Again, there was no significant difference in performance on nonvideo questions. Unfortunately, there was also no difference in performance on those questions testing concepts augmented by video clips. Table 4 indicates that on the second exam the video students scored only .5 percentage points higher than the traditional students on the video questions.

There are many potential explanations for this finding. Again, perhaps we subconsciously overcompensated in the nonvideo sections by trying too hard to insure video concepts were adequately covered. Perhaps the novelty of the use of videos simply wore off, and the students turned off when the laser disc player came on. We wondered if perhaps the students had caught wind of the experiment and the nonvideo sections were trying extra hard to keep up.

On the final exam we repeated the 15 video questions. Here, once again, we found that the students exposed to video performed better on these questions. Table 5 reflects that the video students scored 3.1 percentage points higher than the traditional students on the video questions in the final exam. These results were nearly significant at the 95% level, with a probability of .0575. However, the results were probably largely influenced by the striking results on the first examination. Again there was no significant difference in performance on nonvideo questions.

Discussion

Despite our initial excitement and optimism, our findings indicate that, in this experiment, exposure to video

Table 2
Exam #1—Non-Video Questions (27 each)

Group	N	Mean Score	St Dev
traditional	39	77.1%	9.0
video	77	77.1	9.3
pooled variance	t = .000	DF = 114	Prob = 1.00

Table 3
Exam #1—Video Questions (6 each)

Group	N	Mean Score	St Dev
traditional	39	84.4%	18.7
video	77	93.7	14.8
pooled variance	t=2.91	DF= 114	Prob=.002

Table 4
Exam #2—Video Questions (7 each)

Group	N	Mean Score	St Dev
traditional	37	85.2%	18.3
video	72	85.7	16.7
pooled variance	t=.146	DF= 107	Prob=.442

Table 5
Final Exam Video Questions (13 each)

Group	N	Mean Score	St Dev
traditional	39	89.2%	8.5
video	78	92.3	10.0
pooled variance	t=1.59	DF= 115	Prob=.0575

in the classroom may have had only a minor impact on students' abilities to grasp and retain material. Students in the video sections did do a bit better on average throughout the entire course, though only statistically significant on the first examination. Table 6 shows that the video students performed better than the traditional students in the course by .8 percentage points (significance of 77.4%).[5] The video students also scored higher on graded written work, averaging 85.8% as compared to 84.6% for the control group. But these results were not significant even at the 95% level.

Strangely, there was no indication that the students who were exposed to video clips enjoyed the course more than the others. As a matter of fact, the traditional students rated the course slightly higher than the video students! In an end-of-course critique question, which asked the students to compare their level of enjoyment of this course with others at the Academy on a scale from 1–9 (nine being the best), the video sections gave the course a 7.94 rating, while the traditional sections gave the course a 7.95 rating (not significant at the 95% level).

There are many possible explanations for

our results. First, contrary to the conventional wisdom, video augmentation may not be helpful in enhancing student understanding. If this is the case, it may be more advisable for educational institutions to spend their resources augmenting the effectiveness of teachers rather than purchasing high technology software and hardware.

Second, the videos used in this experiment may not have been adequate in explaining the concepts they were meant to explain. This conclusion in our opinion must be seriously considered, since we believe that most of the laser discs available to us were too elementary for the college level. If this experiment were repeated with well-produced video clips, the results could well be very impressive.

A third, and obvious, conclusion is that our sample was too small. If we had carried out this experiment with 1,000 students, our results on all exams would have been significant at the .05 level assuming similar results.

Finally, the Hawthorn Effect could have been at work. If the students in the traditional sections discovered that an experiment was taking place, they could have studied harder, explaining the less than positive results on the second examination. We do not believe this to be the case, however. At the end of the course, we asked all students to let us know if there was something

Table 6
Final Course Grade Average

Group	N	Mean Score	St Dev
traditional	39	81.7%	5.1
video	78	82.5	5.4
pooled variance	t=.754	DF= 115	Prob=.2265

they did not like about the course, and we specifically asked if there was something about their section that they did not like. We received no indication that students were concerned that they were in the traditional class. While this is not proof that they did not know, it suggests that our findings are the result of some other factor.

Experiments such as this one should be continued. As educators, we must determine whether it is worthwhile to spend large portions of the education budget to purchase high-tech gadgetry. If multimedia equipment assists the learning process, then we should proceed in this direction with haste and enthusiasm. If, however, computers, laser discs, and the like do not assist us in educating today's students in measurable ways, then we should return to the chalkboard, both literally and figuratively, to find better ways to educate. Additionally, these types of experiments will be very useful in producing good video supplements in the classroom, if indeed we find that visual stimulus does enhance learning.

Perhaps the most important lesson that we learned from conducting this experiment is that the use of multimedia technology in the classroom is extraordinarily time consuming. Those who believe that education will be enhanced through the purchase of technology alone are not familiar with the attendant labor costs of such systems. There is a very likely danger that advanced technology costing hundreds of thousands of dollars will remain underused because educators do not have the training or cannot afford the time to use it to its full potential.

In sum, video segments had a small impact on our students' ability to understand and retain concepts of American government. This small attempt to collect data is certainly not the last word on the subject, but earlier pessimistic findings appear on the surface to have been at least tentatively substantiated. ■

Notes

This paper was presented at the 1992 Annual Meeting of the American Political Science Association, Chicago, Illinois.

1. Students are predominantly white males from middle-class families.

2. The main sources for these video clips were the ABC News interactive discs, *Powers of the Congress, Powers of the President,* and *Powers of the Supreme Court;* a preproduction video disc designed to accompany Ken Janda's American government text, *The Challenge of Democracy,* Houghton Mifflin Publisher; an American government disc marketed by Harper-Collins; and various VHS clips collected by members of the department over the years.

3. Statistically this creates a one-tail test for significance.

4. The fact that the students in the video sections performed no better on the non-video questions also suggests that there was no spillover effect or that the use of video would spur a generally higher performance on all questions.

5. In addition to two examinations and a final examination, there were two short papers.

References

Janda, Kenneth. 1992. "Multimedia in Political Science: Sobering Lessons from a Teaching Experiment." *Journal of Educational Multimedia and Hypermedia* 1:341–54.

Spencer, Ken. 1991. "Modes, Media, and Methods: The Search for Educational Effectiveness." *British Journal of Educational Technology* 22:12–22.

Summers, Jerry A. 1990–91. "Effect of Interactivity Upon Student Achievement, Completion Intervals, and Affective Perceptions." *Journal of Educational Technology Systems* 19:53–57.

Why Was This Research Needed?

1. What existing bias do Jordan and Sanchez cite in favor of the idea that videos and other multimedia sources will improve classroom teaching? What are the sources of this expectation?

2. What is the practical rationale for conducting this kind of objective evaluation of "technology-aided instruction"?

3. What are the findings of previous research on this subject? Is the authors' review of the literature

adequate in your view? How might more information be helpful, either about the details of the cited studies or about a broader range of relevant educational research?

How Was the Topic Studied?

1. What were the basic steps in setting up this classroom experiment? Who was in the treatment group? Why was it also necessary to have a control group? How was the control group selected?
2. What are the research and null hypotheses for this study?
3. How would you assess the strengths and weaknesses of the sample selected for this project?
4. What is the exact nature of the experimental intervention? That is, how did the instructors integrate the use of videos into their teaching of American government? How does this differ from other ways that videos could be used in the teaching of such a course?
5. What are the outcomes examined in this experiment? Do you believe the concept of teaching effectiveness was tested appropriately by these measures?
6. Would it have been useful to incorporate a cost dimension in the design of this study? How might you do this?

What Are the Findings?

1. Why is the difference-of-means t test the appropriate measure of statistical significance for the data in Tables 1 through 6?
2. Why does this study use a one-tailed test of statistical significance?
3. Why is t calculated using the pooled variance method?

4. Examine the post-test data in Tables 2 through 6. How would you succinctly describe the *nature* and *magnitude* of the impact of the independent variable on the dependent variable?
5. Why would each of the following factors increase the likelihood of a statistically significant difference between the experimental and control groups in this study: a bigger N, a larger difference between the mean test scores of traditional and video groups, and a smaller standard deviation in test scores within each group? (In considering this question, it could be helpful to review the formula for calculating t.)

What Do the Results Mean?

1. Do the authors do a good job of summarizing the mixed findings resulting from their research? Explain. What factors do they note that may have muted the impact of the classroom videos? What role might there be for the collection of certain kinds of qualitative data to aid in the interpretation of findings?
2. What kind of follow-up study could you propose that would avoid weaknesses of the current study?
3. Imagine that you are a university budgetary official considering a department's request for substantial new investment in multimedia technologies. As support for this request, the department chair submits a study similar to the research presented in this reading. How much of a difference in test outcomes between the experimental and control groups would be necessary for you to agree to the funding request? To what extent is this a question that should, or can, be answered by statistics?

Afterword from Peter M. Sanchez

When we decided to conduct a study to assess the impact of video clips on learning, computers were just becoming popular enough to be used in the classroom and the U.S. Air Force Academy had already begun planning to do that. Of course, at that time the Web as we know it today did not exist and Gopher (a limited all-text search engine) was fairly new. The amount of information we can now access via the Internet has grown by leaps and bounds, so our simple experiment is out of date in many ways. Nevertheless, the use of a computer in the classroom is very similar to our research design because what we wanted to measure was the impact of visual stimulation. We were aware that as technology progressed, the ability to deliver video and still images to students would improve dramatically. We also knew that incorporating such media would be an expensive endeavor, so we decided to see whether visuals would actually enhance a student's ability to understand the concepts that he or she was supposed to take away from the classroom. If we found that learning was not enhanced, then spending lots of money on high-tech equipment would not be economically rational. The professor with chalk and a blackboard would suffice, just as had been the case for many decades.

Our results suggested that technology might not be the panacea some educators envisioned back then. Even so, more than a decade and many technological improvements later, universities are spending hundreds of thousands of dollars to make classrooms fully computerized. We now have access to videos, computers, and overhead projection systems at the touch of a button. These so-called smart classrooms have made it both simpler and more difficult for professors to prepare for class. On one hand, professors have an enormous volume of information available to them and many ways to deliver that information. On the other hand, teaching a class in this high-tech environment requires familiarity with a greater range of materials and a greater knowledge of technology, both hardware and software. All of us who use smart classrooms have had the experience of being unable to get the technology to work during class. When that happens, the professor feels like a deer staring into oncoming headlights! Consequently, many professors still remain wedded to their chalk.

Interestingly enough, even though I feel pretty certain that all of the technology we have at our disposal does not necessarily enhance student learning, I always use computers in my classes to deliver videos, images, and information. I have come to the conclusion that using technology in the classroom is not just a question of whether learning objectives are better met. Computers are now part of our lives, and using them is both fun and important because students must become accustomed to their possibilities. Although students may not attain more learning objectives by being exposed to visual stimulation, they certainly learn that computers are important and can be used in numerous ways to acquire, disseminate, and present various forms of data. This means that in order to fully understand the value of technology in the classroom, the researcher must look into other possible ways in which it can help students. I will leave this endeavor to someone else.

How Americans Responded: A Study of Public Reactions to 9/11/01

Michael Traugott, Ted Brader, Deborah Coral, Richard Curtin, David Featherman, Robert Groves, Martha Hill, James Jackson, Thomas Juster, Robert Kahn, Courtney Kennedy, Donald Kinder, Beth-Ellen Pennell, Matthew Shapiro, Mark Tessler, David Weir, and Robert Willis

The four hijacked jetliners that slammed into the World Trade Center, the Pentagon, and a Pennsylvania field on September 11, 2001, killing almost 3,000 people, dealt a stunning blow to the United States. In addition to the tragic loss of life, the nation sustained heavy economic damage: financial losses quickly climbed into the hundreds of billions of dollars, beginning with property damage and the costs of cleaning up the sites of the attacks and extending to long-term damage to the airline, tourism, and insurance industries (Looney 2002). In response to the attacks, the U.S. government reorganized, creating the new cabinet-level Homeland Security Department, which pulled together government agencies and services such as the Federal Emergency Management Agency and the Coast Guard. And, within a month after the attacks, a decisive new course in American foreign policy had been set, signaled by the onset of bombing and the subsequent invasion of Afghanistan by U.S. and allied forces.

Yet, as many commentators have pointed out, some impacts of September 11 were not tangible. The shock to the American psyche was, in many ways, unprecedented due to the surprising and horrific nature of the attacks. According to the Los Angeles Times, *this was "civilization's modern nightmare," while the* Washington Post *reported that we had witnessed "one of the greatest calamities in American history" (The Guardian 2001). Mental health experts predicted widespread traumatic reactions among the population (Schrader 2001). One author who specializes in the formation of generational psychologies stated the attacks could be the defining event for an entire generation of young Americans, much as Pearl Harbor or the assassination of John F. Kennedy influenced young people of earlier eras (Tarlach 2001).*

It is one thing to speculate about the abstract meaning of historic events in this way, however, and quite another to gauge the consequences in objective terms. What are the key variables to be measured? How might relevant data be collected and organized? Using their How Americans Respond survey, Michael Traugott and his colleagues attempt to tackle these difficult research problems. Their work, presented in the following reading, offers a provocative analysis suggesting answers to many important questions surrounding the public's reaction to the September 11 tragedy. Yet while recognizing the contributions of this study, students should pay close attention to the choices the authors made concerning question wording, survey design, and other aspects of research methodology that shaped and, of necessity, limited the results.

References

The Guardian. 2001. "Attack on America: What the US Papers Say." September 13, 7.

Looney, Robert. 2002. "Economic Costs to the United States Stemming from the 9/11 Attacks." *Strategic Insights* 1 (6). www.ccc.nps.navy.mil/si/aug02/homeland.asp.

Schrader, Ann. 2001. "Impact on Psyches Won't Be Felt for Days." *Denver Post*, September 12, A-18.

Tarlach, Gemma. 2001. "Terrorism Attacks May Define a New Generation's Nation." *Milwaukee Journal Sentinel*, September 12, 3B.

On the afternoon of Tuesday, September 11, 2001, a group of social scientists at the Institute for Social Research (ISR) gathered to consider how they might employ their talents to help the country after the shocking events of that morning. The group included economists, political scientists, psychologists, sociologists, demographers, and survey methodologists. Based upon their previous research experience, each of them proposed hypotheses on aspects of American life and individuals' morale and behavior that were most likely to be affected. While they were relatively confident about expected relationships in the short term, we were uncertain about how temporary or permanent these changes might be or how intertwined and mutually reinforcing they could become.

We assumed a proliferation of media polls would provide the country quick snapshots of reactions to current events, but we also felt the scientific monitoring of the attitudes important to changing behaviors would be overlooked. And so the How Americans Respond (HAR) survey was born. From the beginning, the research had a dual focus: to measure attitudes quickly after the event and to explore the effects of the attack over time with a longitudinal design. To the maximum extent possible, the survey used measures from existing longitudinal data collections in order to facilitate comparisons over time. Whenever possible, HAR sought to compare pre-attack national estimates to post-attack estimates. While the indicators of knowledge, attitudes, and behaviors about the attacks themselves had no possible premeasurements, we designed HAR to function as a monitoring device to see how they would change over time.[1]

A primary focus of the study was the resiliency of the U.S. population. A number of previous national traumas in the United States have been the focus of extended research, and general models of effects have been developed (Barton 1969; Canino, Bravo, and Rubio-Stipec 1990). But those events and study designs differed significantly from what we proposed to do. The most relevant events include the assassination of John F. Kennedy in 1963: the disturbances in urban areas in the late 1960s and early 1970s, and Los Angeles in 1992; and the bombing of the federal building in Oklahoma City in 1995. There have, of course, been numerous natural and man-made disasters that have affected large numbers of citizens in local areas, but they have not had the same kind of national impact as September 11 (e.g., Wilkinson 1983). Other incidents, such as the *Challenger* disaster, have also had national consequences, but without equivalent international implications and the equivalent magnitude of loss.

In our studies, we were concerned about the reaction of the entire nation to the event. The incident itself represented an assault on national principles and ideals and was expected to affect the national psyche; and the news coverage, some of which provided a live, real-time view of events as they unfolded, was graphic and available to a large national audience, including children.

In an incident like Oklahoma City, the direct impact was primarily local and the perpetrators were U.S. citizens.

Most Americans saw it as an isolated event by a single individual who was captured quickly. While there were several news polls conducted after the event (and many more subsequently about a trial and eventual punishment), there was little content that focused on either general social psychological attitudes in the nation or their potential political and economic ramifications. Several studies measured the stress and coping abilities of children (Morland 1999; Pesci 1999; Pfefferbaum et al. 1999; Pfefferbaum et al. 2000), victims and their families (North et al. 1999), and other citizens in the area (Sprang 1999; Tucker et al. 2000). While no studies involved either a national or local panel of citizens, there were indications that symptoms of stress were still present in children living in the vicinity of Oklahoma City seven weeks after the incident (Pfefferbaum et al. 1999).

Some researchers have studied the dynamics and resiliency of attitudes about tolerance and civil liberties but not in relation to an equivalent national tragedy or to attitudes relating to international actors and foreign affairs. Going back to the Stouffer studies (1955), shifts in opinions on tolerance and civil liberties have been studied across years and decades. But very few studies have looked at how rapid these shifts might be across a short period of time when there is a particular triggering event for the change.[2]

The role of the media is a key element in this process. The media are an essential source of information about events (and their meaning) as they unfold, and previous research shows that those with the highest levels of media exposure are most affected psychologically and less likely to recover quickly (Morland 1999; Pesci 1999; Pfefferbaum et al. 2000). Only through repeated measures over time can this hypothesis be tested for September 11 and other related actions that followed.

The issue of the durability of initial reactions, including how they may have changed contemporary American civil society, is important too. Putnam (2002) presents an early summary of survey findings produced close to the September attacks, and he concludes that there is a possibility that both a period effect and a cohort effect could develop among those who were affected

directly by the events as well as by the continuous media coverage of them. He notes, "In the aftermath of September's tragedy, a window of opportunity has opened for a sort of civic renewal that occurs only once or twice a century" (22). Whether this renewal is taking place and how long it might last are key questions for analysts of the public reactions to September 11, and answers may be pursued through longitudinal analysis of the HAR study.

Relevant Findings

One of the most important findings from Wave 1 of HAR was that a substantial number of Americans suffered a lost sense of personal safety and security. This loss was associated statistically with their economic attitudes and behavior, their support for various government policies, and their resulting psychological states. In the initial survey, about half of the respondents said their personal sense of safety and security was reduced "a great deal" or "a good amount," while the other half indicated that it was affected "not too much" or "not at all" (see Figure 1).

Despite the government's actions since the attacks, including military action in Afghanistan and the establishment of the Office of Homeland Security, Americans' level of concern has not changed very much. The basic attitudinal measures were dichotomized to reflect "concerned" and "not concerned" and then compared in Wave 2 to Wave 1. These results, presented in Figure 2, show that 39% of the respondents were "not concerned" at either time, and 37% remained "concerned" six months later. One in eight (13%) were "concerned" in September but were not six months later, while 11% were not "concerned" in Wave 1 but were in Wave 2.

Of course, the Bush administration is currently trying to reassure the public that it is fighting a war on terrorism that will extend far into the future, while trying to maintain an appropriate level of heightened alert about the possibility of additional attacks. In general, it has been difficult to measure the "success" in this effort. The data from Wave 1 show close attention to the media correlated with a shaken sense of personal safety. And there

Figure 1 • Respondents' Perceived Sense of Personal Safety and Security Since September 11, Wave 1

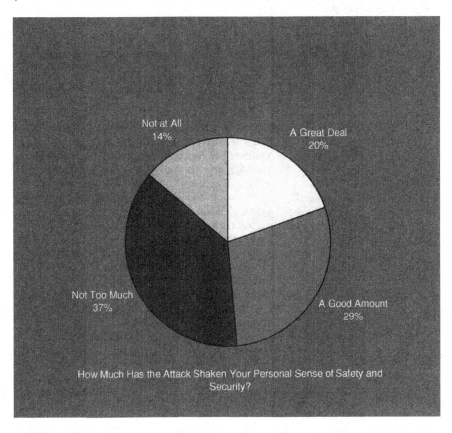

Not at All
14%

A Great Deal
20%

Not Too Much
37%

A Good Amount
29%

How Much Has the Attack Shaken Your Personal Sense of Safety and Security?

was a weaker relationship between attention to news about the war on terrorism, measured in Wave 2, and still feeling shaken or worse off. This is also true in Wave 2 for current attention to television evening news (number of days watched in the last week). However, in Wave 2 a shaken sense of personal safety shows no association with reading the newspaper (number of days read).

Civic Engagement

As in any study that involves indicators of civic engagement, there are a number of ever-present measurement issues. For example, Putnam (2002, 20–21) reports, "Occasional volunteering is up slightly, but regular volunteering (at least twice a month) remains unchanged at

about one in every seven Americans. Compared with figures from immediately after the tragedy, our data suggest that much of the measurable increase in generosity spent itself within a few weeks." Assessments of survey responses like these depend on definitions that are given in the questions, including what a volunteer activity might be and what the relevant time period of reference is.

The HAR question is, "Thinking about the past month, have you spent any time participating in any sort of *volunteer* or charitable activity in your community?" When an AARP survey in 1996 asked a similar question with a time reference of "the past year," 43% of Americans reported that they had engaged in such activity. In both Wave 1 and Wave 2 of HAR, 39% of the respondents indicated that they had done some volunteer

Figure 2 • Changes in Respondents' Perceived Sense of Personal Safety and Security Since September 11, Wave 1 to Wave 2

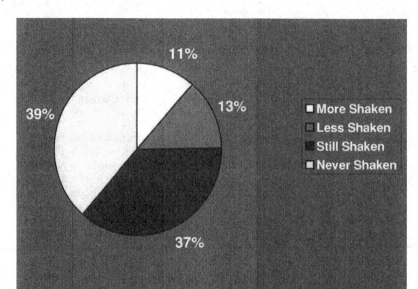

work "in the past month," indicating no significant difference from the earlier time period. When the responses of the *panel* participants are compared, one-quarter of the respondents (26%) indicated volunteering at both points in time and 47% at neither. A total of 15% indicated volunteering in the Wave 1 survey but not at Wave 2, while 12% indicated volunteering at Wave 2 but not at Wave 1. These data certainly do not indicate a surge in volunteering as a response to September 11. However, this reflects only the percentage of people volunteering and says nothing about the time that volunteers spend in such activity.

For a more comprehensive assessment of volunteering, we also asked a follow-up question to those who said they had volunteered about how many hours they spent

volunteering in the past month, and these data suggest a slightly different picture. As illustrated in Table 1, the average number of hours spent volunteering in the preceding month was greater in Wave 2 than in Wave 1, and it may be attributed to an increase in time spent volunteering by those who were already doing so. First-time volunteers in Wave 1 and Wave 2 spent about the same amount of time in the preceding month on this effort (11.7 compared to 12.0 hours). People who volunteered

Table 1
Average Amount of Time Volunteers Spent in That Activity, HAR Wave 1 and Wave 2

Wave 1 Only Volunteers	11.7 hours	(n = 89)[a]
Wave 2 Only Volunteers	12.0 hours	(n = 70)[a]
Wave 1 and 2 Volunteers at Wave 1	16.0 hours	(n = 156)[b]
Wave 1 and 2 Volunteers at Wave 2	21.8 hours	(n = 157)[c]

[a]Not significantly different.
[b]Significantly different from the Wave 1 Only and Wave 2 Only means at p < .05.
[c]Significantly different from the Wave 1 Only, Wave 2 Only, and Wave 1 and 2 Volunteers at Wave 1 means at p < .05.

at both points in time reported more hours at Wave 1 (16.0) and at Wave 2 (21.8 hours). They increased their effort, on average, by 36% (21.8 compared to 16.0), and the time they reportedly spent in volunteering in Wave 2 was about 80% higher than the effort expended by first-time volunteers at either point in time.

Trust in Others

Another measure of civil society is the trust that Americans have in those around them. Putnam reports trust in government data showing that half (51%) of his respondents were more trusting in late 2001 than they had been one year earlier. On the basic item, "Most of the time, people try to be helpful rather than looking out for themselves," there was no difference in the distribution of attitudes measured in HAR in the Wave 1 and Wave 2 cross-sections; two out of three respondents "agreed" or "agreed strongly." Looking at shifts among the panel respondents from Wave 1 to Wave 2, there is a strong correlation (gamma = .40, p < .001) with a slight tendency toward greater agreement at Wave 2.

There are other ways to measure trust. Recent research (Burns and Kinder 2000) shows that trust in others is domain specific. In Wave 2 of HAR, we asked three sets of questions each about trust in "people from other countries," trust in "Americans," and trust in "people in your neighborhood."[3] After September 11, we expected to find that trust in neighbors would be high, followed by trust in Americans, and then trust in foreigners. We constructed three additive scales, and they were intercorrelated, indicating a tendency for some respondents to be generally more trusting than others. However, the scores on the simple additive indexes were distributed quite differently, as shown in Table 2. The mean score for the Trust in Americans index was .34 points (19%) higher than the mean for the Trust in Foreigners index (2.10 compared to 1.76); and the mean Trust in Neighbors index was .49 points (23%) higher than the mean Trust in Americans index and .83 points (47%) higher than the mean Trust in Foreigners index.

The HAR survey suggests that these attitudes may reflect more patriotism and national pride than an opposition to foreigners. While some portion of these attitudes is probably inherently present in most respondents, September 11 undoubtedly played a role in the values measured in HAR. For example, the act of following the news about the war on terrorism "closely" was correlated with the Trust in Americans index (gamma = .16, p < .001), but not significantly with the Trust in Neighbors index (gamma = .08) or Trust in Foreigners index (gamma = .02).

Feelings toward Ethnic and Racial Minorities

Both waves of the HAR survey also contained information from "feeling thermometer" questions that asked respondents how they felt about a variety of ethnic and racial groups. As shown in Figure 3, we found that "American" groups such as African, Hispanic, and even white Americans all received higher ratings in Wave 1 than they had in either the 1998 or the 2000 American National Election Study. These changes in group-favorability ratings are related to attention to the news about the war on terrorism. Those respondents paying close attention to the news on average were more likely to give favorable ratings to every one of these groups in Wave 2, while those who were not paying much attention to such news were less likely to give a positive rating.

Of course several ethnic groups composed of people most closely associated with the attacks on the World

Table 2
Distribution of Trust Index Scores in HAR Wave 2[a]

	Minimum	Maximum	Mean	Standard Deviation	N
Trust in Foreigners	0	3	1.76	1.18	689
Trust in Americans	0	3	2.10	1.04	715
Trust in Neighbors	0	3	2.59	0.83	740

[a]These means are statistically different from each other with p < .05.

Figure 3 • The Evaluation of American Ethnic Groups with Thermometer Ratings, HAR Wave 1

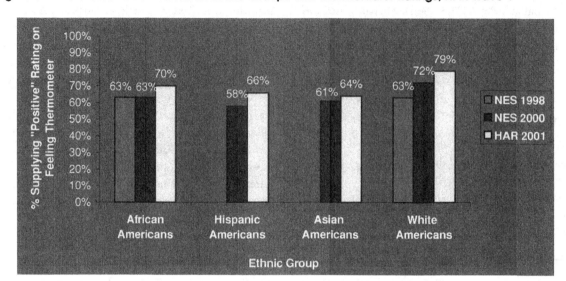

Trade Center received less favorable ratings, measured in the same way. The data presented in Figure 4 show that the percent giving favorable ratings to Middle Eastern ethnic groups in the United States and overseas were generally lower than those for African, Hispanic, Asian, and white Americans. Larger proportions gave favorable ratings to Jewish Americans than to Arab Americans or Muslim Americans. And these proportions were greater in every case than the evaluations for similar groups outside of the United States. These relationships were unchanged in Wave 2 of the HAR study.

Attitudes toward immigrants have changed slightly, however. Last fall, 87% of those surveyed "agreed" or "strongly agreed" that immigrants make America more open to new ideas and cultures, compared to 81% surveyed in March. In Wave 1, about 24% agreed or strongly agreed that immigrants increase U.S. crime rates, compared to 29% surveyed in Wave 2.

Conclusions

The HAR survey results paint a picture of Americans rallying around each other, concerned and even distrustful of some groups of foreigners. This is a kind of patriotism of mutual support more than a jingoistic reaction to all foreigners or even immigrants. The concept of social trust is complex. On the one hand, data from the trust indexes suggest that there is a differentiation among those who can be trusted as a function of proximity to the respondents' daily lives. Respondents place greater trust in neighbors than in Americans generally and in Americans relative to people from other countries. This relationship is mirrored in the favorability data derived from feeling thermometers. Some Americans seem more inclined to help others since September 11. While the number of volunteers does not seem to have grown, the panel data suggest that people who ordinarily help others are spending more time doing so without increased assistance from a new cohort of volunteers.

With additional or different question wordings employed in other studies, we will be able to understand better the conditions and implications of these tendencies. Only continued longitudinal data collection can monitor changes in civic engagement in response to September 11. That is our primary goal with the HAR survey project. ∎

Figure 4 • Ratings of Ethnic Groups in the U.S. and Overseas, HAR Wave 1

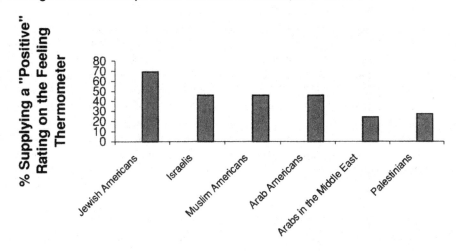

Notes

1. The data for the HAR study derive from a two-wave panel survey. The first wave was conducted in September–October of 2001, and the followup survey was conducted in March–April of 2002. A total of 752 interviews were completed in the first wave of HAR, based upon a nationwide RDD sample. In Wave 2, we recontacted 613 respondents from Wave 1 and conducted new interviews with 151 RDD respondents, for a total sample size of 764 respondents. Each interview lasted approximately 30 minutes on average.

2. One notable exception is a study of English-speaking Canadians' reactions to the assassination of a political figure by French Canadian terrorists which suggests that citizens' restricted views of civil liberties returned to their normal levels by seven months after the incident (Sorrentino and Vidmar 1974).

3. The items included "Generally speaking, would you say that most (people from other countries/Americans/people in your neighborhood) can be trusted or that you can't be too careful in dealing with people?" "Do you think that most of the time (people from other countries/Americans/people in your neighborhood) would try to take advantage of you if they got the chance or would they try to be fair?" and "Would you say that most of the time (people from other countries/Americans/people in your neighborhood) try to be helpful or that they are just looking out for themselves?" A reliabil-

ity analysis for each scale produced alphas of .74 for Trust in Foreigners, .67 for Trust in Americans, and .73 for Trust in Neighbors.

References

Barton, Allen H. 1969. *Communities in Disaster: A Sociological Analysis of Collective Stress Situations.* New York: Doubleday.

Burns, Nancy, and Donald Kinder. 2000. "Social Trust and Democratic Politics: A Report to the National Election Studies Board." Ann Arbor, MI.

Canino, Glorisa, Milagros Bravo, and Maritza Rubio-Stipec. 1990. "The Impact of Disaster on Mental Health: Prospective and Retrospective Analyses." *International Journal of Mental Health* 19:51–69.

Morland, Leslie Anne. 1999. "The Oklahoma City Bombing: An Examination of the Relationship between Exposure to Bomb-related Television and Posttraumatic Stress Symptoms Following a Disaster." Ph.D. diss. Pepperdine University.

North, Carol S., et al. 1999. "Psychiatric Disorders Among Survivors of the Oklahoma City Bombing." *Journal of the American Medical Association* 282:755–62.

Pesci, Marianne. 1999. "The Oklahoma City Bombing: The Relationship among Modality of Trauma Exposure, Gender, and Posttraumatic Stress Symptoms in Adolescents." Ph.D. diss. Pepperdine University.

Pfefferbaum, Betty, et al. 1999. "Clinical Needs Assessment of Middle and High School Students Following the 1995 Oklahoma City Bombing." *American Journal of Psychiatry* 156:1069–74.

Pfefferbaum, Betty, et al. 2000. "Posttraumatic Stress Two Years After the Oklahoma City Bombing in Youths Geographically Distant from the Explosion." *Psychiatry* 63:358–70.

Putnam, Robert. 2002. "Bowling Together." *The American Prospect,* February 11, 20–22.

Sorrentino, R. M., and Neil J. Vidmar. 1974. "Impact on Events: Short- vs. Long-Term Effects of a Crisis." *Public Opinion Quarterly* 38:271–79.

Sprang, Ginny. 1999. "Post-Disaster Stress Following the Oklahoma City Bombing: An Examination of Three Community Groups." *Journal of Interpersonal Violence* 14:169–83.

Stouffer, Samuel A. 1955. *Communism, Conformity, and Civil Liberties.* New York: Doubleday.

Tucker, Phebe, et al. 2000. "Predictors of Post-Traumatic Stress Symptoms in Oklahoma City: Exposure, Social Support, Peri-Traumatic Responses." *The Journal of Behavioral Health Services & Research* 27:406–16.

Wilkinson, C. B. 1983. "Aftermath of a Disaster: Collapse of the Hyatt Regency Skywalks." *American Journal of Psychiatry* 140:1134–39.

Why Was This Research Needed?

1. What contribution to knowledge do these researchers seek to make? How is their study meant to be distinctive from the opinion poll findings published by the mainstream media?
2. How important should the function of social monitoring be for social science researchers? Should this function assume special significance in the face of a national tragedy? Explain.
3. To what extent is the authors' review of previous literature useful for approaching study of the unprecedented event of September 11 and its aftermath?
4. What is the difference between a "period effect" and a "cohort effect" in popular reactions to a national trauma such as September 11?

How Was the Topic Studied?

1. What does it mean to undertake a "longitudinal" analysis? What are the special challenges or pitfalls associated with this form of research?
2. What is a "panel survey"? Review the information provided in note 1. Is the overall design of this study appropriate for the topic? Do you agree with the editorial decision to put these details of the two-wave panel survey in an endnote? Explain.

3. Evaluate the way the general concerns of this study—perceptions of safety and security, civic engagement, trust in others, feelings toward ethnic and racial minorities—were operationalized in the form of specific survey questions. What alternative approaches could you use to ask about the same issues? How might this study's findings have been different if other questions had been asked?

What Are the Findings?

1. At what level of measurement is the variable depicted in Figure 1? Is a pie chart an appropriate way to show the frequency distribution for such a variable? Explain.
2. How were the data in Figure 1 dichotomized and combined with similar data from Wave 2 of this survey to produce Figure 2? Why do you think the authors chose to organize their data in this way? Does this simplification of data result in a possible loss of noteworthy information? Explain. How would you reexpress the pie chart in Figure 2 as a 2 × 2 table?
3. Table 1 presents the average time different groups in the study spent volunteering, but no measures of dispersion (e.g., range, standard deviation) are

reported along with these means. How might such additional information amplify the description of the trends seen in Table 1?

4. What do the p values indicate in Tables 1 and 2?

5. Gamma is a measure of the association between ordinal-level variables. Why is its usage indicated in the comparison of trust scales between Wave 1 and Wave 2 in this survey, as described on p. 99?

6. A "thermometer" rating is a common survey device asking respondents to give their appraisal of an item on a scale from 0 to 100 degrees. Scores greater than 50 are typically interpreted as favorable, or positive, evaluations. The data on attitudes toward different ethnic groups in Figures 3 and 4 are derived from a thermometer-rating approach. Do you think this is a valid measurement tool? Explain. What other approach might you adopt, and why?

What Do the Results Mean?

1. How effective are the authors in summarizing their main findings succinctly in the Conclusions section of their article? In your opinion, what is the most striking finding that comes out of this research?

2. Does this academic study provide a dimension of understanding of the consequences of September 11 that is more credible or more complete than the kinds of commentary you have read in daily newspapers? How would you extend this research? What resources would you need for your investigation?

3. What specific insight from this study into the post–September 11 psychology of Americans could be useful to political leaders? Based on these survey findings, what concerns do you think the president or the secretary of homeland security should be mindful of when addressing the public on the topic of terrorism?

Afterword from Michael Traugott

In order to meet the publication deadline for our *PS* article, we analyzed data from the first two waves of the How Americans Respond (HAR) surveys. While we were eventually able to conduct a third wave in the panel in fall 2002, we were not able to secure funding to do a systematic, continuous monitoring of the American public's response to continued threats of terrorism. This is unfortunate because it was clear that the public had not recovered fully from September 11 after one year, and one of our major goals—to assess Americans' "resilience"—was unfulfilled. Continuous monitoring would have also provided the opportunity to investigate the impact of appeals to the fear of terrorism during the 2004 U.S. presidential campaign and their relationship to reactions to September 11. Researchers missed the chance to make comparative evaluations of "resilience" in the United States in relation to Spain after the March 2004 bombings in Madrid and in relation to the United Kingdom after the July 2005 bombings in London. In addition, researchers could have studied how these events in foreign countries affected Americans' feelings of safety and security.

For the data we were able to collect, the panel design we used gave us much greater analytical power than repeated cross sections. For example, it enabled us to dissect claims about increased volunteerism in the United States. We found that the increased activity was really due to previous volunteers who were devoting more time to volunteer activities, rather than an increase in the number of people doing volunteer work as sometimes had been suggested. We were also able to show in the three-wave panel that individuals who still felt less safe and secure six months after September 11 were the ones most likely to reflect reduced levels of consumer confidence twelve months later.

"The Most Liberal Senator"? Analyzing and Interpreting Congressional Roll Calls

Joshua D. Clinton, Simon Jackman, and Doug Rivers

Americans have a passion for ranking and rating. From the four (or five) star scale used by local movie reviewers to the tabulated product evaluations of national consumer organizations, our society is awash in numerical standings for people, places, and things. People and other popular magazines do a brisk business at the newsstand with their myriad lists that rank the most beautiful, the sexiest, and the best-dressed individuals in our society. Other publications and Web sites provide their own orderings of the most desirable places to live, the best companies to work for, the finest hospitals and doctors, and the best golf courses, beaches, and restaurants. U.S. News and World Report's annual listing of the nation's top colleges and universities has captured widespread attention—and influenced countless prospective first-year students—despite criticism about how the rankings are determined (Thompson 2003). Perhaps the ubiquity of such measurement exercises can be explained by their relationship to core values in our culture—competitiveness, status consciousness, fascination with celebrity, and eagerness to give public recognition for achievement (even if it is only for one's appearance).

Ranking and rating are also popular in the world of public affairs. Scholars, pollsters, and political commentators all have contributed to attempts to pick America's greatest presidents. George Washington, Abraham Lincoln, and Franklin D. Roosevelt do well on most such lists, but there is a lot of variation after that (see, for example, Landy and Milkis 2001). An ambitious multiyear Government Performance Project (2005) assigns grades for how well state governments are doing their jobs. And, in an ironic professional twist, state boards of education and other groups regularly issue "report cards" that evaluate local public schools. No part of government, however, has attracted more scorecards and numerical ratings than the U.S. Congress. Researchers and media groups often rate members of Congress in an effort to objectively assess the leadership, effectiveness, and integrity of lawmakers. Interest groups of all kinds also frequently use rating schemes as a device to inform their constituencies about which senators and representatives are most friendly or hostile to their favored issues and values.

In the following reading, Joshua D. Clinton, Simon Jackman, and Doug Rivers examine an analysis by the influential, nonpartisan National Journal *that labeled John Kerry as the*

Senate's most liberal member. When the magazine published its results in the midst of the 2004 primary campaign, the article created quite a stir. Although it may be tempting to accept such results at face value, rating systems are always simplifications. That is an inherent part of their appeal. But when does simplification turn into distortion? And what is the proper context for interpreting aggregate ratings that characterize a legislator's behavior and philosophy over a period of years? The authors consider these and other questions.

References

Government Performance Project. 2005. *Grading the States 2005.* http://results.gpponline.org.

Landy, Marc, and Sidney Milkis. 2001. *Presidential Greatness.* Lawrence: University Press of Kansas.

Thompson, Nicholas. 2003. "The Best, The Top, The Most." *New York Times,* August 3, sec. 4A, 24.

Scoring lawmakers based upon the votes they cast while serving in Congress is both commonplace and politically consequential. However, scoring legislators' voting records is not without its problems—even when performed by organizations without a specific policy agenda. A telling illustration of the impact that these scores have on political debate recently arose in the 2004 Democratic presidential primaries.

On February 28, 2004, the non-partisan *National Journal* released its analysis of congressional voting for 2003. Of particular interest was the finding that Senator John Kerry—the Democratic nominee for president—was identified as the most liberal senator in 2003 based upon the analysis of 62 key votes. This finding was widely publicized and became the subject of a Democratic presidential debate held the very next night in New York City.

Despite being conducted by a non-partisan source, we show that the ratings (and their subsequent influence) are misleading in at least two respects. First, ignoring the uncertainty associated with the scores is politically consequential; the conclusion of the *National*

Journal (publicized by the press) that Kerry is the most liberal senator in 2003 is doubtful if the votes Kerry missed while campaigning for the Democratic nomination are properly accounted for.

Second, the voting scores were not placed in a proper political context. What made the ratings newsworthy were the scores of the Democratic presidential candidates. But a fairer picture emerges when we consider President Bush's position on issues considered by the Senate. Including President Bush in the analysis significantly changes the political interpretation of the data: Kerry appears to be as liberal as Bush is conservative for the votes that the *National Journal* analyzed in 2003. In short, Kerry's apparent liberalism is only half of the story; the other piece of news is the apparent conservatism of President Bush. Given that we can reasonably expect charges of extremism to be part of the cut and thrust of this year's election campaign, we offer the following analysis as a modest corrective.

Roll Calls and the 2004 Presidential Election (So Far)

Using roll call votes to track lawmakers' behavior is prevalent both in the political arena and in academia. Politically motivated groups such as the Americans for Democratic Action, the American Conservative Union, the Sierra Club, the National Federation of Independent Business, the U.S. Chamber of Commerce, the National Rifle Association, the National Right to Life organization, NARAL, and the AFL-CIO all routinely score legislators according to whether legislators vote in accordance with their respective policy agendas. These resulting scores are used not only to mobilize members and target incumbents in elections (e.g., the Americans for Democratic Action "Zeros and Heroes" list), but the groups also seek to influence lawmakers' votes by publicizing which votes are going to be scored ahead of time. As *CQ Weekly* reports: "interest groups—and members of Congress themselves—use legislative scorecards for much more than reflecting an assessment of each lawmaker's record or mobilizing supporters at the grassroots level at election time. Scorecards, interest groups and lawmakers agree, have become an effective tool of the lobbying trade" (Cochran 2003, 924).

Non-partisan organizations and publications such as Project Vote Smart, the *National Journal,* and *CQ Weekly* also routinely and independently score legislators. Unlike the scores produced by partisan organizations (which are intended to serve political purposes), the scores of non-partisan publications aim to present an objective assessment of lawmakers' voting behavior. While the voting scores given by partisan groups reveal the extent to which a lawmaker agrees with the groups' policy agenda, the scores of non-partisan groups rank a legislator within the political spectrum between two extremes: liberal or conservative. In so doing they provide an important public service. For instance, an interested citizen might well rely on the nonpartisan scores as reasonably unbiased summaries of the ideological positions of their congressional representatives, perhaps with a view to assessing for whom they should vote in the next election.

The scores of ostensibly neutral arbiters like *National Journal* shape political discourse in less passive ways. Precisely because the source is neutral, noteworthy features of the *National Journal* scores attract the attention of the press and the campaigns. In particular, candidates seeking to define one another as extreme and "out-of-step" with voters may use the scores to validate their claims. It is well-known that a "problem for members of Congress seeking the presidency is their extensive voting records, which can—and usually are—deciphered, deconstructed and even distorted by opponents looking to give those positions a negative spin" (Martinez 2004, 458). Evidence from impartial sources often provides the basis for such claims.

The Democratic presidential nominee, Senator John Kerry (MA), is susceptible on this score, if only because his voting history is so long: 6,310 recorded votes cast over 20 years of service in the Senate. Since the candidacy of Lyndon B. Johnson, only two other presidential candidates have had lengthier roll call records (and therefore recorded positions on national issues): Bob Dole and Gerald Ford. As *CQ Weekly* reports: "Republicans

are combing through the 6,310 votes Kerry has cast in the Senate to date, looking for this or that position as an indication that the likely Democratic challenger to President Bush is out of step with mainstream America" (Martinez 2004, 458).

Precisely this opportunity presented itself when the non-partisan *National Journal* issued its ratings of lawmakers for 2003 in February of 2004. The ratings revealed that Kerry was the most "liberal" senator in 2003. In interpreting this result, the *National Journal* wrote, "To be sure, Kerry's ranking as the No. 1 Senate liberal in 2003—and his earning of similar honors three times during his first term, from 1985 to 1990—will probably have opposition researchers licking their chops" (Cohen 2004, 618).

The national impact was immediate. On February 28, 2004—the day after the scores were released [to the media]—Kerry's ranking was reported in the *Boston Herald* ("Liberal Label Sticks; GOP Jumps on Kerry Over Senate Ranking"), the *New York Post* ("Survey: Kerry A Flaming Liberal") and the *Washington Times* ("List Says Kerry Top Senate Liberal"). Kerry's ranking also surfaced during the Democratic presidential debate sponsored by CBS and the *New York Times* held on February 29. Elizabeth Bumiller, a reporter for the *New York Times,* questioned Kerry about his rating (FDCH 2004):

> BUMILLER: The *National Journal,* a respected, non-ideological publication covering Congress . . . has just rated you, Senator Kerry . . . the most liberal senator in the Senate. How can you hope to win with this kind of characterization, in this climate?
>
> KERRY: Because it's a laughable characterization. It's absolutely the most ridiculous thing I've ever seen in my life.
>
> BUMILLER: Are you a liberal?
>
> KERRY: I mean, look, labels are so silly in American politics. I was one of the first Democrats in the United States Senate in 1985 to join with Fritz Hollings in deficit reduction. Now, does that make me a conserva-

tive? I fought to put 100,000 police officers on the streets of America. Am I a conservative?

BUMILLER: But, Senator Kerry, the question is . . .

KERRY: Do you know what they measured in that? First of all, they measured 62 votes. I voted 37 times; 25 votes they didn't even count because I wasn't there to vote for them. Secondly, they counted my voting against the Medicare bill, which is a terrible bill for seniors in America, they called that being liberal. Lots of conservatives voted against that. In addition, they counted my voting against George Bush's tax cut that we can't afford. I thought it was fiscally conservative to vote against George Bush's tax cut. They call it liberal.

BUMILLER: Is this a helpful characterization in this campaign?

KERRY: I think it's the silliest thing I've ever heard.

In addition to Kerry's dismissal of the *National Journal* scores, Senator John Edwards responded: "I don't think anybody in America cares about what some inside-Washington publication says about your ideology." Perhaps. But there is no doubt that the charges as to the "extremism" of both Kerry and Bush will play a critical role in the campaign for president this year.

Since roll call scores permit both the press and partisan groups to characterize (or validate characterizations of) opposition candidates, an understanding of roll call scores is essential in determining the extent to which they should influence political discourse. For example, how much weight should be given to the ratings of the *National Journal* (using a methodology developed by Bill Schneider—a political scientist and senior political analyst for CNN and frequent commentator on contemporary politics) in light of Kerry's criticisms; is Kerry's reaction mere political spin or does it speak to a more serious criticism of the scoring procedure?

Also, how does President Bush rate relative to Kerry? Even if Kerry is among the most liberal senators, the political relevance of this characterization depends upon the extremism of his opponent. For instance, the choice

between a liberal and a moderate is much different than the choice between a liberal and a conservative.

Identifying the Most Liberal Senator(s)

The *National Journal* scores are based on 62 key roll calls from the Senate, and 73 from the House. In reporting its methodology, the *National Journal* notes:

> The ratings rank members of Congress on how they vote relative to each other on a conservative-to-liberal scale in each chamber. The scores are based on law-makers' votes in three areas: economic issues, social issues, and foreign policy. The scores are determined by a computer-assisted calculation that ranks members from one end of the ideological spectrum to the other, based on key votes . . . selected by *National Journal* reporters and editors (Cohen 2004, 615).

In addition to publishing the results in a February 28 cover story entitled "How They Measured Up," the scores are posted on the *National Journal* web site. The most newsworthy result in the rankings is that John Kerry is reported to be more liberal than 97% of the Senate, and more conservative than 4% of the Senate. No other senator is ranked "more liberal" in the *National Journal* rankings. John Edwards (NC) is ranked "second most liberal" by this measure; Edwards is estimated by *National Journal* to be more liberal than 95% of the Senate, and more conservative than 6% of the Senate.

One problem with the rankings is that there are no confidence intervals for the reported scores. It is well-known that the results from public opinion polls are inexact measures of true public opinion and that the error associated with the results must be acknowledged. The same is also true for roll call scores. In fact, the uncertainty that accompanies a voting score (or ought to) is most easily explained using analogies from the realm of public opinion polling. Uncertainty results from using a small number of roll call votes, just as a small sample size induces uncertainty in the results of an opinion poll. There is also the question of validity: the legislator's decision on any analyzed vote may well have been influenced by party pressure, presidential pressure, and/or lobbying by interested groups, and is not a perfect reflection of the legislator's ideology (analogously, survey questions are imperfect, and do not tap respondents' attitudes the way we think they might). Finally, the lawmaker may have missed some votes (i.e., surveys are subject to bias from non-response).

These sources of error have important political consequences for the proper interpretation of Kerry's voting record (indeed, any voting record) and the 2003 *National Journal* scores. As Kerry noted in the CBS/*New York Times* debate, as a result of his presidential campaign, he (and the other Democratic presidential candidates) missed a sizable fraction of the votes that the *National Journal* analyzed. For the 62 key roll calls in the Senate in 2003, the average abstention rate is 2.9%—with 56 senators voting on every analyzed vote and another 23 senators voting on all but one. Interpreting the announced positions of the Bush administration on the 62 votes (as reported in *CQ Weekly*) as evidence of how President Bush would have voted were he in the Senate allows us to compare the percentage of recorded votes by Bush and the Democratic presidential candidates. Table 1 summarizes the findings.

As is immediately evident from Table 1, the Bush administration and the presidential candidates took positions on only some of the analyzed votes. In fact, the two presidential candidates—Bush and Kerry—announced positions or voted only 40% of the time. Kerry was right to suggest in the CBS/*New York Times* primary debate that his absenteeism is consequential—there is far less data with which to estimate his voting score (and those of his fellow presidential candidates) than for the typical senator. Using fewer votes (i.e., smaller sample size) to score Kerry means that Kerry's score will have a larger confidence interval than those of other candidates. Any conclusion about Kerry's voting score and his relative rank ordering in the Senate should be sensitive to this important feature of the roll call data.

To demonstrate both the validity of Kerry's reaction and the importance of reporting confidence intervals for vote scores we first replicate the analysis of the *National Journal* using the method outlined in Clinton, Jackman, and Rivers (2004). The intuition underlying statistical models of legislative voting such as that employed by the *National Journal* and Clinton, Jackman, and Rivers is that each roll call presents each legislator with a choice between a "yea" and a "nay" position. Legislators are presumed to vote for the position most similar to their own ideal policy position/outcome. As a matter of practice, a legislator's voting record probably reflects a number of different influences, including: personal ideology, the ideology of the legislator's constituency, lobbying by interest groups, and pressure from party leaders. Without considerably more data than is available here, the effects of each of these plausible sources of influence cannot be ascertained.[1] Accordingly, our voting scores should not be literally treated as a measure of a senator's personal ideology, but rather as a mix of these possible influences on roll call voting, and, in any event, as a useful summary of the ideological content of a senator's voting record. We normalize the scores such that senators with more liberal voting histories have lower scores, and senators with more conservative voting histories have higher scores.

We present our results in a series of graphs. Figure 1 shows our estimated voting scores for the 100 senators (solid points) along with a 95% confidence interval for each voting score (horizontal bars). Negative scores are associated with more liberal preferred positions and positive scores represent more conservative preferred positions.

Table 1
Absentee Rates, Selected Lawmakers

Lawmaker	Absentee Rate 62 *National Journal* Key Votes
Sen. John Kerry	60%
Sen. Joseph Lieberman	40%
Sen. John Edwards	35%
Sen. Bob Graham	24%
Announced positions of the Bush administration	61%

Figure 1 • Point Estimates and 95% Confidence Intervals Using 62 *National Journal* Key Votes

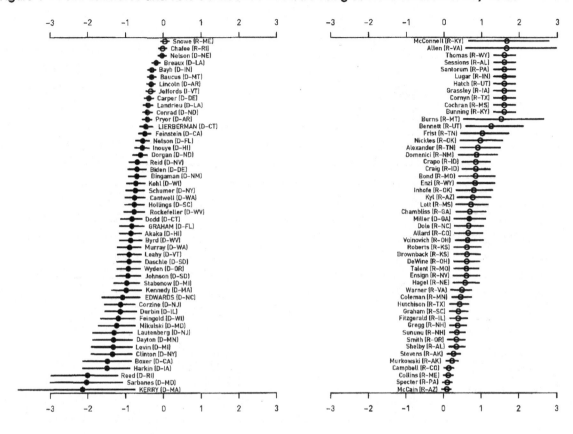

Solid points indicate Democratic senators, generally to the left of Republican senators (open points)—the notable exception being Zell Miller (GA).

We see immediately that some senators' voting scores are estimated with considerably wider confidence intervals than other senators. This is a product of two factors: (1) the relative lack of data resulting from absenteeism—all else equal, the less data we have the wider the confidence intervals—and (2) extremism—all else equal, as ideological extremism increases the confidence interval widens because the voting record becomes less informative (e.g., while the data suggest George Allen (VA) is relatively conservative, since we seldom observe Senator Allen voting for the more liberal position on any given roll call, we do not know precisely how conservative he

is).[2] Both features appear to influence Senator Kerry's score; our best guess is that Kerry is quite liberal, but it is difficult to precisely state "how liberal" given the combination of a one-sided voting record and the prevalence of missing data.

Figure 2 shows the ranks of the estimated voting scores (and associated 95% confidence intervals) for the Senate. Senators have been arranged according to their estimated ideal points. By definition, the ranks and their confidence intervals must lie within 1 and 100 inclusive. Again, solid (open) points indicate the most likely rank for the indicated Democratic (Republican) senator, while the horizontal bars indicate 95% confidence intervals. Given that the voting scores graphed in Figure 1 are estimated with uncertainty, so too will be any rank-ordering

Figure 2 • Rank Ordering and 95% Confidence Intervals Using 62 *National Journal* Key Votes

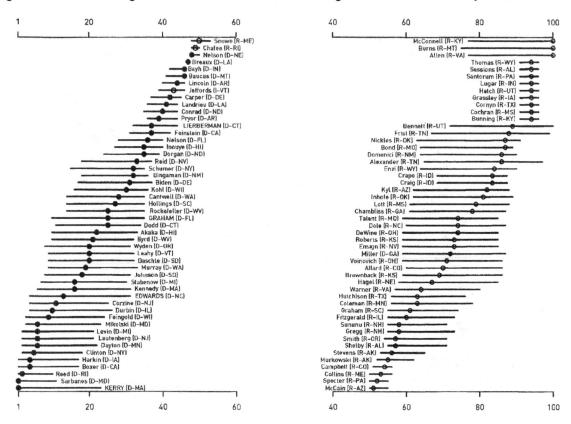

based on these scores. Accordingly, we estimate the probability that a given senator is the most liberal senator (has a rank of 1): only three senators have any appreciable chance of being the most liberal senator, namely Kerry (0.38 probability), Senator Paul Sarbanes of Maryland (0.28), and Senator Jack Reed of Rhode Island (0.24).

We can also compare any two senators to assess the probability that they are statistically distinguishable. For instance, the probability that Senator Edwards has a voting score more conservative (greater) than Senator Kerry's is .90, short of the traditional 95% standard used in social-scientific research but moderately strong evidence nonetheless. The probability that Senator Joseph Lieberman (CT) has a more conservative voting record than Senator Kerry is an overwhelming .998 (which is

the same probability that Lieberman's voting record is more conservative than Edwards').

Note also that Kerry's voting score is indistinguishable from the other senators with nontrivial probabilities of being the most liberal, Senators Sarbanes and Reed: the probabilities that these senators have voting scores more liberal than Kerry's are both .51, or roughly 50–50. That is, while these senators each have a slightly lower probability of being the most liberal senator than does Kerry, Kerry's voting score is indistinguishable from their voting scores (for the 25 roll calls in which Kerry cast a vote—out of the 62 key roll calls analyzed by the *National Journal*—Kerry's voting record is indistinguishable from Sarbanes' and Reed's. Any of these three senators could be the most liberal senator of 2003.

Figure 3 • Rank Ordering and 95% Confidence Intervals Including President Bush Using 62 *National Journal* **Key Votes**

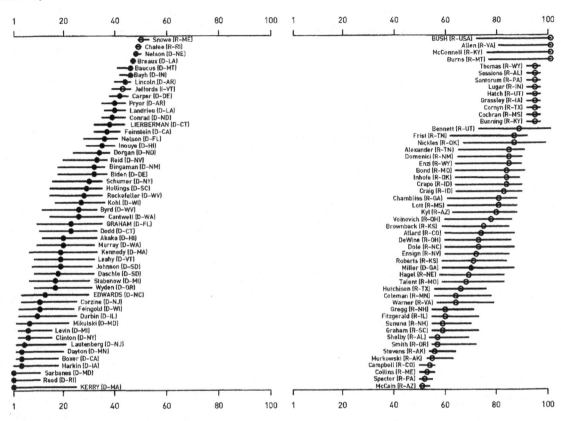

Comparing Bush and Kerry

A second problem with the analysis thus far is that it is silent on the comparison that is arguably most politically consequential—the relative positions of President Bush and Senator Kerry. This comparison is straightforward to make: we compute a voting score for President Bush treating Bush as an additional legislator in the statistical analysis, with a voting record on the *National Journal* key votes given by Bush's announced positions on these votes as reported by *CQ Weekly.* Table 1 reveals that both Kerry and Bush failed to take a position on approximately 60% of the 62 analyzed votes, and so we expect to recover an implied voting score for Bush that has a wide confidence interval.

Figure 3 presents our estimated relative rank ordering for both the 108th Senate and President Bush using the 62 key votes of 2003 identified by the *National Journal.* Bush's implied voting record is at least as conservative as any Republican senator. In fact, 17 Republican senators have voting records that are in complete agreement with Bush's announced positions (ignoring abstentions). The fact that Bush announced positions relatively infrequently (on 24 of 62 key votes) generates considerable uncertainty in the voting score we assign him. In turn, this generates considerable uncertainty in the rank orderings among conservative Republicans, just as Kerry's high rate of absenteeism, coupled with a relatively extreme voting record, generates uncertainty in any assessment of the degree of Kerry's liberalism. The probability that Bush lies to the right of the entire Senate is .41; other contenders for the "most conservative senator" include Senator Mitch McConnell of Kentucky (probability of .18), Senator George Allen of Virginia (.16), and Senator Conrad Burns of Montana (.11).

It is worth repeating that the combination of short and extremely one-sided voting histories means that estimates of legislators' voting scores (and rank orderings) are imprecise. Although the most probable rank ordering supported by the data locates Bush as more conservative than the entire Senate, a conventional 95% confidence interval on Bush's voting score extends far into Republican ranks: in fact, there is better than a 5% chance that Bush is less conservative than as many as 22 senators. Likewise, although the most probable rank ordering supported by the data locates Kerry as more liberal than the rest of the Senate, there is a better than 5% chance that Kerry is less liberal than as many as 16 senators. These confidence intervals are large when one considers that the Senate consists of 100 legislators, underscoring the limits of the available data.

A Longer Horizon: Bush and Kerry in the 107th Congress

The analysis above highlights the difficulties of estimating voting scores for incumbent legislators who are actively seeking the presidency. Campaigning takes these legislators away from Washington, generating considerably high rates of abstention in their voting records in the run up to an election. Indeed, the problem is probably more pernicious: the roll calls that do draw candidates back to Washington to cast votes are not a random subset of roll calls, but are on issues where their votes might have utmost importance for procedural reasons. Party loyalty rather than a genuine ideological position might explain some of these votes. In fact, there is some evidence that supports this notion:

> As John Kerry was preparing to fly to Des Moines to unveil his health care platform on May 15, his well-laid plans for furthering his presidential candidacy were sud-

denly complicated by his day job representing Massachusetts in the United States Senate. The Republican leadership had chosen that day for the climactic votes on President Bush's second major tax cut—sure to be among the defining issues of the 2004 campaign. So, like the other five members of Congress seeking the Democratic presidential nomination, Kerry scrambled his campaign schedule and was on hand to vote against the bill that ultimately became last year's $330 billion, 11 year tax-cut (Kady 2004, 22).

To determine if analyzing more votes in a non-presidential year is (both statistically and politically) consequential we analyze the 498 non-unanimous roll calls of the 107th Senate. Again, we include President Bush in the analysis, adding his announced positions to the roll call data (Bush publicly announced positions on 63 of the 498 non-unanimous roll calls). In contrast to the *National Journal* key votes of 2003, Kerry misses just 15 of the 498 non-unanimous roll calls in the 107th Senate.[3]

Figure 4 presents the rank-ordering and 95% confidence intervals that result from the analysis of this larger data set. Taking this longer time horizon and analyzing more votes in a non-presidential election year reveals a slightly different conclusion. The probability that Kerry is the most liberal senator in the 107th Senate is infinitesimally small. Our best guess is that Kerry is the 16th most liberal senator, and a 95% confidence interval on his rank ranges from the 10th to the 20th most liberal. In contrast, the probability that President Bush is the most conservative lawmaker in the analysis is 31%; other contenders include Republican Senators Jesse Helms (NC, with probability 0.24), Jon Kyl (AZ, 0.20), and Phil Gramm (TX, 0.17). Our best guess is that Bush is more conservative than the entire Senate, but since the president did not take a position on every vote we cannot estimate his score (and rank) with much precision. As a result, a 95% confidence interval over Bush's rank extends from the most conservative to the 27th most conservative.

In summary, with this larger set of data, the conclusion that Kerry is extremely liberal simply is not supported. To be sure, Kerry is more liberal than most senators, and we would unambiguously locate him among the most liberal

Figure 4 • Rank Ordering and 95% Confidence Intervals Including President Bush Using All Non-unanimous Roll Calls from the 107th Senate. *National Journal* **Key Votes**

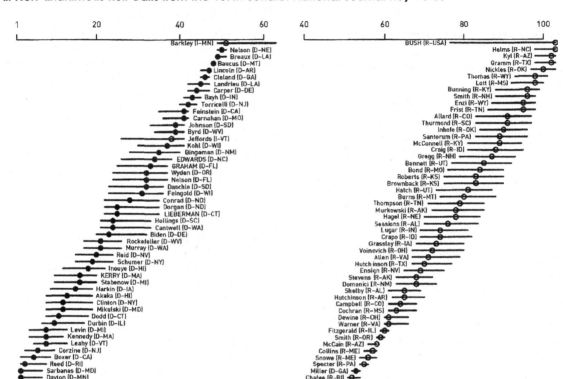

quintile of the Senate. But Kerry is far from being the most liberal senator in the 107th Senate; the late Paul Wellstone (D-MN) is unambiguously to the left of the rest of the 107th Senate. In fact, the only conclusion that is supported by analyses of both the 107th Senate and the 62 votes analyzed by the *National Journal* in the 108th Senate is that Kerry and Bush are among the most liberal and most conservative quintiles, respectively.

Conclusion

A voting score simplifies a legislative voting history into a single number, providing an easily understood and easily communicated basis for comparing legislators. But it is important that voting scorecards be understood in per-

spective. A reanalysis of the 62 key votes studied by the non-partisan *National Journal* [suggests the results] are actually much more ambiguous than reported. The probability that Kerry is the most liberal senator is only 30%—far from the certainty implied by newspaper headlines. Furthermore, using conventional levels of statistical significance, we cannot rule out the possibility that Kerry is actually only the 20th most liberal senator based on the 62 votes in 2003 analyzed by the *National Journal.*

An analysis including the public positions taken by President Bush reveals that Bush lies in the most conservative quintile of senators. Analyses that fail to include President Bush's publicly announced positions fail to provide an appropriate context for interpreting Kerry's score. A more balanced analysis, one that includes both Bush and

Kerry, finds that *both* are extreme relative to the Senate; Kerry is more liberal and Bush more conservative than a large majority of the Senate. This conclusion is confirmed through analysis of votes cast in the 107th Senate.

An additional point on the political context of our findings is worth noting. While it is one thing to find that a Massachusetts senator has a quite liberal voting history, it is arguably of more political significance to discover that the announced positions of the Bush administration generate an implied voting history likely to be the most conservative in the Senate. In short, the Bush administration's apparent conservatism is arguably more politically striking than Kerry's apparent liberalism if we were to compare their voting records with the preferences of the median voter in their nominal constituencies (i.e., Massachusetts for Kerry, and the entire country for Bush).

Political scientists have devoted considerable effort (e.g., Clausen 1973; Kingdon 1989; Poole and Rosenthal 1997; Clinton, Jackman, and Rivers 2004) to analyzing roll call votes and the properties of vote scores for legislators (e.g., Snyder 1992). Given a political environment in which candidates are eager to use information to portray their opponents as extreme, it is important to place any vote scores in a proper context. Just as it is problematic to report poll results without uncertainty assessments, so too is it problematic to report vote scores without accounting for the scores' uncertainty. The characterization of Senator John Kerry as the most liberal senator resulting from the publication of the *National Journal* scores is an oversimplification. In fact, the evidence is a bit more ambiguous than reported, and the context, especially relative to President Bush's corresponding conservatism, is missing. One should not be surprised when journalists do not report or ask for confidence intervals. Confidence intervals are usually considered technical jargon and too complex to explain to the general public. Unfortunately, in this case, they were very relevant to the story. ∎

Notes

1. On this point, and for various attempts to untangle the effects of ideology/constituency/party, see Jackson and Kingdon (1992), Levitt (1996), Snyder and Groseclose (2000), Erikson

and Wright (2001), McCarty, Poole, and Rosenthal (2001), Krehbiel (2003), and Clinton, Jackman, and Rivers (2004).

2. The analogy from an educational setting is the student who gets every question asked of them correct: until the student is asked questions that they answer incorrectly, all we know is that the student is relatively smart, but we lack a precise estimate of how smart the student is in an absolute sense. Indeed, this is one of the motivations behind adaptive testing in standardized tests; i.e., tailoring the difficulty of items to the ability of test-takers, as revealed by their responses to items answered earlier in the test.

3. We also break the voting history of Senator Jim Jeffords (VT) into two pieces, corresponding to his switch from a Republican to an Independent; the data strongly suggest that his voting records changed as a result of this switch.

References

Blomquist, Brian. 2004. "Survey: Kerry a Flaming Liberal," *New York Post,* Feb. 28, 2.

Clausen, Aage. 1973. *How Congressmen Decide: A Policy Focus.* New York: St. Martin's Press.

Clinton, Joshua D., Simon Jackman, and Douglas Rivers. 2004. "The Statistical Analysis of Roll Call Voting: A Unified Approach." *American Political Science Review* 98(2):355–370.

Cohen, Richard E. 2004. "How They Measured Up." *National Journal* 36(Feb. 28): 613–619.

Dinan, Stephen. 2004. "List Says Kerry Top Senate Liberal; Missed Votes Boosted Credentials," *Washington Times,* Feb. 28, A2.

Erikson, Robert S., and Gerald C. Wright. 2001. "Voters, Candidates and Issues in Congressional Elections." In *Congress Reconsidered.* Seventh edition, eds. Lawrence C. Dodd and Bruce I. Oppenheimer. Washington, D.C.: Congressional Quarterly Press.

Federal Document Clearing House (FDCH). 2004. "Democratic Presidential Candidates Participate in Debate Sponsored by CBS News and the *New York Times*." In FDCH Political Transcripts, February 29, 2004. *Academic Universe.* Princeton: Lexis-Nexis.

Guarnino, David R., and Noelle Straub. 2004. "Liberal Label Sticks; GOP Jumps on Kerry Over Senate Ranking," *Boston Herald,* Feb. 28, 16.

Jackson, John E., and John Kingdon. 1992. "Ideology, Interest Group Scores, and Legislative Votes." *American Journal of Political Science* 36(3):805–823.

Kady, Martin II. 2004. "Voting on the Run." *CQ Weekly* 62:22–23.

Kingdon, John W. 1989. *Congressmen's Voting Decisions.* Third edition. Ann Arbor: University of Michigan Press.

Krehbiel, Keith. 2003. "The Coefficient of Party Influence." *Political Analysis* 11:95–103.

Levitt, Stephen. 1996. "How Do Senators Vote? Disentangling the Role of Voter Preferences, Party Affiliation, and Senator Ideology." *American Economic Review* 86:425–441.

Martinez, Gebe. 2004. "GOP Pans for Political Gold in Kerry's Voting Record." *CQ Weekly* 62:458–465.

McCarty, Nolan, Keith T. Poole, and Howard Rosenthal. 2001. "The Hunt for Party Discipline in Congress." *American Political Science Review* 95:673–687.

Poole, Keith, and Howard Rosenthal. 1997. *Congress: A Political-Economic History of Roll Call Voting.* Oxford: Oxford University Press.

Snyder, James M., Jr. 1992. "Artificial Extremism in Interest Group Ratings." *Legislative Studies Quarterly* 17:319–345.

Snyder, James M., Jr., and Tim Groseclose. 2000. "Estimating Party Influence in Congressional Roll Call Voting." *American Journal of Political Science* 44:187–205.

Why Was This Research Needed?

1. What different types of groups rate legislators? How do these groups seek to maximize the impact of their ratings?
2. How can the argument be made that nonpartisan groups perform a public service by rating legislators?
3. According to the *National Journal,* how did Kerry compare with his colleagues on the magazine's "conservative-to-liberal scale"? Include specific results in your answer. What justification do the authors give for undertaking a critical examination of this magazine's rating approach (other than the objections of Kerry, who believed he was mislabeled)?

How Was the Topic Studied?

1. Using the information presented in this reading, explain the *National Journal*'s methodology for determining its scores.
2. By what means do the authors reexamine the roll call data used by the *National Journal*?
3. What main sources of error are the authors concerned with in their analysis?

What Are the Findings?

1. From a statistical point of view, what is the importance of the absentee data presented in Table 1 for the analysis of legislators' voting records?

2. What factors influence a legislator's voting decisions? How do these influences complicate the interpretation of voting records?
3. What is a "95% confidence interval"? Why is the calculation of confidence intervals necessary when generalizing results from a sample to a population? How does this observation apply to the analysis of roll call data?
4. Explain the format and purpose of the graphing technique employed in Figures 1 through 4.
5. Figure 1 shows that U.S. senators have different "point estimates" for the 62 votes analyzed by the *National Journal,* and that there is substantial variation in the precision with which a particular legislator's liberalism or conservatism can be measured. Why must both of these facts be considered when interpreting such scoring data?
6. Based on the information in Figure 2, why do the authors conclude that Kerry is actually one of three senators who might qualify for the distinction of being the Senate's most liberal member?
7. According to Figure 3, where does President Bush stand in comparison with the members of the Senate for these 62 votes? What makes the authors uncertain of this rank order? Why do the authors maintain it is necessary to analyze President Bush's stated issue positions in order to interpret Senator Kerry's voting record properly?

8. Using the results shown in Figure 4, explain how selecting a larger set of voting decisions over a longer time period results in a rank ordering different than the one produced by the *National Journal*. Next, consider the *National Journal*'s 62 vote count and the authors' revised 498 vote count: is one set of data clearly preferable for generating a liberal-to-conservative ranking for Senator Kerry and President Bush? Why?

What Do the Results Mean?

1. After reading this study, what is your overall assessment of the validity of the *National Journal*'s liberal-to-conservative scorecard? Was the public well served by the magazine's publication of its analysis? Explain.

2. How difficult would it be for the public to understand the increased complexity of the alternative rank ordering presented by the authors? Should such findings be reserved only for a specialized audience? Explain.

3. What alternative method would you recommend for gauging a legislator's liberalism or conservatism? Would your method be based on a modified roll call analysis or an entirely different approach? Explain.

4. Now that you understand what goes into creating a roll call ranking, how do you think a lawmaker might manipulate his or her standing?

5. Does this reading make you more or less inclined to believe that the "liberal" and "conservative" labels are useful for analyzing American political behavior? Why?

Afterword from Joshua Clinton

Measurement is central to political science. It concerns the documenting of empirical regularities within the political environment and collecting evidence to investigate generalized explanations. As such, quantifying political concepts is an extremely useful and informative endeavor; it can make precise the meanings of many concepts and provide the means for comparing different conditions and situations. Quantitative descriptions of politics are prevalent in academic discourse and are used increasingly by journalists, politicians, and pundits. However, quantification by itself is not necessarily informative; the implied exactness can be profoundly misleading even when it is performed by impartial sources.

A belief in the importance of rigorous measurement motivated our writing of "The Most Liberal Senator." Interpreting measures of political concepts requires understanding the process that generates the "numbers," expressing how much uncertainty the numbers contain, and defining how the measured actions correspond to the interpretation given to the measure. All these factors affect whether a measure captures what users intend. Unfortunately, this kind of discussion is often overlooked.

Evaluating the appropriateness and limits of measures is critical for questions relevant to political science and politics for many reasons. In contrast to the natural sciences in which many units of measurement are established and agreed upon—in fact, government organizations such as the U.S. National Institute for Standards and Technology partially exist to study measurement issues—measures of political concepts that are objective and agreed upon are rare. For example, what defines a "liberal" (or a "conservative")? Even assuming a consensual definition, the trait of interest (e.g., "liberalness") is, to some extent, intangible and unobservable.

As a result, political scientists often must focus on an observable characteristic or action plausibly related to the trait (e.g., roll call voting behavior) as a substitute for more direct measurement.

Even if agreement is reached on which observable measure is "best"—for example, the use of roll call voting behavior by scholars, interest groups, and the media to summarize political preferences—there is no guarantee the units are objective. Unlike the task of measuring an individual's height, for which the units of measurement are unaffected by the task of measurement, maintaining a distinction between the process and substance of measurement can be problematic for political concepts. For example, the "units" of roll call analysis result from conscious (and often strategic) choices on the part of politicians and those who score the votes. Politicians decide which policies they will allow to come to a vote, whether they will take a position on the vote, and the position they will take. Scholars, journalists, and other organizations decide which roll call votes should count. In short, roll call voting results reflect deliberate choices that are a function of the political environment; the behavior being measured may be influenced (or even distorted) by multiple considerations.

This is not meant to imply that roll call votes are without value. The point is that careful work is required to define precisely what is being measured and what must be assumed for the measure to be valid. The ability to associate a number with a political concept does not guarantee either precision or clarity. Researchers who are not explicit about how the item being counted relates to the underlying political concept may produce extremely misleading results. Although this point is not new—it is equally important to consider how well responses to a survey question measure a respondent's trait of interest—it is critical nonetheless. The difficulty of addressing measurement concerns clearly and concisely can result in even impartial sources suggesting potentially unwarranted (and possibly partial) conclusions.

Political Views from Below: A Survey of Beijing Residents

Yang Zhong, Jie Chen, and John M. Scheb II

In the United States, it is easy to take the availability of public opinion data for granted. Nearly seven decades ago, George Gallup offered a convincing demonstration of the accuracy of political surveys carried out according to proper methods of random sampling (Glynn et al. 1999). Since that time, scientific public opinion research has become a staple in the work of media organizations, academic scholars, and professional consultants who seek to understand the driving forces of politics at the mass level. Although they might not enjoy being interrupted at dinnertime, many Americans willingly express their political likes and dislikes to interviewers, knowing that such information is important to the discourse of public affairs in U.S. society. Without public opinion research of this kind, it would be much more difficult to gain insight into the information, beliefs, and attitudes that define contemporary political culture in the United States. Further, elected leaders regularly monitor public opinion to gauge the general mood of the country as well as popular reactions to specific policy issues and proposals.

The situation is much different within a nondemocratic polity such as China. Public opinion and voting are not touchstones of political legitimacy as they are in the United States, so there is relatively little concern with measuring and reporting public views, and few resources are available for conducting this kind of research. Under these circumstances, the extent of popular discontent with government policies can easily be misread until it boils over into open political protest, as it did in Tiananmen Square in 1989. Partly because of this realization, opinion polling has gained a modest place of importance in China today and is being carried out by both Chinese and foreign researchers (Leow 2001). Although not all political topics are open to investigation, the following reading discusses a kind of research—in this case, conducted by a group of American academics in cooperation with the Public Opinion Research Institute of the People's University in Beijing—that is a good example of the progress being made in documenting the citizens' perspective in China.

The reading is also rich from a quantitative analysis standpoint. Through charts, percentage tables, and analysis of means, authors Yang Zhong, Jie Chen, and John M. Scheb II integrate several techniques in their multifaceted analysis of survey data.

References

Glynn, Carroll J., Susan Herbst, Garrett J. O'Keefe, and
   Robert Y. Shapiro. 1999. *Public Opinion.* Boulder, Colo.:
   Westview Press.
Leow, Jason. 2001. "Public Opinion Starting to Count in
   China." *Straits Times,* December 10.
   http://taiwansecurity.org/News/2001/ST-121001.htm.

With the death of Deng Xiaoping, China's political future is once again in the spotlight. Debate over the viability of the current political regime in China started immediately after the 1989 Tiananmen Square crackdown when the prospects for reform in the People's Republic of China (PRC) and the fate of the Chinese Communist Party (CCP) projected by China watchers were then overwhelmingly pessimistic (Ditmer 1989; Swaine 1989). Eight years after the Tiananmen Square events, the survival of the CCP against all odds (including the aftermath of the collapse of communist regimes in Eastern Europe and the Soviet Union) is in itself no small miracle. The post-Tiananmen political regime in China has by and large been stable. Not only has the CCP survived, it has made impressive economic progress in recent years. This new development has caused a major reassessment of the situation in the PRC among China watchers. Nicholas Kristoff, in the *New York Times* (1993), called the phenomenon of China's rapid economic growth in an authoritarian environment the "riddle of China." One China specialist even posed the question whether China is where Samuel Huntington's "third wave" stopped and whether the PRC would be an exception to the fall of communism worldwide (Nathan 1993).

The most often cited factors accounting for the political tranquillity in the PRC are its remarkable economic growth and its political oppression (Nathan 1993). These two factors are certainly indispensable in understanding developments in China after 1989. However, they fall short of providing a satisfactory and convincing explanation of the "China exception." Economic growth in and of itself does not directly contribute to political stability. In fact, it has been argued that economic development and modernization lead to political instability (Tilly 1973). Further, it is simplistic to argue that the survival of the current communist leadership in the PRC is due mainly to political repression such as arrests and terror. A heavy-handed approach to controlling the population was adopted during the immediate aftermath of the June 4th crackdown in some urban centers. Since then, tight political control has been replaced by a more relaxed approach of dealing with the discontent among the masses, even though the high-profiled dissidents are still either imprisoned or under constant police harassment. It is a fact that criticisms or even cursing of the CCP and its leaders are not uncommon in China today.[1]

Our study, based on a survey of permanent residents of Beijing or residents with Beijing *hukou* (residential registration), explores the mood and feelings of ordinary people in China regarding levels of political interest and democratic values, attitudes toward economic reform, evaluations of government performance in different policy areas, and general levels of satisfaction and confidence. The survey had two purposes: first, we intended to find out what ordinary Beijing residents thought about political issues; second, we tried to map China's political future.

We believe that public opinion affects public policy in China. In a recent book, Allen Liu (1996) argues that post-Mao economic and political reforms came about more as a result of public opinion—which grew too strong for the Communist Party leaders to ignore after the death of Mao—and less as a result of the political motivations of individual leaders. The fact that the Chinese government has made noticeable efforts to control inflation and combat official corruption is evidence that the leaders and their policies are constrained to a certain degree by public opinion.

The Survey

Our survey of Beijing residents was conducted in December 1995 in cooperation with the Public Opinion Research Institute of the People's University in Beijing.[2] A total of 700 permanent Beijing residents 18 and older were sampled using the multistage random sampling procedure.[3] The questionnaire was taken by the interviewer to the randomly chosen individual respondent, was filled out, and then brought by the interviewer back to the survey center. As a result of this survey measure, the response rate was 97%—considerably higher than surveys done in other fashions. The sample is cut right in the middle between the two genders. All age groups (from 18 years old to over 66) and occupation sectors are represented in the sample. Over 75% of the respondents have either a middle school or high school diploma. Nearly 80% of the respondents live in the urban areas of the city. Based upon a comparison between our sample and the 1990 Beijing census, the sampling error of our survey is less than 2% for gender and less than 3% for age.

Since our sample only included permanent residents of Beijing, we do not intend to generalize our findings to the rest of China. But our survey can be regarded as a case study for the special status of Beijing in Chinese politics and history. As the capital of many dynasties and the People's Republic of China, Beijing is often viewed as a special place in the history of China, unparalleled by any other city. Significant historical events such as the May 4th Movement of 1919, the Cultural Revolution of 1966, the April 5th Incident of 1976, and the Tiananmen Square democracy movement of 1989 all started in Beijing. The mood of Beijingers is often regarded as the barometer of the mood of the country. We were particularly interested in examining the mood among Beijing residents six years after the dramatic events of 1989.[4]

ingly apolitical and pragmatic.[5] However, our survey shows that the perception of low level of political interest may be incorrect or exaggerated. As Table 1 shows, about two-thirds of survey respondents are still interested in national affairs, and an even larger number care about Beijing local affairs. Another indication of the level of political interest is the frequency of discussion of politics by citizens. Our survey shows that many people do talk about politics with their family members, relatives, friends, and colleagues. Specifically, about 40% said that they engage in political discussions with others very often, while about 50% said they talk about politics occasionally (see Table 1). Apparently, while they do not often share their thoughts with others, many people are interested in national affairs or Beijing affairs. These findings are not surprising, given the concerns about the leadership succession at the top and the high profiled cases of official corruption, particularly the case of former Beijing Mayor Chen Xitong, in the last two years.

We were also interested in how the demographic factors of our respondents affect their level of political interest. We found that residency, education, age, and income seem to be the factors affecting the respondents' interest in politics. Our findings are very similar to studies on mass political behavior in other countries. Specifically, we find that the level of political interest is higher among urban residents, the more educated, older people, and those with higher incomes. Table 2 clearly shows this pattern when it comes to level of interest in national affairs. The sharpest contrasts are between urban residents

Findings

1. Level of Political Interest and Democratic Values

Nowadays, the Chinese often think of themselves as consumed with making money and disinterested in political and public affairs. With the influence of market economic reforms and the disillusion with democratic reforms, people are said to become increas-

Table 1
Level of Political Interest

	Very Much Interested	Interested	Somewhat Interested	Not Interested	N
National Affairs	13.8%	56.9%	27.3%	2.1%	682
Beijing Affairs	22.6	58.5	17.6	1.3	682

	Whenever We See Each Other	Very Often	Not Often	Never	Can't Tell	N
Discussion of Politics with Others	2.5	40.9	50.6	3.4	2.5	670

Table 2
Interest in National Politics by Residence, Education, Age, and Income

	Very Much Interested	Interested	Somewhat Interested	Not Interested	N
Residence					
Urban*	15.7%	61.7%	21.0%	1.4%	
Rural	5.0	42.9	47.1	5.0	668
Education					
Primary School or Below	9.9	53.1	32.1	4.9	
Middle School	11.2	53.7	31.8	3.3	
High School	15.6	58.3	25.7	0.4	
College	19.0	65.8	13.9	1.3	678
Age					
Young (18–35)	10.0	53.2	34.4	2.3	
Middle (36–55)	14.5	55.7	27.2	2.4	
Old (Over 55)	18.0	65.1	15.7	1.1	682
Monthly Income					
Lower (below 250 yuan)	4.8	37.1	56.5	1.6	
Middle (250–800 yuan)	14.6	58.4	24.8	2.1	
Upper (over 800 yuan)	20.1	64.5	15.3	0.0	643

*Urban residents here include both residents of urban districts of Beijing and residents of urban county towns in Beijing.

and rural residents and between low income people and middle/high income people (see Table 2).

Findings displayed in Table 3 illustrate the complexity in the political attitude toward democracy and civil liberties among Beijing residents. Over 85% of the respondents seem to be tolerant of people with different political views; a majority favors wider press freedom; and an overwhelming majority voice support for a more democratic way of choosing local government officials (see Table 3). However, findings from the next three questions indicate a low level of political efficacy among Beijingers. Seventy percent of the respondents lack confidence in themselves. Most are reluctant to challenge the authorities. And an overwhelming majority of the people we surveyed prefer stability and order to a more free society. Thus, the two sets of results seem to be contradictory. Apparently, Beijingers are in favor of the general and abstract principles of civil liberties and democracy. Yet, their cultural and behavioral pattern is still marked by elitist orientation, deference to authority, and preference for order. We suspect that the contradiction results from

the gap between the two levels of political culture: the cognitive level and the behavioral level. On the cognitive level, buzz words such as "democracy," "freedom," and "liberty" are quite acceptable to the general public—indeed, even the Chinese Constitution is filled with these terms and concepts. Yet, on a deeper level, much longer terms of socialization and experience are needed to change people's behavior in this regard.

2. Attitude toward Economic Reforms

Economic reforms that Deng Xiaoping started in the late 1970s have changed the face of China and made it one of the fastest growing economies in the world. Economic reforms have generally improved the standard of living. Yet, such reforms have also had their downside, such as corruption, inflation, job insecurity, declining welfare programs, and income inequality. What is the impact of the negative drawbacks on people's view on economic reforms? In this survey, we wanted to tap into the opinions about possible economic systems and ownership systems and attitudes toward economic reforms in general. Figure 1 and Figure 2 show an interesting pattern of preferences for economic systems and ownership structures. With regard to economic systems, very few of the people we surveyed prefer a total central planning economy (CPE). Less than 16% of those surveyed are fond of a predominantly CPE. Nearly a quarter of Beijing residents seem to favor a truly mixed economy—half planning and half market economy—indicating they want to have the benefits of both systems. One-third of the respondents favor a predominantly market economy. Another 20% are unsure which system works better for them. The findings indicate that even though many Chinese have embraced the concept of a market economy, most are still uncertain about the adoption of a complete or predominant market

Table 3
General Political Attitudes

	Strongly Agree	Agree	Disagree	Strongly Disagree	N
Regardless of one's political beliefs, he or she is entitled to the same legal rights and protections as is anyone else	39.8%	47.5%	11.2%	1.5%	676
The press should be given more freedom to expose wrong doings such as corruption	68.5	25.8	5.2	0.4	677
Elections to local government positions should be conducted in such a way that there are more than one candidate for each post	49.8	43.8	5.1	1.3	671
The well-being of the country is mainly dependent upon state leaders, not the masses	37.0	34.4	21.8	6.8	675
In general, I don't think I should argue with the authorities even though I believe my idea is correct	22.5	41.0	28.7	7.8	676
I would rather live in an orderly society than in a freer society which is prone to disruptions	61.8	33.0	3.6	1.6	673

economy. It should be pointed out that the official goal of the economic reforms undertaken since the early 1990s has been the introduction of a full market economy. With more than one-third of state enterprises in the red, the fear of losing one's job due to competition in a full-fledge market economy is real for workers in the public sector.

We also found that socialist values are still very strong among Beijing residents when it comes to forms of ownership of means of production. Over 60% of Beijing residents prefer predominant public ownership (see Figure 2). Even a mixed-ownership system gets little support. This finding means that CCP's official policy of maintaining mostly public ownership (i.e., the so-called socialist market economy) has wide popular support.

When asked about the speed of economic reforms, about 40% of respondents seem satisfied with the current speed (see Figure 3). However, nearly one-third of the people we surveyed think the economic reforms are moving quickly or too quickly. Very few think the reforms are moving either slowly or too slowly. Once again, nearly one-quarter of the respondents could not answer the question. These findings show that the public is quite divided on the speed of economic reforms. Many people have been negatively affected by the market-oriented economic reforms and have suffered from the

"pains" in the economic transition even though China's economic reforms have been perceived to be gradual and less radical than the economic reform in the newly democratized Eastern European countries and the former Soviet Union.

When analyzed in terms of social-demographic characteristics, support for particular economic systems varies among different societal groups (see Table 4). Urban and rural residents do not seem to differ in their relative support of different economic systems. But it is telling that a very high percentage of rural residents have no opinion on this issue. It also seems that the more educated are more likely to support a market-oriented economy. Support for a predominantly market economy is the highest among college graduates. This is probably due to the fact that the better educated are better endowed or equipped to compete in a more market-driven economy. It is also clear in Table 4 that people between 18 and 35 years of age give the strongest support to a predominantly market economy. This is primarily because people in this group tend to be better educated, more energetic, and mobility-oriented; and they are less afraid of new challenges. These qualities make them more competitive and marketable in a market-driven economy. We have also found, not surprisingly, that more people in the upper income bracket are supportive of

Figure 1 • Preference of Economic System (N = 680)

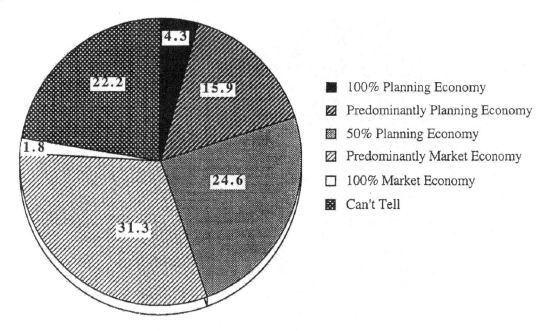

- ■ 100% Planning Economy
- ▨ Predominantly Planning Economy
- ▦ 50% Planning Economy
- ▨ Predominantly Market Economy
- □ 100% Market Economy
- ▨ Can't Tell

Figure 2 • Preference of Economic Ownership System (N = 680)

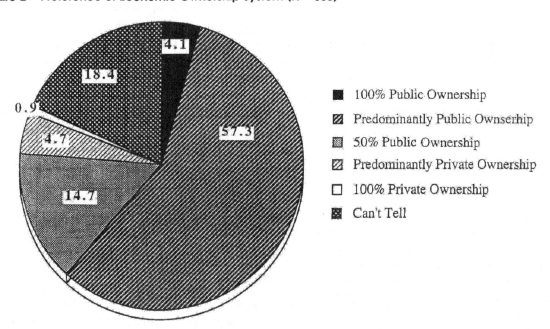

- ■ 100% Public Ownership
- ▨ Predominantly Public Ownserhip
- ▦ 50% Public Ownership
- ▨ Predominantly Private Ownership
- □ 100% Private Ownership
- ▨ Can't Tell

Figure 3 • Attitude toward the Speed of Economic Reform (N = 682)

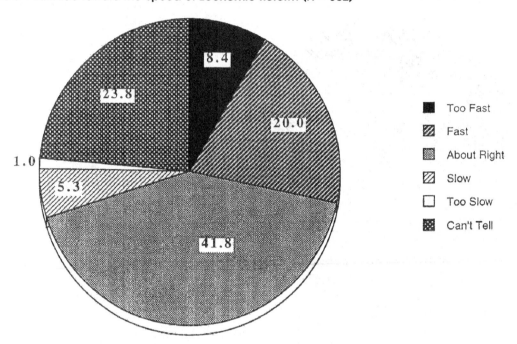

a market economy since they have benefited the most from the market-oriented economic reforms. It is also evident from Table 4 that rural residents and people with primary education or below, in addition to those in the low income bracket, have the lowest efficacy in choosing what kind of economic system they prefer.

3. Evaluation of Government Performance

How do people in Beijing evaluate the performance of the Chinese government? Their evaluation of government performance reflects their level of satisfaction and can be used as one of the predictors of stability in the country. The respondents in our survey were asked to rate the performance of the government in ten policy areas using a scale of 1 to 5 points (1-very poor, 2-poor, 3-fair, 4-good, and 5-very good). The grades given by the sampled Beijing residents are presented in Table 5. The overall evaluation of Chinese government performance by the Beijingers in all ten policy areas is close to fair (or 3-point) level, which is barely a passing grade. The respondents

give the lowest score to government performance in narrowing the income gap. The widening income gap (partly attributable to official corruption) is becoming a major sociopolitical problem in the PRC. The government's effectiveness in controlling inflation was also given a low grade by the respondents in our survey. Substantial numbers of people are unhappy with the government's efforts to improve housing conditions, maintain societal order, and combat pollution. The highest marks were given to the government's performance in implementing family planning and providing national defense, indicating the effectiveness of government policies in these two areas.

Do different demographic and socio-economic groups differ in their evaluation of government performance? To address this question, we used the statistical analysis of variance to detect any such differences. This analysis is designed to examine the variability in the sample in order to determine whether the population means are not equal. The results, presented in Table 6, show that the means between rural residents and urban residents

Table 4
Preference of Economic Systems by Residence, Education, Age, and Income

	100% CPE[1]	Pre[2]-CPE	50% CPE	Pre-ME[3]	100% ME	Can't Tell
Residence (N = 666)						
Urban	3.8%	17.5%	26.0%	33.1%	1.9%	17.7%
Rural	6.4	10.0	17.1	27.1	0.7	38.6
Education (N = 676)						
Primary School or Below	11.1	12.3	18.5	19.9	2.5	35.8
Middle School	4.2	17.5	22.9	25.0	1.3	29.2
High School	2.9	15.9	27.9	35.1	1.8	16.3
College	2.5	15.2	24.1	49.4	2.5	6.3
Age (N = 680)						
Young (18–35)	4.0	10.9	20.8	41.6	1.8	20.8
Middle (36–55)	2.9	15.4	27.2	27.9	1.8	24.6
Old (over 55)	6.4	22.5	25.1	29.4	1.6	20.3
Monthly Income (N = 641)						
Lower (below 25 yuan)	11.3	9.7	9.7	25.8	1.6	41.9
Middle (250–800 yuan)	4.3	17.3	26.8	29.3	1.6	20.6
Upper (over 800 yuan)	0.0	16.0	22.3	44.7	2.1	15.0

Note: 1. Central Planning Economy
      2. Predominantly
      3. Market Economy

Table 5
Evaluation of Government Performance

	1 Very Poor	2 Poor	3 Fair	4 Good	5 Very Good	Average Grade	N
Controlling Inflation	11.3%	36.9%	38.4%	9.4%	3.4%	2.6%	681
Providing Job Security	5.7	26.7	53.3	10.4	3.4	2.8	671
Minimizing Rich-Poor Gap	16.5	43.7	28.5	6.2	4.3	2.4	677
Improving Housing Conditions	8.7	29.7	42.2	13.6	4.9	2.7	677
Maintaining Societal Order	8.7	29.3	39.9	13.5	8.2	2.8	679
Providing Adequate Medical Care	5.7	24.9	45.0	18.3	5.7	2.9	678
Implementing Family Planning	0.9	3.1	18.3	40.4	36.8	4.1	678
Providing Welfare to the Needy	3.7	18.5	48.1	20.4	7.7	2.9	671
Combating Pollution	11.0	35.8	31.5	14.1	7.3	2.7	679
Ensuring a Strong National Defense	1.3	3.4	30.8	33.7	30.6	3.9	679

are indeed different. The rural residents tend to give the government higher marks for its performance in the ten policy areas than urban residents. Also, as indicated in Table 6, people of middle and upper income are more likely to grade the government better than people of lower income. Even though the non-college graduates in our survey rate the government performance slightly higher than the college graduates, the difference is not statisti-

cally significant. Evaluations of government performance remain constant with all age groups.

4. Satisfaction and Confidence

Findings presented in Table 7 are illustrative of the mood of Beijingers and, perhaps, the Chinese people as a whole. On the one hand, it seems that people are extremely dissatisfied with several specific economic and

Table 6
Evaluation of Government Performance (Index) by Residence, Education, Age, and Income

	Mean	F Ratio	Signficance
Residence			
Urban	28.04		
Rural	31.05	23.33	.0000
Education			
Non-College	28.80		
College	27.32	3.59	.0584
Age			
Young (18–35)	28.64		
Middle (36–55)	28.60		
Old (over 55)	28.67	0.01	.9943
Income			
Lower	27.66		
Middle	29.39		
Upper	28.71	5.34	.0050

political areas. An overwhelming majority of our respondents are seriously discontent with the growing disparity among income groups. Over 90% of the people we surveyed either agree or strongly agree that the income differentials are becoming too big. The majority are unhappy with the responsiveness of their government to their concerns. Over 70% of the respondents indicate that their suggestions and complaints made to the government were often ignored. It does not seem that the majority of Beijingers are satisfied with the speed of political reforms in China. Over 80% of the people we surveyed believe that economic reforms far outpace political reforms in the country.

On the other hand, people seem satisfied with the improvements made in their living standard and social status since the reforms began in the late 1970s. Nine in ten of our respondents agree or strongly agree with the statement that since 1978 their living standard has noticeably been improved and seven in ten of those polled agree or strongly agree that their social status has been improved (see Table 7). These findings are consistent with other survey results.[6] This is one indication that economic reforms have achieved considerable success. The general satisfaction with the improvement in living standard and social status in part provides the basis for an overall confidence and optimistic view of China's development in the future. Nearly 85% of our respondents do not believe that

Table 7
Levels of Satisfaction and Confidence

	Strongly Agree	Agree	Disagree	Strongly Disagree	N
The gap between rich and poor is getting too big	56.0%	37.4%	5.9%	0.6%	673
Suggestions and complaints made by the public to the government are often ignored	25.8	46.5	26.4	1.3	675
Economic reforms in China far outpace political reforms	22.6	57.6	18.4	1.3	668
Since the reforms in 1978, my living conditions have noticeably improved	39.3	52.1	7.3	0.4	682
Since the reforms in 1978, my social status has noticeably improved	19.9	49.7	25.3	5.0	672
It is unlikely that China will experience political and social turmoils in the next ten years	29.1	55.2	14.1	1.6	676
I am confident that China will become an economic power in the 21st century	38.0	52.3	8.2	0.9	674

China will experience major sociopolitical turmoil in the next ten years, and 90% are confident that China will become a world-class economic power in the 21st century (see Table 7).

Do the demographic factors play a role in the respondents' level of life satisfaction and confidence about the future? An analysis of variance shows that residence, education, and age do not make any difference in people's satisfaction level and confidence level. The only relevant factor is income level. As indicated in Table 8, the population means are significantly different between three income groups, particularly between the lower income group on the one hand and the middle and upper income groups on the other. It means that people with higher incomes are more satisfied with the improvement in their living standards and their social status. In addition, the more money people make, the more optimistic they are about the prospect of China's development in the future (see Table 8).

Implications

Based on the findings above, we derive the following tentative implications. First, Chinese political culture still tends to be conservative. On the economic front, even though most people in our survey admit that their life has noticeably improved in the reform era, a majority of them still hesitate to endorse the adoption of a predominantly market economy and very few prefer a predominantly private ownership system. Apparently, people remain afraid of the repercussions of the ongoing economic transformation. There does not seem to be a public consensus on the government's goal of eventually adopting a "socialist market economy." Therefore, the Chinese government needs

to be careful in handling the transition from the central planning economy to a market economy. The dissatisfaction with the negative results of the economic reforms partially contributed to the outbreak of the Tiananmen events in 1989.

On the political front, a majority of our respondents still seem to be elitist- and authority-oriented. An overwhelming majority of the respondents in the survey (over 90%) prefer an orderly society to a more free society prone to disruptions. It seems that the public has been buying the "stability first" argument advocated by the Chinese government, partly because people in China witnessed the breakdown of order in many former Soviet republics after the collapse of communism in the former Soviet Union. The relentless efforts by the Chinese leaders to stress the need for stability for continued economic growth and development have struck a chord in the psyche of the Chinese mind which is stigmatized by *luan* (chaos) after more than a century of upheavals, revolutions, and instabilities.

Table 8
Satisfaction and Confidence by Income

	Mean	F Ratio	Significance
1. Since the reforms in 1978, my living conditions have noticeably improved			
Lower Income	3.15		
Middle Income	3.41		
Upper Income	3.45	15.62	.0000
2. Since the reforms in 1978, my social status has noticeably improved			
Lower Income	2.65		
Middle Income	2.93		
Upper Income	3.21	16.88	.0000
3. It is unlikely that China will experience political and social turmoils in the next ten years			
Lower Income	3.02		
Middle Income	3.17		
Upper Income	3.23	4.76	.0088
4. I am confident that China will become an economic power in the 21st century			
Lower Income	3.16		
Middle Income	3.33		
Upper Income	3.51	9.46	.0001

The chaotic Cultural Revolution is still fresh in the minds of many people. This stability- and order-oriented mentality explains, in part, the relative success of the post-Tiananmen regime in controlling China since 1989.

Second, the post-1989 strategy of eudaemonism—that is, making people happy by providing them with material benefits—has partially worked in Beijing. It is apparent from our survey that a majority of the people in Beijing have felt improvements in their living conditions and social status. This high level of life satisfaction leads to relatively high levels of confidence in the further economic development of China. Yet, we also found in our survey that people in Beijing only gave passing grades for the Chinese government's performance in a variety of policy areas. It has been consistently shown in our findings that people with higher incomes are more appreciative of the government's performance record, more satisfied with their life, and more optimistic about the future. We believe this provides part of the answer to the puzzle of the survival of the current political regime in China and the relative political stability in the PRC since the 1989 Tiananmen Square crackdown. As the Chinese government continues to improve the living standard of the people, it will probably increase its political legitimacy. However, what we have also found is that materialism, partially encouraged by the Chinese leaders, has not reduced people's attention to political issues. The majority of the respondents in our survey are still interested in national affairs and more than 40% of them discuss politics with someone else very often. Obviously, since Beijing is the political center of the country, figures concerning levels of political interest for the rest of the country may be lower.

Third, the findings also indicate who are the most likely Beijing supporters of the current Chinese government and who are not. Support for the CCP most likely comes from rural residents and people with higher incomes. As our findings have shown, the rural residents in our survey tend to have lower levels of political interest and efficacy. Hence, it is much easier for the government to control them. Furthermore, it is shown that rural respondents in our survey gave markedly better grades for government performance than their counterparts in the urban areas. It should be noted that peasants in the suburbs of Beijing are generally wealthier and more urban than peasants elsewhere in China. Another group likely to support the current regime in Beijing are those who are better off and have gained materially in the reform era. Conversely, we can speculate that challenges to the CCP may come from the urban areas and people of lower income. The urban poor (many of whom are workers and employees of the near bankrupt state-owned enterprises) may be a major source of instability in the PRC in the future.

The overall picture portrayed in this survey is certainly not all rosy for the Chinese government, but it is far from a gloomy one. If the major findings from our survey of Beijing residents hold true in general for the rest of China, it is hard to imagine that the CCP will encounter major problems and challenges from below in the period of post-Deng power transition. ▪

Notes

Support for this project was provided by the Social Science Research Institute of the University of Tennessee–Knoxville, the University of Wisconsin–River Falls, and the Public Opinion Research Institute of the People's University in Beijing.

1. During two trips to China in the summers of 1994 and 1995, Yang Zhong, one of the authors of this article, personally witnessed people cursing Jiang Zeming and Li Peng at bus stops on several occasions.

2. Doing a good survey in China depends heavily on having a reliable Chinese partner. Public Opinion Research Institute of the People's University in Beijing, which was set up in 1986, was the first of its kind established in the PRC and has done numerous surveys for both Chinese as well as foreign organizations.

3. Seven urban districts and rural counties were randomly chosen after the first stage of sampling. Five residential neighborhoods (*juweihui*) or villages (*cunming weiyuanhui*) were randomly chosen after the second stage of sampling. The third stage of random sampling produced a sample of twenty households from each of the five residential neighborhoods or villages of the seven urban districts or rural counties. One individual was chosen randomly from each household as the respondent at the final stage of sampling in our survey.

4. Two of our papers from this survey, "The Level and Sources of Popular Support for China's Current Authoritarian Regime" and "Assessing Political Support in China: Citizens' Evaluations of Governmental Effectiveness and Legitimacy," are forthcoming in *Communist and Post Communist Studies* and *The Journal of Contemporary China,* respectively.

5. Even the former participants of the Tiananmen Square democracy movement have become pragmatic and materialistic. See "Tiananmen and China's Future: The View Five Years Later," *Current History,* Vol. 93, No. 584 (September 1994), p. 248.

6. For example, according to one survey conducted in the city of Qingdao, Shandong Province, at the end of 1993, 90% of the respondents were satisfied with the supply of goods in the market; 75% of them felt their life was improved. *See People's Daily,* Overseas Edition, May 13, 1994, p. 2. In a Gallup nationwide poll conducted from May 20 to September 15, 1994, pollsters found that more than half of those surveyed expressed satisfaction with their life, among other things, as reported by LI Jianmin and Chuck Lin, "China: A Tough Market, U.S. Survey Says," *Chinese News Digest* (an electronic news magazine), February 19, 1995.

References

Ditmer, L. 1989. "The Tiananmen Massacre." *Problems of Communism* (September–October): 14–15.

Kristof, Nicholas D. 1993. "The Riddle of China: Repression as Standard of Living Soars." *New York Times,* 7 September, A1 and A6.

Liu, Allen P. L. 1996. *Mass Politics in the People's Republic: State and Society in Contemporary China.* Boulder, CO: Westview Press.

Nathan, Andrew. 1993. "China's Path from Communism." *Journal of Democracy* 4 (2): 30.

Swaine, Michael D. 1989. "China Faces the 1990s." *Problems of Communism* (September–October): 20–35.

Tilly, Charles. 1973. "Does Modernization Breed Revolution?" *Comparative Politics* 5 (3): 425–47.

Why Was This Research Needed?

1. What is the "riddle of China" discussed in the introduction to this article?
2. What kinds of factors typically receive attention in explanations of China's political stability? What questions do these authors raise about this perspective?
3. What are the stated objectives of this research? How is the study of public opinion related to these objectives?

How Was the Topic Studied?

1. What are the details of the survey conducted for this study—sample group, sample size, interviewing procedure, response rate?
2. For what reasons do you think the authors used a multistage random sample (described in note 3) rather than a simple random sample? What evidence is there of the accuracy of the data collected according to this methodology?
3. What kinds of demographic and attitudinal variables were included on the survey instrument?

What Are the Findings?

1. Why do the authors consider the data presented in Table 1 to be noteworthy?
2. What are the most important trends that emerge from Table 2? How would you explain the use of row-based percentages? Why did the authors choose this tabulation approach rather than column-based percentages?
3. Do you see any directional relationships in Table 2 between the "interest in national politics" variable and the four demographic factors examined? Describe any positive or negative relationships that you can identify.
4. How might the six survey items listed in Table 3 be combined into a single composite index? What name would you give it? What would be the level of measurement of the new index, and how might

this variable subsequently be used in statistical analysis?

5. Why are the pie charts in Figures 1 and 2 an effective way to present the survey data on citizen preferences regarding economic issues? How do these visuals set up the demographic analysis in Table 4? What kind of chart or graph would you recommend using to reduce the complexity of Table 5?

6. Why do the authors use an analysis of variance procedure to analyze the data in Tables 6 and 7? How do you interpret the significance values reported? How would you calculate the strength of the relationships in these tables? What additional information would such a measure of strength provide?

What Do the Results Mean?

1. What are the authors' main conclusions from this study?

2. What kind of study would you recommend as a follow-up to this research? Would you want to ask different questions of the same sample group? Or would you choose to survey another population to broaden the context of these findings? Explain your answer.

3. What specific lessons for public policy and administration could Chinese leaders derive from the information gathered in this survey? Would carrying out more public opinion research in China contribute to democratization? Explain your conclusion.

Afterword from Yang Zhong

Systematic empirical study of mass political culture and behavior in authoritarian countries has always been difficult, if not impossible. Nonetheless, during the 1970s and 1980s researchers studying the former Soviet Union and Communist Eastern Europe began to employ survey research to examine the attitudes and behavior of ordinary citizens in these countries. However, Western scholarship on Communist China continues to suffer from a lack of empirical study of mass political culture and behavior. The concept of public opinion did not appear in the lexicon of contemporary U.S. Sinology until the 1980s. Rather, the study of Chinese politics has mainly focused on the Chinese elite and formal political institutions and processes.

Thanks to the relaxation of political control since the 1980s, a growing number of China scholars based outside China have been able to conduct survey research inside the country, even though mass public opinion survey research is still a novel enterprise in China and there are many restrictions and limitations for this kind of study. The keys to conducting sound survey research in China include finding reliable and experienced Chinese collaborators, drafting questionnaires skillfully, and designing sampling procedures carefully. The limited volume of political survey research conducted in China has already yielded important information and findings about patterns of political culture and behavior. Our 1995 Beijing survey shows that the city's residents exhibited high levels of political interest, overwhelmingly favored democratic principles, and showed relatively high levels of dissatisfaction with government performance in a number of policy areas. Two of our additional surveys—one conducted in Beijing in 1997 (Zhong, Chen, and Scheb 1998) and the other in rural areas in the southern Jiangsu province of China in 2000 (Zhong 2004)—yielded similar findings. We expect that survey research will become an important part of Chinese political studies in the future as China gradually opens up its political system.

References

Zhong, Yang. 2004. "Political Culture and Participation in the Chinese Countryside: Some Empirical Evidence." *PS: Political Science & Politics* 37 (3): 445–453.

Zhong, Yang, Jie Chen, and John Scheb II. 1998. "Mass Political Culture in Beijing: Findings from Two Public Opinion Surveys." *Asian Survey* 38 (8): 763–783.

Untangled Web:
Internet Use During the 1998 Election

David A. Dulio, Donald L. Goff, and James A. Thurber

According to a report by the Pew Research Center (Rainie, Cornfield, and Horrigan 2005), the Internet was "a key force" in the 2004 U.S. elections. For 75 million Americans, the Internet served as a place to get political information, provided an opportunity to exchange e-mail on political topics, and offered the means to become directly involved in campaign activities as a donor, as a volunteer, or in some other capacity. The Internet now has surpassed radio as a primary source of presidential campaign news for registered voters. Among the heaviest users of this technology—those who have broadband connections at home—the Internet is more important than print newspapers when it comes to receiving political news. The convenience of going online is the major factor behind these upward trends. But Internet users also value the chance to get a broader spectrum of news and views than is available from traditional outlets.

As David A. Dulio, Donald L. Goff, and James A. Thurber demonstrate in the following reading, the 1998 elections marked a turning point in the relationship between politics and the Internet. Two years earlier, during the 1996 elections, professional politicians were just beginning to recognize the Internet's possibilities. Only a small number of candidates had their own Web sites, and those sites were not used very creatively. By 1998, a large majority of candidates for national offices had become online campaigners, and they and their staffs demonstrated greater sophistication about how the Internet could help them get their message out, raise money, and conduct other campaign business. Their efforts laid the groundwork for Howard Dean's great success with the Internet as a campaign tool in 2004.

This Web site study by Dulio, Goff, and Thurber is one of the first attempts to document the details of Internet usage in political campaigning and to explore party differences in emerging online practices. In addition to describing an innovative data collection strategy, this reading illustrates basic techniques of tabular analysis.

Reference

Rainie, L., M. Cornfield, and J. Horrigan. 2005. *The Internet and Campaign 2004*. Washington, D.C.: The Pew Research Center for the People and the Press.

During the 1996 election cycle, candidates for public office began to use the Internet as a campaign tool (Browning 1996; Casey 1996; Rash 1997). As Internet use grew among the general population, it was reasonable to expect that the 1998 election cycle would see increased use of this new medium by political candidates, and new methods and techniques developed to exploit its capabilities.

In increasing numbers, House and Senate candidates campaigned along the information superhighway in 1998. While very few candidates had web sites in previous elections (Browning 1996), by October 1998 more than two-thirds of the candidates for U.S. Senate and for U.S. House open seats had established web sites. In the past, candidate web sites were little more than digital yard signs (Casey 1996). In 1998, candidates enhanced the functionality of their sites, particularly in the solicitation of small-dollar contributions.

Like it or not, the Internet is now a campaign tool that many campaigns employ. Therefore, we believe the manner in which it is used needs to be investigated. In this article we pay particular attention to candidates' solicitation of campaign contributions over the Internet. Our analysis is mostly descriptive as we try to summarize the Internet activity of candidates in a sample of Senate and House races during 1998.

We entered the analysis with some expectations. With the costs of campaigns continuing to climb, we anticipated that campaigns would increasingly use the Internet to solicit and process contributions. We also expected to see campaigns borrowing the best practices from the commercial sector in order to obtain the greatest return from their investment in a web site and the hardware and software associated with it.

Between October 5 and October 16, 1998, we conducted an interactive content analysis of the web sites employed by all the candidates for the U.S. Senate ($N = 68$) and for open seats for the U.S. House of Representatives ($N = 65$).[1] Our analysis was designed to evaluate the ways candidates used their web sites to solicit contributions, and to judge the accessibility of those sites. To find the sites, we used the Alta Vista search engine (www.altavista.com) and the convention of the last name of the candidate plus the word "senate" or "house," depending upon the office sought.[2] If that method failed, we searched via party links. We used a list of 24 questions to evaluate sites with respect to the presence or absence of solicitations for contributions, disclaimers, and whether filters were present to assure that online contributions were secure, valid, and verified.[3] Finally, we evaluated the political nature of the sites to determine sophistication in the use of the medium. Screening for contributions from foreign nationals was taken as evidence of a high level of sophistication.

Overall, more than two-thirds of the 1998 congressional candidates in our sample, 92 of 133, had operating web sites (see Table 1). For the Senate, 75%, or 51 candidates, had web sites. This constituted a dramatic increase from the June figure of 29% (44 of 153 candidates[4]) reported by Kamarck (1998). For House open seats, it was 64%, or 41 of 65 candidates.

Web sites for specific campaigns were hard to find. While the Democratic Senatorial Campaign Committee (DSCC) provided a link to each of their candidates' home pages (www.dssc.org), the National Republican Senatorial Committee (NRSC) limited itself to descriptions of incumbents (www.nrsc.org). On the House side, the Democratic Congressional Campaign Committee (DCCC) provided links to only 51 candidate sites (www.dccc.org), while the National Republican Congressional Committee (NRCC) linked to 155 (www.nrcc.org), significantly less than the total number of candidates each party fielded. Groups not officially affiliated with either party, but using the party name, such as GOP-Net (www.

Table 1
Frequency Distribution of 1998 Candidate Web Sites

	N	Percent
Candidate Web Site Present	92	69.2
No Candidate Web Site Present	41	30.8
Total	133*	100

*68 Senate candidates; 65 House candidates.

gopnet.org), provided more links than the parties themselves. Generally, state party organizations were the most useful for finding candidates from either party in a given state, though the state party sites are by no means uniform in the information they contain or the information they convey (see, e.g., www.va-democrats. com; www.gagop.org). The Republican National Committee (RNC) did not link at all (www.rnc. org), but the Democratic National Committee (DNC) opened a links page in August 1998 to most of their candidates and to their state central committees (www. democrats.org). In sum, we concluded that the national party committees were not the best way for a constituent to find the candidates in his or her district or state. Aldrich (1995) describes an evolution of the parties toward a "party in service," away from the components of Key's (1964) tripartite model, but providing links to candidate sites is apparently not yet part of this service agreement.

Often, the search engine did not return a candidate's campaign web site among the top search results. References to the candidate in the news media, official House or Senate sites, and public interest group symposia generally elicited more hits, and appeared to the search engine to have a higher probability of matching our selection criteria. The few conventions we found for domain names (see note 3) were inconsistently applied. Our interpretation is that domain names are dependent upon availability and the image the campaign consultant wanted to convey.

As an aside, we also looked for counters on the web site, which would indicate how many hits the sites were receiving. Most sites had removed their counters, not installed them, or hidden them. The few remaining counters indicated senators were receiving hits in the range from three to six thousand. House sites received substantially fewer hits. One campaign manager lamented that his candidate's site had been accessed only 26 times—13 of them by the candidate looking to see how many hits there were.[5] While this is nothing more than anecdotal data, from which we do not pretend to draw any conclusions,

it provides further evidence that the Internet has not yet become a major medium for campaigning.

The parties varied little in candidates' overall use of the Internet. Just over 71% of Democrats were on the web compared to 68.2% of Republicans. This finding runs contrary to the conventional wisdom that Republicans are better organized and more technological than Democrats. Incumbents were the most frequent users, with 75.9% having sites; challengers established sites 69% of the time. In open seat races, candidates established web sites 67% of the time.

Following election day, we coded candidates with web sites as winners or losers and added these data to our analysis. We discovered little difference in Internet campaigning between winners and losers. While we found no evidence the Internet is currently a medium that can help determine the outcome of an election, we did find that candidates' web sites may have an effect on other campaign activities, such as fundraising, management, and internal communication.

Upon visiting a site, we conducted a content analysis to determine whether the candidate's campaign used the site to solicit campaign contributions. Nearly 73% of candidates with web sites solicited contributions from visitors in some way.

While we found no evidence the Internet is currently a medium that can help determine the outcome of an election, we did find that candidates' web sites may have an effect on other campaign activities, such as fundraising, management, and internal communication.

An interview with the staff of Robert Torricelli (D-NJ) provided insights into the issues we included in our content analysis. Of the 1996 candidates for national office whom we could identify as having operated a campaign web site, only Torricelli employed a secure online connection to allow for credit card contributions. Results were meager, especially in light of the expenses incurred in encoding and processing the contributions.[6]

Campaigns solicited contributions from web site visitors online in four ways: (1) inviting the contributor to send in a contribution by mail; (2) inviting the donor to download, print, and complete a form, and send in a contribution by mail; (3) asking the donor to pledge to contribute; and (4) encouraging the donor to contribute online.[7] Table 2 reports the use of these four techniques in the 1998 elections. Each technique has its particular strengths and weaknesses.

The first, and simplest, method merely asks the donor/constituent to mail a check into the candidate's headquarters and provides a surface or "snail" mail address for the campaign. The disadvantage to this system is that donors may not provide information required for Federal Election Commission (FEC) reporting, particularly employer and occupation information, which is commonly omitted from reports. An additional disadvantage is that the campaign does not debit the money to its account until the check is received, posted, and cleared by drawing from the bank, a process that continues for weeks after the donor visited the site. Despite these procedural difficulties, slightly more than half of the candidates who solicited contributions, 54%, used this method.

The second method asks the donor to download and print a form to be filled out in long hand and mailed to the headquarters with a check. This format helps solve the miss-ing information problem by having donors supply all the required information on an easily completed and processed form. But the delay in processing and debiting the contribution remains. In one variation, a donor can write in his or her name, address, credit card number and its expiration date, and other information, which the campaign then processes when received (either by surface mail, fax, or email). In this variant, the time from receipt to debit is dramatically reduced, since the campaign can debit the credit card transaction the day of receipt and does not have to wait for a check to clear. A third of the campaigns, 32.8%, used this technique.

The third method of collecting online contributions amounts to taking pledges. In this version, donors fill out an online screen with the necessary name, address, and phone and email information, and the amount pledged. The pledge is then only fulfilled by mailing a check or a credit card number and signature to the campaign. This method allows campaigns to capture a commitment and

Table 2
Types of Web Site Solicitation Techniques

	N	Percent
1. Web site requests donor to mail in a contribution. E.g., "Support Smith for Congress by mailing a donation to . . . ."	36	53.7
2. Solicitation requests the donor to print and send, fax, or email contributor information to the campaign as a pledge. E.g., "Become a member of the Thomas for Congress campaign by donating ____ $5 ____ $10 ____ $25 ____ $50"	32	47.8
3. Campaign requires donor to first contact the campaign, which then sends a solicitation by regular mail. E.g., "Join Senator Jones's reelection campaign by making a campaign contribution. Send your name, address and phone number and we will send you a pledge form."	22	32.8
4. Online solicitation. E.g., "Help Bob Williams become a U.S. Senator by making a contribution on our secure Internet site. Click here."	21	29.9

to at least anticipate cash flow for the coming weeks based upon the commitment. As with all pledge drives, however, a substantial question remains regarding whether pledges taken via the web will ever be collected in great volume. The method allows campaigns to collect important information, however, including the email address of the donor. Nearly half of the campaigns soliciting contributions, 47.8%, used this method.

The fourth method takes advantage of secure transaction technology, known as a secure socket layer (SSL), to collect online contributions using a credit card. An SSL is generally indicated by the letter "s" inserted in the familiar hypertext prefix to a web address, or universal resource locator (URL) (e.g., https://). A "pop-up," or secondary, window usually appears in the browser indicating a secure transaction is about to take place and reappears following the transaction when the donor returns to an unsecure connection. Using this device usually relieves donors' anxiety about posting credit card information on the Internet. The donor enters all the information requested by the donation form and sends it by clicking on a reply button. Often there is a screen on which donors are asked to verify the information they provided. Even though this is, in our opinion, by far the best option, only 30% of the campaigns seeking online contributions used this technique. Nearly 62% of the web sites that permitted online contributions employed a secure connection. However, this summary statistic should not cloud the fact that, of the 133 candidates' web sites investigated, this only amounts to 13. Therefore, we can conclude that this technology, widely used by other e-commerce solicitors, is underused by campaigns.

As with all pledge drives, a substantial question remains regarding whether pledges taken via the web will ever be collected in great volume.

The programs campaigns did use to collect secure online contributions were exclusively commercial off the shelf products (COTS), developed for familiar forms of electronic commerce, such as retail book sales. For the most part, campaigns did not customize these programs. Consequently, the net effect of using these COTS solutions ranges, in our judgment, from, at best, potentially useful to, at worst, potentially illegal.

Use of commercial applications for handling online contributions may facilitate illegal corporate giving because they do not automatically discriminate with regard to the type of credit card used. That is, the software does not screen for whether the card used is corporate or personal. In the commercial world, the issue of using corporate funds to make a purchase remains an issue between the user of the credit card and the corporation which issued the card or authorized its use. In politics, the use of a corporate credit card is illegal if corporate funds are used to pay the debt. That is, corporate contributions are illegal; using a corporate credit card gives an appearance that the donation is an illegal contribution. Campaigns must therefore bear a burden to show, if challenged, that the contribution is in fact legal. Even if it provides disclaimers about the illegality of corporate contributions, the campaign runs a risk of having donors confuse the issue. The smart campaign, consequently, will ask the donor to make an affirmative statement that the card is personal and not corporate.

Even those campaigns that do not solicit online contributions have to worry about illegal corporate contributions. For example, those that ask the donor to simply send in a pledge with a signature and a credit card number (category 3 in Table 2) also must be sure that they do not accept corporate credit card donations if they want to stay within the law. Therefore, we investigated whether or not campaign web sites screened for corporate information in any way at all. This would include screening for corporate credit cards and requiring information about the contributor's occupation and employer to be submitted with any online contribution,[8] for this information to be present on a pledge form that was to be sent (or faxed or emailed), or providing a disclaimer about illegal corporate contributions on the contribution page.

We found, in the aggregate, that only two-thirds of all web sites that solicited contributions required, or even provided a disclaimer regarding, information about the donor's employer (68.8%) or occupation (66.7%). There were no differences across candidate type (incumbent, challenger, or open seat) or type of race (House or Senate). However, Republicans were slightly more likely to ask for information on occupation or employer than Democratic candidates (see Tables 3A and 3B).

A wise campaign will validate credit card numbers before processing them. Given that most credit card processing requires the payment of a batch processing fee, filing false credit card information that has been posted to a campaign web site could potentially impose a large cost to the campaign. But, by using the validation methods that already exist, much like those at the gas pump, the campaign can virtually eliminate this potential nuisance. Yet only three campaigns bothered to validate and verify credit card information submitted online.[9]

Controlling for party, type of race (House or Senate), and type of candidate (incumbent, challenger, or open seat) provided interesting results. Similar to the finding reported above that indicated little difference between Republicans and Democrats in their proclivity to have a web site, we found little difference between the number of Democrats and Republicans that solicited cam-

paign contributions on their web sites—78.7% of Democrats and 66.7% of Republicans. This again contradicts the conventional wisdom that Republicans have more money in campaigns, appeal to the higher socioeconomic status voters (i.e., those who use the web), and are more organized and technological than Democrats. However, the difference cannot be distinguished from zero, so we cannot draw any conclusions. More Senate candidates (78.4% of them) had web sites that solicited contributions than did House candidates (65.9%). Slight differences ($\chi^2 = 4.52$, d.f. = 2, p = .104) appear between types of candidates who solicit contributions online; 86.4% of incumbents, 80% of challengers, but only

Table 3A

Party Differences in Information Gathering on Campaign Web Sites that Solicit Contributions: Occupation

		Democrats	Republicans
Does the web site require compilation of, or provide a disclaimer regarding, FEC-required information about occupation?	Yes	60% (21)	79.3% (23)
	No	40% (14)	20.7% (6)
	Total	100% (35)	100% (29)

Pearson χ^2 = 2.752
d.f. = 1
p = 0.097
Fisher's Exact Test p = .112 (2-tail)

Table 3B

Party Differences in Information Gathering on Campaign Web Sites that Solicit Contributions: Employer

		Democrats	Republicans
Does the website require compilation of, or provide a disclaimer regarding, FEC-required information about employer?	Yes	57.1% (20)	78.6% (23)
	No	42.9% (15)	21.4% (6)
	Total	100% (35)	100% (29)

Pearson χ^2 = 3.214
d.f. = 1
p = 0.073
Fisher's Exact Test p = .106 (2-tail)

64% of open seat candidates who had a web site solicited contributions through their pages.

There is no sure way to systematically determine the success or failure of the solicitation of campaign contributions online. Given the relatively few numbers of acknowledged hits on web sites and the general difficulty in finding them, there were probably few funds raised this year. Comments in the popular press about the race for California's U.S. Senate seat indicated that Barbara Boxer (D), the successful incumbent candidate, raised about $25,000 online and her opponent, Matt Fong (R), raised about $30,000 (Komarow 1998). If accurate, these figures represent a very small percentage—less than 1%—of total spending in the race.

The election of 1998 was the first time a high percentage of campaigns developed web sites, and the first time a number of important campaigns began to experiment with soliciting online contributions. The campaigns in our sample had little experience with the medium. They adopted existing technologies and applications with little or no adaptation to the political environment. Instead, they used the new medium of the Internet to fight the same ground war they have in the past. If the results were not all they hoped, it will be no surprise if they write the medium off as somehow ineffectual. Campaigns must experiment and learn, and then, in the next iteration, use the medium more fully if they are going to reap all of the benefits this technology potentially affords them. As one example, campaigns can use key words to identify themselves more readily to search engines, thus increasing traffic to their site.

Campaigns can also begin to generate email lists of potential supporters whom they might solicit for support or contributions. When they do, they will be able to reduce the cost of their mailings and solicitations dramatically (Bonchek 1996). For example, a first-class solicitation that can cost $3.50 to mail can be sent for only pennies in an email; and information packs sent to PACs, currently costing up to $7.00 apiece—and frequently discarded without being read by PAC administrators—can be digitally scanned and also sent for a few cents via email.

Additionally, candidates and field staff on the road may communicate with headquarters and retrieve documents anywhere there is a laptop and dial up connection. For example, campaigns can solicit potential supporters at, say, the county fair by logging them into the database and processing a credit card all at once, without delay, additional handling, or missing data. Safeguards built into the software can also help prevent potential political gaffes, like failing to report required FEC information, by highly motivated but poorly trained volunteers.

Finally, search engines can now sort, and in a few cases, merge email with physical addresses. The availability of this technology from the search engine companies makes it far more likely that a campaign will be able to identify, with considerable accuracy, a potential district voter, contact that voter, and tailor a message precisely to the identified interest of that voter.[10]

The problem is not the medium. The problem lies with those who know how to manage campaigns using such traditional methods as television advertising, direct mail, and telemessaging but do not yet know how to fully utilize the power of the Internet to reduce costs, identify key supporters regardless of geography, and entice them into visiting a campaign web site. Campaign managers do not, generally, drive traffic to their candidates' sites. Neither do they use the flexibility and mobility that the Internet offers to support the campaign process. They have benchmarked the web against their traditional campaign practices and, in so doing, often found it lacking. Many have criticized the web as "too passive" (Casey 1996).

The Internet offers new ways to manage and improve campaigns. Many of these innovations help make the process more accurate, legal, and democratic. For example, the World Wide Web effectively removes the constraint of distance. Yet campaigns still think largely in terms of geography, in terms of one of Fenno's (1978) four constituencies of intimate, primary, reelection, or geographic. The Internet may add a new category, "virtual political communities," to these time-tested definitions of constituency. For example, the links many southern Republican party and candidate sites provide to groups like the Christian Coalition (e.g., Republican Party of Virginia, www.rpv.org/links.htm) illustrate that there is an Internet network that links interest groups and campaigns in virtual communities that might make a difference in some future races (Rash 1997; Browning 1996).

In 1998, congressional candidates generally underutilized the full potential of the medium of the Internet. A relatively few campaigns began to experiment with new applications, including inviting online solicitations and interactive communication among campaign volunteers and voters, but there is no evidence in our study that its use provided a winning margin in any congressional race. ■

Notes

Funding for this research was provided, in part, by a grant from The Pew Charitable Trusts to American University Center for Congressional and Presidential Studies and Campaign Management Institute in a grant focused on "Improving Campaign Conduct." Names of authors appear in alphabetical order.

1. Candidates for Senate and open House seats were chosen for the competitive nature of the races. We felt that these races would permit us to investigate candidates that were of similar quality, had similar budgets, and were competitive. While this obviously does not hold true for all races or candidates, we feel this strategy is better than the alternatives. We feel this provides for a more objective measure of competitiveness than any "list of competitive races" (such as those found in the Cook Report or the Rothenberg Report).

2. When neither of these techniques produced any results, we tried a few common frames that were part of other site names, such as smithforcongress.org, jones4senate.com, or thomas98.org. We stopped looking for campaign sites after the first 50 sites identified by the search engine on the assumption that if we could not find the site after this amount of searching, a constituent would not look any further either.

3. The evaluation criteria were limited to objective measures in order to limit any bias that could have influenced a subjective analysis. Most of the survey items could be answered yes or no: Does the candidate have a web site? Does the web site solicit campaign contributions? See the Appendix for a complete list of questions.

4. Kamarck's study, conducted in June 1998, included all primary candidates.

5. Interview with Chris Esposito, campaign manager, Dennis Moore for Congress Campaign, October 9, 1998, Kansas City, KS.

6. Successfully managing the transaction fees associated with credit card use will be a major problem for campaigns for two reasons. First, banks negotiate the rate for the credit card debitor based upon experience. Since campaigns usually lack experience, they pay at the highest rates. Second, fees for batch processing are assessed regardless of the amount of the contribution. A daily batch processing fee of $50 may therefore be more than a single contribution processed that day. Interview with James P. Fox, chief of staff for Senator Robert Torricelli, May 19, 1998.

7. These categories are not mutually exclusive; many sites incorporated two or more of the methods described. However, we found no additional variants and believe the four methods are an exhaustive list.

8. To complete the analysis, we entered spurious information that matched the entry format. For example, when prompted to provide a credit card number, name, address, phone number, occupation, or employer, we entered "John Doe" data. We could then determine whether the site would accept this invalid information and process it, or whether it would attempt to verify and reject it.

9. By illustrating these points we do not intend to provide or endorse online tricks that campaigns might use to undermine or derail, legally or financially, each others' campaigns.

10. Privacy is an important issue embedded in the use of this technology. Many Internet service providers and content providers are trying to sort out privacy issues with respect to the use of their existing data bases. Currently, senders must determine whether potential recipients are willing to accept such messages prior to their being sent. "Spamming," the practice of sending mass emails on an unsolicited basis, is regarded both as a major breach of Internet etiquette and as likely to be counterproductive to the sender.

References

Aldrich, John A. 1995. *Why Parties?* Chicago: University of Chicago Press.
Bonchek, Mark S. 1996. "Grassroots in Cyberspace." Harvard University Political Participation Project. Manuscript.

Browning, Grahame. 1996. *Electronic Democracy: Using the Internet to Influence American Politics.* Wilton, CT: Pemberton Press.

Casey, Chris. 1996. *The Hill on the Net: Congress Enters the Information Age.* Boston: AP Professional.

Fenno, Richard F. 1978. *Homestyle: House Members in their Districts.* Glenview, IL: Scott, Foresman.

Kamarck, Elaine. 1998. "Campaigning on the Internet in the Off Year Elections of 1998." *Visions of Governance in the Twenty-*

First Century <www.ksg.harvard.edu/visions/agenda.htm>. December 23, 1998.

Key, V. O. 1964. *Politics, Parties, and Pressure Groups.* New York: Thomas Crowell.

Komarow, Steve. 1998. "Politicians Take First Steps into Medium that May Hold Huge Potential in Elections." *USA Today,* November 4.

Rash, Wayne, Jr. 1997. *Politics on the Net: Wiring the Political Process.* New York: W. H. Freeman.

Appendix

Evaluation criteria used at each site

1. Is there a campaign web site?
   yes   no
2. If so, does it solicit campaign contributions?
   yes   no
3. If so, does it request the donor to contact the campaign (either by mail or email) in order to send the donor more information about contributions?
   yes   no
4. Does it request the contributor to mail in a contribution?
   yes   no
5. Does it request the donor to print a form from the web site and then mail in a contribution?
   yes   no
6. Does it permit online contributions?
   yes   no
7. Does it provide for a secure connection to protect the contributor (i.e., https://)?
   yes   no
8. Does it screen for corporate credit cards?
   yes   no
9. Does it screen for foreign contributors?
   yes   no
10. Does it require FEC reporting information regarding employer (either on screen or in the form the donor has to fill out)?
    yes   no
11. Does it require FEC reporting information regarding occupation (either on screen or in the form the donor has to fill out)?
    yes   no
12. Does it link to the national party site?
    yes   no
13. Does the national party site link to the candidate site?
    yes   no
14. Does it link to the state party site or vice versa?
    yes   no
15. Does the state party site link to the candidate site?
    yes   no

16. Does it link to other candidates' sites?
    yes   no
17. Does it link to special interest sites or vice versa?
    yes   no
18. Do special interest sites link to specific candidate sites?
    yes   no
19. Is there a disclaimer regarding the deductibility of the contribution present?
    yes   no
20. Is there a disclaimer regarding illegal corporate contributions on the screen?
    yes   no
21. Is there a disclaimer about foreign contributions on the screen?
    yes   no
22. Does it bounce back invalid or incomplete information?
    yes   no
23. Does it validate credit card numbers?
    yes   no
24. Is there a minimum contribution?
    yes   no

Why Was This Research Needed?

1. What relevance does the development of a new communication medium like the Internet have for the field of politics?
2. What do the authors mean by characterizing their analysis as "mostly descriptive"? When is description an important contribution to scholarship on a topic? Explain the distinction between description and hypothesis testing.
3. What expectations did the authors have in undertaking this study?

How Was the Topic Studied?

1. What is the database for this study? What challenges did the authors face in collecting their data?
2. What does it mean to develop a "coding scheme" as part of research methodology? What specific items of information did the authors code for each campaign Web site they examined?
3. How have the authors tried to limit the possibility that the time frame within which a study like this is carried out could shape the results?

What Are the Findings?

1. What is the prevalence of Web site creation among the political candidates in this study? To what extent is political party a variable that helps to explain which candidates had Web sites? What is the impact of other independent variables on Web site creation?
2. What do the authors conclude about the association between Internet use and election results? Are you satisfied that their method of analysis is sufficient to answer this question? Explain.
3. Why is the solicitation of campaign contributions via Web sites such a complex topic for investigation? What are the authors' main descriptive findings concerning such solicitations? Why do the research data reported in this study raise questions about the legality of contributions collected through campaign Web sites?
4. What bivariate relationships are examined in Tables 3A and 3B? What measures of significance are reported? By what standard do these measures indicate that neither relationship is significant?

5. Chi-square is a statistic generated by comparing observed and expected frequencies in a table. Calculate the expected frequency in row 1, column 1 of Table 3A. Under what assumption is this value "expected"? Based on what you know about the way that the chi-square statistic is calculated, what changes in the distribution of numbers within Tables 3A and 3B would have improved the chance of a significant result?

6. What do the authors mean when they write that they "controlled for" party, type of race, and type of candidate in extending their bivariate analysis? How do the results of this control analysis strengthen the original conclusion that party is not a significant factor in Web site fundraising practices?

What Do the Results Mean?

1. Based only on the results of this study, would you say that the medium of the Internet will help standardize political campaigning in the United States? Explain.

2. If you were to update this study today, what additional areas of online campaign activity would you examine? Why?

3. Why might it be worthwhile to look at the impact of rival candidates' Web sites on each other? Describe how you would design a research study for this topic.

Afterword from David A. Dulio

The Internet certainly made headlines during the 2004 presidential campaign, beginning with Howard Dean's fundraising success early in the race for the Democratic Party's nomination. The Internet will likely be part of the story of future elections as well, as candidates, parties, and professional consultants find more innovative ways to harness this modern electioneering tool. Things have certainly changed since 1998 when we wrote about the Web's role in that year's congressional elections. For instance, we noted that in the U.S. Senate race in California, Sen. Barbara Boxer and her opponent Matt Fong took advantage of the Web to raise $25,000 and $30,000, respectively. Those amounts are a drop in the bucket compared with what candidates can raise today via the Web—in one financial quarter of 2003, Dean raised roughly $4 million on the Web, and in his bid for the Republican Party's nomination four years earlier, Sen. John McCain raised millions online. In addition, readers of this volume will likely be surprised at how few campaigns took advantage of the Internet during 1998 and by how little we as political scientists knew about the Web (this holds true not only for our piece, but also for others that were published around the same time).

It is nice, however, to see that some of the predictions we made in the article actually turned out to be true. For instance, we noted that campaign staff in the field might want to communicate with campaign headquarters when talking to potential volunteers or voters. In 2004, campaign and party volunteers on both sides used handheld devices to enter data into databases when they walked precincts around the country for voter-contact and get-out-the-vote purposes. We also noted that campaigns might want to use e-mail to tailor specific messages to voters with certain characteristics. Again, in 2004, this was done by candidates' campaigns, parties, and outside interest groups.

Looking back at the research we conducted can also provide important information for future investigations of any kind. Here, there are at least three points that should be noted. First, take note of the (relatively) simple statistics that we employed in our analysis. As we point out in the article, much of our work was descriptive; we also used some chi-square statistics to note associations between variables. Researchers should not fall into the trap of always trying to use fancy statistical techniques when they are not needed; researchers should use statistics that are appropriate for the data they have collected. In addition, when a phenomenon has not been studied heavily in the past, description can go a long way toward helping readers understand that phenomenon.

Second, the cliché "hindsight is 20/20" applies here and to many other research projects. In this project, we were already at the candidates' Web sites, but we only asked a few questions in our content analysis. If we had done some additional data collection, we could have investigated additional research questions. The lesson here is to collect as much data as you can with the time and resources you have, because you never know what great research questions and hypotheses you may want to investigate.

Lastly, this piece illustrates the importance of continuing to collect data over time so you have a time series. We all move on to different research projects, but looking back we wish that we had collected data on these and other questions in subsequent election cycles so that we could replicate the study and track any changes that occur over time. Comparisons across the election cycles from 1998 through 2004 and beyond would make great projects.

Tuning In, Tuning Out: The Strange Disappearance of Social Capital in America

Robert D. Putnam

Robert Putnam is that rare academic whose work is of vital interest to scholars as well as a broad public audience. The concept of "social capital" examined by Putnam in his celebrated book Bowling Alone *(2000) has provided a compelling intellectual stimulus for researchers interested in such topics as economic growth, public health, crime, community well-being, and democratic performance. At the same time, it has influenced the thinking of political leaders in the United States and abroad, among them Bill Clinton and Tony Blair (Lloyd 2001). Not just a theoretician, Putnam seeks to be a key player in the movement to strengthen local civic life in the United States. His Saguaro Seminar at Harvard University's Kennedy School of Government was founded as a vehicle for "develop[ing] a handful of far-reaching, actionable ideas to significantly increase Americans' connectedness to one another and to community institutions" (www.ksg.harvard.edu/saguaro).*

One way to understand the far-reaching impact of Putnam's work is in terms of the variables he has chosen to study and their resonance with contemporary social concerns. Although research on social capital, defined as the cooperation resulting from networks of formal and informal ties among people, dates back to the early twentieth century, Putnam has devoted himself to measuring the concept in a contemporary context and to exploring its causes and consequences. The following reading, in which Putnam presents an early formulation of his research results in an address before the American Political Science Association, demonstrates that the erosion of social capital presents a challenging puzzle for empirical analysis. In a society that has changed in so many ways over recent decades, how do researchers isolate those forces that are responsible for undermining the communal nature of American life?

Putnam approaches this problem as a detective attempting to solve a crime. First he lines up his suspects, then he weighs the evidence and counterevidence relevant to each. Putnam's painstaking selection of variables, his systematic use of controls to test the validity of quantitative findings, and his visual presentation of longitudinal and other data all exemplify valuable techniques for students seeking to understand the logic and applications of multivariate analysis.

References

Lloyd, John. 2001. "Let Us All Go and Bowl Together." *The Financial Times,* April 14, 3.

Putnam, Robert. 2000. *Bowling Alone: The Collapse and Revival of American Community.* New York: Simon and Schuster.

It is a daunting honor to deliver the inaugural Pool Lecture. Ithiel de Sola Pool was a brilliant, broad-gauged scholar whose interests ranged from the Nazi elite to direct satellite broadcasting, from the first rigorous computer simulation of electoral behavior to the development of network theory, from which he invented "small world" research. He helped found the field of political communications. A graduate of the University of Chicago's political science department during its classic golden age, and first chair of the MIT political science department, Pool must also have been a remarkable teacher, for his students continue to contribute to our understanding of technology, communications, and political behavior. When I accepted this honor, I did not guess how close my own inquiry would lead me to Pool's own professional turf. I shall return to the contemporary relevance of Pool's insights at the conclusion of this talk.

For the last year or so, I have been wrestling with a difficult mystery. It is, if I am right, a puzzle of some importance to the future of American democracy. It is a classic brain-teaser, with a corpus delicti, a crime scene strewn with clues, and many potential suspects. As in all good detective stories, however, some plausible miscreants turn out to have impeccable alibis, and some important clues hint at portentous developments that occurred long before the curtain rose. Moreover, like Agatha Christie's *Murder on the Orient Express,* this crime may have had more than one perpetrator, so that we shall need to sort out ringleaders from accomplices. Finally, I need to make clear at the outset that I am not yet sure that I have solved the mystery. In that sense, this lecture represents work-in-progress. I have a prime suspect that I am prepared to indict, but the evidence is not yet strong enough to convict, so I invite your help in sifting clues.

Theories and Measures of Social Capital

Allow me to set the scene by saying a word or two about my own recent work.[1] Several years ago I conducted research on the arcane topic of local government in Italy (Putnam 1993). That study concluded that the performance of government and other social institutions is powerfully influenced by citizen engagement in community affairs, or what (following Coleman 1990) I termed *social capital.* I am now seeking to apply that set of ideas and insights to the urgent problems of contemporary American public life.

By "social capital," I mean features of social life—networks, norms, and trust—that enable participants to act together more effectively to pursue shared objectives. Whether or not their shared goals are praiseworthy is, of course, entirely another matter. To the extent that the norms, networks, and trust link substantial sectors of the community and span underlying social cleavages—to the extent that the social capital is of a "bridging" sort—then the enhanced cooperation is likely to serve broader interests and to be widely welcomed. On the other hand, groups like the Michigan militia or youth gangs also embody a kind of social capital, for these networks and norms, too, enable members to cooperate more effectively, albeit to the detriment of the wider community.

Social capital, in short, refers to social connections and the attendant norms and trust. Who benefits from these connections, norms, and trust—the individual, the wider community, or some faction within the community—must be determined empirically, not definitionally.[2] Sorting out the multiple effects of different forms of social capital is clearly a crucial task, although it is not one that I can address here. For present purposes, I am concerned with forms of social capital that, generally speaking, serve civic ends.

Social capital in this sense is closely related to political participation in the conventional sense, but these terms are not synonymous. Political participation refers to our relations with political institutions. Social capital refers to our relations with one another. Sending a check to a PAC is an act of political participation, but it does not embody or create social capital. Bowling in a league or having coffee with a friend embodies and creates social capital, though these are not acts of political participation. (A grassroots political movement or a traditional urban machine is a social capital-intensive form of political participation.) I use the term "civic engagement" to refer to people's connections with the life of their communities, not merely with politics. Civic engagement is correlated with political participation in a narrower sense, but whether they move in lock-step is an empirical question, not a logical certitude. Some forms of individualized political participation, such as check-writing, for example, might be rising at the same time that social connectedness was on the wane. Similarly, although social trust—trust in other people—and political trust—trust in political authorities—might be empirically related, they are logically quite distinct. I might well trust my neighbors without trusting city hall, or vice versa.

The theory of social capital presumes that, generally speaking, the more we connect with other people, the more we trust them, and vice versa. At least in the contexts I have so far explored, this presumption generally turns out to be true: social trust and civic engagement are strongly correlated. That is, with or without controls for education, age, income, race, gender, and so on, people who join are people who trust.[3] Moreover, this is true across different countries, and across different states in the United States, as well as across individuals, and it is true of all sorts of groups.[4] Sorting out which way causation flows—whether joining causes trusting or trusting causes joining—is complicated both theoretically and methodologically, although John Brehm and Wendy Rahn (1995) report evidence that the causation flows mainly from joining to trusting. Be that as it may, civic connections and social trust move together. Which way are they moving?

Bowling Alone: Trends in Civic Engagement

Evidence from a number of independent sources strongly suggests that America's stock of social capital has been shrinking for more than a quarter century.

- Membership records of such diverse organizations as the PTA, the Elks club, the League of Women Voters, the Red Cross, labor unions, and even bowling leagues show that participation in many conventional voluntary associations has declined by roughly 25% to 50% over the last two to three decades (Putnam 1995, 1996).

- Surveys of the time budgets of average Americans in 1965, 1975, and 1985, in which national samples of men and women recorded every single activity undertaken during the course of a day, imply that the time we spend on informal socializing and visiting is down (perhaps by one quarter) since 1965, and that the time we devote to clubs and organizations is down even more sharply (probably by roughly half) over this period.[5]

- While Americans' interest in politics has been stable or even growing over the last three decades, and some forms of participation that require moving a pen, such as signing petitions and writing checks, have increased significantly, many measures of collective participation have fallen sharply (Rosenstone and Hansen 1993; Putnam 1996), including attending a rally or speech (off 36% between 1973 and 1993), attending a meeting on town or school affairs (off 39%), or working for a political party (off 56%).

- Evidence from the General Social Survey (GSS) demonstrates, at all levels of education and among both men and women, a drop of roughly one-quarter in group membership since 1974 and a drop of roughly one-third in social trust since 1972.[6] Moreover, as Figure 1 illustrates, slumping membership has afflicted all sorts of groups, from sports clubs and professional associations to literary discussion groups and labor unions.[7] Only nationality groups, hobby and garden clubs, and the catch-all category of "other" seem to have resisted the ebbing tide. Furthermore, Gallup polls report that church attendance fell by roughly 15% during the 1960s and has remained at that lower level ever since, while data from the National

Figure 1 • Membership Trends (1974–1994) by Type of Group (education controlled)

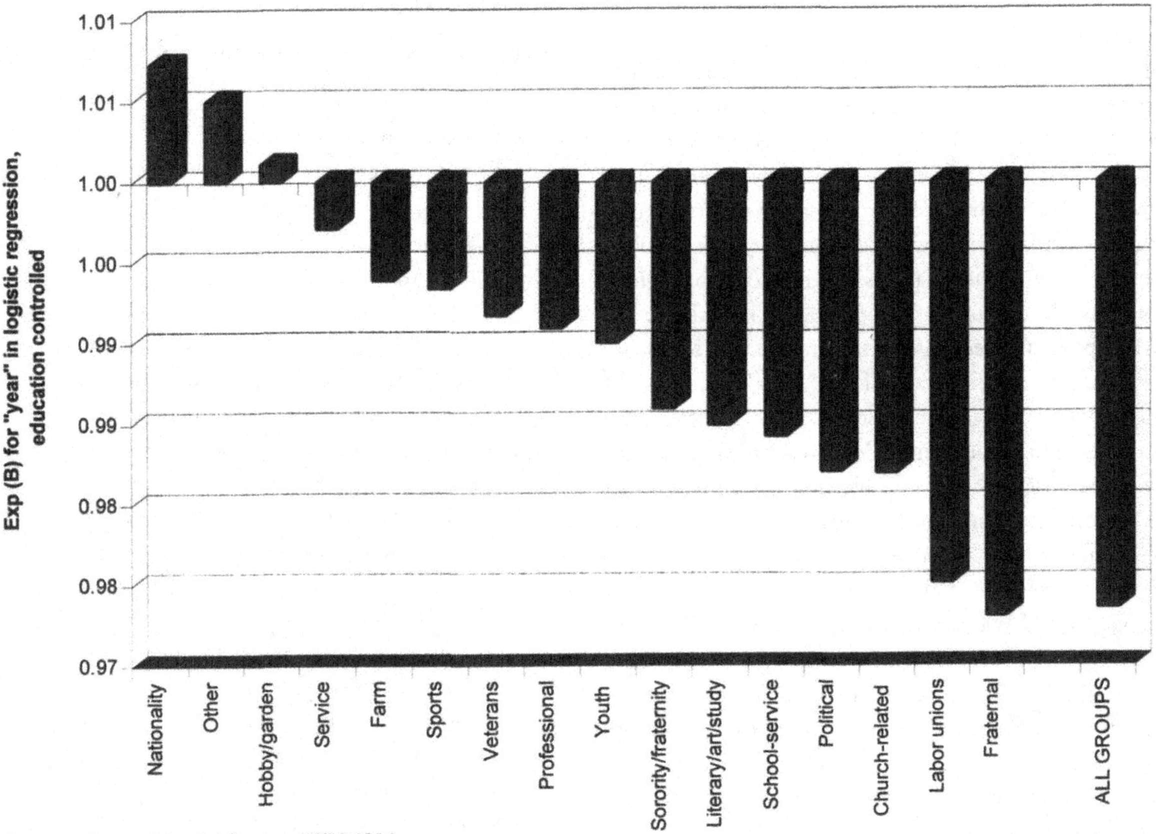

Source: General Social Survey, 1974-1994

Opinion Research Center suggest that the decline continued during the 1970s and 1980s and by now amounts to roughly 30% (Putnam 1996).

Each of these approaches to the problem of measuring trends in civic engagement has advantages and drawbacks. Membership records offer long-term coverage and reasonable precision, but they may underrepresent newer, more vibrant organizations. Time budgets capture real investments of time and energy in both formal and informal settings, not merely nominal membership, but the available data are episodic and drawn from relatively small samples that are not entirely comparable across time. Surveys are more comprehensive in their coverage of various types of groups, but (apart from church attendance) comparable trend data are available only since the mid-1970s, a decade or more after the putative downturn began, so they may understate the full decline. No single source is perfect for testing the hypothesized decline in social connectedness, although the consistency across different measuring rods is striking.

A fuller audit of American social capital would need to account for apparent counter-trends.[8] Some observers believe, for example, that support groups and neighborhood watch groups are proliferating, and few deny that the last several decades have witnessed explosive growth in interest groups represented in Washington. The growth of "mailing list" organizations, like the American Association of Retired People or the Sierra Club, although highly sig-nificant in political (and commercial) terms, is not really a counter-example to the supposed decline in social con-nectedness, however, since these are not really associations in which members meet one another. Their members' ties are to common symbols and ideologies, but not to each other. These organizations are sufficiently different from classical "secondary" associations as to deserve a new rubric—perhaps "tertiary" associations. Similarly, although most secondary associations are not-for-profit, most prominent nonprofits (from Harvard University to the Metropolitan Opera) are bureaucracies, not secondary associations, so the growth of the "Third Sector" is not tantamount to a growth in social connectedness. With due regard to various kinds of counter-evidence, I believe that the weight of the available evidence confirms that Americans today are significantly less engaged with their communities than was true a generation ago.

Of course, lots of civic activity is still visible in our communities. American civil society is not moribund. In-deed, evidence suggests that America still outranks many other countries in the degree of our community involve-ment and social trust (Putnam 1996). But if we compare ourselves, not with other countries but with our parents, the best available evidence suggests that we are less con-nected with one another.

This prologue poses a number of important questions that merit further debate:

- Is it true that America's stock of social capital has diminished?
- Does it matter?
- What can we do about it?

The answer to the first two questions is, I believe, "yes," but I cannot address them further in this setting. Answering the third question—which ultimately concerns me most—depends, at least in part, on first understanding the *causes* of the strange malady afflicting American civic life. This is the mystery I seek to unravel here: Why, be-ginning in the 1960s and accelerating in the 1970s and 1980s, did the fabric of American community life begin to fray? Why are more Americans bowling alone?

Explaining the Erosion of Social Capital

Many possible answers have been suggested for this puzzle:

- Busyness and time pressure
- Economic hard times (or, according to alternative theories, material affluence)
- Residential mobility
- Suburbanization
- The movement of women into the paid labor force and the stresses of two-career families
- Disruption of marriage and family ties
- Changes in the structure of the American econ-omy, such as the rise of chain stores, branch firms, and the service sector
- The Sixties (most of which actually happened in the Seventies), including
  — Vietnam, Watergate, and disillusion with public life
  — The cultural revolt against authority (sex, drugs, and so on)
- Growth of the welfare state
- The civil rights revolution
- Television, the electronic revolution, and other technological changes

Most respectable mystery writers would hesitate to tally up this many plausible suspects, no matter how en-ergetic the fictional detective. I am not yet in a position to address all these theories—certainly not in any defin-itive form—but we must begin to winnow the list. To be sure, a social trend as pervasive as the one we are inves-tigating probably has multiple causes, so our task is to assess the relative importance of such factors as these.

A solution, even a partial one, to our mystery must pass several tests.

Is the proposed explanatory factor correlated with trust and civic engagement? If not, it is difficult to see why that factor should even be placed in the lineup. For example, many women have entered the paid labor force during the period in question, but if working women turned out to be more engaged in community life than housewives, it would be harder to attribute the downturn in community organizations to the rise of two-career families.

Is the correlation spurious? If parents, for example, were more likely to be joiners than childless people, that might be an important clue. However, if the correlation between parental status and civic engagement turned out to be entirely spurious, due to the effects of (say) age, we would have to remove the declining birth rate from our list of suspects.

Is the proposed explanatory factor changing in the relevant way? Suppose, for instance, that people who often move have shallower community roots. That could be an important part of the answer to our mystery *only if* residential mobility itself had risen during this period.

Is the proposed explanatory factor vulnerable to the claim that it might be the result *of civic disengagement, not the cause?* For example, even if newspaper readership were closely correlated with civic engagement across individuals and across time, we would need to weigh the possibility that reduced newspaper circulation is the result (not the cause) of disengagement.

Against that set of benchmarks, let us consider various potential influences on social capital formation.

Education

Human capital and social capital are closely related, for education has a very powerful effect on trust and associational membership, as well as many other forms of social and political participation. Education is by far the strongest correlate that I have discovered of civic engagement in all its forms, including social trust and membership in many different types of groups.[9] In fact, as Figure 2 illustrates, the relationship between education and civic engagement is a curvilinear one of increasing returns. The last two years of college make twice as much difference to trust and group membership as the first two years of high school. The four years of education between 14 and 18 total years have *ten times more impact* on trust and membership than the first four years of formal education. The same basic pattern applies to both men and women, and to all races and generations. Edu-

cation, in short, is an extremely powerful predictor of civic engagement.

Sorting out just why education has such a massive effect on social connectedness would require a book, not a mere lecture.[10] Education is in part a proxy for social class and economic differences, but when income, social status, and education are used together to predict trust and group membership, education continues to be the primary influence. (Income and satisfaction with one's personal financial situation both have a significant independent effect.) In short, highly educated people are much more likely to be joiners and trusters, partly because they are better off economically, but mostly because of the skills, resources, and inclinations that were imparted to them at home and in school.

It is widely recognized that Americans today are better educated than our parents and grandparents. It is less often appreciated how massively and rapidly this trend has transformed the educational composition of the adult population during just the last two decades. Since 1972, the proportion of all adults with fewer than 12 years of education has been cut in half, falling from 40% to 18%, while the proportion with more than 12 years has nearly doubled, rising from 28% to 50%, as the generation of Americans educated around the turn of this century (most of whom did not finish high school) passed from the scene and were replaced by the baby boomers and their successors (most of whom attended college).

Thus, education boosts civic engagement sharply, and educational levels have risen massively. Unfortunately, these two undeniable facts only deepen our central mystery. By itself, the rise in educational levels should have *increased* social capital during the last 20 years by 15–20%, even assuming that the effects of education were merely linear. (Taking account of the curvilinear effect in Figure 1, the rise in trusting and joining should have been even greater, as Americans moved up the accelerating curve.) By contrast, however, the actual GSS figures show a net *decline* since the early 1970s of roughly the same magnitude (trust by about 20–25%, memberships by about 15–20%). The relative declines in social capital are similar *within* each educational category—roughly 25% in group

Figure 2 • Social Trust and Group Membership by Years of Education

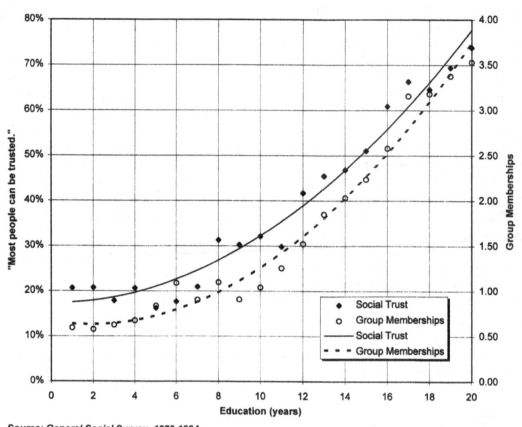

Source: General Social Survey, 1972-1994

memberships and roughly 30% in social trust since the early 1970s, and probably even more since the early 1960s.

Thus, this first investigative foray leaves us more mystified than before. We may nevertheless draw two useful conclusions from these findings, one methodological and one substantive:

1. Since education has such a powerful effect on civic engagement and social trust, we need to take account of educational differences in our exploration of other possible factors, in order to be sure that we do not confuse the consequences of education with the possible effects of other variables.[11]
2. Whatever forces lie behind the slump in civic engagement and social trust, those forces have affected

all levels in American society.[12] Social capital has eroded among the one in every twelve Americans who have enjoyed the advantages (material and intellectual) of graduate study; it has eroded among the one in every eight Americans who did not even make it into high school; and it has eroded among all the strata in between. The mysterious disengagement of the last quarter century seems to have afflicted all echelons of our society.

Pressures of Time and Money

Americans certainly *feel* busier now than a generation ago: the proportion of us who report feeling "always rushed" jumped by half between the mid-1960s and the mid-1990s (Robinson and Godbey 1995). Probably the most obvious suspect behind our tendency to drop out of community affairs is pervasive busyness. And lurking nearby in the shadows are those endemic economic pressures so much discussed nowadays—job insecurity and declining real wages, especially among the lower two-thirds of the income distribution.

Yet, however culpable busyness and economic insecurity may appear at first glance, it is hard to find any incriminating evidence. In fact, the balance of the evidence argues that pressures of time and money are apparently *not* important contributors to the puzzle we seek to solve.

In the first place, time budget studies do *not* confirm the thesis that Americans are, on average, working longer than a generation ago. On the contrary, Robinson and Godbey (1995) report a five-hour per week *gain* in free time for the average American between 1965 and 1985, due partly to reduced time spent on housework and partly to earlier retirement. Their claim that Americans have more leisure time now than several decades ago is, to be sure, contested by other observers. Schor (1991), for example, reports evidence that our work hours are lengthening, especially for women. Whatever the resolution of that controversy, however, the thesis that attributes civic disengagement to longer workdays is rendered much less plausible by looking at the correlation between work hours, on the one hand, and social trust and group membership, on the other.

The available evidence strongly suggests that, in fact, long hours on the job are *not* associated with lessened involvement in civic life or reduced social trust. Quite the reverse: results from the General Social Survey show that employed people belong to somewhat *more* groups than those outside the paid labor force. Even more striking is the fact that among workers, longer hours are linked to *more* civic engagement, not less.[13] This surprising discovery is fully consistent with evidence from the time budget studies. Robinson (1990a) reports that, unsurprisingly, people who spend more time at work do feel more rushed, and these harried souls do spend less time eating, sleeping, reading books, engaging in hobbies,

and just doing nothing. Compared to the rest of the population, they also spend a lot less time watching television—almost 30% less. However, they do *not* spend less time on organizational activity. In short, those who work longer forego *Nightline,* but not the Kiwanis club, *ER,* but not the Red Cross.

I do not conclude from the positive correlation between group membership and work hours that working longer actually *causes* greater civic involvement—there are too many uncontrolled variables here for that—but merely that hard work does not *prevent* civic engagement. Moreover, the nationwide falloff in joining and trusting is perfectly mirrored among full-time workers, among part-time workers, and among those outside the paid labor force. So if people are dropping out of community life, long hours do not seem to be the reason.

If time pressure is not the culprit we seek, how about financial pressures? It is true that people with lower incomes and those who feel financially strapped are less engaged in community life and less trusting than those who are better off, even holding education constant. On the other hand, the downtrends in social trust and civic engagement are entirely visible at all levels in the income hierarchy, with no sign whatever that they are concentrated among those who have borne the brunt of the economic distress of the last two decades. Quite the contrary, the declines in engagement and trust are actually somewhat greater among the more affluent segments of the American public than among the poor and middle-income wage-earners. Furthermore, controlling for both real income and financial satisfaction does little to attenuate the fall in civic engagement and social trust. In short, neither objective nor subjective economic well-being has inoculated Americans against the virus of civic disengagement; if anything, affluence has slightly exacerbated the problem.

I cannot absolutely rule out the possibility that some part of the erosion of social capital in recent years might be linked to a more generalized sense of economic insecurity that may have affected all Americans, nor do I argue that economic distress *never* causes disengagement. Studies of the unemployed during and after the

Great Depression (Jahoda, Lazarsfeld, and Zeisel 1933; Ginzberg 1943; Wilcock and Franke 1963) have described a tendency for them to disengage from community life. However, the basic patterns in the contemporary evidence are inconsistent with any simple economic explanation for our central puzzle. Pressures of time and money may be a part of the backdrop, but neither can be a principal culprit.[14]

Mobility and Suburbanization

Many studies have found that residential stability and such related phenomena as homeownership are associated with greater civic engagement. At an earlier stage in this investigation (Putnam 1995, 30), I observed that "mobility, like frequent repotting of plants, tends to disrupt root systems, and it takes time for an uprooted individual to put down new roots." I must now report, however, that further inquiry fully exonerates residential mobility from any responsibility for our fading civic engagement. Data from the U.S. Bureau of the Census 1995 (and earlier years) show that rates of residential mobility have been remarkably constant over the last half century. In fact, to the extent that there has been any change at all, both long-distance and short-distance mobility have *declined* over the last five decades. During the 1950s, 20% of Americans changed residence each year and 6.9% annually moved across county borders; during the 1990s, the comparable figures are 17% and 6.6%. Americans, in short, are today slightly *more* rooted residentially than a generation ago. If the verdict on the economic distress interpretation had to be nuanced, the verdict on mobility is unequivocal. This theory is simply wrong.

But if moving itself has not eroded our social capital, what about the possibility that we have moved to places—especially the suburbs—that are less congenial to social connectedness? To test this theory, we must first examine the correlation between place of residence and social capital. In fact, social connectedness does differ by community type, but the differences turn out to be modest and in directions that are inconsistent with the theory.

Controlling for such demographic characteristics as education, age, income, work status, and race, citizens of the nation's 12 largest metropolitan areas (particularly their central cities, but also their suburbs) are roughly 10% less trusting and report 10–20% fewer group memberships than residents of other cities and towns (and their suburbs). Meanwhile, residents of very small towns and rural areas are (in accord with some hoary stereotypes) slightly more trusting and civically engaged than other Americans. Unsurprisingly, the prominence of different *types* of groups does vary significantly by location: major cities have more political and nationality clubs; smaller cities more fraternal, service, hobby, veterans, and church groups; and rural areas more agricultural organizations. But overall rates of associational memberships are not very different.

Moreover, this pallid pattern cannot account for our central puzzle. In the first place, there is virtually no correlation between gains in population and losses in social capital, either across states or across localities of different sizes. Even taking into account the educational and social backgrounds of those who have moved there, the suburbs have faintly higher levels of trust and civic engagement than their respective central cities, a fact that *ceteris paribus* should have produced growth, not decay, in social capital over the last generation. The central point, however, is that the downtrends in trusting and joining are virtually identical everywhere—in cities, big and small, in suburbs, in small towns, and in the countryside.

There are, of course, suburbs and suburbs. Evanston is not Levittown is not Sun City. The evidence available does not allow us to determine whether different types of suburban living have different effects on civic connections and social trust. However, these data do rule out the thesis that suburbanization per se has caused the erosion of America's social capital. In this respect, size of place is like mobility—a cross-sectional correlate that cannot explain our trend. Both where we live and how long we've lived there matter for social capital, but neither explains why it is eroding everywhere.

The Changing Role of Women

Most of our mothers were housewives, and most of them invested heavily in social capital formation—a jargony way of referring to untold, unpaid hours in church suppers, PTA meetings, neighborhood coffee klatches, and visits to friends and relatives. The movement of women out of the home and into the paid labor force is probably the most portentous social change of the last half century. However welcome and overdue the feminist revolution may be, it is hard to believe that it has had no impact on social connectedness. Could this be the primary reason for the decline of social capital over the last generation?

Some patterns in the available survey evidence seem to support this claim. All things considered, women belong to somewhat fewer voluntary associations than men (Edwards, Edwards, and Watts 1984 and the sources cited there; more recent GSS data confirm this finding). On the other hand, time budget studies suggest that women spend more time on those groups and more time in informal social connecting than men (Robinson and Godbey 1995). Although the absolute declines in joining and trusting are approximately equivalent among men and women, the relative declines are somewhat greater among women. Controlling for education, memberships among men have declined at a rate of about 10–15% a decade, compared to about 20–25% a decade for women. The time budget data, too, strongly suggest that the decline in organizational involvement in recent years is concentrated among women. These sorts of facts, coupled with the obvious transformation in the professional role of women over this same period, led me in previous work to suppose that the emergence of two-career families might be the most important single factor in the erosion of social capital.

As we saw earlier, however, work status itself seems to have little net impact on group membership or on trust. Housewives belong to different types of groups than do working women (more PTAs, for example, and fewer professional associations), but in the aggregate working women are actually members of slightly more voluntary associations.[15] Moreover, the overall declines in civic engagement are somewhat greater among housewives than among employed women. Comparison of time budget data between 1965 and 1985 (Robinson and Godbey 1995) seems to show that employed women as a group are actually spending more time on organizations than before,

while nonemployed women are spending less. This same study suggests that the major decline in informal socializing since 1965 has also been concentrated among nonemployed women. The central fact, of course, is that the overall trends are down for all categories of women (and for men, too—even bachelors), but the figures suggest that women who work full-time actually may have been more resistant to the slump than those who do not.

Thus, although women appear to have borne a disproportionate share of the decline in civic engagement over the last two decades, it is not easy to find any micro-level data that tie that fact directly to their entry into the labor force. It is hard to control for selection bias in these data, of course, because women who have chosen to enter the workforce doubtless differ in many respects from women who have chosen to stay home. Perhaps one reason that community involvement appears to be rising among working women and declining among housewives is that precisely the sort of women who, in an earlier era, were most involved with their communities have been disproportionately likely to enter the workforce, thus simultaneously lowering the average level of civic engagement among the remaining homemakers and raising the average among women in the workplace. Obviously, we have not been running a great national controlled experiment on the effects of work on women's civic engagement, and in any event the patterns in the data are not entirely clear. Contrary to my own earlier speculations, however, I can find little evidence to support the hypothesis that the movement of women into the workplace over the last generation has played a major role in the reduction of social connectedness and civic engagement. On the other hand, I have no clear alternative explanation for the fact that the relative declines are greater among women than among men. Since this evidence is at best circumstantial, perhaps the best interim judgment here is the famous Scots verdict: not proven.

Marriage and Family

Another widely discussed social trend that more or less coincides with the downturn in civic engagement is the breakdown of the traditional family unit—mom, dad, and the kids. Since the family itself is, by some accounts, a key form of social capital, perhaps its eclipse is part of the explanation for the reduction in joining and trusting in the wider community. What does the evidence show?

First of all, evidence of the loosening of family bonds is unequivocal. In addition to the century-long increase in divorce rates (which accelerated in the mid-1960s to the mid-1970s and then leveled off), and the more recent increase in single-parent families, the incidence of one-person households has more than doubled since 1950, in part because of the rising number of widows living alone (Caplow, Bahr, Modell, and Chadwick 1991, 47, 106, 113). The net effect of all these changes, as reflected in the General Social Survey, is that the proportion of all American adults who are currently unmarried climbed from 28% in 1974 to 48% in 1994.

Second, married men and women do rank somewhat higher on both our measures of social capital. That is, controlling for education, age, race, and so on, single people—both men and women, divorced, separated, and never-married—are significantly less trusting and less engaged civically than married people.[16] Roughly speaking, married men and women are about a third more trusting and belong to about 15–25% more groups than comparable single men and women. (Widows and widowers are more like married people than single people in this comparison.)

In short, successful marriage (especially if the family unit includes children) is statistically associated with greater social trust and civic engagement. Thus, some part of the decline in both trust and membership is tied to the decline in marriage. To be sure, the direction of causality behind this correlation may be complicated, since it is conceivable that loners and paranoids are harder to live with. If so, divorce may in some degree be the consequence, not the cause, of lower social capital. Probably the most reasonable summary of these arrays of data, however, is that the decline in successful marriage is a significant, though modest part of the reason for declining trust and lower group membership. On the other hand, changes in family structure cannot be a major part of our story, since the overall declines in joining and trusting are substantial even among the happily married.

My own verdict (based in part on additional evidence to be introduced later) is that the disintegration of marriage is probably an accessory to the crime, but not the major villain of the piece.

The Rise of the Welfare State

Circumstantial evidence, particularly the timing of the downturn in social connectedness, has suggested to some observers (for example, Fukuyama 1995, 313–14) that an important cause—perhaps even *the* cause—of civic disengagement is big government and the growth of the welfare state. By "crowding out" private initiative, it is argued, state intervention has subverted civil society. This is a much larger topic than I can address in detail here, but a word or two may be appropriate.

On the one hand, some government policies have almost certainly had the effect of destroying social capital. For example, the so-called "slum clearance" policies of the 1950s and 1960s replaced physical capital, but destroyed social capital, by disrupting existing community ties. It is also conceivable that certain social expenditures and tax policies may have created disincentives for civic-minded philanthropy. On the other hand, it is much harder to see which government policies might be responsible for the decline in bowling leagues and literary clubs.

One empirical approach to this issue is to examine differences in civic engagement and public policy across different political jurisdictions to see whether swollen government leads to shriveled social capital. Among the U.S. states, however, differences in social capital appear essentially uncorrelated with various measures of welfare spending or government size.[17] Citizens in free-spending states are no less trusting or engaged than citizens in frugal ones. Cross-national comparison can also shed light on this question. Among 19 OECD countries for which data on social trust and group membership are available from the 1990–1991 World Values Survey, these indicators of social capital are, if anything, *positively* correlated with the size of the state.[18] This simple bivariate analysis, of course, cannot tell us whether social connectedness encourages welfare spending, whether the welfare state fosters civic engagement, or whether both are the result of some other unmeasured factor(s). Sorting out the underlying causal connections would require much more thorough analysis. However, even this simple finding is not easily reconciled with the notion that big government undermines social capital.

Race and the Civil Rights Revolution

Race is such an absolutely fundamental feature of American social history that nearly every other feature of our society is connected to it in some way. Thus, it seems intuitively plausible that race might somehow have played a role in the erosion of social capital over the last generation. In fact, some observers (both black and white) have noted that the decline in social connectedness and social trust began just after the greatest successes of the civil rights revolution of the 1960s. To some, that coincidence has suggested the possibility of a kind of sociological "white flight," as legal desegregation of civic life led whites to withdraw from community associations.

Like the theory about the welfare state, this racial interpretation of the destruction of social capital is highly controversial and can hardly be settled within the compass of these brief remarks. Nevertheless, the basic facts are these.

First, racial differences in associational membership are not large. At least until the 1980s, controlling for educational and income differences, blacks actually belonged to more associations on average than whites, essentially because they were more likely than comparably situated whites to belong to religious and ethnic organizations and no less likely to belong to any other type of group.[19] On the other hand, racial differences in social trust are very large indeed, even taking into account differences in education, income, and so on. On average, during the 1972–94 period, controlling for educational differences, about 17% of blacks endorsed the view that "most people can be trusted," as compared to about 45% of whites, and about 27% of respondents of other races.[20] These racial differences in social trust, of course,

reflect not collective paranoia, but real experiences over many generations.

Second, the erosion of social capital has affected all races. In fact, during the 1980s the downturns in both joining and trusting were even greater among blacks (and other racial minorities) than among the white majority. This fact is inconsistent with the thesis that "white flight" is a significant cause of civic disengagement, since black Americans have been dropping out of religious and civic organizations at least as rapidly as white Americans. Even more important, the pace of disengagement among whites has been uncorrelated with racial intolerance or support for segregation. Avowedly racist or segregationist whites have been no quicker to drop out of community organizations during this period than more tolerant whites. Figure 3 presents illustrative evidence, its three parallel slopes showing that the decline in group membership is essentially identical among whites who favor segregation, whites who oppose it, and blacks.[21]

This evidence is far from conclusive, of course, but it does shift the burden of proof onto those who believe that racism is a primary explanation for growing civic disengagement over the last quarter century, however virulent racism continues to be in American society.[22] This evidence also suggests that reversing the civil rights gains of the last 30 years would do nothing to reverse the social capital losses.

Generational Effects

Our efforts thus far to localize the sources of civic disengagement have been singularly unfruitful. The downtrends are uniform across the major categories of American society—among men and among women; in central cities, in suburbs, and in small towns; among the wealthy, the poor, and the middle class; among blacks, whites, and other ethnic groups; in the North, in the South, on both coasts, and in the heartland. One notable exception to this uniformity, however, involves age. In all our statistical analyses, age is second only to education as a predictor of all forms of civic engagement and trust. Older people belong to more organizations than young people,

Figure 3 • Group Membership by Race and Racism, 1974–1994 (education controlled)

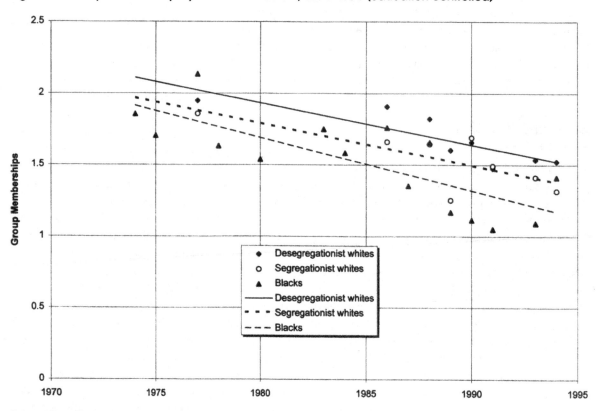

Source: General Social Survey, 1972-1994
Equal weighting of three educational categories.
White segregationism measured by support for racial segregation in social club.

and they are less misanthropic. Older Americans also vote more often and read newspapers more frequently, two other forms of civic engagement closely correlated with joining and trusting.

Figure 4 shows the basic pattern—civic involvement appears to rise more or less steadily from early adulthood toward a plateau in middle age, from which it declines only late in life. This humpback pattern, familiar from many analyses of social participation, including time-budget studies (Robinson and Godbey 1995), seems naturally to represent the arc of life's engagements. Most observers have interpreted this pattern as a life cycle phenomenon, and so, at first, did I.

Evidence from the General Social Survey enables us to follow individual cohorts as they age. If the rising lines in Figure 4 represent deepening civic engagement with age, then we should be able to track this same deepening engagement as we follow, for example, the first of the baby boomers—born in 1947—as they aged from 25 in 1972 (the first year of the GSS) to 47 in 1994 (the latest year available). Startlingly, however, such an analysis, repeated for successive birth cohorts, produces virtually no evidence of such life cycle changes in civic engagement. In fact, as various generations moved through the period between 1972 and 1994, their levels of trust and membership more often fell

Figure 4 • Civic Engagement by Age (education controlled)

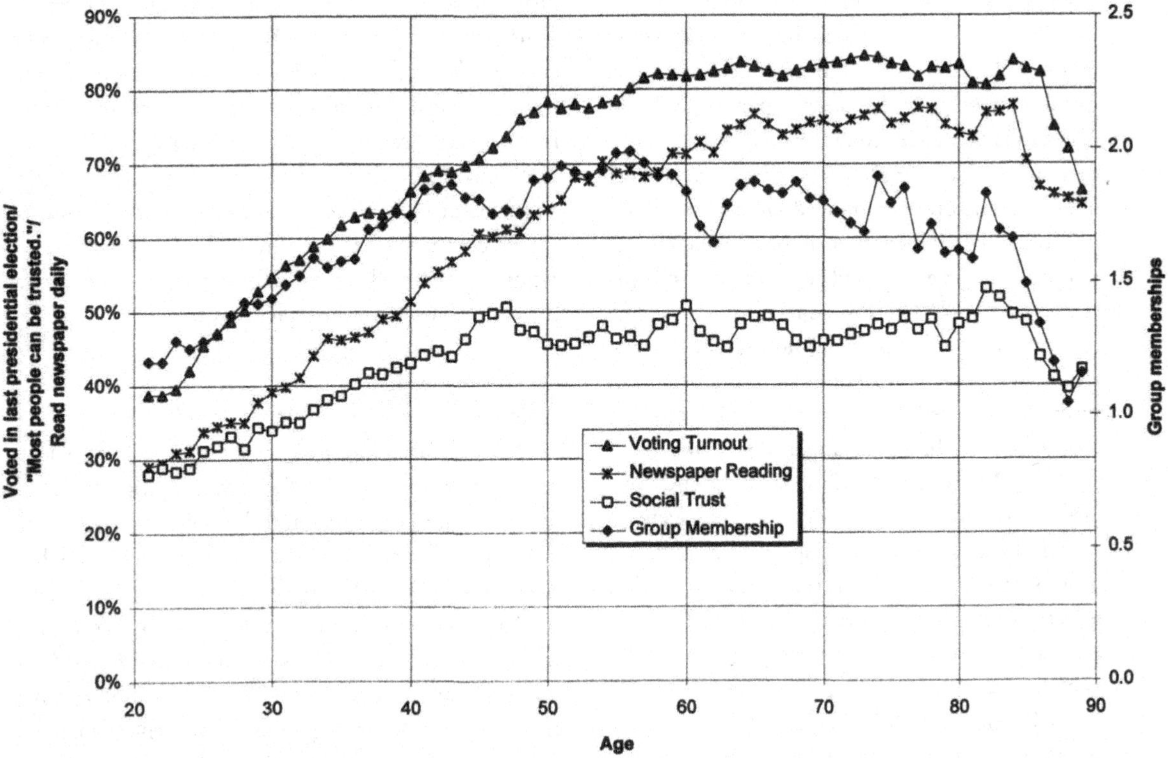

Source: General Social Survey, 1972-1994
Respondents aged 21-89. Three-year moving averages.
Equal weighting of three educational categories.

than rose, reflecting a more or less simultaneous de-cline in civic engagement among young and old alike, particularly during the second half of the 1980s. But that downtrend obviously cannot explain why, through-out the period, older Americans were always more trusting and engaged. In fact, the only reliable life cycle effect visible in these data is a withdrawal from civic engagement very late in life, as we move through our 80s.

The central paradox posed by these patterns is this: Older people are consistently more engaged and trust-ing than younger people, yet we do not become more engaged and trusting as we age. What's going on here?

Time and age are notoriously ambiguous in their effects on social behavior. Social scientists have learned to distinguish three contrasting phenomena:

1. *Life-cycle effects* represent differences attributable to stage of life. In this case individuals change as they age, but since the effects of aging are, in the aggre-gate, neatly balanced by the "demographic metabo-lism" of births and deaths, life cycle effects produce no aggregate change. Everyone's close-focus eye-sight worsens as we age, but the aggregate demand for reading glasses changes little.

2. *Period effects* affect all people who live through a given era, regardless of their age.[23] Period effects

can produce both individual and aggregate change, often quickly and enduringly, without any age-related differences. The sharp drop in trust in government between 1965 and 1975, for example, was almost entirely this sort of period effect, as Americans of all ages changed their minds about their leaders' trustworthiness. Similarly, as just noted, a modest portion of the decline in social capital during the 1980s appears to be a period effect.

3. *Generational effects,* as described in Karl Mannheim's classic essay on "The Problem of Generations," represent the fact that "[i]ndividuals who belong to the same generation, who share the same year of birth, are endowed, to that extent, with a common location in the historical dimension of the social process" (Mannheim 1952, 290). Like life cycle effects (and unlike typical period effects), generational effects show up as disparities among age groups at a single point in time, but like period effects (and unlike life cycle effects) generational effects produce real social change, as successive generations, enduringly "imprinted" with divergent outlooks, enter and leave the population. In pure generational effects, no individual ever changes, but society does.

At least since the landmark essay by Converse (1976), social scientists have recognized that to sort out life cycle, period, and generational effects requires sensitivity to a priori plausibility, "side knowledge," and parsimony, not merely good data and sophisticated math. In effect, cohort analysis inevitably involves more unknowns than equations. With some common sense, some knowledge of history, and some use of Ockham's razor, however, it is possible to exclude some alternatives and focus on more plausible interpretations.

Returning to our conundrum, how could older people today be more engaged and trusting, if they did not become more engaged and trusting as they aged? The key to this paradox, as David Butler and Donald Stokes (1974) observed in another context, is to ask, not *how old people are,* but *when they were young.* Figure 5 addresses this reformulated question, displaying various measures of

civic engagement according to the respondents' year of birth.[24] (Figure 5 includes data on voting from the National Election Studies, since Miller 1992 and Miller and Shanks 1995 have drawn on that data to demonstrate powerful generational effects on turnout, and it is instructive to see how parallel are the patterns that they discovered for voting turnout and the patterns for civic engagement that concern us here.[25] The figure also includes data on social trust from the National Election Studies, which will prove useful in parsing generational, life cycle, and period interpretations.)

The Long Civic Generation

In effect, Figure 5 lines up Americans from left to right according to their date of birth, beginning with those born in the last third of the nineteenth century and continuing across to the generation of their great-grandchildren, born in the last third of the twentieth century. As we begin moving along this queue from left to right—from those raised around the turn of the century to those raised during the Roaring Twenties, and so on—we find relatively high and unevenly rising levels of civic engagement and social trust. Then rather abruptly, however, we encounter signs of reduced community involvement, starting with men and women born in the early 1930s. Remarkably, this downward trend in joining, trusting, voting, and newspaper reading continues almost uninterruptedly for nearly 40 years. The trajectories for the various different indicators of civic engagement are strikingly parallel: each shows a high, sometimes rising plateau for people born and raised during the first third of the century; each shows a turning point in the cohorts born around 1930; and each then shows a more or less constant decline down to the cohorts born during the 1960s.[26]

By any standard, these intergenerational differences are extraordinary. Compare, for example, the generation born in the early 1920s with the generation of their grandchildren born in the late 1960s. Controlling for educational disparities, members of the generation born in the 1920s belong to almost twice as many civic associations as those born in the late 1960s (roughly 1.9 memberships

Figure 5 • Social Capital and Civic Engagement by Generation (education controlled)

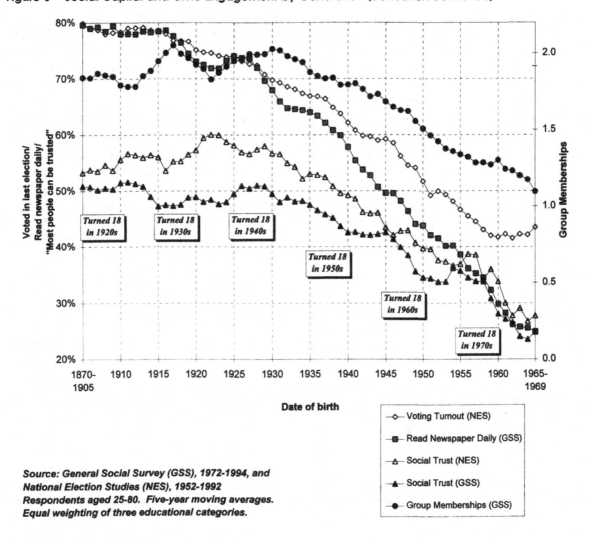

*Source: General Social Survey (GSS), 1972-1994, and
National Election Studies (NES), 1952-1992
Respondents aged 25-80. Five-year moving averages.
Equal weighting of three educational categories.*

per capita, compared to roughly 1.1 memberships per capita). The grandparents are more than twice as likely to trust other people (50–60% compared with 25% for the grandchildren). They vote at nearly double the rate of the most recent cohorts (roughly 75% compared with 40–45%), and they read newspapers almost three times as often (70–80% read a paper daily compared with 25–30%). And bear in mind that we have found no evidence that the youngest generation will come to match

their grandparent's higher levels of civic engagement as they grow older.

Thus, read not as life cycle effects, but rather as generational effects, the age-related patterns in our data suggest a radically different interpretation of our basic puzzle. Deciphered with this key, Figure 5 depicts a long "civic" generation, born roughly between 1910 and 1940, a broad group of people substantially more engaged in community affairs and substantially more trusting than those younger than they.[27] The culminating point of this civic generation is the cohort born in 1925–1930, who attended grade school during the Great Depression, spent World War II in high school (or on the battlefield), first voted in 1948 or 1952, set up housekeeping in the 1950s, and watched their first television when they were in their late twenties. Since national surveying began, this cohort has been exceptionally civic: voting more, joining more, reading newspapers more, trusting more. As the distinguished sociologist Charles Tilly (born in 1928) said in commenting on an early version of this essay, "we are the last suckers."

To help in interpreting the historical contexts within which these successive generations of Americans matured, Figure 5 also indicates the decade within which each cohort came of age. Thus, we can see that each generation who reached adulthood since the 1940s has been less engaged in community affairs than its immediate predecessor.

Further confirmation of this *generational* interpretation comes from a comparison of the two parallel lines that chart responses to an identical question about social trust, posed first in the National Election Studies (mainly between 1964 and 1976) and then in the General Social Survey between 1972 and 1994.[28] If the greater trust expressed by Americans born earlier in the century represented a *life cycle* effect, then the graph from the GSS surveys (conducted when these cohorts were, on average, 10 years older) should have been some distance *above* the NES line. In fact, the GSS line lies about 5–10% *below* the NES line. That downward shift almost surely represents a *period* effect that depressed social trust among all cohorts during the 1980s.[29] That downward period effect, however, is substantially more modest than the large generational differences already noted.

In short, the most parsimonious interpretation of the age-related differences in civic engagement is that they represent a powerful reduction in civic engagement among Americans who came of age in the decades after World War II, as well as some modest additional disengagement that affected all cohorts during the 1980s. These patterns hint that being raised after World War II was a quite different experience from being raised before

that watershed. It is as though the postwar generations were exposed to some mysterious X-ray that permanently and increasingly rendered them less likely to connect with the community. Whatever that force might have been, *it*—rather than anything that happened during the 1970s and 1980s—accounts for most of the civic disengagement that lies at the core of our mystery.

But if this reinterpretation of our puzzle is correct, why did it take so long for the effects of that mysterious X-ray to become manifest? If the underlying causes of civic disengagement can be traced to the 1940s and 1950s, why did the effects become conspicuous in PTA meetings and Masonic lodges, in the volunteer lists of the Red Cross and the Boy Scouts, and in polling stations and church pews and bowling alleys across the land only during the 1960s, 1970s, and 1980s?

The visible effects of this generational disengagement were delayed for several decades by two important factors:

1. The postwar boom in college enrollments boosted massive numbers of Americans up the sloping curve of civic engagement traced in Figure 2. Miller and Shanks (1995) observe that the postwar expansion of educational opportunities "forestalled a cataclysmic drop" in voting turnout, and it had a similar delaying effect on civic disengagement more generally.

2. The full effects of generational developments generally appear several decades after their onset, because it takes that long for a given generation to become numerically dominant in the adult population. Only after the mid-1960s did significant numbers of the "post-civic generation" reach adulthood, supplanting older, more civic cohorts. Figure 6 illustrates this generational accounting. The long civic generation (born between 1910 and 1940) reached its zenith in 1960, when it comprised 62% of those who chose between John Kennedy and Richard Nixon. By the time that Bill Clinton was elected president in 1992, that cohort's share in the electorate had been cut precisely in half.

Figure 6 • The Rise and Decline of a "Civic" Generation

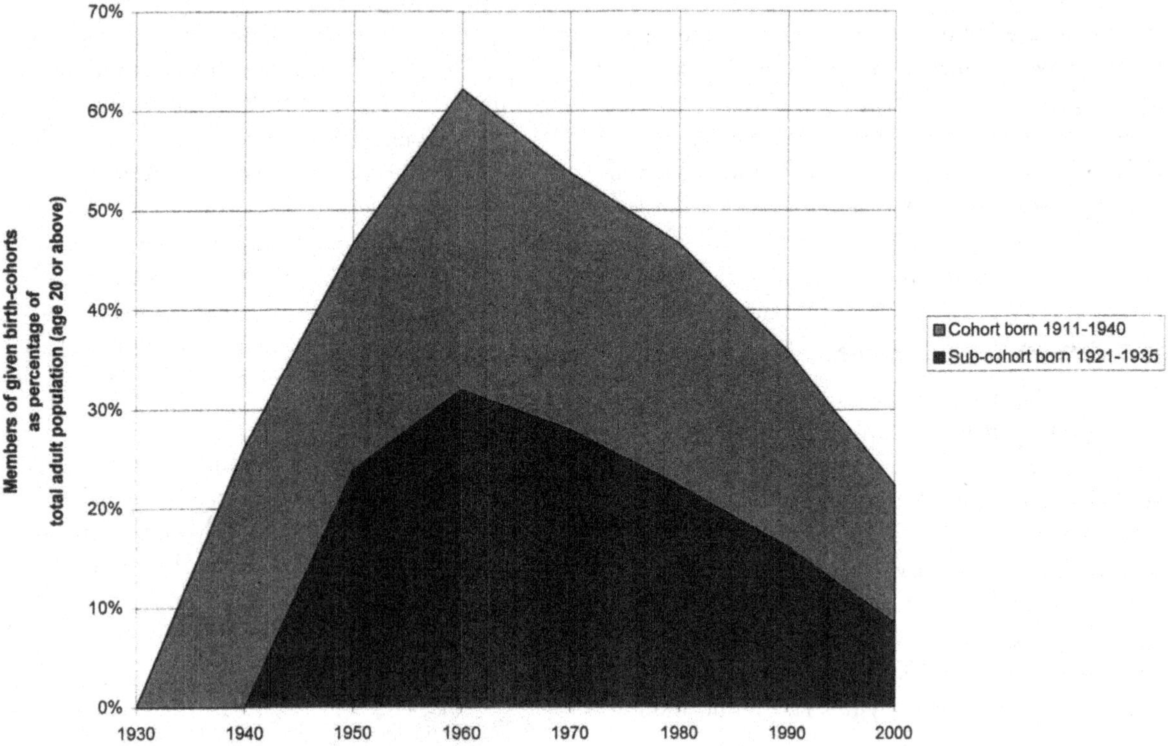

Source: Calculated from U.S. Census Bureau, Current Population Reports.

Conversely, over the last two decades (from 1974 to 1994) boomers and X-ers (that is, Americans born after 1946) have grown as a fraction of the adult population from 24% to 60%.

In short, the very decades that have seen a national deterioration in social capital are the same decades during which the numerical dominance of a trusting and civic generation has been replaced by the dominion of "post-civic" cohorts. Moreover, although the long civic generation has enjoyed unprecedented life expectancy, allowing its members to contribute more than their share to American social capital in recent decades, they are now passing from the scene. Even the youngest members of that generation will reach retirement age within

the next few years. Thus, a generational analysis leads almost inevitably to the conclusion that the national slump in trust and engagement is likely to continue, regardless of whether the more modest "period effect" depression of the 1980s continues.

More than two decades ago, just as the first signs of disengagement were beginning to appear in American politics, Ithiel de Sola Pool (1973, 818–21) observed that the central issue would be—it was then too soon to judge, as he rightly noted—whether the development represented a temporary change in the weather or a more enduring change in the climate. It now appears that much of the change whose initial signs he spotted did in fact reflect a climatic shift. Moreover, just as the erosion of the ozone layer was detected only many years after the proliferation of the chlorofluorocarbons that caused it, so too the erosion of America's social capital became visible only several decades after the underlying process had begun. Like Minerva's owl that flies at dusk, we come to appreciate how important the long civic generation has been to American community life just as its members are retiring. Unless America experiences a dramatic upward boost in civic engagement (a favorable "period effect") in the next few years, Americans in 2010 will join, trust, and vote even less than we do today.

The Puzzle Reformulated

To say that civic disengagement in contemporary America is in large measure generational merely reformulates our central puzzle. We now know that much of the cause of our lonely bowling probably dates to the 1940s and 1950s, rather than to the 1960s and 1970s. What could have been the mysterious anti-civic "X-ray" that affected Americans who came of age after World War II and whose effects progressively deepened at least into the 1970s?[30]

A number of superficially plausible candidates fail to fit the timing required by this new formulation of our mystery.

- Family instability seems to have an ironclad alibi for what we have now identified as the critical period, for the generational decline in civic engagement began with the children of the maritally stable 1940s and 1950s.[31] The divorce rate in America actually fell after 1945, and the sharpest jump in the divorce rate did not occur until the 1970s, long after the cohorts who show the sharpest declines in civic engagement and social trust had left home. Similarly, working mothers are exonerated by this re-specification of our problem, for the plunge in civicness among children of the 1940s, 1950s, and 1960s happened while mom was still at home.

- Our new formulation of the puzzle opens the possibility that the *Zeitgeist* of national unity and patriotism that culminated in 1945 might have reinforced civicmindedness. On the other hand, it is hard to assign any consistent role to the Cold War and the Bomb, since the anti-civic trend appears to have deepened steadily from the 1940s to the 1970s, in no obvious harmony with the rhythms of world affairs. Nor is it easy to construct an interpretation of Figure 5 in which the cultural vicissitudes of "the Sixties" could play a significant role.

- Neither economic adversity nor affluence can easily be tied to the generational decline in civic engagement, since the slump seems to have affected in equal measure those who came of age in the placid Fifties, the booming Sixties, and the busted Seventies.

I have discovered only one prominent suspect against whom circumstantial evidence can be mounted, and in this case, it turns out, some directly incriminating evidence has also turned up. This is not the occasion to lay out the full case for the prosecution, nor to review rebuttal evidence for the defense. However, I want to illustrate the sort of evidence that justifies indictment. The culprit is television.

First, the timing fits. The long civic generation was the last cohort of Americans to grow up without television, for television flashed into American society like lightning in the 1950s. In 1950 barely 10% of American homes had television sets, but by 1959 90% did, probably the fastest diffusion of a technological innovation ever recorded. The reverberations from this lightning bolt continued for decades, as viewing hours per capita grew by 17–20% during the 1960s and by an additional 7–8% during the 1970s. In the early years, TV watching was concentrated among the less educated sectors of the population, but during the 1970s the viewing time of the more educated sectors of the population began to converge upward. Television viewing increases with age, particularly upon retirement, but each generation since the introduction of television has begun its life cycle at a higher starting point. By 1995, viewing per TV household was more than 50% higher than it had been in the 1950s.[32]

Most studies estimate that the average American now watches roughly four hours per day.[33] Robinson (1990b), using the more conservative time-budget technique for determining how people allocate their time, offers an estimate closer to three hours per day, but concludes that as a primary activity, television absorbs 40% of the average American's free time, an increase of about one-third since 1965. Moreover, multiple sets have proliferated: by the late 1980s, three quarters of all U.S. homes had more than one set (Comstock 1989), and these numbers too are rising steadily, allowing ever more private viewing. In short, as Robinson and Godbey (1995) conclude, "television is the 800-pound gorilla of leisure time." This massive change in the way Americans spend our days and nights occurred precisely during the years of generational civic disengagement.

Evidence of a link between the arrival of television and the erosion of social connections is, however, not merely circumstantial. The links between civic engagement and television viewing can instructively be compared with the links between civic engagement and newspaper reading. The basic contrast is straightforward: newspaper reading is associated with high social capital, TV viewing with low social capital.

Controlling for education, income, age, race, place of residence, work status, and gender, TV viewing is strongly and negatively related to social trust and group membership, whereas the same correlations with newspaper reading are positive. Figure 7 shows that within every educational category, heavy readers are avid joiners,

Figure 7 • Group Membership by Newspaper Readership and Education

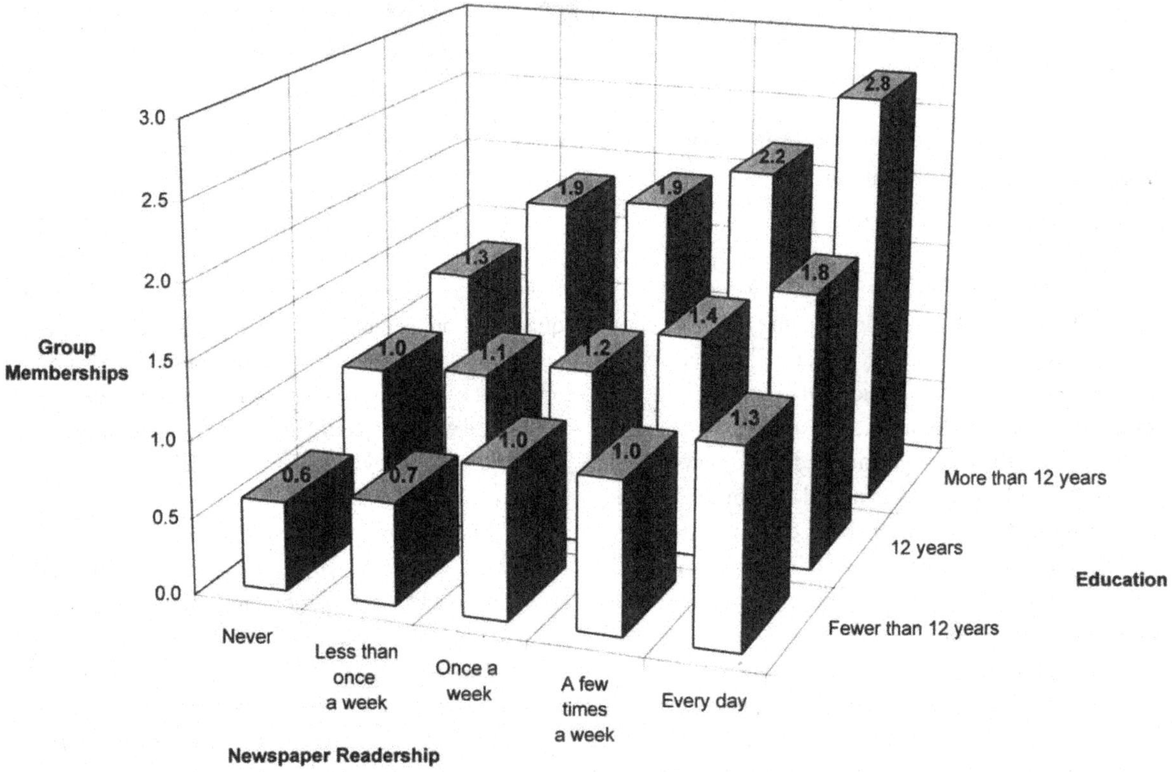

Source: General Social Survey, 1974-1994

Figure 8 • Group Membership by Television Viewing and Education

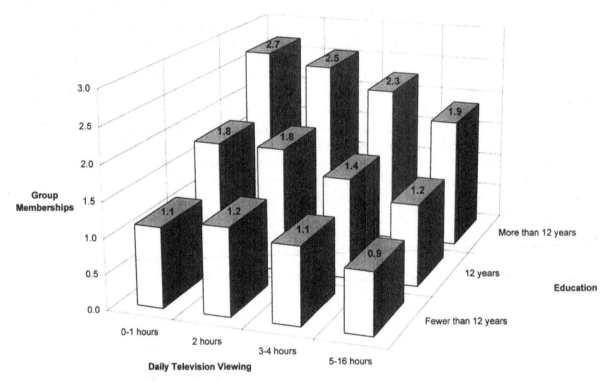

Source: General Social Survey, 1974-1994

whereas Figure 8 shows that heavy viewers are more likely to be loners.[34] Viewing and reading are themselves uncorrelated—some people do lots of both, some do little of either—but Figure 9 shows that (controlling for education, as always) "pure readers" (that is, people who watch less TV than average and read more newspapers than average) belong to 76% more civic organizations than "pure viewers." Precisely the same pattern applies to other indicators of civic engagement, including social trust and voting turnout. "Pure readers," for example, are 55% more trusting than "pure viewers."[35]

In other words, each hour spent viewing television is associated with less social trust and less group membership, while each hour reading a newspaper is associated with more. An increase in television viewing of the magnitude that the United States has experienced in the last

four decades might directly account for as much as one-quarter to one-half of the total drop in social capital, even without taking into account, for example, the indirect effects of television viewing on newspaper readership or the cumulative effects of "life-time" viewing hours.[36]

How might television destroy social capital?

• *Time displacement.* Even though there are only 24 hours in everyone's day, most forms of social and media participation are positively correlated. People who listen to lots of classical music are more likely, not less likely, than others to attend Cubs games. Television is the principal exception to this generalization—the only leisure activity that seems to inhibit participation outside the home. TV watching comes at the expense of

Figure 9 • Group Membership by Media Usage (education controlled)

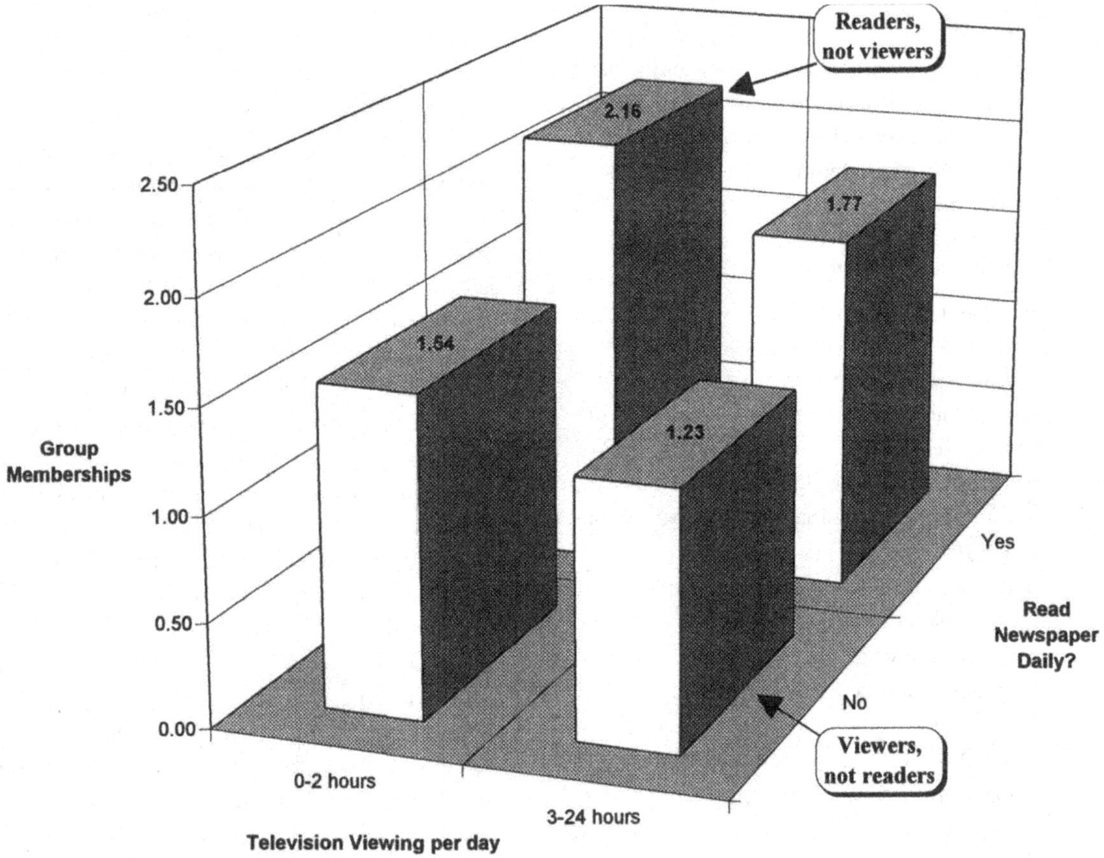

Source: General Social Survey, 1974-1994
Entries based on three equally
weighted educational categories.

nearly every social activity outside the home, especially social gatherings and informal conversations (Comstock et al 1978; Comstock 1989; Bower 1985; and Robinson and Godbey 1995). TV viewers are homebodies.

Most studies that report a negative correlation between television watching and community involvement (including my Figure 7) are ambiguous with respect to causality, because they merely compare different individuals at a single time. However, one important quasi-experimental study

of the introduction of television in three Canadian towns (Williams 1986) found the same pattern at the aggregate level across time: a major effect of television's arrival was the reduction in participation in social, recreational, and community activities among people of all ages. In short, television is privatizing our leisure time.

- *Effects on the outlooks of viewers.* An impressive body of literature, gathered under the rubric of the "mean world effect," suggests that heavy watchers of TV are unusually skeptical about the benevolence of other people—overestimating crime rates, for example. This body of literature has generated much debate about the underlying causal patterns, with skeptics suggesting that misanthropy may foster couch-potato behavior rather than the reverse. While awaiting better experimental evidence, however, a reasonable interim judgment is that heavy television watching may well increase pessimism about human nature (Gerbner et al 1980; Dobb and MacDonald 1979; Hirsch 1980; Hughes 1980; and Comstock 1989, 265–69). Perhaps, too, as social critics have long argued, both the medium and the message have more basic effects on our ways of interacting with the world and with one another. Television may induce passivity, as Postman (1985) has claimed, and it may even change our fundamental physical and social perceptions, as Meyrowitz (1985) has suggested.

- *Effects on children.* TV occupies an extraordinary part of children's lives—consuming about 40 hours per week on average. Viewing is especially high among pre-adolescents, but it remains high among younger adolescents: time-budget studies (Carnegie Council on Adolescent Development 1993, 5, citing Timmer et al. 1985) suggest that among youngsters aged 9–14 television consumes as much time as *all other discretionary activities combined,* including playing, hobbies, clubs, outdoor activities, informal visiting, and just hanging out. The effects of television on childhood socialization have, of course, been hotly debated for more than three decades. The most reasonable conclusion from a welter of sometimes conflicting results appears to be that heavy television watching probably increases aggressiveness (although perhaps not actual violence), that it probably reduces school achievement, and that it is statistically associated with "psychosocial malfunctioning," although how much of this effect is self-selection and how much causal remains much debated (Condry 1993). The evidence is, as I have said, not yet enough to convict, but the defense has a lot of explaining to do.

Conclusion

Ithiel de Sola Pool's posthumous book, *Technologies Without Borders* (1990), is a prescient work, astonishingly relevant to our current national debates about the complicated links among technology, public policy, and culture. Pool defended what he called "soft technological determinism." Revolutions in communications technologies have profoundly affected social life and culture, as the printing press helped bring on the Reformation. Pool concluded that the electronic revolution in communications technology, whose outlines he traced well before most of us were even aware of the impending changes, was the first major technological advance in centuries that would have a profoundly decentralizing and fragmenting effect on society and culture.

Pool hoped that the result might be "community without contiguity." As a classic liberal, he welcomed the benefits of technological change for individual freedom, and, in part, I share that enthusiasm. Those of us who bemoan the decline of community in contemporary America need to be sensitive to the liberating gains achieved during the same decades. We need to avoid an uncritical nostalgia for the Fifties. On the other hand, some of the same freedom-friendly technologies whose rise Pool predicted may indeed be undermining our connections with one another and with our communities. I suspect that Pool would have been open to that argument, too, for one of Pool's most talented protégés, Samuel Popkin (1991, 226–31), has argued that the rise of television and the correlative decline of social interaction have impaired American political discourse. The last line in Pool's last book (1990, 262) is this: "We may suspect that [the technological trends that we can anticipate] will promote individualism and will make it harder, not easier, to govern and organize a coherent society."

Pool's technological determinism was "soft" precisely because he recognized that social values can condition the effects of technology. In the end this perspective invites us not merely to consider how technology is privatizing our lives—if, as it seems to me, it is—but to ask whether we entirely like the result, and if not, what we might do about it. But that is a topic for another day. ∎

Notes

1. I wish to thank several researchers for sharing valuable unpublished work on related themes: John Brehm and Wendy Rahn (1995); Warren Miller and Merrill Shanks (1995); John Robinson and Geoffrey Godbey (1995); and Eric Uslaner (1995). Professor Uslaner was generous in helping track down some elusive data and commenting on an earlier draft. I also wish to thank a fine team of research assistants, including Jay Braatz, Maryann Barakso, Karen Ferree, Archon Fung, Louise Kennedy, Jeff Kling, Kimberly Lochner, Karen Rothkin, and Mark Warren. Support for the research project from which this study derives has been provided by the Aspen Institute, Carnegie Corporation, the Ford, Kovler, Norman, and Rockefeller foundations, and Harvard University.

2. In this respect I deviate slightly from James Coleman's "functional" definition of social capital. See Coleman (1990): 300–21.

3. The results reported in this paragraph and throughout the paper, unless otherwise indicated, are derived from the General Social Survey. These exceptionally useful data derive from a series of scientific surveys of the adult American population, conducted nearly every year since 1972 by the National Opinion Research Center, under the direction of James A. Davis and Tom W. Smith. The cumulative sample size is approximately 32,000, although the questions on trust and group membership that are at the focus of our inquiry have not been asked of all respondents in all years. Our measure of trust derives from this question: "Generally speaking, would you say that most people can be trusted, or that you can't be too careful in dealing with people?"; for this question, N = 22390. For evidence confirming the power of this simple measure of social trust, see Uslaner (1995). Our measure of group membership derives from this question: "Now we would like to know something about the groups or organizations to which individuals belong. Here is a list of various organizations. Could you tell me whether or not you are a member of each type?" The list includes fraternal groups, service clubs, veterans' groups, political clubs, labor unions, sports groups, youth groups, school service groups, hobby or garden clubs, social fraternities or sororities, nationality groups, farm organizations, literary, arts, discussion or study groups, professional or academic societies, church-affiliated groups, and any other groups. For this question, N = 19326. Neither of these questions, of course, is a perfect measure of social capital. In particular, our measure of multiple memberships refers not to total groups, but to total *types* of groups. On the other hand, "noise" in data generally depresses observed correlations below the "true" value, so our findings are more likely to understate than to exaggerate patterns in the "real world."

4. Across the 35 countries for which data are available from the World Values Survey (1990–91), the correlation between the average number of associational memberships and endorsement of the view that "most people can be trusted" is r .65. Across the 42 states for which adequate samples are available in the General Social Survey (1972–1994), the comparable correlation is r .71. Across individuals in the General Social Survey (1972–1994), controlling for education, race, and age, social trust is significantly and separately correlated with membership in political clubs, literary groups, sports clubs, hobby and garden clubs, youth groups, school service groups, and other associations. The correlation with social trust is insignificant only for veterans groups, labor unions, and nationality groups.

5. The 1965 sample, which was limited to nonretired residents of cities between 30,000 and 280,000 population, was not precisely equivalent to the later national samples, so appropriate adjustments need to be made to ensure comparability. For the 1965–1975 comparison, see Robinson (1981, 125). For the 1975–1985 comparison (but apparently without adjustment for the 1965 sampling peculiarities), see Cutler (1990). Somewhat smaller declines are reported in Robinson and Godbey (1995), although it is unclear whether they correct for the sampling differences. Additional work to refine these cross-time comparisons is required and is currently underway.

6. Trust in political authorities—and indeed in many social institutions—has also declined sharply over the last three decades, but that is conceptually a distinct trend. As we shall see later, the etiology of the slump in social trust is quite different from the etiology of the decline in political trust.

7. For reasons explained below, Figure 1 reports trends for membership in various types of groups, *controlling for* the respondent's education level.

8. Some commentaries on "Bowling Alone" have been careless, however, in reporting apparent membership growth. *The Economist* (1995, 22), for example, celebrated a recent rebound in total membership in parent-teacher organizations, without acknowledging that this rebound is almost entirely attributable to the growing number of children. The fraction of parents who belong to PTAs has regained virtually none of the 50% fall that this metric registered between 1960 and 1975. Despite talk about the growth of "support groups," another

oft-cited counter-example, I know of no statistical substantiation for this claim. One might even ask whether the vaunted rise in neighborhood watch groups might not represent only a partial, artificial replacement for the vanished social capital of traditional neighborhoods—a kind of sociological Astroturf, suitable only where you can't grow the real thing. See also Glenn (1987, S124) for survey evidence of "an increased tendency for individuals to withdraw allegiance from . . . anything outside of themselves."

9. The only exceptions are farm groups, labor unions, and veterans' organizations, whose members have slightly less formal education than the average American. Interestingly, sports clubs are *not* an exception; college graduates are nearly three times more likely to belong to a sports group than are high school drop-outs. Education is un-correlated with church attendance, but positively correlated with membership in church-related groups.

10. For a thorough recent investigation of the role of education in accounting for differences in political participation, see Verba, Schlozman, and Brady (1995).

11. As a practical matter, all subsequent statistical presentations here implement this precept by equally weighing respondents from three broad educational categories—those with fewer than 12 years of formal schooling, those with exactly 12 years, and those with more than 12 years. Conveniently, this categorization happens to slice the 1972–1994 GSS sample into nearly equal thirds. The use of more sophisticated mathematical techniques to control for educational differences would alter none of the central conclusions of this essay.

12. The downturns in both joining and trusting seem to be somewhat greater among Americans on the middle rungs of the educational ladder—high school graduates and college dropouts—than among those at the very top and bottom of the educational hierarchy, but the differences are not great, and the trends are statistically significant at all levels.

13. This is true with or without controls for education and year of survey. The patterns among men and women on this score are not identical, for women who work part-time appear to be somewhat more civically engaged and socially trusting than either those who work full-time or those who do not work outside the home at all. Whatever we make of this intriguing anomaly, which apparently does not appear in the time budget data (Robinson and Godbey 1995) and which has no counterpart in the male half of the population, it cannot account for our basic puzzle, since female part-time workers constitute a relatively

small fraction of the American population, and the fraction is growing, not declining. Between the first half of the 1970s and the first half of the 1990s, according to the GSS data, the fraction of the total adult population constituted by female part-time workers rose from about 8% to about 10%.

14. Evidence on generational differences presented below reinforces this conclusion.

15. Robinson and Godbey (1995), however, report that nonemployed women still spend more time on activity in voluntary associations than their employed counterparts.

16. Multivariate analysis hints that one major reason why divorce lowers connectedness is that it lowers family income, which in turn reduces civic engagement.

17. I have set aside this issue for fuller treatment in later work. However, I note for the record that (1) state-level differences in social trust and group membership are substantial, closely intercorrelated, and reasonably stable, at least over the period from the 1970s to the 1990s, and (2) those differences are surprisingly closely correlated ($R^2 = .52$) with the measure of "state political culture" invented by Elazar (1966), and refined by Sharkansky (1969), based on descriptive accounts of state politics during the 1950s and traceable in turn to patterns of immigration during the nineteenth century and before.

18. Public expenditure as a percentage of GDP in 1989 is correlated r −.29 with 1990–1991 trust and r −.48 with 1990–1991 associational memberships.

19. For broadly similar conclusions, see Verba, Schlozman, and Brady (1995, 241–47) and the sources cited there.

20. As elsewhere in this essay, "controlling for educational differences" here means averaging the average scores for respondents with fewer than 12 years of schooling, with exactly 12 years, and with more than 12 years, respectively.

21. White support for segregation in Figure 3 is measured by responses to this question in the General Social Survey: "If you and your friends belonged to a social club that would not let Blacks join, would you try to change the rules so that Blacks could join?" Essentially identical results obtain if we measure white racism instead by support for antimiscegenation laws or for residential segregation.

22. As we shall see in a moment, much civic disengagement actually appears to be generational, affecting people born after 1930, but not those born before. If this phenomenon represented white flight from integrated community life after the civil rights revolution, it is difficult to see why the trend should be so much more marked among those who came of age in the

more tolerant 1960s and 1970s, and hardly visible at all among those who came of age in the first half of the century, when American society was objectively more segregated and subjectively more racist.

23. Period effects that affect only people of a specific age shade into generational effects, which is why Converse, when summarizing these age-related effects, refers to "two-and-a-half" types, rather than the conventional three types.

24. To exclude the life cycle effects in the last years of life, Figure 5 excludes respondents over 80. To avoid well-known problems in reliably sampling young adults, as discussed by Converse (1976), Figure 5 also excludes respondents aged under 25. To offset the relatively small year-by-year samples and to control for educational differences, Figure 5 charts five-year moving averages across the three educational categories used in this essay.

25. I learned of the Miller/Shanks argument only after discovering generational differences in civic engagement in the General Social Survey data, but their findings and mine are strikingly consistent.

26. Too few respondents born in the late nineteenth century appear in surveys conducted in the 1970s and 1980s for us to discern differences among successive birth cohorts with great reliability. However, those scant data (not broken out in Figure 5) suggest that the turn of the century might have been an era of rising civic engagement. Similarly, too few respondents born after 1970 have yet appeared in national surveys for us to be confident about their distinctive generational profile, although the slender results so far seem to suggest that the 40-year generational plunge in civic engagement might be bottoming out. However, even if this turns out to be true, it will be several decades before that development could arrest the aggregate drop in civic engagement, for reasons subsequently explained in the text.

27. Members of the 1910–1940 generation also seem more civic than their elders, at least to judge by the outlooks of the relatively few men and women born in the late nineteenth century who appeared in our samples.

28. The question on social trust appeared biennially in the NES from 1964 to 1976 and then reappeared in 1992. I have included the 1992 NES interviews in the analysis in order to obtain estimates for cohorts too young to have appeared in the earlier surveys.

29. Additional analysis of indicators of civic engagement in the GSS, not reported in detail here, confirms this downward shift during the 1980s.

30. I record here one theory attributed variously to Robert Salisbury (1985), Gerald Gamm, and Simon and Garfunkel. Devotees of our national pastime will recall that Joe Dimaggio signed with the Yankees in 1936, just as the last of the long civic generation was beginning to follow the game, and he turned center field over to Mickey Mantle in 1951, just as the last of "the suckers" reached legal maturity. Almost simultaneously, the Braves, the Athletics, the Browns, the Senators, the Dodgers, and the Giants deserted cities that had been their homes since the late nineteenth century. By the time Mantle in turn left the Yankees in 1968, much of the damage to civic loyalty had been done. This interpretation explains why Mrs. Robinson's plaintive query that year about Joltin' Joe's whereabouts evoked such widespread emotion. A deconstructionist analysis of social capital's decline would highlight the final haunting lamentation, "our nation turns its *lonely* eyes to you" [emphasis added].

31. This exoneration applies to the possible effects of divorce on children, not to its effects on the couple themselves, as discussed earlier in this essay.

32. For introductions to the massive literature on the sociology of television, see Bower (1985), Comstock et al. (1978), Comstock (1989), and Graber (1993). The figures on viewing hours in the text are from Bower (1985, 33) and *Public Perspective* (1995, 47). Cohort differences are reported in Bower (1985, 46).

33. This figure excludes periods in which television is merely playing in the background. Comstock (1989, 17) reports that "on any fall day in the late 1980s, the set in the average television owning household was on for about eight hours."

34. In fact, multiple regression analysis, predicting civic engagement from television viewing and education, suggests that heavy TV watching is one important reason *why* less educated people are less engaged in the life of their communities. Controlling for differential TV exposure significantly reduces the correlation between education and engagement.

35. Controlling for education, 45% of respondents who watch TV two hours or less a day and read newspapers daily say that "most people can be trusted," as compared to 29% of respondents who watch TV three hours or more a day and do not read a newspaper daily.

36. Newspaper circulation (per household) has dropped by more than half since its peak in 1947. To be sure, it is not clear which way the tie between newspaper reading and civic involvement works, since disengagement might itself dampen one's interest in community news. But the two trends are clearly linked.

References

Bower, Robert T. 1985. *The Changing Television Audience in America.* New York: Columbia University Press.

Brehm, John, and Wendy Rahn. 1995. "An Audit of the Deficit in Social Capital." Durham, NC: Duke University. Unpublished manuscript.

Butler, David, and Donald Stokes. 1974. *Political Change in Britain: The Evolution of Electoral Choice,* 2nd ed. New York: St. Martin's.

Caplow, Theodore, Howard M. Bahr, John Modell, and Bruce A. Chadwick. 1991. *Recent Social Trends in the United States: 1960–1990.* Montreal: McGill–Queen's University Press.

Carnegie Council on Adolescent Development. 1993. *A Matter of Time: Risk and Opportunity in the Nonschool Hours: Executive Summary.* New York: Carnegie Corporation of New York.

Coleman, James. 1990. *Foundations of Social Theory.* Cambridge, MA: Harvard University Press.

Comstock, George. 1989. *The Evolution of American Television.* Newbury Park, CA: Sage.

Comstock, George, Steven Chaffee, Natan Katzman, Maxwell McCombs, and Donald Roberts. 1978. *Television and Human Behavior.* New York: Columbia University Press.

Condry, John. 1993. "Thief of Time, Unfaithful Servant: Television and the American Child," *Daedalus* 122 (Winter): 259–78.

Converse, Philip E. 1976. *The Dynamics of Party Support: Cohort-Analyzing Party Identification.* Beverly Hills, CA: Sage.

Cutler, Blaine. 1990. "Where Does the Free Time Go?" *American Demographics* (November): 36–39.

Davis, James Allan, and Tom W. Smith. *General Social Surveys, 1972–1994.* [machine readable data file]. Principal Investigator, James A. Davis; Director and Co-Principal Investigator, Tom W. Smith. NORC ed. Chicago: National Opinion Research Center, producer, 1994; Storrs, CT: The Roper Center for Public Opinion Research, University of Connecticut, distributor.

Dobb, Anthony N., and Glenn F. Macdonald. 1979. "Television Viewing and Fear of Victimization: Is the Relationship Causal?" *Journal of Personality and Social Psychology* 37: 170–79.

Edwards, Patricia Klobus, John N. Edwards, and Ann DeWitt Watts, "Women, Work, and Social Participation." *Journal of Voluntary Action Research* 13 (January–March, 1984), 7–22.

Elazar, Daniel J. 1966. *American Federalism: A View from the States.* New York: Crowell.

Fukuyama, Francis. 1995. *Trust: The Social Virtues and the Creation of Prosperity.* New York: The Free Press.

Gerbner, George, Larry Gross, Michael Morgan, and Nancy Signorielli. 1980. "The 'Mainstreaming' of America: Violence Profile No. 11," *Journal of Communication* 30 (Summer): 10–29.

Ginzberg, Eli. 1943. *The Unemployed.* New York: Harper and Brothers.

Glenn, Norval D. 1987. "Social Trends in the United States: Evidence from Sample Surveys." *Public Opinion Quarterly* 51: S109–S126.

Graber, Doris A. 1993. *Mass Media and American Politics.* Washington, DC: CQ Press.

Hirsch, Paul M. "The 'Scary World' of the Nonviewer and Other Anomalies: A Re-analysis of Gerbner et al.'s Findings on Cultivation Analysis, Part I," *Communication Research* 7 (October): 403–56.

Hughes, Michael. 1980. "The Fruits of Cultivation Analysis: A Re-examination of the Effects of Television Watching on Fear of Victimization, Alienation, and the Approval of Violence." *Public Opinion Quarterly* 44: 287–303.

Jahoda, Marie, Paul Lazarsfeld, and Hans Zeisel. 1933. *Marienthal.* Chicago: Aldine-Atherton.

Mannheim, Karl. 1952. "The Problem of Generations." In *Essays on the Sociology of Knowledge,* ed. Paul Kecskemeti. New York: Oxford University Press: 276–322.

Meyrowitz, Joshua. 1985. *No Sense of Place: The Impact of Electronic Media on Social Behavior.* New York: Oxford University Press.

Miller, Warren E. 1992. "The Puzzle Transformed: Explaining Declining Turnout." *Political Behavior* 14: 1–43.

Miller, Warren F., and J. Merrill Shanks. 1995. *The American Voter Reconsidered.* Tempe, AZ: Arizona State University. Unpublished manuscript.

Pool, Ithiel de Sola. 1973. "Public Opinion." In *Handbook of Communication,* ed. Ithiel de Sola Pool et al. Chicago: Rand McNally: 779–835.

Pool, Ithiel de Sola. 1990. *Technologies Without Boundaries: On Telecommunications in a Global Age.* Cambridge, MA: Harvard University Press.

Popkin, Samuel L. 1991. *The Reasoning Voter.* Chicago: University of Chicago Press.

Postman, Neil. 1985. *Amusing Ourselves to Death: Public Discourse in the Age of Show Business.* New York: Viking-Penguin Books.

Public Perspective. 1995. "People, Opinion, and Polls: American Popular Culture." 6 (August/September): 37–48.

Putnam, Robert D. 1993. *Making Democracy Work: Civic Traditions in Modern Italy.* Princeton, NJ: Princeton University Press.

Putnam, Robert D. 1995. "Bowling Alone, Revisited," *The Responsive Community* (Spring): 18–33.

Putnam, Robert D. 1996. "Bowling Alone: Democracy in America at the End of the Twentieth Century," forthcoming in a collective volume edited by Axel Hadenius. New York: Cambridge University Press.

Robinson, John. 1981. "Television and Leisure Time: A New Scenario," *Journal of Communication* 31 (Winter): 120–30.

Robinson, John. 1990a. "The Time Squeeze." *American Demographics* (February).

Robinson, John. 1990b. "I Love My TV." *American Demographics* (September): 24–27.

Robinson, John, and Geoffrey Godbey. 1995. *Time for Life.* College Park, MD: University of Maryland. Unpublished manuscript.

Rosenstone, Steven J., and John Mark Hansen. 1993. *Mobilization, Participation, and Democracy in America.* New York: Macmillan.

Salisbury, Robert H. 1985. "Blame Dismal World Conditions on . . . Baseball." *Miami Herald,* May 18, 27A.

Schor, Juliet. 1991. *The Overworked American.* New York: Basic Books.

Sharkansky, Ira. 1969. "The Utility of Elazar's Political Culture." *Polity* 2: 66–83.

The Economist. 1995. "The Solitary Bowler." 334 (18 February): 21–22.

Timmer, S. G., J. Eccles, and I. O'Brien. 1985. "How Children Use Time." In *Time, Goods, and Well-Being,* ed. F. T. Juster and F. B. Stafford. Ann Arbor, MI: University of Michigan, Institute for Social Research.

U.S. Bureau of the Census. 1995 (and earlier years). *Current Population Reports.* Washington, D.C.

Uslaner, Eric M. 1995. "Faith, Hope, and Charity: Social Capital, Trust, and Collective Action." College Park, MD: University of Maryland. Unpublished manuscript.

Verba, Sidney, Kay Lehman Schlozman, and Henry E. Brady. 1995. *Voice and Equality: Civic Volunteerism in American Politics.* Cambridge, MA: Harvard University Press.

Wilcock, Richard, and Walter H. Franke. 1963. *Unwanted Workers.* New York: Free Press of Glencoe.

Williams, Tannis Macbeth, ed. 1986. *The Impact of Television: A Natural Experiment in Three Communities.* New York: Academic Press.

Why Was This Research Needed?

1. In what way is Putnam's work on social capital in contemporary America rooted in his previous research abroad?
2. Putnam presents social capital as a variable having different possible forms and components. What difficulties does this complexity create for use of the concept in empirical research?
3. What is meant by the term *civic engagement*? What is the nature of the relationship between social capital and civic engagement, according to the author?
4. What central question does Putnam attempt to answer in his analysis?

How Was the Topic Studied?

1. What are the different sources of data in this study?
2. What independent variables does the author assess in trying to explain the erosion of social capital? What are his four criteria for judging the relevance of each variable he examines?
3. Why is the concept of statistical control crucial for this type of study? Explain Putnam's decision to use education as a standard control variable throughout his quantitative analysis.

What Are the Findings?

1. What kinds of evidence point to the decline of social capital in the United States during the last part of the twentieth century? How clearly does Putnam sketch this picture of decline?

2. What does it mean to say that education has a curvilinear relationship with civic engagement? Summarize the information presented in Figure 2.

3. What is the hypothesized relationship between economic factors and community involvement? Does Putnam's analysis strengthen or undermine this hypothesis?

4. What trends lead the author to qualify his earlier assumptions about the impact of residential mobility on civic engagement?

5. While the author is not convinced that increases in the number of women in the workplace have caused declines in civic engagement, he resists coming to any final conclusions regarding this trend. What makes this such a difficult topic to analyze?

6. Concerning changes in the institution of marriage and declining social capital, Putnam writes that "the disintegration of marriage is probably an accessory to the crime, but not the major villain of the piece." What does this statement mean?

7. How do interstate and cross-national comparisons lead to Putnam's rejection of the assertion that big government and the growth of the welfare state have undermined social capital?

8. What is the relationship between race and social capital according to the data in this study?

9. What is the distinction among life cycle effects, period effects, and generational effects when considering the connection between age and civic engagement? Why do the trends in Figure 5 focus Putnam's attention on the years after World War II as the formative era for changes in civic engagement?

10. What factor does Putnam ultimately identify as the likely major culprit in his mystery? What data analyses does he use to support this conclusion?

What Do the Results Mean?

1. How persuasive did you find the author's claims about Americans' increasing disengagement from civic life? Are there other variables you would propose measuring that are relevant to this issue?

2. Putnam's analysis is shaped, in part, by the kinds of information available to him in existing databases. Pick one of the independent variables in this study and explain how you would collect original data in a study of your own design to test the validity of the findings reported here. For example, how might data from a panel study taking repeated measurements of the same study group over time be useful?

3. Did you find the argument about the "privatizing" impact of TV watching in our culture plausible? What kinds of analysis would you propose for examining the civic engagement effects of different kinds of TV watching, such as news versus entertainment versus sports programs?

4. Why do you think Putnam's work has proved to be of such great interest to political leaders in the United States and elsewhere? If you were an elected official, how might the concepts of civic engagement and social capital be relevant for public policy development and rhetorical discourse? Do you think the decline of social capital is an issue more likely to be of concern to liberals or conservatives?

Afterword from Robert D. Putnam

More than a decade ago, I began to explore changes in Americans' civic engagement and social connectedness (for which I borrowed the term *social capital*) and the impact of those changes on U.S. communities and democracy. My initial findings, suggesting a remarkable decline in social capital nationwide, appeared in a 1995 article called "Bowling Alone" in the *Journal of Democracy*. A year later, *PS* published "Tuning In, Tuning Out: The Strange Disappearance of Social Capital in America," a preliminary investigation of explanations for the decline. Four years later I published a book-length treatment of the issue, drawing on a much richer range of evidence (Putnam 2000).

These writings—along with work by other scholars, some predating mine—triggered a massive international debate that has proved one of the most fecund controversies in recent scholarly and public life. Last year, after a decade of exponential growth, scholarly articles about social capital were appearing at a rate approaching one a day. Not all the research supported my thesis—far from it! Here I present a not-entirely-impartial assessment of what that debate has shown about four central questions raised by the original articles.

1. What has happened to civic engagement and social capital in America over the last 30 to 40 years?

The first wave of critical commentary suggested that I had missed some crucial countertrends, such as the rise of soccer teams and self-help groups; if only we looked more closely, the picture would supposedly not be so dire. But as I reported in *Bowling Alone,* the more data I gathered, the more dismal the picture became. Although disputes continue along the margins, this controversy has moved toward a broad consensus that the initial reaction of the American public to the debate was correct and that of the critics was wrong: We are, in fact, less civically engaged and socially connected than our parents were.

2. Why the decline?

"Tuning In, Tuning Out" identified several suspects, including a World War II generational effect, the movement of women into the workplace, and so on, although many read my argument as essentially monocausal—television as the root of all evil. Subsequent research supported many of the article's hypotheses, but I now think that my analysis overlooked three important factors: the growth of inequality, the growth of diversity, and the decay of mobilizing organizations. (I'm currently engaged in research on some of those omitted forces.)

3. Does it matter?

Most public commentators assumed all along that if civic engagement were, in fact, declining, it would be big news. Social scientists have been appropriately more cautious, wanting incontrovertible evidence that social capital is actually a cause, and not merely a correlate, of the benefits I claimed—better schools, longer lives, more responsive government, and so on. It is premature to render a final verdict on this still-heated debate, although I expect that more sophisticated research will, in the end, vindicate the importance of social connectivity for American politics and society. However, because correlation does not prove causation, and because experimental methods are difficult to apply with respect to broad hypotheses like these, rigorous tests of the consequences of social capital will not be easy.

4. What can we do about it?

The weakest part of my original argument was the paucity of solutions, and it remains so despite the creative insights of many people and my own efforts (Putnam, Feldstein, and Cohen 2003). That American democracy seems even less healthy today than it did a decade ago suggests that my diagnosis was right—and that practicable ideas for revitalizing American civic life are needed more urgently than ever.

References

Putnam, Robert D. 2000. *Bowling Alone: The Collapse and Revival of American Community.* New York: Simon and Schuster.

Putnam, Robert D., and Lewis Feldstein with Don Cohen. 2003. *Better Together: Restoring the American Community.* New York: Simon and Schuster.

Note: This afterword was adapted by the author from Putnam, Robert D. 2005. "1996: The Civic Enigma." *The American Prospect Online,* May 22. Used by permission of the author and publisher.

14

Choosing Canada? The 1995 Quebec Sovereignty Referendum

Harold D. Clarke and Allan Kornberg

When the citizens of Quebec went to the polls on October 30, 1995, the occasion could hardly have been more momentous. A referendum item on the ballot asked them to vote on the political identity of their province: the question to be decided was one of sovereignty, and it was uncertain what voting yes or no might mean for Quebec's future relationship with the rest of Canada. The referendum was the culmination of a longstanding historical tension between Canada's English- and French-speaking communities. Quebec nationalists viewed the vote as a means of preserving their province's distinctive Francophone culture. Others in the province feared the consequences—political, economic, and social—that might result from a withdrawal from the Canadian federation. With the stakes so high, voter participation in the referendum was expected to be virtually universal, and it was: 94 percent of those eligible voted. Once the votes were tallied, the outcome was remarkably close: 49.4 percent voted in favor of sovereignty, 50.6 percent against.

This was the second of two popular votes against separatism since 1980 (Brown 1996). The 1995 referendum was a serious political setback for the Quebec sovereignty movement, raising doubts about when—and under what conditions—the majority of Quebec's population would support this issue. From a political science research standpoint, the referendum also posed a variety of questions of interpretation. What was the relationship between voters' attitudes toward sovereignty and their feelings about a possible association between an independent Quebec and Canada? Were there patterns in how different demographic groups, particularly Francophone versus non-Francophone citizens, viewed the referendum? Did general perceptions about government and politics in Canada contribute to this voting outcome? How did voters' reactions to the political leaders at the forefront of the referendum debate influence the results?

In the following reading, Harold D. Clarke and Allan Kornberg address these questions. Students should note the various sources of data the authors use in providing their historical background of the Quebec sovereignty issue, in tracking changes in public opinion over the months leading up to the referendum, and in analyzing the final voting outcome. The article also provides a good illustration of how to construct an explanatory model based on several variables, in this case, both short- and long-term forces are hypothesized to affect a citizen's voting choice. Finally, the authors use the technique of multiple regression in a cumulative manner, showing the increasing power of their model overall as variables are entered in stages.

Reference

Brown, Craig, ed. 1996. *The Illustrated History of Canada.* Toronto: Lester Publishing.

". . . [T]he battle for the country is not over. And it will not be until we have one."

Quebec Premier Jacques Parizeau,
October 30, 1995

In his recent book on the many puzzles of Canadian nationalism, Richard Gwyn (1995, 9) notes that more Canadians (97%) cite their own country as the best in the world than do citizens of any other country. Notwithstanding this coup and the fact that Canada is one of the world's oldest continuously functioning democracies, in an October 30, 1995 referendum, the citizens of Quebec were again asked (as they had been in May 1980) to vote *oui* or *non* on a proposal that would secure the political independence of Quebec. Although Quebeckers rejected the 1980 sovereignty proposal by a three to two margin, the 1995 sovereignty proposal failed by the proverbial eyelash. Why a country described by British writer Jan Morris as "all in all, on the whole, the most admirable on earth" (cited in Gwyn 1995, 51) should periodically appear on the brink of falling apart is a question that has engaged us because of our longstanding interest in the conditions under which democratic political systems are sustained over time.

It can be argued that many of the conditions associated with the emergence and development of a democracy were already obtained in 1867 when the new Dominion of Canada was created by an act of the British parliament. *Inter alia,* these included a Westminster-model parliamen-

tary government, the rule of law, nascent political parties and free, competitive elections. However, as we have argued elsewhere (Kornberg and Clarke 1992, 12–19), the downside of "Confederation" (as the establishment of the Canadian state is termed) was that it either laid the groundwork for, or exacerbated, many of the national integration problems Canada has experienced. The poor "fit" between the country's geographic, social, and economic realities and its political institutions and processes is said to have generated and sustained ongoing center-periphery conflicts, fueled Anglophone-Francophone sociocultural disputes, and inhibited the development of a distinct and unifying national identity (e.g., Lipset 1990; Schwartz 1974). Of these, the most sustained and troubling problems have been strong regional cleavages based upon economic particularisms (the Western provinces), and sociocultural and linguistic ones (Quebec).

In Quebec, these reinforcing cleavages nurtured the growth of Québécois nationalism. After World War II, such nationalism evolved from an inward-looking, defensive posture to a confident, assertive one insisting that governmental power was required to foster Québécois language and culture, and to end Québécois economic domination (Cook 1995; McRoberts 1988). The "Quiet Revolution" of the early 1960s focused on securing greater provincial powers for Quebec within Confederation, but soon more radical voices demanded a sovereign state. In 1968, former provincial Liberal cabinet minister, Réne Lévesque, founded the Parti Québécois (PQ) as a "synthesis of all valid perspectives" in order to achieve that aim by democratic means. Pursuing an *étapiste* (step-by-step) strategy, the PQ's goal of a "ballot box revolution" became a serious threat to the continued integrity of Canada when the party won the 1976 provincial election. The PQ's subsequent 1980 sovereignty referendum failed in part because then-prime minister Pierre Trudeau offered Quebeckers a "renewed federalism" that seemingly promised to satisfy nationalist aspirations within the framework of a revised Canadian constitution. Although a new constitution became a reality in 1982, the PQ government of Quebec refused to endorse it (Russell 1992, ch. 3; see also Cairns 1992).

The PQ's defeat in the 1985 provincial election paved the way for the 1987 Meech Lake Constitutional Accord formulated by Progressive Conservative Prime Minister Brian Mulroney and the ten provincial premiers (Monahan 1991). In addition to several other constitutional revisions, the Accord recognized Quebec as a "distinct society" within Canada. However, its failure to secure ratification by all ten provinces within a proscribed three-year period sparked another constitutional crisis and revived separatist sentiments in Quebec. Lucien Bouchard, a cabinet minister in the Mulroney government, resigned and formed a new party, the Bloc Québécois (BQ), to work for Quebec sovereignty in the federal political arena.

The failure of Meech Lake and the revival of separatism set in motion a series of events that propelled Prime Minister Mulroney to attempt yet another constitutional deal. The resulting Charlottetown Accord was designed to satisfy everyone, e.g., Quebec would be recognized as a distinct society and would have a guaranteed 25% of House of Commons seats, and the Western provinces would get a revised Senate. But, it also dissatisfied everyone, and was badly defeated when voted on in a national referendum in October 1992 (LeDuc 1993). Also contributing to its failure was a serious economic recession for which the Mulroney government, the Accord's principal champion, was held responsible by many Canadians (Clarke and Kornberg 1994). Some observers speculated that the era of "mega constitutional politics" (Russell 1993) was over.

However, the irate electorate then vented its wrath on Prime Minister Mulroney's successor, Kim Campbell, and her government by handing the Conservatives a crushing defeat in the 1993 federal election (Clarke et al. 1996). Although the Liberals led by Jean Chrétien won a parliamentary majority, two new parties, the Bloc Québécois and Reform, gained large numbers of seats in Quebec and the West, respectively. The new parties' regionally concentrated strength and the fact that the BQ became the official opposition in parliament, indicated that another constitutional crisis might be in the offing. The PQ victory in the subsequent September 1994 Quebec provincial election, and the announcement by PQ leader, Premier Jacques Parizeau, that his government would hold another sovereignty referendum within a year, signaled that the crisis had arrived.

The Dynamics of the Referendum Campaign

After assuming office, the Parti Québécois began to lay the political groundwork for a sovereignty referendum. As in the run-up to the 1980 referendum, the PQ tried to convince voters that sovereignty would not cost them the economic benefits and important social programs that came with membership in the Canadian political system. However, despite these efforts, public opinion polls were not encouraging; throughout the winter and spring of 1995, majorities (typically sizable ones) of those expressing an opinion repeatedly voiced their opposition to sovereignty[1] (see Figure 1). Indeed, given the apparent likelihood that a sovereignty proposal would be soundly defeated, it was widely speculated that Premier Parizeau might postpone the referendum, perhaps indefinitely.

The weakness of the sovereignty option among the Quebec electorate in opinion polls encouraged the federal government to maintain the "strict silence" strategy it had adopted after the PQ's election victory. This strategy was premised on two considerations. First, the apparent lack of public enthusiasm for sovereignty indicated that there was no need to develop counter proposals for constitutional change that would appeal to Quebec voters. Not offering such proposals seemed wise; the two recent failures (Meech Lake, Charlottetown) to secure agreement on constitutional revision suggested that such proposals could well backfire and reinvigorate separatist sentiments. Moreover, given Prime Minister Chrétien's prominent role in negotiations on the 1982 constitutional agreement that Quebec had refused to sign, many Quebeckers might not trust his offers of yet another variant of "renewed federalism" such as the federal Liberals had promised before the 1980 referendum.

Second, although former prime minister Pierre Trudeau had enjoyed widespread popularity in Quebec in 1980,

Figure 1 • Support for and Opposition to Sovereignty, the Quebec Electorate, March–October 1995

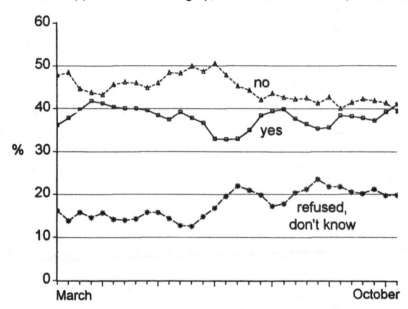

the large Francophone majority was decidedly luke-warm about Chrétien in 1995.[2] The prime minister probably calculated that he would do more harm than good by involving himself in a campaign that might never take place.

A postponement announcement never came, however. Rather, recognizing that his predecessor, René Lévesque, had delayed a sovereignty referendum for three and one-half years waiting for an opinion tide that never rose, Parizeau pressed ahead with plans for a ballot sometime in late 1995. Then, in June, the PQ moved to bolster public support by announcing and widely publicizing an agreement reached with its federal ally, the Bloc Québé-cois, and the small Action Démocratique du Québec Party, to conduct a united campaign for sovereignty. The agreement not only signaled an end to public bickering among the PQ and BQ, but it also paved the way for BQ chieftain, Lucien Bouchard, to assume a leading role in the campaign. Unlike Parizeau, Bouchard was a very popular figure among Francophone Quebeckers,[3] and his heightened involvement in the contest promised to give a much-needed boost to the sovereignty cause.

Another important element in the PQ strategy was to craft a referendum proposal that would allay fears about possible negative consequences of sovereignty. As in 1980, the Péquistes tried to defuse the "profitable federalism" ar-guments advanced by those wishing to keep Quebec in Canada by developing a softly-worded question that sug-gested voters could "have their cake and eat it too"—they could be residents of a sovereign Quebec that continued to provide the security that went with being Canadian citizens. The proposal's wording thus implied that a sov-ereign Quebec might be able to maintain economic and political ties with Canada: "Do you agree that Quebec should become sovereign, after having made a formal offer to Canada for a new Economic and Political Part-nership, within the scope of the Bill respecting the Fu-ture of Quebec and of the agreement signed on June 12, 1995?" The date for a referendum on this question was set for October 30.

The PQ strategy worked. Polls conducted during the summer showed support for sovereignty moving upward into the mid- to high-40% range (Figure 2). In Septem-ber, the sovereignty camp reinforced its growing mo-

**Figure 2 • Support for Sovereignty, With and Without Reallocation of Refusals and "Don't Knows,"
March–October 1995**

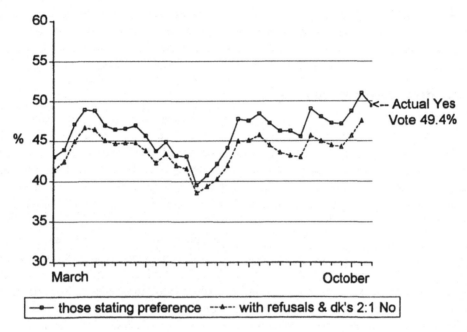

mentum by announcing that Lucien Bouchard would assume direct leadership of the *oui* campaign. Support for sovereignty increased again and, as polling day approached, surveys showed that a pro-sovereignty majority was a very real possibility. Whether or not sovereignty would occur depended in part on the sizable undeclared group (refusals and don't knows). This group increased over the summer (Figure 1) and, although there was little solid evidence to buttress the claim, some pollsters and media pundits speculated that it contained a 2:1 ratio of hidden *non* supporters (see Figure 2). This possibility notwithstanding, what only a few months earlier had seemed an easy victory for the federalist forces had now clearly turned into a dramatic struggle that would determine the future of one of the world's oldest democracies.

When it became apparent that Quebeckers might actually opt to leave Canada, the federal government abandoned its "strict silence" strategy. In late September, Prime Minister Chrétien made an emotional speech in parliament in which he declared that he would not allow

Canada to be shattered by a narrow majority on an ambiguous question. In a widely publicized speech a few days later, Finance Minister Paul Martin Jr. forcefully stated that Canada would *not* enter into economic partnership with a sovereign Quebec and, moreover, if they voted for sovereignty, Quebeckers would be treated as "foreigners" by Canada. Other federalist supporters claimed that a yes vote would mean that Quebeckers would be made to pay their share of Canada's onerous national debt, they would lose their eligibility to participate in Canadian social programs, their Canadian passports would be revoked, they would no longer be free to elect representatives to the national parliament, they would no longer be defended by the Canadian armed forces, and they might lose large portions of Quebec to aboriginal peoples. In the closing days of the campaign, when it became clear that support for sovereignty was not waning, the prime minister went on national television to appeal directly to Quebeckers not to take the fatal step of destroying Canada. The penultimate act in the drama occurred over the last weekend before the balloting when thousands of people from all parts of the country participated in a massive rally in Montreal to demonstrate the depth of their affection for a Canada that included Quebec and Québécois.

What If They Held a Referendum and Everybody Came?

During the pre-referendum wave of our referendum voting survey,[4] daily updates of the marginals for the voting turnout question consistently revealed that 95–97% indicated that they intended to cast a ballot. In the event, fully 93.5% voted, 18% more than had participated in the Charlottetown Accord referendum three years earlier. As our survey and opinion polls also predicted, the actual division of the vote was extremely close. The result was a razor-thin victory for the *non* side, with 50.6% of the valid votes being *non*'s and 49.4%, *oui*'s. However, in terms of *total* votes cast, *neither side won.* The gap was merely 52,000 votes, some 34,000 less than the number of spoiled ballots.[5]

Why did Quebeckers vote as they did, and why was the 1995 outcome so much closer than that of the first sovereignty referendum in 1980? A simple, but incomplete, answer to these questions is that when voters went to the polls in 1995 their opinions on both sovereignty with an economic and political association with the rest of Canada and full independence for Quebec were very different from what they had been 15 years earlier. In our 1995 pre-referendum survey, a large majority (63%) of respondents said they were either "very" (39%) or "somewhat" (24%) favorably disposed to sovereignty *combined with* a continuing association with Canada (Figure 3A). The comparable percentages in 1980 were only 25% and 22%, respectively.[6] Responses to a question posing the starker choice of independence for Quebec without mention of association with Canada had shifted dramatically as well. In 1980, only 25% indicated that they were very or somewhat favorable to outright independence, whereas in 1995 fully 46% did so (Figure 3B). The latter figure is important because it suggests that even if the federalist

forces had been fully successful in convincing Quebeckers that a *oui* vote was in fact a vote for independence *without* association, the percentage of the electorate favoring complete dissolution of Quebec's ties with Canada had moved close to the 50% mark in the 15 years since the last sovereignty referendum. Our survey indicates that fully 97% of this pro-independence group intended to vote *oui.*

Although federalists worked to construe its meaning differently, the referendum question was about sovereignty *combined with* a continuing association with the rest of Canada. Attitudes towards this option were strongly, but *imperfectly,* correlated with referendum voting. The percentages of *oui* voters among persons who were very favorable towards sovereignty with association was 90%, and among those who were somewhat or very *un*favorable, the percentages were 14% and 4%, respectively. Among a fourth group, persons who were somewhat favorable towards sovereignty with association, the division was closer, with 64% stating that they would vote *oui,* and 36%, *non.* These lukewarm *souverainistes* constituted a significant segment (22%) of the electorate and, given the extremely close result of the referendum, their failure to offer overwhelming support for the *oui* side was consequential.

A multivariate, multistage model is required to provide a deeper understanding of the forces affecting referendum voting behavior. In previous research (Kornberg and Clarke 1992, ch. 5; see also Pammett et al. 1983), we have argued that variables measuring public support for Canada's national political authorities, regime, and community should occupy central positions in such a model. Other important variables gauge voters' assessments of federal government performance in managing the economy and other salient policy areas, their evaluations of the equity-fairness of the operation of Canada's polity and society, their judgments of the performance of the Canadian political system as a democracy, and their reactions to the alternative democratic political system implied by the Péquiste option of a sovereign Quebec. We also have argued the importance of recognizing that referendums such as that on Quebec sovereignty

Figure 3

A. Attitudes Toward Quebec Sovereignty with Association with Canada 1980, 1995

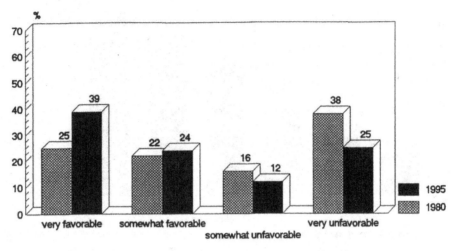

B. Attitudes Toward Quebec Independence 1980, 1995

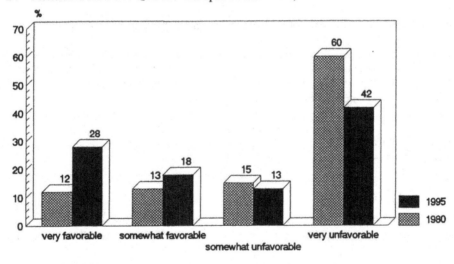

are held in political contexts where voters choose between alternatives advocated by competing groups of politicians with highly salient public images (Clarke and Kornberg 1994; see also Brulé 1992; Franklin, Marsh, and McLaren 1994). Thus, variables tapping voters' attitudes towards the leaders of the *oui* campaign, Bouchard and Parizeau, as well as their feelings about Prime Minister Chrétien and the federal Liberal government are relevant. Finally, several demographic variables (age, education, gender, income, language) index identification with and membership in important social groups in the electorate.[7]

Figure 4 • Explanatory Power as Types of Variables Added to Referendum Vote Model

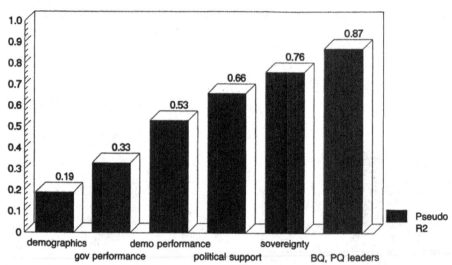

Key—Variables Included at Each Stage

demographics: age cohorts (18–24, 25–33, 34–47, 48–56, 57–65, 66 and older), annual family income, gender, language community (Francophone, non-Francophone), level of formal education.

gov performance: evaluations of federal government performance, evaluations of equity-fairness of Canada's political system and society.

demo performance: evaluations of the performance of Canada as a democracy, political efficacy in federal and provincial politics, expectations re: the relative performance of Canada and a sovereign Quebec as democratic political system.

political support: support for Canada's national political community, regime and authorities.

sovereignty: attitudes towards a sovereign Quebec with an economic and political partnership with Canada.

BQ, PQ leaders: feelings about Lucien Bouchard and Jacques Parizeau.

Probit analyses reveal that many of these variables influenced the vote either directly or indirectly. A simple baseline model using demographic variables as the only predictors yields a pseudo R^2 of .19 (Figure 4), a figure consistent with the fact that although non-Francophone voters were massively opposed to sovereignty (only 9% voted *oui*), Francophones were deeply divided (61% voted *oui*). The explanatory power of the model increases as other types of variables are considered, such that when all of them *except* attitudes towards sovereignty and Bouchard and Parizeau are employed, the R^2 is .66 and 89% of the voters are correctly classified. Adding atti-

tudes towards sovereignty with continuing association raises the R^2 to .76 and the percentage of correctly classified to 92%. However, *controlling for all of these factors,* voters' feelings about the leaders of the *oui* side, Bouchard and Parizeau, mattered. Variables measuring feelings about Bouchard and Parizeau are statistically significant ($p < .001$) and properly (positively) signed in the fully specified model, and their inclusion boosts the R^2 to .87, with 95% being correctly classified.

It is thus apparent that even a fundamental "system-level" choice such as that offered to the Quebec electorate in the 1995 sovereignty referendum cannot be fully explained without knowledge of voters' feelings about the principal advocates of the competing alternatives. Given the extraordinarily narrow division of the vote, what would have been the outcome if Quebeckers felt differently about these politicians? To answer this question, we construct scenarios in which public feelings about federal political authorities (Prime Minister Chrétien, the federal Liberal Party) and Premier Parizeau were set at the levels recorded by their predecessors at the time of the 1980 referendum. As noted, unlike their counterparts in 1995, former Prime Minister Trudeau and his federal Liberal government enjoyed widespread popularity in 1980. This also was true of former Quebec premier, Réne Lévesque.[8] The scenarios focus on the Francophone subset (18% of the electorate) in the group of voters who were "somewhat" favorable towards sovereignty. As noted, this group had significant percentages of both *oui* and *non* voters. Other variables in the vote model, except gender, are set at their mean values. Since women were less likely than men to cast a *oui* ballot,[9] we compute vote probabilities for the two gender groups separately.

The results show that the probability of a *oui* vote varies substantially for both men and women, depending upon voters' feelings about federal authorities and Premier Parizeau. For example, if Parizeau had been as popular as Lévesque, the probability of a *oui* vote among women increases by 13%, and among men by 11%. In contrast, if the prime minister and the federal Liberal government had been as popular as Trudeau and his government but feelings about Parizeau were unchanged, the probability of voting *oui* would have decreased by 26% for women and 24% for men. If both the federal and provincial authorities had enjoyed 1980 popularity levels, the probability of a *oui* vote would have decreased by 10% for women and by 8% for men. Taking into consideration the size of the groups in question indicates that *all* of these changes in vote probabilities would have changed the referendum outcome. For example, if the prime minister and his government were more warmly received, but Parizeau had remained relatively unpopular, the margin of defeat would have been significantly larger (approximately 5%). However, if Parizeau's sup-

port had equaled Lévesque's and feelings for the federal authorities were unchanged, the referendum would have narrowly passed—and Canada would have failed.

The Referendum Nobody Won

In his nationally televised speech after the referendum outcome was publically known, Prime Minister Chrétien said, "The people have spoken, and it is time to accept that verdict" (Wilson-Smith 1995). Unfortunately for the federalist forces, the verdict could hardly have been more ambiguous—the *non* majority of valid votes was minuscule and, as noted, neither side gained a majority of the total votes cast. Although the *souverainistes* were bitterly disappointed, the result gave them hope that they could eventually win. The Péquistes remain in power in Quebec (the next provincial election does not need to be held until 1999) and this will provide them with an extended window of opportunity to hold yet another sovereignty referendum should they choose to do so.

As our analyses of the dynamics of public opinion in the run-up to the 1995 referendum and factors affecting voting behavior in that contest indicate, the outcome of another referendum is highly uncertain. Although support for sovereignty is partly a product of highly inertial long-term forces, it also is driven partly by mutable short-term reactions to the competing politicians on both sides of the issue. In this regard, Premier Parizeau's bitter post-referendum comment that his cherished *oui* majority was frustrated by a combination of "money and the ethnic vote" (Wilson-Smith 1995) is only part of the story. To be sure, corporate interests worked to defeat sovereignty and an overwhelming majority of non-Francophones voted *non*. However, as shown above, Parizeau also could have blamed himself for the loss—his unpopularity with the electorate (including Francophones) helped to defeat sovereignty in 1995.

Parizeau has now resigned. His successor as premier of Quebec, Lucien Bouchard, is a far more popular figure and, like Parizeau, he is deeply dedicated to sovereignty. It remains to be seen if he can sustain popularity as his government grapples with the many problems confronting late 20th century Quebec. If he can, Parizeau may decide to hold yet another sovereignty referendum in the near future and, as the 1995 result shows, the possibility that he might obtain a *oui* majority is very real. In the meantime, Canada's crisis of political support continues. The 1995 sovereignty referendum was a contest nobody won. ∎

Notes

1. The data in Figures 1 and 2 are three week moving averages based on Canadian Facts' weekly Multifacts surveys. We wish to thank Peter Wearing, Senior Project Director, Canadian Facts, for making these data available to us.

2. In 1980 Trudeau's mean score on a 100-point feeling thermometer was 68 among Francophones and 69 among non-Francophones. In 1995, Chrétien's scores were 40 among Francophones and 68 among non-Francophones. His mean score among all Quebeckers was 44.

3. Bouchard's mean feeling thermometer score was 64 among Francophones, 28 among non-Francophones, and 59 among the entire Quebec electorate. Parizeau's scores among these three groups were much lower—48, 20, and 44, respectively.

4. CATI telephone interviews, averaging 37 minutes in length, were conducted by Canadian Facts with a representative sample of 1,005 Quebeckers 18 years of age or older. Details concerning sample design and other technical aspects of the survey are available upon request. The research was funded by NSF grant SBR-9514385.

5. A nontrivial percentage of Quebeckers who typically spoil their ballots in federal and provincial elections, e.g., 3.33% and 1.96%, respectively, did so in the 1993 federal and 1994 provincial elections (*Élections 94: Rapport des résultats officiels du scrutin:* p. 51; *Thirty-Fifth General Election 1993 Official Voting Results: Synopsis:* Table 3, p. 23; see also Feigert 1989). However, after the referendum charges were made that pro-sovereignty vote scrutineers had intentionally rejected ballots in areas, particularly in non-Francophone parts of Montreal, where opposition to sovereignty was very strong.

6. The 1980 Quebec referendum study was conducted in conjunction with the 1979 and 1980 Canadian national elections studies (principal investigators: Harold D. Clarke, Jane Jenson, Lawrence LeDuc, and Jon H. Pammett). The data are available from the ICPSR Data Archive, University of Michigan (ICPSR Study #8079).

7. In the interest of space, information on the construction of the several variables used in this analysis is not presented here. This information is available from Clarke's homepage on the World Wide Web (http://www.psci.unt.edu/hclarke/), and a printed copy is available upon request. See also Kornberg and Clarke (1992: chs. 2, 3, 4).

8. In 1980, the mean scores (100-point feeling thermometers) for federal political authorities (Trudeau + the federal Liberal Party/2) were 66 among Francophones and 68 among non-Francophones. Lévesque's scores were 61 and 34, respectively.

9. In the entire electorate, the percentages of *oui* voters by gender were: men, 59%; women, 47%. The comparable percentages among Francophones were 66% and 56%, respectively, and among non-Francophones, 9% and 7%.

References

Brulé, Michel. 1992. "France After Maastricht." *The Public Perspective* November/December:28–30.

Cairns, Alan C. 1992. *Charter versus Federalism: The Dilemmas of Constitutional Reform.* Toronto: McClelland and Stewart.

Clarke, Harold D., and Allan Kornberg. 1994. "The Politics and Economics of Constitutional Choice: Voting in Canada's 1992 National Referendum." *Journal of Politics* 56:940–62.

Clarke, Harold D., Jane Jenson, Lawrence LeDuc, and Jon H. Pammett. 1996. *Absent Mandate: Canadian Electoral Politics in an Era of Restructuring.* Toronto: Gage.

Cook, Ramsay. 1995. *Canada, Quebec and the Uses of Nationalism.* 2nd ed. Toronto: McClelland and Stewart.

Élections 94: Rapport des résultats officiels du scrutin. 1994. Québec: Le Directueur général des élections du Québec.

Feigert, Frank. 1989. *Canada Votes: 1935–1988.* Durham: Duke University Press.

Franklin, Mark N., Michael Marsh, and Lauren McLaren. 1994. "Uncorking the Bottle: Popular Opposition to European Unification in the Wake of Maastricht." *Journal of Common Market Studies* 32:455–72.

Gwyn, Richard. 1995. *Nationalism Without Walls: The Unbearable Lightness of Being Canadian.* Toronto: McClelland and Stewart.

Kornberg, Allan, and Harold D. Clarke, eds. 1983. *Political Support in Canada: The Crisis Years.* Durham: Duke University Press.

Kornberg, Allan, and Harold D. Clarke. 1992. *Citizens and Community: Political Support in a Representative Democracy.* New York: Cambridge University Press.

LeDuc, Lawrence. 1993. "Canada's Constitutional Referendum of 1992: A Great Big No." *Electoral Studies* 12:257–63.

Lipset, Seymour Martin. 1990. *Continental Divide: The Values and Institutions of the United States and Canada.* New York: Routledge.

McRoberts, Kenneth. 1988. *Quebec: Social Change and Political Crisis.* 3rd ed. Toronto: McClelland and Stewart.

Monahan, Patrick J. 1991. *Meech Lake: The Inside Story.* Toronto: University of Toronto Press.

Pammett, Jon H. et al. 1983. "Political Support and Voting Behavior in the Quebec Referendum." In *Political Support in Canada: The Crisis Years,* ed. Allan Kornberg and Harold D. Clarke. Durham: Duke University Press.

Russell, Peter H. 1992. *Constitutional Odyssey: Can Canadians Be a Sovereign People?* Toronto: University of Toronto Press.

Russell, Peter H. 1993. "The End of Mega Constitutional Politics in Canada?" *PS: Political Science & Politics.* March:33–37.

Schwartz, Mildred A. 1974. *Politics and Territory: The Sociology of Regional Persistence in Canada.* Montreal: McGill-Queen's University Press.

Thirty-Fifth General Election 1993 Official Voting Results: Synopsis. 1993. Ottawa: Chief Electoral Officer of Canada.

Wilson-Smith, Anthony. 1995. "A House Divided." *Macleans.* November 13:14–16.

Why Was This Research Needed?

1. How is this study of Quebec relevant to broader questions concerning the establishment and maintenance of democratic regimes?

2. How does the background information the authors provide concerning Canadian history help clarify their research project?

3. What short-term political forces led to the scheduling of Quebec's 1995 referendum? How did the authors' awareness of these forces sharpen the focus of their analysis?

How Was the Topic Studied?

1. How do Clarke and Kornberg use existing public opinion poll data in setting the stage for their own analysis of attitudes surrounding the referendum?

2. Authors sometimes make supplemental information available to readers who wish to see the full details of how a particular survey was carried out and what items were included on the questionnaire. How do Clarke and Kornberg do this? How might the presentation of research methodology in this article have benefited by including more technical information? In what way would such details be important for a researcher intent on building upon Clarke and Kornberg's work?

3. Diagram the multivariate model of voting behavior developed by these authors.

What Are the Findings?

1. Why do you think the authors chose a line graph to display the series of public opinion data provided in Figures 1 and 2? How else could these same data be organized or displayed to highlight a particular trend or comparison?

2. Why are the bar charts in Figure 3 an effective means to contrast the change in attitudes toward Quebec sovereignty and Quebec independence between 1980 and 1995? Based on the data in Figure 3, summarize this change as succinctly as possible in your own words.

3. The concept of statistical "control" is pivotal to the multiple regression technique used in this analysis. What does it mean to say that each independent variable's impact has been assessed while *controlling* for other variables in the equation?

4. In its pure form, multiple regression is meant for use with interval-level variables. How does the dependent variable in this model depart from that assumption? What adaptation of the multiple regression technique have the authors used for this situation?

5. A "fully specified" model would provide the reader with both the overall power of a multiple regression and information about the influence, significance, and strength of each independent variable. What are some of the additional statistics that would be reported in a fully specified version of the Referendum Vote Model? How might these statistics enhance your understanding of why Quebeckers voted as they did?

6. The authors report a final (pseudo) R^2 value of .87 for their model (see Figure 4). Explain the meaning of this statistic in a simple sentence.

What Do the Results Mean?

1. Although the explanatory power of this model is impressive, the model does not fully account for why the citizens of Quebec voted as they did in 1995. What other independent variables do you believe could have been added to this multiple regression equation? State your research hypothesis for each.

2. How could pro-sovereignty activists use the results of a research study like this to improve their chances of success in a future referendum campaign?

3. After this referendum was decided by an extremely close vote, the Canadian federal government passed a law stating that sovereignty in Quebec could only be chosen by a "clear majority" of the province's voters. From a democratic theory standpoint, what arguments can you make for and against this decision? If the Canadian House of Commons hired you to be a technical consultant, what numerical standard(s) would you suggest for operationalizing this concept of a "clear majority" in a future referendum campaign?

Afterword from Harold Clarke and Allan Kornberg

Our decision to study the October 1995 Quebec sovereignty referendum was driven by two principal considerations. First, the sovereignty referendum was clearly a major political event in the life and times of one of the world's oldest and, arguably, most successful democracies. A large-scale study of the public's political attitudes and behavior at the time of the referendum would make a valuable contribution to the historical record. Second, such a study would enable us to continue research that we had been conducting since the late 1970s on the causes and consequences of political support in Canada and other mature democracies (see, e.g., Kornberg and Clarke 1992). The sovereignty referendum provided an opportunity to test a number of rival hypotheses about the determinants of support for national political regimes and communities that we had developed in our earlier work. Situations in which voters are asked to make highly consequential regime- and community-level political choices are not easily simulated in laboratory settings. The Quebec sovereignty referendum was high-stakes, real-world politics, and high-quality observational research was required.

The study design we employed involved pre- and post-referendum computer-assisted telephone interviews (CATI) with large representative samples of the Quebec electorate and adults living in the rest of Canada. A twelve-page mail-back questionnaire was also sent to all the post-referendum respondents. Doing pre- and post-referendum surveys in Quebec provided leverage for making inferences regarding the flow of causality from political attitudes to referendum choices. In addition, it enabled us to monitor reactions to the referendum outcome.

In this regard, Quebeckers were not the only ones that mattered. A *oui* vote in the referendum would give the Parti Québécois the warrant it needed to attempt to negotiate sovereignty with the federal government. But the latter's likely reaction was unknown—would the feds fold and accommodate the separatists' demands, or would they take a hard-line approach and deny the legitimacy of the referendum? Would tanks and troops appear in the streets of Montreal and Quebec City as they had during the 1970 "October crisis"? Public opinion in the rest of Canada would be a crucial factor when the feds were deciding how to respond. Accordingly, Canadians outside Quebec were significant players in the referendum drama, and it would be very useful to gauge their political attitudes and opinions before and after the vote.

It has been ten years since the referendum. After the sovereignty proposal was defeated, support for Quebec independence declined, and many Canadian academics and media pundits were quick to claim that the "separatist dragon" had been slain. Our research suggested these claims were premature, owing more to wishful thinking than sound social science. There is a very strong age gradient in Quebeckers' political identities, with younger people being much more likely to identify themselves as "Québécois" rather than as Canadians (see Clarke, Kornberg, and Wearing 2000). Support for sovereignty similarly tends to be greater at younger ages, and there is strong, albeit circumstantial, evidence that these relationships reflect generational, not merely life cycle, differences. If so, there is a large latent base of support for sovereignty, a base that can be mobilized by a combination of precipitating events and charismatic political leadership. The current "sponsorship scandal"—which concerns the misuse, by some Quebec Liberals, of money paid by the Canadian federal government between 1996 and 2001 to advertise the concept of national unity in Quebec—is exactly such an event and, as anticipated, support for sovereignty has surged since the scandal broke in early 2004 (Clarke, Kornberg, MacLeod, and Scotto 2005).

Looking back, are there aspects of our research we would have done differently? The answer is "Sure—but show us the money!" With additional funding, we would have established a long-term panel in Quebec to track the dynamics of political identities and other key determinants of support for sovereignty over time. We also would have instituted a long-running set of monthly surveys to monitor the aggregate dynamics of public opinion and political support in the province and the rest of Canada. In our judgment, investing in long-term survey research projects should be very high on the wish list for twenty-first century political science. Such projects are the political science equivalents of the Voyager spacecraft, the Hubble telescope, or—with suitable experiments included—Fermilab or the European Organization for Nuclear Research's (CERN) Large Hadron Collider. Students of political choice have many important, longstanding research questions; well-developed theoretical perspectives that inform competing models that address these questions; and advanced statistical methods for adjudicating among the rival models. What we currently lack are the requisite data.

To be sure, surveys conducted at the time of national elections or major polity-shaping events such as the Quebec sovereignty referendum can be very useful. Ultimately, however, they are not adequate to the tasks we would like to address. Until more and better data become available, significant controversies will remain unresolved, and the resurgence of public support for highly consequential political movements such as Quebec sovereignty will continue to occasion surprise among those who could know better.

References

Clarke, Harold D., Allan Kornberg, John MacLeod, and Thomas Scotto. 2005. "Too Close to Call: Political Choice in Canada, 2004." *PS: Political Science & Politics* 38 (April): 247–253.

Clarke, Harold D., Allan Kornberg, and Peter Wearing. 2000. *A Polity on the Edge: Canada and the Politics of Fragmentation.* Toronto: Broadview Press.

Kornberg, Allan, and Harold D. Clarke. 1992. *Citizens and Community: Political Support in a Representative Democracy.* New York: Cambridge University Press.

Forecasting Presidential Nominations, or My Model Worked Just Fine, Thank You

William G. Mayer

The past few years have not been kind to political forecasters. On election night in 2000, the major networks prematurely awarded Al Gore a victory in Florida. However, after several recounts and court decisions, the state entered George Bush's victory column. Two years later, during the midterm congressional elections, a computer crash stymied the consortium of news organizations that rely on exit polling of voters to predict election results. Then, in 2004, a number of polling organizations misgauged the presidential contest again, either proclaiming it a dead heat or anticipating a victory for the challenger, John Kerry, as late as a few days before the election (Memmott 2004). Embarrassments like these have been a wake-up call for the journalistic-academic-professional complex involved in political forecasting, forcing a reexamination of the way information is collected and the factors that are considered when making projections.

Given the risk of error, a political scientist might be forgiven a little boastfulness when his personal forecasting model proves accurate. In the following reading, William G. Mayer is concerned with predicting presidential nominations, not final election results. He approaches the task as a social scientist, rather than as a pollster, by constructing a statistical model based on an understanding of parties' nominating behavior. Developing this kind of model involves a sequence of steps: formulating a theory, collecting and analyzing the data, making a prediction, and testing the accuracy of results (Fair 2002). If a model turns out to be inaccurate, then it must be adjusted and tested again. Here, Mayer is testing the success of his presidential nomination predictions over the period from 1980 through 2000, and he is quite pleased with the findings.

The primary quantitative technique illustrated in this reading is multiple regression analysis. Its value as a tool for making political predictions is another example of the versatility of this statistical approach, which is so widely used in political science research.

References

Fair, Ray C. 2002. *Predicting Presidential Elections and Other Things.* Stanford: Stanford University Press.

Memmott, Mark. 2004. "Predictions Burn Pollsters, Pundits—Again." *USA Today,* November 14. www. usatoday.com/news/politicselections/vote2004/2004-11-03-polls-burn-pundits_x.htm (accessed August 8, 2005).

For most Americans, the 2000 elections will be remembered as the Year of the Great Recount in Florida. Contemporary political science being what it is, political scientists are more likely to remember 2000 as the Year when the Forecasting Models Went Crash. Of the seven major presidential forecasting models presented at the 2000 American Political Science Association Annual Meeting, *all seven* forecast a comfortable Gore victory, with a median prediction that Gore would win 55% of the two-party popular vote.

Yet, not every forecasting model went bust in 2000. Seven years ago, I published an article presenting what was then the only model ever developed for forecasting presidential *nomination* races (Mayer 1996).[1] Three contested nomination races have occurred since that time, and my model has worked well in every instance. The purpose of this article is two-fold: to examine the model's performance in 1996 and 2000; and to discuss what the model reveals about the nature of contemporary presidential nominations.

The Basic Model

The original model was based on data from seven contested nomination races that took place between 1980 and 1992. One of these, the Republican race in 1992, was never seriously in doubt; no one reasonably expected Pat Buchanan to defeat incumbent President George Bush. But the other six races each featured a serious battle for a major party's presidential nomination, with considerable uncertainty (and a lot of inaccurate predictions) as to how it would turn out. Were there any indicators that might have enabled us to predict the winning candidates before the actual voting and delegate selection commenced? As it turns out, there were two such indicators, both available in January or early February of the election year, which pointed out the winner in five of the six contested races (six of seven if one includes the Bush-Buchanan battle).

The first of these indicators was the candidates' relative standing in polls of the national party electorate. For at least a year before the first caucus or primary takes place, polling organizations routinely ask national samples of Democrats and Republicans whom they would prefer as their party's next presidential candidate. (In everything that follows, I use data drawn from the Gallup polls, partly because the Gallup organization has a very good track record for doing careful, unbiased survey work, and partly because Gallup is the only organization I know of that has asked questions on this topic continuously over the last two decades.) My interest here is on the last such poll before the start of delegate selection activities—meaning, in most years, the last poll before the Iowa caucuses. As shown in the top half of Table 1, the candidate who was leading in this poll went on to win the nomination in five of the six cases.

The second indicator is the candidates' relative success in raising campaign money. Under the federal campaign finance laws that have been in effect since 1974, all active candidates for the presidential nomination are required to submit periodic reports detailing how much money they have raised and spent. Here, my focus is on the total amount of money that each candidate had raised (technically, their net receipts) by December 31 of the *year before* the election. And again, in five of the six cases, the leading money raiser went on to win the nomination (see Table 1).

To allow for easier comparison with general election forecasting efforts, I then combined these two indicators into a regression equation in order to generate a numerical prediction of each candidate's success in the actual primaries. The dependent variable in this equation is the percentage of the total vote won by each candidate in all presidential primaries held by that candidate's party during the entire nomination season. In the 1992 Democratic nomi-

Table 1
National Poll Standings and Pre-Election Fund-Raising Results as Predictors of Presidential Nominations

A. Poll Standings

Year	Party	Candidate leading in the last poll before the Iowa caucuses	Eventual Nominee
1980	Republican	Reagan	Reagan
1980	Democratic	Carter	Carter
1984	Democratic	Mondale	Mondale
1988	Republican	Bush	Bush
1988	Democratic	Hart	Dukakis
1992	Republican	Bush	Bush
1992	Democratic	Clinton	Clinton

B. Fund-Raising Totals

Year	Party	Candidate raising the most money prior to the year of the election	Eventual Nominee
1980	Republican	Connally	Reagan
1980	Democratic	Carter	Carter
1984	Democratic	Mondale	Mondale
1988	Republican	Bush	Bush
1988	Democratic	Dukakis	Dukakis
1992	Republican	Bush	Bush
1992	Democratic	Clinton	Clinton

nation contest, for example, 39 different primaries were held at which a total of 20,239,385 presidential preference votes were cast. Bill Clinton received 10,482,411 of these votes, or 51.8%; Jerry Brown had 4,071,232 votes, or 20.1%; Paul Tsongas received 18.1%; and so on.

Two independent variables were used to predict these primary vote shares. The first is the percentage of party identifiers who supported each candidate in the last national Gallup poll before the Iowa caucuses. The second is the total amount of money each candidate raised before the election year, divided by the largest amount of money

raised by any candidate in that party's nomination race.[2]

The results, based on data from 1980 through 1992, are shown in the first column of figures in Table 2. (For a fuller discussion, see Mayer 1992, 51–53.) As I noted in my original article, a number of factors would seem to make presidential nomination races inherently more difficult to predict than general elections: the larger number of serious candidates in the contest; the sequential nature of the process; and the absence of such stabilizing forces as party identification.[3] That said, the model does a quite commendable job of accounting for the variation in how candidates fared in the presidential primaries. And most importantly, the model correctly forecasts the winning candidate in five of the six races.

Forecasting the 1996 and 2000 Races

So much for the past. As an old Chinese proverb notes, "To prophesy is extremely difficult—especially about the future." The acid test for models of this sort is how well they fare *after* publication.

Table 3 provides the relevant data for 1996: the results of the last national poll of Republican party identifiers before the Iowa caucuses; and how much money each Republican candidate had raised as of December 31, 1995. Both predictors (and the equation-based fore-

Table 2
Regression Equations for Predicting Primary Vote Shares

	1980–1992	1980–1996	1980–2000
Regression Coefficents			
National poll standings	.94 (.14)	.99 (.13)	1.05 (.11)
Total funds raised	.02 (.08)	.00 (.07)	−.02 (.06)
Constant	1.31 (3.37)	1.57 (3.13)	1.72 (2.66)
R^2	.70	.72	.77
Adjusted R^2	.69	.70	.77
SEE	11.93	11.50	10.91
N	38	44	52

Table 3

Presidential Nomination Predictors in the 1996 Republican Nomination Race

A. Presidential Nomination Preferences of National Republican Identifiers	
Dole	47%
Forbes	16
Gramm	8
Buchanan	7
Alexander	3
Lugar	3

B. Total Net Receipts Through the End of 1995	
Dole	$24,611,816
Gramm	20,758,066
Forbes	17,973,910
Alexander	11,516,266
Buchanan	7,222,685
Lugar	5,903,326

C. Model Forecasts		
	Predicted Vote	Actual Vote
Dole	47.5%	58.5%
Buchanan	8.5	21.6
Forbes	17.8	10.2
Alexander	5.1	3.5
Lugar	4.6	0.9
Gramm	10.5	0.5

Source: Poll results are taken from the Gallup Poll, survey of January 26–29, 1996. Fund-raising totals are derived from the individual candidate reports submitted to the Federal Election Commission. Actual primary vote percentages come from *America Votes*.

casts) point unambiguously to Robert Dole; and after a number of stumbles, and in spite of a rather lackluster campaign, Dole did indeed win the 1996 Republican presidential nomination.[4]

Table 4 provides comparable information on the 2000 nomination races. On the Democratic side, Al Gore led Bill Bradley in both the polls and total in fundraising (though rather narrowly in the latter case). And, of course, Gore also eventually won the nomination. George W. Bush had an even more daunting lead over the rest of the Republican field. Though the Texas governor made the race closer than it might otherwise have been by running

a remarkably ill-conceived campaign in New Hampshire, it was ultimately he, and not John McCain, who became the Republican standard-bearer.

What It Means

What, in general, can we learn from election forecasting models? In many cases, I would argue, the answer is: not much. Far too often, forecasting work seems to be low on theory and high on crude empiricism. Variables are added or modified just because they lead to higher R^2 values or lower standard errors of estimate—exactly the sorts of things we all tell our introductory methods classes *not* to do. (For a striking exception—and a wonderful example of what can be done with these models, see Campbell 2000.)

In contrast, I developed my model with the primary purpose of making a series of arguments about the basic dynamics of the contemporary nomination process. And it is these arguments, I think, that have held up particularly well through the 1996 and 2000 election cycles.

1. The contemporary presidential nomination process is unusually favorable to frontrunners

If this point now seems widely accepted, it was most certainly not that way when I first formulated the model. To the contrary, for at least two decades after the rules were re-written in the early 1970s, the conventional wisdom was precisely the opposite: that the new system offered great advantages to outsiders and insurgents. As Robert Scheer of the *Los Angeles Times* put it, "There's a special problem with the drawn out system of primaries and caucuses. What it allows is for an unknown to get in" (Foley et al. 1980, 44).

But it wasn't just those dreaded journalists and pundits who reached this conclusion. The same verdict was pronounced in some of the very best academic writing on the subject. One of the best-known models of the primary election process is that of Brady and Johnston

Table 4
Presidential Nomination Predictors in the 2000 Nomination Races

Democrats		Republicans	
A. Presidential Nomination Preferences of National Party Identifiers			
Gore	60%	Bush	63%
Bradley	27	McCain	19
		Forbes	6
		Bauer	2
		Keyes	1
		Hatch	1
B. Total Net Receipts Through the End of 1999			
Gore	$27,847,335	Bush	$67,630,541
Bradley	27,465,950	Forbes	34,150,997
		McCain	15,532,082
		Bauer	8,761,166
		Keyes	4,483,505
		Hatch	2,285,829

C. Model Forecasts					
	Predicted Vote	Actual Vote		Predicted Vote	Actual Vote
Gore	61.0%	75.7%	Bush	63.9%	63.2%
Bradley	28.3	19.9	McCain	20.4	29.8
			Forbes	7.5	0.7
			Bauer	3.6	0.4
			Keyes	2.6	5.3
			Hatch	2.6	0.1

Source: Poll results are taken from the Gallup Poll, survey of January 17–19, 2000. Fundraising totals are derived from the individual candidate reports submitted to the Federal Election Commission.

national public figures" (287). James Ceaser (1982), who approached these issues from a more historical and theoretical perspective, pronounced a similar verdict: "When the effects of sequence in the primaries and the influence of the media are taken into consideration, the nominating campaign often becomes not simply a test among established national contenders, but an occasion for outsiders to make their reputation during the campaign itself. In this respect, the current system is more open than the pure convention system and the mixed nominating system" (95).

(1987). As they conclude in the very last sentence of their article: "The lesson, then, of this analysis is that being the favorite is a mixed blessing, and one might better be a newcomer with media appeal and a little luck in Iowa or New Hampshire" (184). Larry Bartels (1988) ended his award-winning book on presidential primaries on a similar note. Characterizing the current system as one with a "remarkable openness to new candidates," he added, "In many political systems positions of party leadership are earned through decades of toil in the party organization. In contemporary American politics the same positions are sometimes seized, almost literally overnight, by candidates with negligible party credentials and very short histories as

In almost every recent nomination race, the candidate who ultimately won was the person leading before any of the delegates were selected.

From the late 1970s through the early 1990s, academic writing about the presidential nomination process was saturated with this perspective. (In addition to the sources just quoted, see Sundquist 1980, 193–94; Mann 1985, 35–36; Keeter and Zukin 1983, 190–93; and King 1981.) Even in the mid- and late 1990s, many scholars continued to argue, as Mackenzie (1996) did in his book on political reform, that "[The contemporary presidential nomination] process has a strong tendency to promote the candidacies of outsiders who have little or no Washington experience and who are often strangers to the leading members of their own party" (50).

The most important point of my excursion into election forecasting was to assert the opposite: that in almost every recent nomination race, the candidate who ultimately won was the person leading before any of the delegates were selected. Indeed, in seven of the last 10 contested nomination races, the eventual nominee was leading in the national polls for at least a year before the Iowa caucuses. To say the least, this is not a system characterized by its openness to new faces.

2. As a factor in the presidential nomination process, momentum is greatly overrated

If the pre-race frontrunner usually wins, then one must also conclude that momentum is nowhere near the overwhelming force that it is frequently portrayed to be. Momentum can be compared to a roller-coaster ride: it provides a lot of thrills and excitement, but in the end it leaves us exactly where we started. And so it is in presidential politics: after all the effects of momentum have come and gone, the person who started out ahead almost always finishes ahead. Put another way, if you're interested in figuring out why John McCain went from 15% to 34% in the national polls within five days of his New Hampshire victory, momentum clearly provides the best explanation. But if your main interest is in who finally wins the nomination, momentum is really of very little help at all. Not since Jimmy Carter's campaign in 1976 has a momentum-driven candidacy been successful.

3. Frontrunners almost invariably stumble at some point in the process—but these mistakes, for all the media attention they receive, are rarely fatal

If frontrunners usually triumph in the end, their road to the nomination is never an entirely smooth one. Bad stuff happens. Bob Dole lost the New Hampshire, Delaware, and Arizona primaries; George Bush lost in New Hampshire and Michigan; and Al Gore spent the better part of 1999 squandering his lead in both the

polls and in fundraising (on Gore's early missteps, see Mayer 2001, 23–26). But all of these candidates also had real strengths that were not entirely overwhelmed by a few weeks of bad campaign-related publicity. Each recovered his footing—rather quickly, in fact—and ultimately racked up a long string of victories in the presidential primaries.

4. The longer we live under the current system, the more we learn about it—and this, too, works to the advantage of frontrunners

There are a number of reasons why Jimmy Carter won the 1976 Democratic nomination against a series of better-known and better-financed opponents, but one of the most important is simply that the nomination process was then new and not very well understood. Carter and his advisors figured out what it took to win in the new environment; many of his chief opponents (in particular, Henry Jackson) were less astute. But the longer the current system endures, the more its basic quirks and tendencies have become a matter of common knowledge. The net effect of all this learning and experience has been to create a fair amount of uniformity in basic campaign strategy—and thus to neutralize the advantage that any one candidate can derive from "playing the game" better than his or her opponents. And if campaign strategy *doesn't* matter, presidential nomination races will be decided more and more on the basis of such fundamental factors as popularity and money—resources that frontrunners, almost by definition, will have in greater supply than their competitors.

A good example of how campaign learning works against outsiders and insurgents is provided by the contrast in how two early frontrunners—Walter Mondale and Robert Dole—dealt with opponents who tried to ride a "better than expected" showing in Iowa to a breakthrough win in New Hampshire. When Mondale scored a resounding victory in the 1984 Iowa caucuses, he and his campaign strategists fully expected that win to propel them to another win eight days later in New Hampshire, where Mondale was already well ahead in the polls. In fact, the candidate with the momentum turned out to be Gary Hart, who had finished 30 percentage points behind Mondale in Iowa but had nevertheless managed to convince the press that he was now Mondale's chief rival. What is noteworthy for our purposes is that the Mondale campaign never really saw it coming until the very end (see Germond and Witcover 1985, 161–68). In particular, they made no sustained attempt to attack Hart until the day *after* New Hampshire, by which time Hart's impressive win in the Granite State almost completely transformed the character of the race. In the end, it took the Mondale campaign four more months of hard fighting before they finally, narrowly defeated Hart.

In 1996, Dole faced a quite similar predicament. After winning in Iowa (though by a considerably less decisive margin than Mondale), Dole, too, found that victory did little or nothing to help his standing in New Hampshire. Instead, according to all the polls, the momentum went to Pat Buchanan, who finished second in Iowa, and, even more, to Lamar Alexander, who had finished third. In one set of tracking polls, Alexander's support in New Hampshire went from 5% on the day before Iowa to 18% four days after the primary. But here the parallel breaks down, for the Dole campaign knew quite well what had happened to Mondale and, recognizing the peril they faced, did not wait for their opponents' momentum to snowball. The Dole strategists felt that Buchanan was not a long-term threat to win the nomination—but Alexander was. Hence, on the final weekend before the New Hampshire vote, they launched an all-out attack on the former Tennessee governor. And it worked: Alexander's momentum stalled, he finished third in New Hampshire, and he never again was a serious factor in the 1996 Republican nomination race. In the 13 primaries held between New Hampshire and Alexander's withdrawal, he averaged just 9% of the vote (for further details, see Mayer 1997). Instead of having to fight a prolonged battle against a fresh face with a tidal wave of momentum, the Dole campaign stopped Alexander before he ever gained traction.

The effect of money on primary voting, holding initial poll standings constant, is essentially zero.

---

5. Money helps, but it's definitely not the whole ball game

Though a great deal of attention is always focused on candidate fundraising, the clear thrust of this model is that, unless a candidate also has a strong base of support among ordinary, rank-and-file party voters, a huge warchest will not get a candidate very far. Indeed, according to all three equations in Table 2, the effect of money on primary voting, holding initial poll standings constant, is essentially zero. The same moral emerges, on a more anecdotal level, from a listing of all the candidates who were very successful fundraisers in the year before the election, but then fared dismally once the actual primary voting began: John Connally in 1980, John Glenn in 1984, Pat Robertson in 1988, Phil Gramm in 1996, Steve Forbes in both 1996 and 2000, and even, to some extent, Bill Bradley.

In a number of ways, these statistics probably understate the true role of money in the presidential nomination process. On the one hand, the model does not include (it was not designed to) the role that money might have played in helping a candidate become the frontrunner or remain in that position. On the other side, there is obviously a strong correlation between these two variables, such that frontrunners are generally guaranteed to be at least reasonably successful fundraisers. As noted in the original article, an interesting test case would be to see how a candidate fared who had a large lead in the polls but couldn't raise a decent warchest. But in the races examined here, there is no such candidate.

And on to 2004

The final column in Table 2 provides the most recent version of my forecasting model, reestimated to include all the data from 1980 through 2000. In the meantime, I am pursuing research that pushes the model both forward and backward in time: forward to see how much of a race's final outcome is determined by the results in Iowa and New Hampshire, backward to examine the dynamics of candidate support during the invisible primary.

Notes

1. Several other models have since been put forward. See, in particular, Adkins and Dowdle 2000; and Steger 2000.

2. For example, in the 1992 Democratic nomination contest, the largest fund-raiser during 1991 was Bill Clinton, who raised $3,304,000; Clinton thus received a score of 100 on this variable. Paul Tsongas, who raised $2,630,000, received a score of 79.6. Jerry Brown, with total receipts of $1,034,000, was assigned a value of 31.3.

3. As Adkins and Dowdle (2000) have shown, however, the accuracy of these forecasts can be considerably improved simply by adding in the results of the New Hampshire primary.

4. Though the publication date for my article is listed as 1996, it is important to note that the book in which it was published actually appeared in late 1995. In addition, an all-but-identical version of the book chapter was presented as a paper at the 1994 meeting of the Northeastern Political Science Association. Thus, the results shown here for the 1996 Republican nomination race are a genuine *prediction*, not an after-the-fact rationalization.

References

Adkins, Randall E., and Andrew J. Dowdle. 2000. "Break Out the Mint Juleps? Is New Hampshire the 'Primary' Culprit Limiting Presidential Nomination Forecasts?" *American Politics Quarterly* 28:251–69.

Bartels, Larry. 1988. *Presidential Primaries and the Dynamics of Public Choice.* Princeton, NJ: Princeton University Press.

Brady, Henry E., and Richard Johnston. 1987. "What's the Primary Message: Horse Race or Issue Journalism?" In *Media and Momentum: The New Hampshire Primary and Nomination Politics*, ed. Gary R. Orren and Nelson W. Polsby. Chatham, NJ: Chatham House.

Campbell, James E. 2000. *The American Campaign: U.S. Presidential Campaigns and the National Vote.* College Station: Texas A&M University Press.

Ceaser, James W. 1982. *Reforming the Reforms: A Critical Analysis of the Presidential Selection Process.* Cambridge, MA: Ballinger.

Foley, John, Dennis A. Britton, and Eugene B. Everett Jr. 1980. *Nominating a President: The Process and the Press.* New York: Praeger.

Germond, Jack W., and Jules Witcover. 1985. *Wake Us When It's Over.* New York: Macmillan.

Hagen, Michael G., and William G. Mayer. 2000. "The Modern Politics of Presidential Selection: How Changing the Rules Really Did Change the Game." In *In Pursuit of the White House 2000: How We Select Our Presidential Nominees*, ed. William G. Mayer. New York: Chatham House.

Keeter, Scott, and Cliff Zukin. 1983. *Uninformed Choice: The Failure of the New Presidential Nominating System.* New York: Praeger.

King, Anthony. 1981. "How Not to Select Presidential Candidates: A View from Europe." In *The American Elections of 1980*, ed. Austin Ranney. Washington, DC: American Enterprise Institute.

Mackenzie, G. Calvin. 1996. *The Irony of Reform: Roots of American Political Disenchantment.* Boulder, CO: Westview.

Mann, Thomas E. 1985. "Should the Presidential Nominating System Be Changed (Again)?" In *Before Nomination: Our Primary Problems*, ed. George Grassmuck. Washington, DC: American Enterprise Institute.

Mayer, William G. 1996. "Forecasting Presidential Nominations." In *In Pursuit of the White House: How We Choose Our Presidential Nominees*, ed. William G. Mayer. Chatham, NJ: Chatham House.

Mayer, William G. 1997. "The Presidential Nominations." In *The Election of 1996: Reports and Interpretations*, ed. Gerald M. Pomper. Chatham, NJ: Chatham House.

Mayer, William G. 2001. "The Presidential Nominations." In *The Election of 2000: Reports and Interpretations*, ed. Gerald M. Pomper. New York: Chatham House.

Steger, Wayne P. 2000. "Do Primary Voters Draw from a Stacked Deck? Presidential Nominations in an Era of Candidate-Centered Campaigns." *Presidential Studies Quarterly* 30 (December): 727–53.

Sundquist, James L. 1980. "The Crisis of Competence in Our National Government." *Political Science Quarterly* 95:183–208.

Why Was This Research Needed?

1. What is a social science "model"? How does a model explain and predict a dependent variable?
2. Does a model have to be error-free to be judged a success? Explain.
3. How much attention have political scientists given to forecasting presidential nominations? What is Mayer's contribution to this area of research?
4. Why does Mayer believe it may be more difficult to predict presidential nominations than presidential elections?

How Was the Topic Studied?

1. What data were used in the initial development of this forecasting model? From what sources were the data taken?
2. What two independent variables are included in the model? Explain the theoretical rationale for specifying these variables as predictive factors in the presidential nomination process.
3. What is the dependent variable in this model?
4. What does it mean to say that a multiple regression equation calculates the *simultaneous* and *independent* effects of the independent variables on the dependent variable? Explain your answer in the context of this forecasting study.

What Are the Findings?

1. What is the initial multiple regression equation for Mayer's presidential nomination forecasting model?
2. What measure indicates the overall success of this model? Explain how this measure should be interpreted. Does the model improve or worsen in its accuracy when the 1996 and 2000 elections are added into the calculations?
3. The sign of the regression coefficient for Total Funds Raised changes as more years of data are entered into the model. How does this sign change affect the interpretation of this variable's impact on voting results?
4. Table 2 lists partial regression coefficients for each independent variable, along with their standard errors in parentheses. Using this information, what calculation could you perform to determine the significance of each of the independent variables?
5. Tables 3 and 4 compare predicted and actual votes for the Republican and Democratic primary candidates in 1996 and 2000. Why do you think the model's degree of error (as a proportion of actual vote received) is generally greater for the candidates who did not win? What might this indicate about a possible pitfall of the model?

What Do the Results Mean?

1. What does Mayer mean when he writes that a number of other election forecasting models are guilty of "crude empiricism"? For what reason does he maintain that his own forecasting approach is innocent of this charge?
2. How do the findings of this study contradict other scholarly writings on the nominating process?
3. What ideas do you have for improving this forecasting model? Would you retain the fundraising variable? Are there other independent variables you would want to test and, if so, why?

Afterword from William G. Mayer

This article was written in 2003, at which point the forecasting model described here had successfully predicted the outcome of the last three contested presidential nomination races. Given the celebratory, self-confident tone of the article, it was perhaps inevitable that the model would not work in 2004.

Table A1 shows the two predictor variables as they applied to the 2004 Democratic nomination contest: the amount of money that each major candidate had raised by the end of 2003, and the results of the last Gallup Poll of national nomination preferences taken before the Iowa caucuses. Howard Dean was leading the field on both indicators—but John Kerry won the Democratic nomination. What does this indicate about my forecasting model and about the enterprise of election forecasting in general?

When a model's predictions fail to work out, there are a number of alternatives open to the analyst besides completely abandoning the model. One is to qualify or correct it: perhaps it holds only in certain types of cases or one of its variables needs to be slightly redefined. In this case, although Howard Dean led in the final nomination preference poll, his support was substantially lower than the level that every other nominee-to-be had enjoyed at that stage of the race. As shown in Table A2, those candidates who went on to win their party's nomination all had at least 40 percent—and frequently a lot more than that—in the final pre-Iowa poll. By contrast, Howard Dean and Gary Hart each had the support of only about 25 percent of their party's voters—and both then lost their party's nomination.

In the context of a competitive presidential nomination race, there is an enormous difference between having 40 percent of the

Table A1
Pre-Election Predictors of the 2004 Democratic Nomination Contest

A. Funds raised by the End of 2003	
Howard Dean	$41,038,025
John Kerry	23,362,373
Richard Gephardt	16,531,291
John Edwards	14,540,690
Joseph Lieberman	13,923,862
Wesley Clark	13,720,807

B. Standing in the Final National Gallup Poll of Nomination Preferences	
Howard Dean	25%
Wesley Clark	19
John Kerry	9
Joseph Lieberman	8
Richard Gephardt	7
John Edwards	6

Source: Fund-raising figures are taken from the candidate reports submitted to the Federal Election Commission, available at www.fec.gov. Gallup results are taken from the survey of January 9–11, 2004.

potential vote and having 25 percent. As I noted in my original presentation of this model (see Mayer 1996, 55–60), every candidate makes a few mistakes or encounters a few mishaps during his nomination campaign—which often lead to a noticeable loss of support in the national polls. But a candidate backed by 40 or 50 percent of his party's identifiers can endure this sort of setback and still go on to win. In the 2000 Republican contest, for example, John McCain unexpectedly trounced front-runner George Bush in the New Hampshire primary. In the first national poll conducted after New Hampshire, Bush's support dropped by 9 percentage points, and McCain's increased by 19 points. But because Bush had been so far ahead of McCain before New Hampshire, he still led McCain 56 percent to 34 percent in the national polls even after the Granite State had had its say. When a candidate has only 25 percent in the polls, however, even a small decline can prove fatal to his prospects. After his losses in Iowa and New Hampshire, Dean's support dropped a total of 11 percentage points. It is difficult to win a lot of primaries with only 14 percent of the potential vote.

One moral of the 2004 Democratic contest, then, may be that the pre-Iowa polls are an accurate predictor of the eventual nominee *only if the leading candidate has at least 40 percent of the vote in the final poll.* Levels of support significantly below 40 percent indicate that the race is still up for grabs, and that the winner will be the candidate who does best in the early stages of the race, especially in Iowa and New Hampshire.

The other lesson is that election forecasting models should be interpreted not as establishing invariable, law-like truths but as showing the general tendencies of a political process. The principal purpose of my original forecasting article was to show that, contrary to the then-conventional wisdom, the new post-reform nomination process was not very favorable to outsider and long-shot candidates—the nomination was usually won by the early front-runner. The 2004 results notwithstanding, these generalizations have clearly held up in a substantial majority of recent nomination races.

Table A2

Level of Support Received by the Leading Candidate in the Final Pre-Iowa Nomination Preference Poll

Race	Leading Candidate	Level of Support	Eventual Nominee
1992 Republican	Bush	84%	Bush
2000 Republican	Bush	63	Bush
2000 Democratic	Gore	60	Gore
1980 Democratic	Carter	51	Carter
1984 Democratic	Mondale	49	Mondale
1996 Republican	Dole	47	Dole
1988 Republican	Bush	45	Bush
1992 Democratic	Clinton	42	Clinton
1980 Republican	Reagan	41	Reagan
2004 Democratic	Dean	25	Kerry
1980 Democratic	Hart	23	Dukakis

Reference

Mayer, William G. 1996. "Forecasting Presidential Nominations." In *In Pursuit of the White House: How We Choose Our Presidential Nominees,* ed. William G. Mayer, 44–71. Chatham, N.J.: Chatham House.

Monica Lewinsky's Contribution to Political Science

John R. Zaller

She was a psychology major, just out of college, who decided to explore a budding interest in government. With the help of a family friend who was also a major contributor to the Democratic Party, Monica Lewinsky gained a coveted position as a White House intern (Leen 1998). Within about five months, she had become involved in an intimate relationship with the president of the United States. The liaison lasted, on and off, from November 1995 through December 1997. Then, on January 21, 1998, the Washington Post *and other major news organizations let the world in on the secret by reporting on an investigation of President Bill Clinton by independent counsel Kenneth Starr (*Washington Post *1998). Whatever she had gained from her internship experiences, Lewinsky's real education on the subject of American politics—and that special interaction known as executive-congressional relations—was about to begin. Eventually, the scandal fueled a Republican quest for Clinton's impeachment and removal from office, which the president managed to escape only when the final Senate vote was taken. (Although the House approved two articles of impeachment, the Senate vote did not reach the two-thirds threshold required for conviction.) However, Clinton's power in office was greatly diminished for the rest of his term, as was his future standing in the history books.*

For the same reasons that Monica Lewinsky emerged as a central figure on the national political scene, she also became a "phenomenon" of note in political science. Once her discussions commenced with prosecutor Starr, Lewinsky's private indiscretion was transformed into a public issue, and popular interest in the controversy quickly rose to fever pitch. One national opinion study in February 1998 found that 93.2 percent of Americans could identify Monica Lewinsky as the White House intern with whom Clinton was linked. By contrast, only 13 percent knew that Clinton had signed a Republican welfare overhaul bill in 1996 and only 26 percent could correctly characterize the president's position on health care reform, which were the two foremost domestic policy priorities of his first term (Lewis, Morgan, and Jhally 1998). From a political science standpoint, there were two immediate questions: How much damage to Clinton was caused by the great and sudden notoriety of the Lewinsky scandal? How were reactions to the scandal moderated by other attitudes toward the Clinton presidency?

As John Zaller explains in this reading, Monica Lewinsky presented political scientists with a valuable opportunity to investigate the basis of public opinion formation toward the American presidency, in particular the roles of such factors as "media politics" versus "political substance." Zaller begins by focusing on the period after the Lewinsky story broke in January 1998. Then he broadens his analysis to consider the vagaries of presidential popularity more generally in the post–World War II period. This reading shows how competing theoretical explanations can be examined by means of empirical data analysis. It also provides a straightforward application of the technique of multiple regression as a tool for enhancing historical understanding.

References

Leen, J. 1998. "Lewinsky: Two Coasts, Two Lives, Many Images." *Washington Post,* January 24, A1.

Lewis, J., M. Morgan, and S. Jhally. 1998. "Libertine or Liberal? The Real Scandal of What People Know about President Clinton." Department of Communication, University of Massachusetts–Amherst, February 10. www.umass.edu/communication/resources/special_reports/lewinsky_scandal/scandalreport.shtml.

Washington Post. 1998. "Time Line." September 13, A32.

The bounce in President Clinton's job ratings that occurred in the initial 10 days of the Lewinsky imbroglio may offer as much insight into the dynamics of public opinion as any single event in recent memory. What it shows is not just the power of a booming economy to buttress presidential popularity. It shows, more generally, the importance of political substance, as against media hype, in American politics. Even when, as occurred in this case, public opinion is initially responsive to media reports of scandal, the public's concern with actual political achievement reasserts itself. This lesson, which was not nearly so clear before the Lewinsky matter as it is now, not only deepens our understanding of American politics. It also tends, as I argue in the second half of this article, to undermine the importance of one

large branch of public opinion research, buttress the importance of another, and point toward some new research questions.

Whatever else may have transpired by the time this article gets into print, the Lewinsky poll bounce is something worth pondering. In a half-dozen commercial polls taken in the period just before the story broke, Clinton's job approval rating averaged about 60%. Ten days later, following intensive coverage of the story and Clinton's State of the Union address, presidential support was about 10 percentage points higher.[1] The fact that no analyst of public opinion could have credibly predicted this outcome makes the poll bounce especially important to examine. It is, in statistical parlance, a high leverage case.

I begin my analysis with an attempt to establish the parameters of the initial public response to the Lewinsky matter. Toward this end, the results of some three dozen commercial polls, gleaned from published sources, are summarized in Table 1. Although question wordings differ somewhat, all poll results refer to approval of Clinton's job performance as president. Also reported in Table 1 are the results of a content analysis of network TV news coverage during this period.

The content analysis, as shown in the top three rows of the table, gives average minutes of each network news program that were favorable or unfavorable to Clinton. Favorable references include Clinton's denials, attacks on Independent Prosecutor Ken Starr, statements of support for Clinton, and any other information (including non-scandal information) that might tend to enhance public support for the president. Unfavorable references include all statements indicating that the president had an affair with Lewinsky or tried to cover it up, attacks on Clinton or defense of Starr, and any other information that might tend to undermine public support for Clinton. I emphasize that, although journalists played a major role in creating the Lewinsky imbroglio, other actors, notably politicians, initiated some of the information that was reported.

What the content analysis shows is that the frenzy began with two days of heavily negative coverage, but that coverage was relatively balanced after that (given that the matter continued to attract media attention at

Table 1
Trends in Presidential Job Approval in the Initial Phase of the Lewinsky Matter

	Pre-event Baseline	Jan. 21 Story Breaks	22	23	24	25	26	27 Before Speech	27 After Speech	28	29	30	31	Feb. 1	Change
TV News Content															
Positive news minutes		0.7	2.0	4.2	2.5	2.4	2.9	4.9	—	4.6	1.9	4.0			
Negative news minutes		7.9	8.3	5.3	5.2	1.6	5.3	3.4	—	1.5	2.4	2.4			
Net news (positive minus negative)		−7.2	−6.3	−1.1	−2.8	+0.8	−2.5	+1.5		+3.1	−0.4	+1.6			
Phase I: Initial Frenzy (first two days)															
NBC News	62 (1/18/98)		61												−1
CBS News–*NYT*	58 (1/18)		55												−3
ABC News	62 (1/13)				57										−6
Time/CNN	59 (1/15)			52											−7
Newsweek	61 (1/18)			54											−7
Gallup	60 (1/18)				58										−2
ABC News–*Wash. Post*	59 (1/19)			51											−8
Phase II: Charge & Counter-charge (up to State of Union)															
NBC			61			61	63								+2
CBS News/*NYT*			55		56	56	57								+2
ABC News					57	59	60								+3
Gallup					58	60	59	67							+9
Phase III: State of Union address															
ABC News							60		60						0
NBC							63		68						+5
CBS News (respondents telephoned ahead to watch speech)									73						16?
Phase IV: Coverage of State of Union address															
Gallup									67	67				69	+2
CBS News							57			73				72	+15
ABC News							60				68	69			+9
Los Angeles Times					59								68		+9
Time/CNN				52							68				+16
Averages:	60		58	53	56	59	60	67	67	70	68	69	68	72	

Note: For sources of polls, see a PC Excel 5.0 file labeled "Lewpols" on my webpage, http://www.sscnet.ucla.edu/polisci/faculty/zaller/. Sizes and designs of polls vary.

all). In fact, if the first two days are removed, the remaining period has about as many positive minutes as negative ones, including two days on which Clinton's coverage was decidedly positive.

I have divided the poll data into four partially overlapping periods. As the table indicates, the first two days of heavily negative scandal reportage had a considerable impact on public opinion. On the basis of a half-dozen polls, Clinton's public support seems to have dropped about six or seven points.[2]

The scandal broke on a Wednesday, with the most heavily negative coverage on that day and Thursday. From Friday on, coverage was more balanced and public support for the president rose. By Monday, Clinton had regained everything lost in the first two days, and in Tuesday's Gallup poll, support for the President rose above pre-Lewinsky levels. There were two notable events in this period, both of which were amply reported on TV news. The first was Clinton's appearance on camera on Monday to make an emotional denial of a sexual relationship with Lewinsky; the other was Hillary Clinton's appearance on NBC's *Today Show* on Tuesday morning, where she charged the existence of a right-wing conspiracy against her husband.

If there is any particular spike in the data, it is the Tuesday Gallup poll, which was taken between six and nine in the evening and was therefore able to reflect news of Hillary Clinton's appearance on the *Today Show* that morning. Indeed, the poll was taken just as or just after many Americans were getting news of Mrs. Clinton's appearance; it may therefore, as other polls hint, have overstated its lasting importance on opinion. This poll showed a gain of eight percentage points from the day before, a difference that is statistically significant on a two-tailed test.[3]

Clinton's State of the Union address occurred on Tuesday evening, the end of the seventh day since the Lewinsky story broke. The speech attracted an unusually large audience, presumably because people wanted to see how the crisis-stricken president would perform. According to virtually all the pundits, he performed extremely well. "Good speech, too bad," as one commentator put it.[4]

Two national surveys were taken immediately after the speech. From baselines on the day before the speech—and therefore before Hillary Clinton's charge of a right-wing conspiracy—one survey showed no change and the other showed a gain of five points, for an average gain of 2.5%.[5] There was also a CBS poll involving reinterviews with a panel of respondents who had been asked by telephone to watch the speech so that they could be polled afterward. This survey found that Clinton's post-speech job approval rating was 73%. No immediate prespeech baseline for this poll is available, but if we take the best baseline we have—Clinton's 57% job approval in the CBS-*New York Times* poll from the day before the speech—then the combination of the speech and Mrs. Clinton's defense netted the president some 16 percentage points in support.

A little back-of-the-envelope arithmetic shows that these two sets of post-speech results—an average 2.5% gain in two polls and a 16-point gain among those asked to watch the speech—are not as far apart as they might seem. According to the Nielsen research firm, 53.1 million Americans saw the speech ("TV Ratings for Speech," 1998). This is a lot of people, but only about 25% of the adult population. If 16% of the 25% who watched the speech became more supportive of the president, the overall increase in public support would be only 4.0 percentage points ($.16 \times .25 = .04$). If we assume that viewership of the speech was higher than 25% among those asked to watch it in preparation for a survey but still well under 100%, there is no real disagreement among the three polls on the size of the "speech plus Hillary" effect.

From the bottom panel of Table 1, it appears that public support for Clinton rose another three or so points after the State of the Union, perhaps in response to favorable news coverage of that event. But this gain, if real, is apparently small in relation to gains that had already occurred.

It is tempting to pursue more detailed analyses of particular events, but I have already pressed dangerously close to the limits of the data. Instead, I will step back and offer a somewhat less detailed and, I therefore hope, safer summary: In response to sharply negative media coverage of the Lewinsky matter, public support for the president fell. But support rebounded and then surpassed its initial level as the president, his wife, and their allies fought back.

One point seems especially clear and important: In the period in which Clinton's support fell about 7 percentage points, media coverage was sharply negative, but in the period in which he gained back those 7 points and added an additional 8 to 10 points of support, coverage was essentially balanced. Thus, while media coverage of the Lewinsky matter explains part of the opinion change that occurred, it cannot explain all of it. In particular, the notion that the public responded mechanically to media coverage cannot explain how Clinton ended up with higher job approval ratings than he began with. Additional explanation is needed.

An obvious possibility is to argue that the public makes a distinction between approving the way the president does his job and approving of the president as a person. There is, as it happens, some evidence for this view, but not a great deal. The president's personal favorability ratings fell more sharply than his job approval ratings and also recovered less well. In three NBC News polls, Clinton's favorability ratings were 57% before the Lewinsky matter broke, 40% after three days of scandal coverage, and 50% after the State of the Union. In what is apparently the only other set of surveys that made three such soundings of opinion, *Time*-CNN found that Clinton's favorability ratings went from 60% to 50% and then back to 60%.[6]

These data on favorability seem to me to do little to alleviate the mystery of Clinton's bounce in job approval ratings, since they show essentially the same trend. Even if we were examining the favorability data alone, we would still be hard-pressed to explain why Clinton, who looked nothing like a teflon president when he was pressing for gays in the military and health reform, stood up to the scandal coverage as well as he did. Nor could we explain why, amidst continued media attention to scandal, he actually recouped most of his initial loss.

Another argument might be that Clinton's specific defense against the allegations of sex and cover-up was simply very persuasive. But I find this hard to swallow—not because I disbelieve Clinton, but because he presented so little evidence to support his side and got so little support from witnesses that were in a position to give it. In particular, Clinton got no help from Lewinsky herself, who was semi-publicly negotiating a plea bargain with the independent prosecutor throughout this period. As I parse Clinton's defense, it has consisted of two flat assertions: "I didn't do it" and "my enemies are out to get me."

If the public believed this defense, it was because it wanted to. I suggest, therefore, that we consider the political context that presumably made the public want to believe Clinton's defense, namely, his record of achievement in office. Clinton made an excellent statement of this record in his State of the Union address. Although the address reached too few people and came too late to explain the bulk of Clinton's recovery in the polls, it is reasonable to suppose that the presidential record that the speech touted was well-known to the majority of the public.

Clinton's speech was, first of all, a celebration of a list of "accomplishments" that would be any president's dream: The economy was the strongest in 25 years, the federal budget was on the verge of balance for the first time in 20 years, crime was falling for the first time in living memory, and the country was at peace. In the main section of the speech, the president proposed a series of programs designed to appeal to the ideological center, as exemplified by a plan to use surplus funds to put Social Security on a sound footing, improve public education, and build more highways. Thus, what the president trumpeted in his speech—and what he would presumably continue by remaining in office—was a record of peace, prosperity, and moderation. Or, more succinctly, it was a record of "political substance." This record was so unassailable that, to much of what the president said in the State of the Union, the Republican leadership could only offer polite applause.

Can political substance, thus defined, move public opinion? Certainly it can. Thanks to a distinguished series of studies—including Key (1966), Kramer (1971), Mueller (1971), Fiorina (1981), and Rosenstone (1983)—political scientists have been aware of the importance of "bottom line" politics for some time. Brody's (1991) work on presidential popularity, which stresses the effects of "outcomes" news coverage on approval, points in the same direction. In light of this, it seems entirely plausible to suggest that the poll bounce that Clinton got at the time of the Lewinsky matter was driven by the same thing that drives presidential election outcomes and presidential popularity in general—political substance. It was not admiration for Bill Clinton's character that first buttressed and then boosted his approval ratings. It was the public's reaction to the delivery of outcomes and policies that the public wants.

This argument is much more than a claim that "It's the economy, stupid." In fact, Clinton's economic performance has been only middling through most of his presidency. Taking the average four-year growth in Real Disposable Income (RDI) for every president elected from 1948 on, Clinton's first term economy ranks tenth of 13. If presidential terms are rank-ordered by growth in the

12-month period prior to Election Day, Clinton's first term is still a mediocre tenth of 13 since World War II. Only recently has Clinton's economic performance become as strong as he described it in his State of the Union.

If Clinton's economy cannot by itself explain why he won by nine percentage points over Bob Dole in 1996, neither can it explain trends in his approval ratings. One big but easy-to-overlook factor is peace, which is a virtual prerequisite for popular support. Popular support for Presidents Truman and Johnson was so damaged by bloody wars that, despite reasonably good economies, they chose not to run for reelection.[7] Clinton's administration has not only avoided war, it has enjoyed a very notable success in Bosnia, for which the president was nominated for a Nobel Peace Prize.

The other big and also easy-to-overlook plus for Clinton is his ideological moderation. This is a factor that scholars, with the exceptions of Rosenstone (1983) and Alesina et al. (1993), have too often ignored. Let me first show anecdotally how moderation affected Clinton's support and then, insofar as possible, make a systematic case.

Since gays in the military and the debacle of health care reform, Clinton has hewed to centrist policies, including ones, like welfare reform (and NAFTA earlier on), that are hard for Democratic presidents to endorse. In his confrontation with the Republican Congress over balancing the budget, it was the president, rather than the Republicans, who held middle ground. And finally, after two decades of massive budget deficits, the president has, by means of an initially unpopular budget package in his first term, helped bring the centrist goal of a balanced budget within apparent grasp.

Consistent with the notion that moderation matters is this fragment of hard evidence: President Clinton's approval ratings were weaker at the midpoint of his first term, when the economy was stronger but he identified himself with noncentrist policies, than at the end of his first term, when the economy was weaker but he had remade himself as a policy moderate. Clinton's average job approval rating in Gallup polls taken in the sixth, seventh, and eighth quarters averaged 44.3% and the average percent change in RDI in these same quarters was 4.7%. In quarters fourteen through sixteen, these figures were 55.5% and 1.5%.

Systematic evidence that policy moderation affects presidential popularity is, as far as I know, non-existent. But as regards presidential elections, the evidence, though limited, is clear. The only published evidence comes from Rosenstone's *Forecasting Presidential Elections* (1983), which finds centrism to be a major determinant of cross-state and cross-time voting. In another cut at this problem, my research assistant rated each of the candidates in elections from 1948 to 1996 on a seven-point scale, running from liberal (+3) to conservative (−3). The ratings of each pair of candidates were then summed to produce a measure of relative distance from the center—i.e., a measure of relative extremism—such that higher scores indicated greater relative distance from the midpoint by the candidate of the incumbent party. For example, Lyndon Johnson was rated +2 in 1964 and Barry Goldwater as −3, so that Goldwater was one point further from the center than Johnson. Obviously, such ratings are subject to error and bias. But I note that they were developed in connection with another project (press bias in presidential primaries), and that they correlate highly with the ratings of Rosenstone with which they overlap. These ratings also correlate well with a new set of ideological location scores produced by Poole (forthcoming) for presidential candidates who earlier served in Congress.[8]

The results for a standard voting model are shown in Table 2. War is coded as "1" in 1952 and 1968 and "0" otherwise. Economic performance is measured as average percent change in RDI in the four quarters prior to the election; that is, in the 12th through 15th quarters of each term. As examination of the regression coefficients in Table 2 shows, ideological extremism rivals economic performance as a determinant of vote for the incumbent party. Being one point closer to the center on a seven-point ideology scale (as Johnson was in 1964) is worth about 3 percentage points of the vote; by way of comparison, each additional percent of growth in RDI is worth about 2.1 percentage points. Finally, war costs the incumbent party about 4.5 percentage points of the vote.[9]

Table 2
The Effect of Peace, Prosperity, and Moderation on
Presidential Vote, 1948–1996

	B	S.E.	Two-sided p-value
War (52, 68=1, else=0)	−4.5	2.3	.04
Real Disposable Income[a] (range: 0% to 7.7%)	2.1	0.40	.001
Relative Extremism (see text)	−3.3	1.0	.005
Constant	43.6		
Adjusted r-square	.77		
N=	13		

Note: Dependent variable is percentage of the two-party vote for the incumbent party candidate.
[a]From *Survey of Current Business,* August, 1997, Table 4, p. 164–67.

From all this I conclude that peace, prosperity, and moderation very heavily influence the dynamics of presidential support, probably in matters of presidential popularity and certainly in general elections, for Clinton as well as for other presidents. What the Lewinsky bounce adds to this conclusion is confidence. Although evidence of the importance of political substance has been accumulating for some three decades, no one could have predicted that Clinton would survive the opening round of the Lewinsky affair nearly so well as he did. This is because it has never been quite so starkly clear just how relentlessly the majority of voters can stay focused on the bottom line. Nor, to my knowledge, has it ever been quite so clear that it is possible for public opinion and media opinion to go marching off in opposing directions.

To argue, as I am, that the public stays focused on a bottom line consisting of peace, prosperity, and moderation is not to say that the public is either wise or virtuous. For one thing, its sense of substance seems, in the aggregate, rather amoral—usually more like "what have you done for me lately" than "social justice." Nor is it clear that its decision criteria are very sophisticated. Suppose, for example, that the Watergate investigation of Richard Nixon had taken place in the context of Bill Clinton's booming economy rather than, as was the case,

in the context of gasoline shortages and "stagflation" (the combination of high inflation and high unemployment). Would Nixon have been forced from office under these circumstances? Or, if Clinton were saddled with Nixon's economy, would Clinton be, at this point, on the verge of impeachment? These are, I believe, real questions, and the fact that they are does not speak well for the public's wisdom or virtue.

Perhaps future events will shed clearer light on these questions. From the vantage point of early April, when this essay is being finalized, I am keenly aware that issues relating to Lewinsky, Whitewater, and Paula Jones have by no means reached a conclusion. If clear evidence of sexual harassment, perjury, or obstruction of justice emerges, the public might still turn on Clinton. If so, one's judgment of public opinion would need to be more favorable: It waits for clear evidence before reaching a verdict, and it is, after all, concerned with higher values. My personal hunch, however, is that public support for Clinton will be more affected by future performance of the economy than by the clarity of the evidence concerning the charges against him.

I said in opening this article, the Lewinsky affair buttresses some work in political science and undermines the importance of other work. The tradition of studies on economic and retrospective voting, which maintains that the public responds to the substance of party performance, seems strengthened by the Lewinsky matter. On the other hand, the tradition of studies that focuses on the mass media, political psychology, and elite influence, including such diverse studies as Edelman's *Symbolic Uses of Politics* (1964) and my own *Nature and Origins of Mass Opinion* (1992), seems somewhat weaker. It is reasonable to contend that the ground has shifted beneath these two traditions in a way that scholars will need to accommodate. However poorly informed, psychologically driven, and "mass mediated" public opinion may be, it is capable of recognizing and focusing on its own conception of what matters. This is not a conclusion that comes naturally to the second tradition.

Let me amplify the nature of the aspersion I have just cast. A major development in American politics in the last 50 to 100 years has been the rise of what has been variously called *The Rhetorical Presidency* (Tulis 1987), the "political spectacle" (Edelman 1988) and, more simply, Media Politics. This form of politics stands in contrast to an older model of politics, Party Politics. The defining feature of what I prefer to call Media Politics is *the attempt to govern on the basis of words and images that diffuse through the mass media.* This communication—whether in the form of presidential speeches, press conferences, TV ads, media frenzies, spin, or ordinary news—creates a sort of virtual reality whose effects are arguably quite real and important. Typical of the attitude that prevails in this style of politics is Republican strategist Frank Luntz's assessment of the events I have just analyzed: "The problem with [the Lewinsky matter] is we are not going to learn the real impact for years. . . . It's going to leave an indelible mark on our psyche but I don't know what the mark will be . . ." (quoted in Connolly and Edsall 1998). Freely translated, what Luntz is saying is: "It may take us in the spin business a little time to figure out how to play this, but you can be sure we'll keep it alive until we come up with something that works for our side."

As a Republican strategist, Luntz has an obvious partisan interest in taking this view. But his occupational interest is equally great. He and his colleagues in both parties have an interest in "constructing" a public discourse in which events like the Lewinsky affair are important and in which political substance—in the sense of peace, prosperity, and moderation—is unimportant, except insofar as it is useful to emphasize it.

A sizeable part of political science has organized itself to study this new political style. My analysis of the Lewinsky affair, however, suggests that political science not go too far down this road, since old-fashioned political substance of the kind that party competition brings to the fore is not only thriving in the media age, but quite likely still dominant.

This is not to say that the new style of Media Politics is without importance. If only for the resources it consumes and the public attention it commands, Media Politics matters. More, perhaps, than we would like, Media Politics defines our political culture. But beyond that, the effects of Media Politics on political outcomes must be demonstrated on a case-by-case basis, because sometimes the effects are real and lasting and other times they are not.

One illuminating example of Media Politics that produced lasting effects is Gerald Ford's pardon of Richard Nixon in 1974. Coverage of the event was, of course, overwhelmingly negative. On the basis of the same coding categories as in Table 1, Ford got 11 minutes of negative coverage on the network news on the night following the pardon, as against two minutes of positive coverage. The next night, these figures were 10 and two minutes. Reporters were by no means the only source of the bad news. In the first two news days after the pardon, 12 Democratic members of Congress, including the House Speaker and Senate Majority Leader, were quoted on the network news attacking Ford, and within the first week the Democratic Congress passed a resolution condemning the pardon. Three Republican leaders also criticized Ford. In these circumstances, Ford's approval rating fell 17 percentage points in the first two days and about 30 points over the longer run.

The contrast with the Lewinsky case is striking. In the first two days of this case, only three Republican members of Congress, none from the leadership, were willing to be quoted on network TV news attacking Clinton— and not for want of opportunity. Reporters were scouring Capitol Hill for volunteers, but politicians (including Democratic politicians) were playing it safe. Thus, the media were forced to shoulder a much larger part of the Lewinsky story on their own. In these quite different circumstances, Clinton suffered limited short-term damage and made gains over the longer run.

It is a tempting conclusion that when the partisan opposition joins a media frenzy, the two together can move public opinion, but that the media alone cannot do it. But even if systematic research were to establish that this pattern is general, there would still be an obvious concern: Namely, that opposition politicians attack when they see an opportunity to score points and hold fire otherwise. By this account, Democratic politicians attacked Ford because they knew the attacks would play well, but Republican politicians refrained from attacking Clinton because they feared the attacks would backfire. If this argument is considered plausible, as I think it must be, it further underscores the central claim of this essay: That American politics tends to be driven more by political substance—in this case, public disapproval of the pardon of Nixon—than by the antics of Media Politics. It also points to a difficult future research problem: Sorting out whether partisan attacks and other media messages are the causes of public attitudes or their hidden (i.e., endogenous) effects. Surely, the answer is some of both.

Another media frenzy from the Ford administration is worth a brief look. When Ford stated in the second presidential debate that "there is no Soviet domination of Eastern Europe," the mass audience hardly noticed but reporters instantly saw the remark as a gaffe. Polls showed that, citizens polled immediately after the debate judged 44% to 33% that Ford had won. Once the media frenzy of this famous gaffe had run its course, however, the public's judgment was reversed: Several days after the debate, the public thought by a margin of 62-17% that Carter had won. More significantly, Ford also lost ground in straw poll surveys on how people intended to vote. But by about 10 days later, Ford's poll standing had recovered and the gaffe was left for political scientists to ponder (Chaffee and Sears 1979; Sabato 1993, 127–29).

According to a study by Daron Shaw (1995), this pattern is typical. Media frenzies over gaffes and alleged gaffes in presidential campaigns do affect public support for the candidates, but only briefly. The time it takes public opinion to bounce back may, as in the Ford example, disrupt a candidate's momentum and perhaps thereby affect the election, but the lasting direct effect of most media frenzies tends to be nil.

One way to think about this pattern is to assume that there is some "natural" level of support for candidates that is determined by political fundamentals such as the strength of the economy, the candidates' positions on issues, and other such matters. Media frenzies can briefly undermine a candidate's natural level of support, but cannot permanently lower it. Thus, what happened to Clinton in the Lewinsky matter is similar to what happens to candidates who misstep in elections; he recovered from the initial attack. The fact that Clinton gained back more support than he lost is harder to explain in these terms, but I offer the following conjecture: In nonelectoral periods, the public tunes out from politics, failing, *inter alia,* to keep its evaluation of presidential performance fully up-to-date. But when, as in the early days of the Lewinsky matter, Clinton's capacity to remain in office came into question, the public took stock and reached a conclusion that led to higher levels of overall support for the threatened leader.

These observations suggest a rough generalization about when media frenzies have lasting effects on opinion and when they don't: The closer media frenzies get to what I am calling political substance, the more likely the effects are to be lasting. The example of Ford's pardon of Nixon would seem to fit this pattern. To take one other example, it seems likely that sympathetic press coverage of attacks by racist southerners on peaceful civil rights protesters in the 1960s had an important effect on northern opinion and thereby congressional action. This was exactly what the Rev. Martin Luther King Jr. expected to happen, and it had lasting importance.

One lesson for political science from the Lewinsky poll bounce, then, is that more attention needs to be given to the general question of when Media Politics (in the sense of trying to mobilize public support through mass communication) matters and when it doesn't, and to do so in a manner that doesn't presuppose the answer. A current research project of Larry Bartels shows how this can be done: With a measure of the "real economy" from the Commerce Department and a measure of the "media economy" from content analysis of media coverage, he hopes to find out which has more influence on presidential approval. Among the auxiliary variables whose impact on presidential approval he will assess is the white-collar unemployment rate in Manhattan. The results will be interesting however they come out.

Another lesson for political science from the Lewinsky poll bounce is that the public is, within broad limits, functionally indifferent to presidential character. "Don't Ask, Don't Tell," as my colleague Art Stein summarizes the mass attitude. Given this, it seems appropriate to consider carefully whether research on the public's assessment of presidential character really helps us to understand the dynamics of American politics.

Contrary to this suggestion, it might be argued that private sexual misbehavior is different from public character, especially in light of changing sexual mores in this area, and that voters' assessments of public character will remain important. Perhaps. But if we view the character issue more broadly, it seems unlikely that voter concern about character has ever been very great. For example, Richard Nixon's peculiar shortcomings were deeply felt by a large number of voters from the moment he stepped onto the national stage in the 1940s. Further, the concerns about Nixon's public character were more serious than any that have been raised about Clinton's. Yet Nixon was elected to the presidency twice, once over Hubert Humphrey, a man whose sterling character has been almost universally acknowledged. Nixon's campaign against Humphrey was, of course, framed by urban riots and a stalemated war in Asia, and in these circumstances, Nixon chose to emphasize substance rather than character. "When you're in trouble," he told voters, "you don't turn to the men who got you in trouble to get you out of it. I say we can't be led in the '70s by the men who stumbled in the '60s."[10] Voters agreed with this emphasis, as they almost always do.

Notes

Thanks to Larry Bartels, Dick Brody, Mo Fiorina, Fred Greenstein, John Petrocik, and Daron Shaw for advice on early drafts of this paper.

1. Documentation of the sources of polls cited in this paper may be found in a PC Excel 5.0 file labeled "Lewpols" on my web page (www.sscnet.ucla.edu/polisci/faculty/zaller).

The polls used in determining the overall effect of the Lewinsky matter are: ABC News-*Washington Post,* January 19 and 31, job approval rates of 59% and 67%; ABC News, January 13 and 30, job approval of 62% and 69%; CBS News, January 18 and February 1, 58% and 72%; *Newsweek,* January 18 and 30, 61% and 70%; *Time*-CNN, January 15 and 31, 59% and 72%; *U.S. News and World Report,* January 11 and February 1, 58% and 66%. In cases in which polling occurred over several days, the date given is for the final day. Although wordings of the questions differ, all refer more or less directly to Clinton's job performance rather than to the Lewinsky matter *per se.*

2. Gallup conducted a poll on the afternoon of the first day of the episode, prior to the evening news. This poll showed Clinton's support rising to 62% from 60% two days earlier. However, I do not count this poll on the grounds that, although the story had broken at the time of the poll, few Americans could yet have learned about it.

3. The sizes of the two surveys were 864 and 672.

4. Peter Jennings, quoting an anonymous politician.

5. The baseline for the ABC poll was actually January 25–26, with a sample of 1,023. The size of the ABC post-speech survey was 528. The NBC pre- and post-speech surveys both have reported sizes of 405.

6. For sources of these and other favorability polls, see the PC Excel file labeled "Lewpols" on my webpage (www.sscnet.ucla.edu/polisci/faculty/zaller).

7. President Bush showed that short, successful wars that cost few American lives do not harm popularity; but neither are they much help over the longer run.

8. Full details of the ideological coding are available upon request.

9. Though going beyond the direct evidence, this analysis suggests that Clinton's confrontation with Congress over the budget in early 1996, in which he reestablished his reputation as a defender of centrist policies, may have been as important to his November win as the economy.

10. Quoted in *Newsweek,* November 4, 1968, p. 28.

References

Alesina, Alberto, John Londregan, and Howard Rosenthal. 1993. "A Model of the Political Economy of the United States." *American Political Science Review* 87 (1): 12–33.

Brody, Richard. 1991. *Assessing the President: The Media, Elite Opinion, and Public Support.* Stanford: Stanford University Press.

Chaffee, Steven, and David Sears. 1979. "Uses and Effects of the 1976 Presidential Debates: An Overview of Empirical Studies." In *The Great Debates: Carter vs. Ford,* ed. Sidney Kraus. Bloomington: University of Indiana Press.

Connolly, Ceci, and Thomas B. Edsall. 1998. "Political Pros Looking for Explanations: Public Reaction Seems to Rewrite the Rules." *Washington Post,* February 9, A6.

Edelman, Murray. 1964. *Symbolic Uses of Politics.* Urbana: University of Illinois Press.

———. 1988. *Constructing the Political Spectacle.* Chicago: University of Chicago Press.

Fiorina, Morris. 1981. *Retrospective Voting in American National Elections.* New Haven: Yale University Press.

Key, V. O., Jr. 1966. *The Responsible Electorate: Rationality in Presidential Voting, 1936–60.* New York: Vintage.

Kramer, Gerald H. 1971. "Short-Term Fluctuations in U.S. Voting Behavior, 1896–1964." *American Political Science Review* 65 (1): 131–43.

Mueller, John. 1973. *War, Presidents, and Public Opinion.* New York: Wiley.

Poole, Keith. Forthcoming. "Recovering a Basic Space from a Set of Issue Scales." *American Journal of Political Science* 42(August).

Rosenstone, Steven. 1983. *Forecasting Presidential Elections.* New Haven: Yale University Press.

Sabato, Larry. 1993. *Feeding Frenzy: How Attack Journalism Has Transformed American Politics.* New York: Free Press.

Shaw, Daron. 1995. "Strong Persuasion? The Effect of Campaigns in U.S. Presidential Elections." Ph.D diss. UCLA.

Tulis, Jeffrey. 1987. *The Rhetorical Presidency.* Princeton: Princeton University Press.

"TV Ratings from Speech." 1998. *Los Angeles Times,* January 29, A11.

Zaller, John. 1992. *Nature and Origins of Mass Opinion.* Cambridge: Cambridge University Press.

Why Was This Research Needed?

1. What does the "Lewinsky poll bounce" refer to at the beginning of this reading? What makes it of special interest for political scientists who study public opinion?
2. Explain what Zaller means by a "high leverage case."
3. What are the two main branches of public opinion research, as categorized by this author?
4. Zaller does not follow a conventional format for presenting this research, which would begin with the formal statement of a hypothesis. How would you describe his alternative stylistic approach?

How Was the Topic Studied?

1. What kinds of sources were used in the preparation of Table 1? What method did the author use to complete his content analysis of network news programs in order to create three variables for this study?

2. Describe how the data in Table 1 could be presented in one or more graphs. What would be the advantages and disadvantages of using graphs instead of this kind of table?
3. What kinds of questions are important to ask about the methods and content of the many opinion polls reported in Table 1?
4. By what means does Zaller estimate the boost in ratings that Clinton received as a result of his State of the Union address? Why is it difficult to separate this "speech effect" from the "Hillary effect"?
5. What data did the author use to generate the multiple regression analysis for this study?

What Are the Findings?

1. How does the author summarize the complex data in Table 1? Why is he cautious about not going beyond "the limits of the data"? Are you

persuaded by his interpretation of the poll numbers?

2. Why does the author believe the job approval data gathered for this study fail to confirm the claim that media coverage determined Clinton's approval ratings in the period after the Lewinsky story broke?

3. What is the distinction between measuring a president's "favorability" and a president's "job performance"? Why must both of these elements of public opinion be considered when attempting to explain views of Clinton?

4. Given the importance Zaller attributes to President Clinton's State of the Union address, it would be interesting to consider additional information that could bolster or undermine his interpretation. If you had the opportunity at the time of the speech itself, what kinds of research about the impacts of this address would you conduct to evaluate, or refine, Zaller's perspective? What bivariate analyses might be relevant to this question?

5. Table 2 reports the regression coefficient b but not the standardized regression coefficient beta.

How would knowing the values of beta for this research help you interpret the results?

6. Using the method Zaller describes in this article, predict the percentage of the presidential vote that would be won by an incumbent party candidate who rated +2 on the political extremism scale, during a time of war, after an average change of 5% in the nation's real disposable income.

7. Which independent variables in Table 2 are significant? How do you know this?

8. What is the overall strength of the relationship calculated by the adjusted R^2 in Table 2?

What Do the Results Mean?

1. Why do the findings of this research lead the author to critique his own previous research in the field of public opinion?

2. What implications does this study have concerning the legitimacy of leadership in democratic societies?

3. If you were advising a president (or other top political executive) caught in the middle of a media scandal, what strategic recommendations would you make based on this research?

Zog for Albania, Edward for Estonia, and Monarchs for All the Rest? The Royal Road to Prosperity, Democracy, and World Peace

Jeremy D. Mayer and Lee Sigelman

Comparative politics, one of the major subfields of political science, is concerned with the laws, institutions of government, political behavior, and public policies of countries around the world (Zahariadis 1996). Developing frameworks of description and analysis that encompass the community of nation-states provides valuable insight into the forces of convergence and divergence across varied political systems. Rudyard Kipling, in his poem "The English Flag," asked, "And what should they know of England who only England know?" Comparative politics is, in its way, the political science discipline's response to the challenge of cosmopolitanism that is implicit in this question.

The emphasis on comparison in the study of comparative politics has encouraged many researchers to quantify national indicators for the purpose of statistical analysis. Many countries routinely collect similar kinds of numerical information with regard to government spending, the operation of electoral systems, criminal justice matters, and the provision of education and social welfare services. Moreover, scholars' desire for a better understanding of political culture, as both a stimulus and an outcome of governmental process, has led to ambitious data-building projects focusing on public opinion in a cross-national context. The theoretical possibilities of comparative quantitative analysis are virtually unlimited for such investigations can incorporate a broad range of variables, including regime type, structures of governance, population makeup, and policy actions.

This reading by Jeremy D. Mayer and Lee Sigelman is a useful, if quirky, illustration of the application of quantitative techniques to comparative political analysis. The question addressed by these authors is simply stated: what are the social and political benefits of a monarchical form of government? The methods and results of this study, however, are far from simple. Ironically, as determined by a sophisticated multivariate model, monarchies are statistically associated with the functioning of healthy democracies through a variety of indirect relationships. The authors draw conclusions from these findings that are likely to surprise you.

Reference

Zahariadis, Nikolaos. 1996. *Theory, Case, and Method in Comparative Politics.* New York: Harcourt.

Down with Communists, we want a king!

Albanian demonstrators in Tirana's central square,
rioting for the return of King Zog

Monarchy has been the predominant form of governance throughout recorded history, and its hegemony extended well into the twentieth century. On the eve of World War I, only four nations in Europe, and none of any consequence (France, Portugal, San Marino, and Switzerland), were not monarchies. Today, however, democracy reigns, and monarchs are widely seen, in the words of the American writer Austin O'Malley, as "a vermiform appendix: useless when quiet; when obtrusive, in danger of removal" (quoted in Esar 1962, 140), or even as the capstone of a sinister conspiracy. "The Royal Family stands at the pinnacle of the class system, and its wealth is linked to the creation of poverty and need," charges British Marxist Mark Kirby (1998, 37). For antimonarchists, the crown is not only a symbol but also a source of centuries-old class domination, social injustice, and imperialism, a wasteful frippery at best (Came 1998) and a malignant atavism at worst (Nairn 1994). Thus, the forces of blond egalitarianism have humbled the Nordic royalty by replacing their horse-drawn carriages with bicycles, and the British have reduced their nobility to guiding hordes of T-shirted, gum-snapping American tourists through their ancestral homes in order to make ends meet. In Australia, "progressive" forces have succeeded in scheduling a referendum in 1999 on whether the current head of state, Queen Elizabeth, should be replaced by an illustrious Australian—if one can be found.

Though an endangered species, monarchs are by no means extinct. On five of the world's six inhabited continents, monarchs (emirs and emiras, emperors and empresses, grand dukes and duchesses, kings and queens, princes and princesses, sultans and sultanas) still preside over nations large and small. Indeed, there are signs that monarchy may even be undergoing something of a renaissance. In 1994, the Estonian Royalist Party, holders of almost 10% of the seats in the national parliament, offered to crown Britain's Prince Edward as the King of Estonia, because of their admiration for "him . . . , Britain, its monarchy, democracy and culture" and, presumably, because he had so little else to do.[1] Three years later, the untimely death of the dazzling Diana stirred a lachrymose tidal wave. Then, in 1998, came the once-unimaginable spectacle of a Russian leader repentantly sanctioning the interment of the remains of Tsar Nicholas II in the Cathedral of St. Peter and St. Paul.

Avid appreciation of the merits of monarchy lives on in Central and Eastern Europe, in particular, and especially in Albania, Romania, Russia, and Serbia. This is not difficult to fathom. The last time some of these nations experienced a sustained period of independence, stability, and prosperity, a monarch sat atop the government. So, while the Estonians' longing to be ruled by a member of the British royal family may conjure up quaint images of the crackpot scheme hatched by the Duchy of Grand Fenwick in *The Mouse That Roared,* the fervor for monarchy in the new democracies is real. Cynics dismiss it as silly, nostalgic romanticism, but could it instead be an altogether rational manifestation of the universal desire to live well and be governed well? Although the royal road has generally been bypassed in the twentieth century, might it be the surest route to societal well-being and good government in the new millennium?

Data and Methods

To find out, we formulated and tested a statistical model based on the data Muller and Seligson (1994) assembled for their analysis of the link between political culture and democratic performance in 27 Western societies. The ultimate dependent variable in our model was a rating of each country's democratic performance during the 1980s.[2] Posited as immediately prior to democratic performance in the chain of causality were three interrelated dimensions of national political culture: the percentage of the public proclaiming support for revolutionary change, the percentage expressing concern about threats from internal subversion, and the percentage endorsing the idea that most of their fellow citizens were trustworthy. The intuitions underlying this portion of the model were that democracy is not apt to thrive in countries whose citizens clamor for revolution, fear internal subversion, and distrust one another. In turn, we posited as causally prior to these components of political culture three interrelated structural conditions: national wealth (as indicated by per capita gross domestic product), socioeconomic equality (as indicated, inversely, by the income share of the top 20% of the nation's households), and past democratic performance (as indicated by the nation's democratic performance rating during the 1970s). That is, we hypothesized that a culture supportive of democracy would be more likely to flourish in nations that were more prosperous, where wealth was less concentrated, and where democratic institutions had functioned well in the recent past.

To this seven-variable model we added, as the key element, a dummy variable indicating whether the nation was a monarchy (1) or not (0). Of the 27 nations in the analysis, 11 were monarchies; these 11 represent almost 40% of the world's 28 remaining ruling dynasties.[3] We specified monarchy as causally prior to every other variable in the model in order to test its impact on the contemporary structural and cultural requisites of democracy and on democracy itself.

Findings

As shown in the first section of Table 1, several of the variables just described were significant predictors of democratic performance: national democratic performance ratings in the 1980s were significantly higher in nations where the public was less worried about internal subversion and less supportive of revolution, where the top 20% commanded a smaller share of the income, and where na-

Table 1

Models of the Impact of Monarchy on Societal Well-Being and Democracy

	b	t
Democracy 1981–90 (Adjusted R² = .83)		
Monarchy	-5.57	0.13
Income inequality	-2.06	-3.42*
GDP per capita	-.001	-0.44
Democracy 1972–80	.28	1.51*
Interpersonal trust	.04	0.13
Concern about subversion	-.54	-1.79*
Support for revolution	-1.04	-1.62*
Constant	181.00	4.21*
Support for Revolution (Adjusted R² = .38)		
Monarchy	-3.73	-1.52*
Income inequality	-.21	-0.84
GDP per capita	.001	1.79
Democracy 1972–80	-.21	-3.43*
Constant	28.40	1.71*
Concern about Subversion (Adjusted R² = .07)		
Monarchy	.64	0.13
Income inequality	.18	0.37
GDP per capita	.001	0.65
Democracy 1972–80	.13	1.09
Constant	-1.92	-0.06
Interpersonal Trust (Adjusted R² = .26)		
Monarchy	15.16	2.73*
Income inequality	.56	1.00
GDP per capita	-.001	-0.54
Democracy 1972–80	.22	1.62*
Constant	-7.01	-0.19
GDP per capita (Adjusted R² = .37)		
Monarchy	$3619.43	3.89*
Constant	$4202.27	7.14*
Income Inequality (Adjusted R² = .47)		
Monarchy	-12.26	-4.68*
Constant	51.94	31.33*
Democracy 1972–80 (Adjusted R² = .24)		
Monarchy	28.28	2.96*
Constant	66.27	10.95*

*t < .10, one-tailed.

Figure 1 • Significant Causal Links

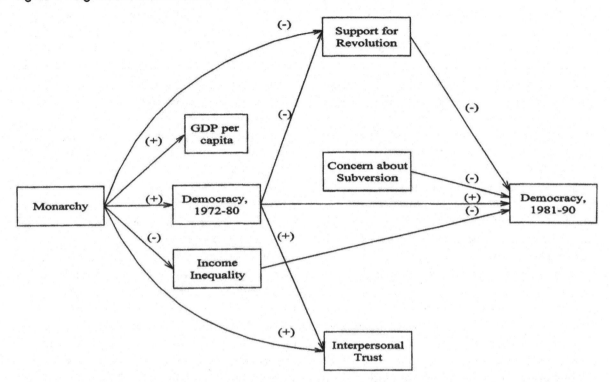

tional democratic performance ratings in the 1970s had been higher. As its omission from this list implies, monarchy was not among the significant predictors. Indeed, it had essentially no independent effect on democratic performance in the 1980s (t = 0.13).

This does not mean, however, that monarchy was inconsequential—far from it. To see why, consider the remaining significant causal links in Table 1, which are shown graphically in Figure 1. These demonstrate the causal impact of monarchy on five of the six intermediate variables in the model. Other factors being equal, in monarchies, public support for revolution was significantly less widespread, interpersonal trust was significantly higher, per capita wealth was significantly greater, income was significantly less concentrated, and the political system had been significantly more democratic during the 1970s. Recalling the data shown in the first section of Table 1, three of these factors—public support

for revolution, income inequality, and democratic performance in the 1970s—themselves significantly affected democratic performance in the 1980s, and the fourth factor—interpersonal trust—helped sustain a climate of personal and political civility. As a consequence, even though monarchy had no direct effect on democratic performance in the 1980s, it consistently bolstered the conditions that, themselves, promoted democracy and it consistently weakened the conditions that, themselves, undermined democracy.

Discussion

Political scientists, whose learned treatises on the requisites of societal well-being and good government have been responsible for felling millions of trees, have heretofore sacrificed remarkably little wood to advance the study of monarchy or, for that matter, to advance monarchy itself.

However, to judge from the results reported above, both monarchy and the study thereof are causes well worth advancing.

Of all the salubrious consequences of monarchy documented here, none will occasion greater consternation among antimonarchists than the observed leveling of incomes. Leftists wedded to the malevolent image of monarchy as "the instrument of the plutocratic establishment . . . which has been successfully deployed to legitimize an unjust and inequitable social structure" (Wilson 1989, 152) obviously have it all wrong, as they would have recognized long ago if they had read their Marx more carefully. Marx argued that during the historical evolution of feudalism the king acted as a check on, not a tool of, the aristocracy. By the same token, in modern times, the royalty serves as a check on the greed of rapacious capitalist barons by demonstrating that class is a function not merely of wealth but also of selective breeding and upbringing, and by embodying for the lower classes the beneficence of their betters. A strategic implication of our findings, then, is that, in many countries, the forces of progressivism and conservatism should join hands in the fight to restore monarchy, which not only spurs the egalitarian distribution of wealth coveted by the former, but also maintains the sense of traditional order valued by the latter.

Political scientists, whose learned treatises on the requisites of societal well-being and good government have been responsible for felling millions of trees, have heretofore sacrificed remarkably little wood to advance the study of monarchy or, for that matter, to advance monarchy itself.

The cultured role model of, and the unstinting acts of *noblesse oblige* by, royal families not only help prevent overconcentration of wealth and conspicuous consumption, but also augment the national stock of interpersonal trust. As even one of the British monarchy's most strident critics concedes, the monarchy is of key importance in "binding together the disparate ethnic populations of the UK into a non-ethnically-based British nationality" (Kirby 1998, 37). Belgians Jean, Jan, and Johannes may have little else in common, but under the unifying spell of King Albert II each can trust the others to return his lost wallet, to obey the speed limit, and to give his all—chocolate, waffle iron, or whatever—for the commonweal.

Our findings also expose the illogic of measures currently underway in Britain and elsewhere to slash the royal purse. This pecuniary assault may save a paltry few tens of millions each year, but its penny-wisdom is far outweighed by its pound-foolishness. In the first place, the cost of maintaining the royals in the manner to which they have become accustomed pales in comparison to the intangible benefits of greater interpersonal trust, a more egalitarian income distribution, panethnic unity, and stronger democracy. More concretely, the enrichment of the national treasury is where kings and queens undeniably earn their pelf. According to data collected for Table 1, having a monarch adds $3619.43 per capita each year to a nation's gross domestic product—many times the annual budget for the wages of liveried footmen, the purchase of new polo mallets, the drycleaning of ermine robes, and the other essentials of the royal lifestyle.

What nation would not want to take advantage of all these royal boons? Of course, some logistical problems remain to be settled before a suitable royal family can be identified for every one of the scores of nations that would benefit therefrom. The Estonian Edwardians and Albanian Zogistas have already made their preferences known, and, fortunately, decades of determined in-breeding among the crowned heads of Europe have produced scores of royal relatives available for consignment, including more double cousins than would be found even in a random sample of Arkansans.

Happily, even those misguided nations that elect not to follow the royal road stand to profit from a rediffusion of monarchy, in the form of a worldwide peace dividend. Political science has convincingly established that democracy leads to peace (Brown, Lynn-Jones, and Miller 1995). As we have demonstrated, monarchy leads to democracy. If every nation crowned just one little monarch, then what a peaceful world this would be! ■

Notes

1. In a typically arch statement, a spokesman for Buckingham Palace termed this "a charming but unlikely idea" (Hardman 1994).

2. For details concerning this measure and the other measures described in this paragraph, see Muller and Seligson (1994).

3. This classification was based on the Summer 1998 "Special Royals Issue" of *Life* magazine. A valuable methodological lesson for political scientists is that they should remain alert while standing in line at the grocery counter. A definitional issue arose for two countries. Although Elizabeth II is the official head of state of both Australia and Canada and is featured prominently on their currency and postage stamps, we were concerned that royalism might not be as deeply ingrained in these two countries as in other monarchies. Needless to say, our decision to classify both nations as monarchies was made for purely theoretical reasons. The fact that this decision bolstered the strength of our findings was wholly irrelevant.

References

Brown, Michael E., Sean M. Lynn-Jones, and Steven E. Miller. 1995. *Debating the Democratic Peace.* Cambridge, MA: MIT Press.

Came, Barry, 1998. "Downsizing Royalty." *Maclean's,* March 23, 32–34.

Esar, Evan, ed. 1962. *Dictionary of Humorous Quotations.* New York: Paperback Library.

Hardman, Robert. 1994. "Royal Confusion over Estonian Role for Prince." *The Daily Telegraph,* July 11.

Kirby, Mark. 1998. "Death of a Princess." *Capital and Class* (Spring): 29–41.

Muller, Edward N., and Mitchell A. Seligson. 1994. "Civic Culture and Democracy: The Question of Causal Relationship." *American Political Science Review* 88 (September): 635–52.

Nairn, Thomas. 1994. *The Enchanted Glass: Britain and Its Monarchy.* London: Vintage.

Wilson, Edgar. 1989. *The Myths of British Monarchy.* London: Journeyman Press.

Why Was This Research Needed?

1. What presence do monarchies have in the contemporary political world? According to Mayer and Sigelman, what forces seem to be calling for renewed attention to monarchy as a viable form of governance?

2. How does this study relate to previous research on the subject of democratic performance?

How Was the Topic Studied?

1. From what previously published research were the data in this study derived?

2. What hypotheses guided the authors' selection of variables for this study?

3. What three measures of political culture do the authors include in their multivariate analysis? Why would it be useful to know the actual wording of the questions for these survey items? What is the meaning of the ultimate dependent variable, "democratic performance"? What additional kinds of information could the authors have provided to explain this measure?

4. Note 3 discusses a quandary that arose in the coding of data. What larger point does this humorous note make about the potential loss of objectivity when data are organized for quantitative analysis?

5. How is the technique of multiple regression used in this research? How many different regression equations were estimated?

What Are the Findings?

1. Which of the statistics presented in Table 1 tells us about the nature of the relationship between the independent and dependent variables? The

significance of the independent variables? The overall strength of the respective equations?

2. The first set of regression results in Table 1 indicates that the partial slope b between Income Inequality and Democracy is −2.06. Explain what this means. (Be sure to include the concept of statistical control in the wording of your answer.)

3. Explain why the authors treat the Monarchy item as a "dummy variable." How does the interpretation of the partial slope calculations for Monarchy differ from those for other variables that are proper numerical scales?

4. Explain why some of the larger b values in Table 1 are not significant, while certain smaller b values are significant.

5. Why did the authors carry out one-tailed tests of significance? How does their standard for rejecting the null hypothesis differ from most statistical studies? What might justify the approach they have adopted in this case?

6. Overall, does the fully specified model do a good job of explaining democratic performance during the 1980s among the countries in this study? Why or why not?

7. How does Figure 1 help clarify the detailed regression findings in Table 1? Look at the relationship paths in this figure. Why do the authors conclude that the presence of a monarchy has no direct effect on democratic performance, although it is a factor that operates through other variables to promote democracy?

What Do the Results Mean?

1. What do you think of the authors' (tongue-in-cheek) assessment that the establishment of new monarchies could advance social well-being in countries around the world? What is the flaw in this argument?

2. What does this research reveal about the need to exercise caution in using statistical associations as actionable truths in politics? What considerations help indicate when the external manipulation of a research variable would be justifiable?

Afterword from Jeremy Mayer

In this puckish bit of political science whimsy, my coauthor and I sought to establish that monarchy leads to democracy. We found that monarchy's impact on democracy is indirect; it has no measurable impact on the current level of democracy in a country. Rather, its influence is felt on three variables that do eventually affect the level of democracy in a country: income inequality, prior era democracy, and per capita wealth. A series of bivariate regressions showed that the binary variable monarchy/nonmonarchy among the twenty-seven nations studied seems to influence these three factors, and these three factors, in turn, influence whether a country is currently democratic. We presumed that monarchy would be causally prior to all other variables, thus justifying the path analysis shown in the article's figure.

Our intention going into this piece was to be humorous, and we deliberately reported results that we believed to be spurious. The article shows that statistical analyses unguided by thoughtful theory can be persuasive on the surface, while ultimately lacking substance. It is far more likely that the effect of monarchy upon these variables is a product of some third factor. For example, monarchies tend to persist as increasingly irrelevant appendages in countries that have not experienced widespread societal upheaval, and thus they remain wealthier than other countries. Monarchies tend to fall in nations that undergo economic collapse, final military defeat, or civil war. Even in those systems in which the monarchy has more impact upon governmental and economic decisions, what we may actually be observing is the long-term impact of more effective royal rule; those countries whose royals were both influential and incompetent are those in which royals lost their jobs and sometimes their lives. Royal families may survive in countries in which the monarchs have tended to be slightly more competent than the average Bourbon.

It is, of course, possible that some of the effects we showed are real, and that constitutional monarchy is a political system that has some nonspurious impact upon democratic values in particular countries. Certainly, the impressive number of monarchist Web sites that have cited this article approvingly shows that there is a population around the world eager to believe the best about monarchy, even if it means demonstrating a remarkable immunity to sarcasm. In the years since our article, few countries have turned to monarchy as the road to democracy, although for a brief period it looked as though our newly liberated brethren in Afghanistan would enthrone their octogenarian former king Zahir Shah as a figure head monarch, but nothing came of it. Nor did the exiled heir to the Hashemite kingdom of Iraq receive the royal welcome when he journeyed back to liberated Iraq in 2003. Why no attempt to leverage monarchy to bring democracy to Iraq or Afghanistan? Obviously, President Bush is more statistically sophisticated than is commonly known, and realizes that the connection between monarchy and democracy is largely spurious.

Mixing and Matching: The Effect on Student Performance of Teaching Assistants of the Same Gender

Daniel M. Butler and Ray Christensen

The status of women in the field of political science has recently emerged as an important disciplinary concern. In July 2005, the American Political Science Association released a major report entitled Women's Advancement in Political Science *(2005) that documents the relatively low number of women among full-time political science faculty members (only about one-quarter of the total). Further, the slowly rising trend toward hiring more women as assistant professors in political science departments has now reached a plateau. Yet women and men do not seem to have different levels of interest in the study of politics. Similar numbers of both sexes enter college as political science majors, and nearly half of all political science doctoral degrees are awarded to women.*

The many factors related to the current discrepancy in professional outcomes for men and women in political science are beyond the scope of this brief introduction. Suffice it to say that ample reason exists to explore the topic of gender bias as it may be operating in any aspect of the political science environment, whether inside or outside the classroom. The following reading by Daniel M. Butler and Ray Christensen is relevant to this issue in two ways. First, the authors consider the impact of statistical course content on male versus female undergraduate political science students. Second, they examine the way a gender match between students and their teaching assistants may affect student performance.

Butler and Christensen make use of a collection of student- and course-based variables in testing the different facets of their problem. Of special interest is their adaptation of the regression technique to accommodate categorical data as both independent and dependent measures in the analysis.

Reference

American Political Science Association. 2005. *Women's Advancement in Political Science: A Report of the APSA Workshop on the Advancement of Women in Academic Political Science in the United States.* Washington, D.C.: American Political Science Association. www.apsanet.org/imgtest/womeninpoliticalscience.pdf.

In *Failing at Fairness,* Sadker and Sadker (1994) provide extensive evidence that America's school system has systematically discriminated against girls and women. In areas that boys are encouraged to excel, girls are denied opportunities. They are taught to speak quietly, to defer to boys, to avoid math and science, and to value neatness over innovation and appearance over intelligence (Sadker and Sadker 1994, 13). Girls consistently outperform boys in elementary school but lag behind them by the time they graduate. Sadker and Sadker show that discrimination does not end with high school graduation, but follows female students through their college careers.

How are political science departments doing? Though roughly half of political science majors are women, are they systematically discriminated against? Two comprehensive reports on women in political science have documented gender discrimination in graduate schools and in the hiring and promotion of women faculty (Committee on the Status of Women in the Profession 1992, 2001). However, these reports only briefly address issues of gender discrimination in the undergraduate classroom.

We are surprised by the relative lack of attention paid to issues of gender discrimination in undergraduate teaching because our jobs, our departments, and our universities exist to teach undergraduates. Potential gender discrimination in undergraduate teaching is an especially important issue at our university where our political science major attracts more men than women, raising the question of whether gender discrimination contributes to this pattern.[1] Thus, we hope to contribute to a discussion of gender discrimination in undergraduate teaching by identifying obstacles women face in political science today and testing for the presence of those obstacles in an undergraduate classroom setting.

We find evidence to support claims that the content of political science courses, specifically statistics, may create barriers for women. We also find support for the claim that women teaching assistants effectively motivate women students. Surprisingly, however, we find that the gender match between a teaching assistant and a student appears largely irrelevant for student performance.

Women seem to be more motivated to complete a course when their teaching assistant is a woman, but we find no consistent evidence that women perform better on course assignments when they are taught by a woman.

Hypotheses

It would be difficult to make a comprehensive list of all the potential obstacles female political science students face. We have condensed the extensive literature on gender discrimination to three distinct hypotheses that were testable and seemed appropriate for a study of gender discrimination in undergraduate political science courses.

Our first hypothesis concerns role model effects, the primary concern of the report on gender and the profession. Female instructors may inspire female students to perform better. Ehrenberg (1997) and his associates carried out the most prominent research project in this area. Using data from the National Educational Longitudinal Study of 1988, they concluded that student performance had little association with the match between the students' race, gender, and ethnicity, and that of the teacher's. Although the Ehrenberg study concluded that a gender match of the instructor and student did not affect student performance, we have decided to test this hypothesis for several reasons. First, there has not been any follow-up research on their findings. Second, the Ehrenberg study looked at students in high school, not college. Third, we can obtain information about students taking courses that was not available to Ehrenberg and his colleagues, allowing us to control for different factors. Finally, we have the advantage of looking at students' performance on a variety of course assignments. We expect that the role model effect would be greatest on assignments that require a close interaction between a student and a teaching assistant and weakest on assignments in which the interaction with the teaching assistant was less important. Thus, a multiple choice exam in a large lecture class should be less influenced by the role model effect of the gender of the teaching assistant while an intense writing and research assignment that required multiple interactions with a teaching assistant should exhibit a greater role model effect.

A second hypothesis comes out of studies about the relationship between gender and course content. Recent studies suggest that in math young girls perform as well as boys do; however, over time fewer girls continue in advanced math courses because of a lack of encouragement and tracking practices (Leahey and Guo 2001; Weber 2001, 147–48). By the time students enter college, women have developed adverse attitudes toward math, affecting their performance in math-related areas (Nosek et al. 2002). In contrast, Fox and Ronkowski (1997) show a gender advantage for women in tasks that are spelled out with clarity. We expect that political science classes that use extensive math or statistics might exhibit a gender disadvantage for women students.

A final hypothesis is derived from descriptions of a "chilly learning environment." Men volunteer comments more than women; men are called on more than women; instructors learn the names of men faster than they learn the names of women (Banks 1988). Similarly, topics typically chosen by men and styles of argumentation used by men are favored in political science and other disciplines (Andersen and Miller 1997; Taber et. al. 1988; Banks 1988, 138). Though one female teaching assistant could not correct for all of these biases, we expect that a female teaching assistant is less likely to contribute to this type of a biased learning environment, somewhat counteracting the effects of the discipline, the content of the course, and the male gender of the professors teaching the course.

Data

We saw an excellent opportunity to examine these hypotheses by collecting data on the performance of more than 600 students who took the course "Political Inquiry" over a three-year period. This course is a required, introductory course that emphasizes writing, library research, research designs, and statistics. The course meets three times a week; two of those meetings are lectures by the professor and the third is an hour-long lab taught by an undergraduate teaching assistant. The lecture class has from 120 to 160 students; the labs have from 10 to 20 students with each teaching assistant teaching two labs during a se-

mester. Students write weekly papers including an essay on a theory and a review of an article; several research designs; and exercises on grammar, style, library research, statistics, and citation style. The teaching assistants' main responsibility during labs is to explain the writing assignments. They also grade these assignments, administer quizzes, review the week's lectures, answer questions, and handle all complaints about grading.

The unusually prominent role of teaching assistants in this course provided an excellent test case to assess gender discrimination. The best course in which to test the effect of the gender of an instructor would be a nearly identical course taught by a variety of instructors. For example, different sections of a calculus course that used the same textbook and same exam would create an excellent test of the effect of the gender of the instructor because differences in the course structure and evaluations are minimized. Unfortunately, there are very few, if any, political science courses that are taught in such a nearly identical manner. Typically, political science courses with the same course title will vary in the amount and type of reading, assignments, and exam formats.

Thus, our study of teaching assistants seems appropriate for an analysis of the gender effects of an instructor. All students take the same identical course with identical readings, exams, and writing assignments. Only the gender of the teaching assistant varies from one lab to the next. Furthermore, the role of teaching assistants in our course is more like that of an instructor than a typical teaching assistant. The teaching assistants explain the writing assignments, work closely with students on those assignments, grade the assignments, and handle student complaints about grading, making the teaching assistants nearly equivalent to instructors in the course.

A wide range of factors have been linked to discrimination, oppression, and barriers in society and the classroom. Weber (2001) examines factors thought to contribute to discrimination based on race, class, gender, and sexuality. In our course, societal norms, university practices, assigned texts, the discipline of political science, and the white, male, upper middle class characteristics of the two professors of the course could all potentially contribute to the presence of discriminatory practices and attitudes.[2] Nevertheless, in our study we attempt to hold these factors constant by selecting a course in which these factors do not vary. In our results we recognize the constant effect of these other factors while simultaneously drawing conclusions about the impact of gender matching between students and teaching assistants.

In addition, the nature of the class controls for self-selection. "Political Inquiry" is a required course for the political science major; very few students choose to take the course as an elective. More importantly, students cannot choose their teaching assistant. Because they register for a lab section without knowing who their teaching assistant will be, student lab assignments are made regardless of any preference the students might have concerning the gender of their instructors. We checked for the random nature of the gender of the teaching assistant by running a cross-tabulation on the gender of the student against that of the teaching assistant. The chi-square value was 0.3889 with a probability significance level of .53. This is strong evidence that gender did not play a role in deciding which lab students registered for.

There are three other advantages to using this course for our analysis. First, in most of the semesters studied in the course teaching assistants used a blind-grading system. The anonymity of students was protected through the use of code names, preventing overt bias in grading for or against individual students or groups of students. Second, the course has a reputation among students as being the most rigorous of the courses in the major.[3] If women are discouraged from being political science majors, a likely place for that discouragement to occur is in this course. Finally, our course data have both objective and subjective measures of student performance. The course grade is based primarily on the writing assignments (subjective) and a multiple-choice final exam (objective). In our analysis we regress both of these measures on the same set of independent variables. The different nature of these two measures allows us to test between several different hypotheses of gender discrimination.

The role model effect could be manifest as either a general or a specific influence. Generally, women students with female teaching assistants would be more enthusiastic about the overall course. They would be more likely to complete the course and more likely to do better on all course assignments. Specifically, the role model effect might appear more strongly on writing assignments for which students work closely with their teaching assistants. In contrast, having a female teaching assistant should be less relevant for performance on the final exam which covers material from class lectures and is only tangentially related to the teaching assistant led lab sections.

The course content suggests that women will do worse in the class, regardless of the gender of the professor or teaching assistant, but the exam is more heavily weighted toward statistics and the assignments are more heavily weighted toward writing and specific task-oriented activities, leading to the conclusion that women should do better (regardless of the gender of their teaching assistant) on the assignments and worse on the final.

Unfortunately, hypotheses derived from observations about a "chilly" learning environment mirror those of the role model hypothesis. Women students should do better on all course work if their teaching assistant is female because there will be less of a "chilly" learning environment for those students. This advantage should be greatest for the writing assignments where the interaction with the teaching assistants is extensive, and least for the exam where the interaction with the teaching assistants is much less important.

Model

Our first analysis is of students who fail to complete the course. We define this term broadly as any student who failed to take the final exam or received less than a total of 40% on their combined writing assignments. We analyze in a logistic regression the dependent variable "complete the course" which is coded as 1 for all students who met the minimal requirements for course completion and 0 for those who did not.

Our most important independent variable was the gender match between a student and his or her teaching assistant. We divided students into four categories: male students with a male teaching assistant, male students with a female teaching assistant, female students with a male teaching assistant, and female students with a female teaching assistant. To avoid problems of multi-collinearity, we excluded the category of male students with male teaching assistants from this and subsequent regressions. We also included several other control variables, including the student's prior GPA, year in school, age, credit hours currently enrolled in, marital status, and U.S. citizenship.[4]

We included GPA since performance in past classes is a measure of both innate ability and work ethic.[5] Students who have done well in previous classes should perform well in their current classes. We included the number of credit hours a student took because the course requires many time consuming writing assignments. Students with fewer credits have more time to study, extremely important for rewriting and revising their writing assignments. Similarly, we included a variable for marital status because we believed that married students, on average, would be more serious about their course work than unmarried students. We also expected year in school to be correlated with class performance; more advanced students should do better in the class, with the possible exception of seniors who may have delayed taking this introductory class until their final year of school for reasons that might be correlated with a poorer performance in the class. Finally, we included a dummy variable to capture whether or not the student was a citizen of a country where English is the native language. Citizenship is a surrogate measure for being a native speaker of English. We expect native speakers to do better in the course, especially on writing assignments.

During the five semesters that the data set covers, two different professors took turns teaching the course and 15 teaching assistants taught various lab sections. With both of the professors and each of the teaching assistants there are certain unobserved characteristics associated with him or her that affect the performance of his or her students. To control for this unobserved heterogeneity, we included dummy variables for one of the professors and for 14 of the 15 teaching assistants. The dummy variable for the professors proved to be significant, as were several of the dummy variables for the teaching assistants. To minimize visual confusion and to keep the tables from becoming too cluttered we do not include the dummy variables for the professor and teaching assistants in our regression results.

Initially there were 669 observations; however, two students never signed up for a lab section, so the working data set has 667 observations. Of these 667 students, 82 or 12.3% failed to complete the course.

Descriptive Statistics

Of the 669 students, 64.9% were male, and 73% took the class from a male teaching assistant (Table 1). Most of the students were single (81.1%) and were U.S. citizens (96.7%). While students from each stage of their college careers were represented in the sample, juniors were the largest group (38.7%). Prior to taking the course, the average GPA for the students was a 3.16. On average, a student in the course was enrolled in 14 cred-

Table 1
Descriptive Statistics for Selected Variables

Variable	Minimum	Maximum	Mean	Median	Standard Deviation
Credits	3	21	14.0	14.0	2.14
GPA	.73	4.0	3.16	3.23	.55
TA Experience 1 = Experienced	0	1	.37	0	.48
Marital Status 1 = Married	0	1	.19	0	.39
Country 1 = English	0	1	.97	1	.18
Age	17	49	21.9	22	2.37
Final Exam	0	91	60.9	62	15.7
Assignment Total	3.9	98	67.7	72.5	18.5

its during the semester. Finally, the average score on the final exam was 60.9%, and the average score on their combined written assignments was 67.7%.[6]

Regression Results

In a logistic regression of 30 independent variables on the dependent variable of whether or not a student completed the course, only two variables achieved levels of statistical significance: the GPA of the student and a dummy variable for female students in labs with male teaching assistants.[7] To facilitate interpretation of the coefficients in this regression, we calculated predicted values for four observations which had the median value for each of the independent variables but varied the four possible matches of student and teaching assistant gender.[8] The percent predicted to complete the class for each group are as follows:

Women in labs with male teaching assistants:	88.3%
Women in labs with female teaching assistants:	96.3%
Men in labs with male teaching assistants:	95.2%
Men in labs with female teaching assistants:	94.5%

These findings support other studies that have found that the gender of the instructor matters to students. Rothenstein (1995) found that increasing numbers of female faculty members were related to the increased likelihood that female students will get an advanced degree. Neumark and Gardecki (1998) found that female Ph.D. students with female advisors did not enjoy any improved job placement when compared with female Ph.D. students who had male advisors. At the same time, they found that female Ph.D. students with female advisors were able to finish their dissertations much more quickly. Rothenstein, Nuemark, and Gardecki and others have all found that female students with female instructors are more motivated to study.

We continued our analysis of the effect of instructor gender by assessing student perform-ance for the 585 students who completed the course. We analyzed separately two dependent variables: the students' final exam scores and their combined scores on all of their written assignments. The final exam score is a percent correct on a 100-question, multiple choice exam. The maximum possible on all of the writing assignments combined was 650 points. To facilitate interpretation of the regression results and comparison between them, we divided the point total on the assignments for each student by 6.5, measuring both variables as a score out of 100 points possible. We included the same battery of independent variables.

After controlling for fixed effects by including dummy variables for the teaching assistants and the professor, most of the results came out as expected. (See Tables 2 and 3.) The number of credit hours was the only variable with a different coefficient value than we had initially expected. Students taking more credits actually did better on course assignments. Perhaps credit hours operates as a surrogate measure for the number of hours employed. Students who take fewer credits may work more hours, and those taking more credits may work few hours or not at all. In addition, students with higher GPAs do

Table 2
Regressing Final Exam Scores on Demographic Variables

Independent Variables	coefficients	standard errors
Constant	.3	4.8
Women in male labs	−2.3	1.2
Women in female labs	−5.3	3.5
Men in female labs	−1.6	3.3
U.S. citizen	2.8	2.3
Married	2.1*	1.0
GPA	14.8*	.8
Credits	.6*	.2
Sophomores	−0.04	1.2
Juniors	−0.2	1.0
First year students	−0.8	2.3
Age 17–18	−1.5	2.3
Age 19	−3.0*	1.5
Age 22–25	−3.7*	1.1
Age 26 and older	−8.2*	2.5

Adjusted R Square .43

*statistically significant at the .05 level

Table 3
Regressing Scores of Written Assignments on Demographic Variables

Independent Variables	coefficients	standard errors
Constant	18.4*	5.6
Women in male labs	−2.5	1.4
Women in female labs	−1.1	4.1
Men in female labs	2.6	3.9
U.S. citizen	3.9	2.6
Married	2.4*	1.2
GPA	14.4*	.9
Credits	.3	.2
Sophomores	2.8*	1.4
Juniors	2.2	1.1
First year students	−5.4*	2.7
Age 17–18	.4	2.7
Age 19	.2	1.7
Age 22–25	−0.8	1.3
Age 26 and older	−5.1	2.9

Adjusted R Square .40

*statistically significant at the .05 level

better, as do married students. U.S. citizens also have the strongest advantage on writing assignments as we predicted. First year students consistently earn the lowest grades, and sophomores and juniors outperform seniors on written assignments with all three grades earning similar exam scores. Students age 20–21 generally outperform students in other age cohorts.

The values of the coefficients regarding the gender match are interesting. On both assignments and finals men do better than women and the gap between men and women does not narrow for writing assignments, contrary to the course content hypothesis. In addition, the gender of the teaching assistant does not produce a clear effect on student performance. For example, men do 2.3% better than women on the final exam for students who have male teaching assistants, but for students who have female teaching assistants, the male advantage increases to 3.7%. We found similar results when we analyzed assignments. In labs with male teaching assistants, men on average earn grades that are 2.5% better than women in those same labs, but in labs with female teaching assistants men on average earn scores 3.7% better than women. These findings do not show an advantage for women with

female teaching assistants, and this lack of advantage is nearly identical for both exams and writing assignments.

In both regressions, men with male teaching assistants served as the baseline. On assignments, it was true that women with female teaching assistants earned higher grades (1.4%) than women with male teaching assistants. However, men with female teaching assistants also earned higher grades (2.6%) than men in labs taught by male teaching assistants. On final exams women on average did 3% better if they had a male teaching assistant, but men also did 1.6% better if they had a male teaching assistant. Students with female teaching assistants did better on assignments, regardless of their gender, and students with male teaching assistants did better on the final, regardless of their gender. In all cases, however, average scores for men were consistently higher than the scores for women in the same categories of labs.

These results, however, rarely reached levels of statistical significance for matching the gender of the student with the teaching assistant, raising questions about the robustness of our findings.[9] Further analysis of separate regressions run for each individual teaching assistant underscores this concern. In these 15 separate regressions there are no consistent differences between the gender of the teaching assistant and the performance of students of the same gender. For example, six of the nine male teaching assistants had men outperforming women on writing assignments, and three of six women teaching assistants showed a similar male advantage. On the final, men did better for five of the nine male teaching assistants and for four of the six female teaching assistants. Similarly, women did relatively better on assignments than on the final (in comparison to the average male performance) for two of the six female teaching assistants but also for four of the nine male teaching assistants.

Finally, for most of the teaching assistants there was not a large differential between the average performance of women relative to men on the objectively graded final compared with the subjectively graded writing assignments. The four largest differentials occurred in two male and two female teaching assistants' results. However, one male and one female both had women doing better than men on assignments but men doing better than women on the exam. The other male teaching assistant had men doing better on assignments with women doing better on exams. The remaining female teaching assistant had men doing better on both assignments and exams with a much larger male advantage on assignments. These inconsistent results suggest that the gender of the instructor may not be a significant factor in student performance.

Though our results support the more general claims of the role model hypothesis (women with female teaching assistants are more likely to finish the course), the specific claims of the role model hypothesis and the "chilly learning environment" hypothesis are not supported. The actual performance of students is not consistently or significantly affected by the gender of the students' teaching assistant. As mentioned above, the Ehrenberg (1997) study found similar results; being the same gender is not related to improved performance.

Our study also provides strong support to the claim that the nature of the course and its content create a bias that favors male students. We were puzzled, however, that the male advantage persisted even in writing assignments and detailed task specific assignments that the literature suggests women excel in. Perhaps the combination of both types of assignments in the same course makes it difficult to compartmentalize the assignments, causing a greater similarity between the types of assignments than would be found if the assignments were given separately in different courses.

Conclusion

We have articulated some of the obstacles that women political science students still face. Barriers to women in courses that rely heavily on math or statistics cannot easily be eliminated by changes in only one college course. Though the main work needs to be done when students

are younger, it is still important that college instructors encourage students, especially women, to pursue statistics and mathematics. Along with encouraging women to study statistics, instructors can try to follow Fox and Ronkowski's (1999) advice to use methods that will better reach female students.

While our findings seem to suggest that women with female teaching assistants (and by implication instructors) do not necessarily learn the material better, they also suggest a strong motivational component of female instructors acting as role models. Female students with female teaching assistants were more likely to finish the course. As women continue to play an increasingly important role in politics, political science faculty should redouble their efforts to eliminate teaching practices that advantage one gender over the other. Faculties with increased numbers of female faculty will be more effective at motivating their female students to finish their programs and play a meaningful role in the world. ∎

Notes

1. BYU is part of a category of the "Protestant Schools" that in general have more men expressing interest in majoring in political science than women (Mann 1996). At BYU approximately 38% of political science majors are women, in contrast to the national average of about 50% women.

2. A cursory analysis of teaching evaluations suggests the overt discriminatory impact of professors is negligible. The overall evaluation of the professor by women students was slightly higher than the evaluation given by male students (6.0 vs. 5.9 on a 7.0 point scale). In addition, student responses to the question "Does the instructor respond respectfully to student questions and viewpoints?" were identical for both male and female students (6.1).

3. A reflection of BYU's religious nature and the reputation of the course is a recent student evaluation suggesting that the course be renumbered as Political Science 666.

4. Age and year in school are both controlled for because of the unique situation at BYU where most male students take two years out of their university education for church service at the age of 19.

5. We also had a measure of ACT scores, but it performed worse than GPA, suggesting that for this course, GPA rather

than ACT scores is a better predictor of class performance. In addition, using ACT scores did not change the results for class performance compared to the gender match between student and teaching assistant.

6. The average scores for the final and the assignments include the students who failed to complete the course. For students who took the course during their first semester at BYU, prior GPA is measured as their GPA during that first semester.

7. The 30 independent variables include 14 dummy variables for specific teaching assistants, three dummy variables for years in school, and four for age groupings. There are three dummy variables for student gender-teaching assistant gender combinations, and single dummy variables for the professor, marital status, country of origin, and teaching assistant experience. There are also two variables for student GPA and credit hours taken.

8. For dummy variables we used the mean value rather than the median value. However, using the mean value produces nearly identical results. Females in male labs have a predicted completion rate of 86.2% and females in female labs have a predicted rate of 95.5%.

9. For the category of women in labs with male teaching assistants, the level of statistical significance was between a probability of .05 and .10 for both regressions.

References

Andersen, Kristi, and Elizabeth D. Miller, 1997. "Gender and Student Evaluation of Teaching." *PS: Political Science and Politics* 30 (June): 216–18.

Banks, Taunya Lovell. 1988. "Gender Bias in the Classroom." *Journal of Legal Education* 38 (March–June): 137–46.

Committee on the Status of Women in the Profession. 1992. "Improving the Status of Women in Political Science: A Report with Recommendations." *PS: Political Science and Politics* 25 (September): 547–54.

Committee on the Status of Women in the Profession. 2001. "The Status of Women in Political Science: Female Participation in the Professoriate and the Study of Women and Politics in the Discipline." *PS: Political Science and Politics* 34 (June): 319–26.

Ehrenberg, Ronald G., Daniel D. Godharber, and Dominic J. Brewer. 1995. "Do Teachers' Race, Gender, and Ethnicity Matter? Evidence from the National Educational Longitudinal Study of 1988." *Industrial and Labor Relations Review* 48 (April): 547–61.

Fox, Richard L., and Shirley A. Ronkowski. 1997. "Learning Styles of Political Science Students." *PS: Political Science and Politics* 30 (December): 732–37.

Leahey, Erin, and Guang Guo. 2001. "Gender Differences in Mathematical Trajectories." *Social Forces* 80 (December): 713–32.

Mann, Sheilah. 1996. "Political Science Departments Report Declines in Enrollments and Majors in Recent Years." *PS: Political Science and Politics* 29 (September): 527.

Neumark, David, and Rosella Gardecki. 1998. "Women Helping Women? Role Model and Mentoring Effect on Female Ph.D. Students in Economics." *The Journal of Human Resources* 33 (winter): 240–46.

Nosek, Brian, Mahzarin R. Banaji, and Anthony G. Greenwald. 2002. "Math = Male, Me = Female, Therefore Math Not = Me." *Journal of Personality & Social Psychology* 83 (July): 44–59.

Robst, J., J. Keil, and D. Russo. 1998. "Effect of Gender Composition of Faculty on Student Retention." *Economics of Education Review* 17 (September): 429–39.

Rothstein, D. S. 1995. "Do Female Faculty Influence Student's Educational and Labor Market Attainments?" *Industrial and Labor Relations Review* 48:515–30.

Sadker, Mayra, and David Sadker. 1994. *Failing at Fairness: How America's Schools Cheat Girls.* New York: Charles Scribner's Sons.

Taber, Janet, et al. 1998. "Project: Gender, Legal Education, and the Legal Profession: An Empirical Study of Stanford Law Students and Graduates." *Stanford Law Review* 40 (May): 1209–97.

Weber, Lynn. 2001. *Understanding Race, Class, Gender, and Sexuality: A Conceptual Framework.* New York: McGraw-Hill.

Why Was This Research Needed?

1. According to past research, in what ways have girls and women been discriminated against in the education system?
2. How thoroughly has the issue of gender discrimination in political science been studied? What is the primary focus of the research published to date?
3. How does the university where this study was based depart from national norms regarding political science enrollment trends? What might explain this discrepancy? Do you think this pattern enhances or detracts from the value of this study setting?
4. What three hypotheses do the authors formulate to guide this study at the outset? How do they describe the potential contributions of their research in the context of existing findings?

How Was The Topic Studied?

1. What is the size of the sample for this study? How was the sample selected? In what ways do the authors justify the suitability of the sample for the special purposes of this research?
2. Why do the authors claim that teaching assistants provide a good focus for looking at gender effects in political science education? How does the study design control for extraneous factors related to gender-based discrimination?
3. Explain how the authors used the chi-square technique to confirm the randomization of male and female students assigned to different teaching assistants.
4. Regression analysis is conventionally reserved for interval, or continuous, data. In this study, what is the level of measurement of the dependent variable "complete the course"? How is logistic regression used to incorporate this variable into a regression framework?
5. Which independent variables in the study are categorical in nature? Explain how these variables are accommodated in data analysis through the creation of dummy variables.
6. What control variables did the authors include in this study and why were these specific choices made?

What Are the Findings?

1. Which independent variables are most important in explaining whether students finished this political science course? How were the regression equation results used to generate the estimated course completion rates for women and men, with and without same-sex teaching assistants? Describe how a graph could be used to display these course completion comparisons effectively.
2. What are the two methods in this study for gauging student performance?
3. Based on the statistical data for coefficients and standard errors in Tables 2 and 3, how could you confirm the significance findings reported by using either a t test or a confidence interval calculation?
4. Summarize the multivariate model that results when only the significant independent variables from Tables 2 and 3 are included. Which statistic indicates that the two original models were about equally successful in explaining the variation in final exam scores and written assignments among students?
5. Overall, what is the statistical evidence for and against the hypothesis that instructor gender affected student performance in this study?

What Do the Results Mean?

1. Based on the mixed findings in this study, what changes in your own political science department would you recommend, if any? Should there be a mathematics prerequisite for students entering a course like "Political Inquiry"? What additional

course-related assistance could be made available to students? Do you think that mentoring of younger students by older students of the same gender is an idea worth trying? Explain.

2. Would you support the idea of giving students more control in choosing the teaching assistants they are assigned to in a course? Summarize the pro and con arguments.

3. Are there any steps that undergraduate political science students can take to help recruit female professors into their departments?

4. Outline an original research study investigating the factors that promote or hinder the success of undergraduate political science students who are women. Would such a study be feasible to carry out in your college or university's department?

Afterword from Daniel M. Butler and Ray Christensen

There are two particularly noteworthy features of our article as it relates to the research process. First, we were able to get leverage on our question because we exploited a natural experiment that limited the concerns of self-selection bias. The data came from a course that was required for all political science majors but does not attract students from other departments. Even more importantly, the students signed up for their lab sections without knowing who their teaching assistant (TA) would be. Thus it is reasonable to assume that the treatment of interest (the gender match between TA and student) was randomly assigned as in an experiment. As noted in the article, we used a chi-square test to see if the assignment of the treatment was random and found that it was.

The second noteworthy point is that like most research, ours was an iterative process. We had not initially included in our analysis the logit regression for likelihood of dropping out of the course, which is arguably our most interesting finding. However, when we ran a chi-square test for the gender sorting into TA sections, we decided to run a similar chi-square test for those who failed to finish the course. We found, to our initial surprise, that there was an effect resulting from the match between the gender of the student and the gender of the TA. As a more robust test of that initial finding, we ran a logit regression because the variable of interest was dichotomous; the results of that regression are in the final article.

Moral Issues and Voter Decision Making in the 2004 Presidential Election

D. Sunshine Hillygus and Todd G. Shields

Political science and journalism are closely related fields. When it comes to the arena of politics, they share an interest in the same topics, make use of many of the same concepts, and have a common goal of improving the quality of public life in the United States. The fields overlap in other ways as well. A political science education can provide good preparation for a career in journalism, while political scientists depend on news reporting to keep up-to-date with events at home and abroad. Political scientists and journalists interact in many different settings—at professional conferences, on public affairs panels convened by the media, at events on college campuses—and it is hard to say which group benefits more from such contact.

However, political science and journalism are based on fundamentally different working methods. When interpreting the news, journalists typically depend on personal sources, short-term fact gathering, and a synthesis of impressions based on professional experience. Political scientists have more time to compile and analyze the data they choose for a certain research question, and their interpretations are informed by theory as well as the findings of previous scholars. A crucial test for political science and its empirical methods is whether it produces results that go deeper, or are more reliable, than the products of journalism.

As D. Sunshine Hillygus and Todd G. Shields note in the introduction to the following reading, George W. Bush's victory in the 2004 presidential contest stimulated a lot of commentary in the press about the powerful impact of "moral issues." Encouraging this interpretation were the results of exit polls that asked a sample of voters about this topic. Juan Williams, a FOX news analyst and correspondent for National Public Radio, summarized a commonly held view when he observed: "Just look at the exit polls, they indicate that the number one issue was morality and I think that comes as a stunner to the Kerry campaign and for much of blue-state America" (Vlahos 2004). Nonetheless, as Hillygus and Shields show, systematic empirical analysis—making use of better data and more sophisticated quantitative methods—does not support the conclusion that moral issues were a decisive factor in the campaign, especially when compared with other leading issues that voters cared about.

Ever since the advent of survey research made individual voter decision making a researchable topic, studying election outcomes has been a central concern of the discipline of political science (Almond 1996). This reading serves as a good primer in contemporary methods of election analysis. It also features the logit statistical technique as a means of calculating the probability of voting for Bush over Kerry based on issue preferences.

References

Almond, Gabriel. 1996. "Political Science: The History of the Discipline." In *A New Handbook of Political Science,* ed. Robert E. Goodin and Hans-Dieter Klingermann, 50–96. New York: Oxford University Press.

Vlahos, Kelley Beaucar. 2004. "'Values' Help Shape Bush Re-Election." FOX News, November 4. www.foxnews.com/story/0,2933,137535,00.html.

President Bush's victory, the approval of every anti-gay marriage amendment on statewide ballots and an emphasis on "moral values" among voters showed the power of churchgoing Americans in this election and threw the nation's religious divide into stark relief.

Associated Press, November 4, 2004

Although the 2004 presidential election was predicted to be razor close, Republican President George W. Bush became the first candidate to win a majority of the popular vote since his father in 1988. Bush's coattails extended to the U.S. Congress as well, with Republican gains in both the Senate and the House of Representatives. Journalists and pundits immediately attributed Republican success to the now ubiquitous "values voters" explanation—voters supported Bush because they shared his socially conservative values. Bush had emphasized his Christian faith throughout the campaign, and a widely reported exit poll found that voters thought "morals" were the most important problem facing the nation. The success of gay marriage bans in 11 states seemed to further affirm the prominence of moral values in voters' decision making. With these indicators suggesting that value issues, like gay marriage and abortion, were the catalyst behind President Bush's

re-election, it seemed that the president rode to victory on a wave of values voters who had all but escaped the notice of even the most careful political observers until Election Day. Surprisingly, the role of the economy, the war in Iraq, and a host of other plausible interpretations of the 2004 presidential election received comparatively little attention in the national media—where analysts seemed almost unanimously preoccupied with moral values. Tucker Carlson, then co-host of CNN's *Crossfire,* concluded on November 5, 2004, "Three days after the presidential election, it is clear that it was not the war on terror, but the issue of what we're calling moral values that drove President Bush and other Republicans to victory this week."[1]

In this study, we examine voter decision making in the 2004 presidential race, evaluating the influence of the "moral issues" of gay marriage and abortion on individual vote choice relative to competing factors such as party identification, retrospective evaluations of the economy, and the Iraq war. Using a new national post-election survey, we find that opinions about gay marriage and abortion were far from the most important predictors of vote choice, and had no effect on voter decision making among Independents, respondents in battleground states, or even among respondents in states with an anti-gay marriage initiative on the ballot. Rather, only in the South did either issue have an independent effect on vote choice, and even here the effect was minimal in comparison to that of attitudes toward the economy, the Iraq war, and terrorism.

The Exit Polls

The conclusion that citizens based their presidential vote largely on the basis of morals was first suggested by the results of a single question from the 2004 exit polls.[2] The question asked 7,000 voters what they believed was the most important issue in their vote for president. The now familiar results presented in Table 1 report 22% of exit poll respondents believed moral values was the most important issue, and 80% of these voters cast ballots for Bush. Comparatively, no other category received as many responses. With more voters choosing moral

Table 1
Most Important Issue by Presidential Vote

Most Important Issue	Respondent Voted For:		
	Bush	Kerry	Nader
Taxes (5%)	57%	43%	0%
Education (4%)	26	73	.
Iraq (15%)	26	73	0
Terrorism (19%)	86	14	0
Economy/Jobs (20%)	18	80	0
Moral Values (22%)	80	18	1
Health Care (8%)	23	77	.

Source: 2004 Exit Poll.

values over any other response category, observers quickly concluded that gay marriage and abortion must have been the prime mover of vote decisions in the 2004 presidential election.

Also contributing to the conclusion that "morality" was the most important consideration in voters' minds was the success of gay marriage bans on the ballot in 11 states.[3] While there was substantial variation in the initiatives, there was popular support for prohibiting gay marriage in every state where citizens were able to vote on the issue.[4] Further, each of the initiatives passed by significant margins—between 57% to 86% of the electorate—even in the so-called blue states of Oregon and Michigan. In the strategically important battleground states, especially Ohio, the gay marriage issue was thought to dominate nearly every other consideration. Anecdotal stories abound about the efforts of the Bush campaign and Christian conservatives to emphasize the gay marriage issue. Across America, church marquees read (and pastors preached) "On Tuesday, vote God."[5] The Baptist convention set out to counter the alleged impact of MTV's "Rock-the-Vote" with their own blend of music and politics they called "Redeem-the-Vote." There were reports that some traditionally Democratic African Americans mobilized for Bush solely on the basis of the gay marriage issue (Shapiro 2004).

Although gay marriage was the moral value issue most prominently featured in the 2004 presidential election, we would be remiss to ignore the perennial hot button issue of abortion. The abortion issue received somewhat less campaign coverage, but it is decidedly an issue that most expect to be an important part of the values vote. Abramowitz (1995) concluded that abortion had a dramatic influence in the 1992 election—even though Governor Bill Clinton campaigned predominantly on the importance of the economy. The role of abortion in the 2004 campaign was highlighted when some Bishops in the Catholic Church were outspoken about their unwillingness to allow Senator John Kerry to participate in communion because of his pro-choice platform, and other church officials declared that it would be a sin to vote for a pro-choice candidate.[6] Archbishop Charles J. Chaput of Colorado, among several others, argued that Catholics voting for pro-choice candidates were sinners who were "cooperating in evil."[7]

Criticism of the Values Voters Interpretation

Following the flurry of media reports concluding that moral values, and gay marriage and abortion in particular, were the primary explanation for Bush's re-election, a number of academics have pointed out several problems with the moral values interpretation (Burden 2004; Jacobs 2004; Fiorina 2004). First, there are certainly reasons to challenge the validity of the exit poll question itself. The question asked respondents about the most important issue in their vote for president. In this context, what do moral values as a "national problem" mean? Is it some combination of gay marriage and abortion policy? Alternatively, do moral values also reflect opposition to Kerry's perceived flip-flopping or President Bush's decision to invade Iraq? Moral values as a response category is hardly comparable to the more specific policy and political issues listed as alternative answers to the question. In this context, moral values can be defined any number of ways, making it very difficult to draw meaningful conclusions about what voters meant when they selected it as an important issue (Fiorina 2004).[8] Moreover, although moral values was the modal response, the proportion of voters selecting moral values is not statistically different from the proportion selecting the economy (20%), and is not substantially greater than the proportion selecting terrorism (19%) and the war in Iraq (15%). So, even if we were to define moral values by the policy issues of gay marriage and abortion, these numbers suggest that these may have been just one of many voter considerations in 2004.

Further, while gay marriage was generally cited in the media as the most likely issue behind the comparatively ambiguous category of "morals/values," the same exit polls indicate that a majority of voters (59%) favored either civil unions (34%) or legal marriage (25%) for same-sex couples. The exit polls also indicate that the electorate generally cast ballots in line with their party identification: 89% of Democrats voted for Kerry and 93% of Republicans voted for Bush. While the importance of party identification for vote choice was established by political scientists nearly a half century ago (Campbell et al. 1960), and recent evidence suggests that the effect may have grown in recent elections (Bartels 2000), the mass media generally failed to acknowledge the importance of party identification in the 2004 presidential election. Jacobs (2004) concludes, "the preoccupation with moral values and then the postmortems on John Kerry's strategy and personal limitations as a candidate has distracted attention from the two most important and enduring influences on voting—the economy and partisanship."[9] Burden (2004) similarly argues that national security concerns, not moral values, appear to explain changes in Bush support between 2000 and 2004.

Although there are growing doubts about the values voters hypothesis, existing empirical challenges have had to rely on aggregate data and can therefore not definitively test competing explanations of individual decision making.[10] In the absence of such an analysis, the moral values conclusion continues to hold sway in the media. In fact, general discussion in the media and among many political observers continues to revolve around morality and values—even to the point where some evangelicals have called on President Bush to "pay them back" for the election victory that they provided.[11]

Data

Ultimately, the explanations presented by the media, pundits, and even some scholars are, so far, incomplete. They fall short because they have not tested the values voters hypothesis with individual level data controlling for potential alternative explanations. In other words, do policy preferences about gay marriage and abortion have an effect on individual vote choice independent of party identification, ideology, and other prominent issues? To offer a more complete evaluation of the importance of values in the 2004 presidential election, we analyze data from a nationally representative post-election survey of more than 2,800 respondents. This post-election survey was designed to gauge public opinion on a wide variety of policy issues that tend to differentiate the political parties, and thus promises to provide an improved understanding of the role of political issues in campaigns, political evaluations, and political participation.

The Blair Center 2004 Presidential Election Survey is nationally representative and randomly sampled from the Knowledge Networks (KN) Internet panel.[12] The KN panel consists of a national random sample of households recruited by random-digit dialing (RDD), who either have been provided Internet access through their own computer or are given a WebTV console in exchange for completing 3–4 surveys per month. Thus, although surveys are conducted over the Internet, respondents are representative of the U.S. population.[13] By using a random probability sample for initial contact and installing web access for respondents without it, KN overcomes the most common shortfall of other Internet surveys; the KN method eliminates non-Internet coverage bias and allows researchers to accurately gauge the potential for self-selection and non-response bias.[14]

Findings

Given the importance that existing explanations of the 2004 presidential election placed on the issue of gay marriage, we begin by presenting attitudes toward gay marriage as measured by our post-election survey (question wording for this and other issues reported in the

Figure 1 • Comparison of Issue Importance

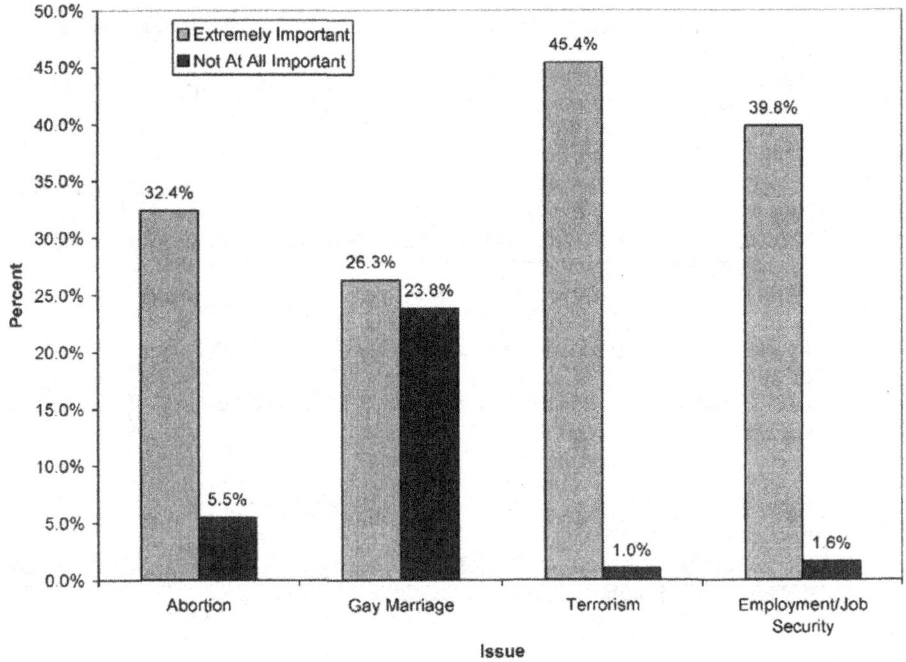

Note: The other possible responses—"very important," "moderately important," and "slightly important"—are not reported in the graph but similarly suggest that gay marriage was not the most important issue.

Appendix).[15] Similar to other studies, we find that a majority of respondents in our survey opposed gay marriage (54%), while 31% supported marriage between same-sex couples, and 14% indicated they neither opposed nor supported homosexual marriage.[16] Even though a majority of citizens expressed anti-gay marriage positions, when asked to rate the importance of various issues, respondents indicated that gay marriage was, on average, far less important than other prominent political issues. As shown in Figure 1, respondents were more likely to indicate that abortion, terrorism, the economy, and job security were more important than gay marriage, and a substantial number of respondents indicated that gay marriage was "not at all important." In fact, our survey asked about the importance of some 15 different political issues, and only the issue of tort reform was considered less important on average.

To begin our investigation into the alternative explanations of the 2004 election, we look at vote choice by party identification and the issues noted above. Figure 2 reports the percentage of respondents voting for Bush (over Kerry) by party identification and issue preferences. For example, in the first set of bars we see that 86.9% of Republicans who supported gay marriage voted for Bush, as did 39.2% of Independents, and just 3.2% of Democrats. Stated differently, the majority of both Democrats and Independents who supported gay marriage voted for Kerry (96.8% and 60.8%, respectively). More interesting, of course, is that among Republicans who supported gay marriage, just 13.1% defected to Kerry. In other words, the vast majority of Republicans who disagreed with Bush on the issue of gay marriage still remained loyal to their party's candidate.

Comparing the relationship between issue preferences and vote choice, we find several interesting patterns. First,

Figure 2 • Percent Voting for Bush by Issue Position and Party Identification

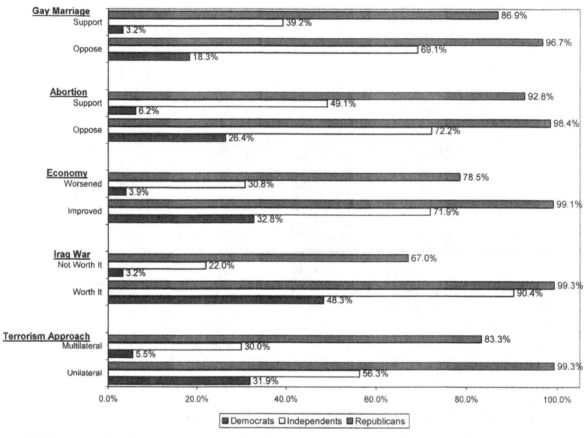

Note: The Democrat and Republican measures do not include leaners. Those with neutral positions are excluded.

these data show that both Democrats and Republicans were exceedingly loyal to their party's candidate *regardless of their position on the issues*. In fact, we could not find a single issue where a majority of partisans voted against their party's candidate—even when they disagreed with the candidate on that issue. Looking specifically at attitudes about gay marriage, just 18.3% of Democrats *opposed* to gay marriage defected to Bush, while only 13.1% of Republicans *supporting* gay marriage defected to Kerry. It is also interesting to note that across all issues, Republicans were consistently more loyal to their party candidate than were Democrats, an asymmetry identified in previous elections as well (Hillygus and Jackman 2003).

Democrats who held issue positions at odds with their candidate appear to have been somewhat more willing to defect from their party and vote for Bush.

This overall pattern of party loyalty should not obscure the fact that there were notable variations in party defections by issue. In comparing defections and loyalty across the various issues, gay marriage and abortion were far less likely to discriminate vote choice than were opinions on the war in Iraq and the economy. In contrast to the rather small rates of defection on the issue of gay marriage reported above, some 33% of Republicans who believed the Iraq war was "not worth the costs" voted for Kerry, while 48.3% of Democrats who believed the Iraq war was "was worth the costs" voted for Bush. Likewise, 21.5% of Republicans who believed the economy had gotten worse in the last year voted for Kerry; while 32.8% of Democrats who believed the economy had improved voted for Bush. Thus, partisans who disagreed with their party on the issue of the Iraq war, terrorism, or the economy were more likely to defect than were partisans who disagreed with their party on the issue of gay marriage or abortion.

Similar to their partisan counterparts, the issue that best discriminated vote choice among Independents was evaluations of the Iraq war. A whopping 90.4% of Independents who thought the Iraq war was worth the costs supported Bush on Election Day, compared to just 22% who thought the Iraq war was not worth the costs—a 68.2% point gap. Among Independents who believed the economy had improved over the past year, 71.9% voted for Bush while only 30.8% who believed the economy had declined over the past year did—a 41.1% point gap. In contrast, the vote gap was far smaller for the issues of gay marriage (29.9% points) and abortion (23.1% points). In other words, opinions about the economy and the war in Iraq did a better job of differentiating vote choice (for both Independents and partisans) than either gay marriage or abortion attitudes.

Although the data presented in Figure 2 provide an initial test of the importance of gay marriage in shaping vote choice, a more rigorous examination simultaneously controls for alternative explanations. To do this, we estimate a multivariate logit model predicting a vote for Bush (over Kerry), allowing us to compare the effects of the economy, evaluations of the war in Iraq, abortion, approaches to terrorism, and gay marriage.[17] For controls, we include standard demographic and political variables, including income, gender, race (black indicator variable), party identification (including leaners), and ideology.[18]

In addition to examining the effect of moral issues on vote choice in the general population, we also look at the importance of these issues among various groups where values-based voting may have been particularly influential in shaping election outcomes in 2004. The first model predicts vote choice among all respondents in the survey. The second model restricts the analysis to only those living in the South[19]—the Bible Belt so heavily courted with moral values messages during the campaign. The third model is estimated for political independents, who might be expected to weigh issue-based considerations more heavily than party loyalties. The fourth model is estimated for respondents living in battleground states, with the rationale that the election outcomes were ultimately decided by votes in a relatively few number of swing states.[20] Given the intensity of the race in battleground states, voters there likely had more issue information than voters in other states, so we might expect issues to play a more prominent role in decision making in battleground states. In the final model, we estimate the effect of gay marriage and other issues for just those respondents living in states with gay marriage ban initiatives on the ballot. The results are presented in Table 2.

Examining the results for all respondents (Model 1), we see that several issues were significant predictors of voting for Bush (over Kerry). Specifically, respondents' evaluations of the war in Iraq and the economy, and opinions about a multilateral approach to terrorism were all significant predictors of vote choice—even controlling for demographics, party identification, and ideology. Notably, opinions on the Iraq war had the largest effect, with a coefficient more than four times that of gay marriage, and even larger than the effect of party identification.[21] In other words, Republicans were indeed significantly more likely than Democrats to vote for Bush, but the difference was not as large as that between respondents who believed the Iraq war was worth it and those who did not. Likewise, self-identifying conservatives were more likely to vote for Bush than self-identifying liberals, but the size of the effect is again smaller than retrospective evaluations of the Iraq war or the economy. With respect to the effects of demographic characteristics, it is worth noting the absence of a gender gap—controlling for all else, women were no more likely to support Kerry than were men. The well-documented racial gap remains, with African Americans significantly more likely to vote for Kerry over Bush. This effect is strongest in battleground states,

Table 2
Logit Models Predicting Vote for Bush (over Kerry)

	Model 1: All Voters		Model 2: South		Model 3: Independents		Model 4: Battleground States		Model 5: Ballot Initiative States	
	B	SE	B	SE	B	SE	B	SE	B	SE
Iraq	3.99*	.38	4.00*	.59	3.81*	.62	6.22*	.97	4.49*	4.49
Terrorism Approach	2.59*	.47	2.14*	.75	3.45*	.81	3.25*	1.06	1.22	1.21
Economy	3.52*	.49	3.52*	.81	3.15*	.77	2.52*	1.13	3.41*	1.19
Abortion	1.01*	.35	.75	.54	.66	.59	1.26	.76	1.19	.79
Gay Marriage	.91*	.30	1.32*	.49	.52	.49	1.03	.68	1.21	.71
Female	.36	.22	.56	.36	−.14	.36	.03	.47	.55	1.09
African American	−1.02*	.38	−1.18*	.55	−.63	.68	−2.8*	1.31	−.23	.09
Married	.30	.24	.11	.37	1.09*	.39	.27	.54	1.14	.64
Income	.68	.56	1.07	.93	−.32	.95	−1.01	1.43	1.24	1.33
Ideology	2.89*	.68	1.61	1.07	2.85*	1.38	2.79	1.45	4.56*	1.66
Party Identification	3.36*	.27	3.82*	.44	3.54*	.59	3.85*	.60	2.80*	.64
Constant	−8.46*	.63	−8.0*	.94	−8.17	1.13	−8.55*	1.40	−10.48*	1.77
Reduction in Error	.879		.907		.799		.910		.880	
Pseudo R^2	.88		.89		.83		.91		.87	
% Correctly Predicted	94.2		95.6		90.9		95.6		94.4	
N	2011		1313		889		735		480	

Notes: Dependent variable is coded as Bush = 1, Kerry = 0. All variables have been rescaled to range from 0 to 1. * $p <= .05$. Reduction in Error calculated by (%correctly predicted-%modal)/(100-%modal).

perhaps reflecting Kerry's concentrated campaign efforts at targeting blacks in those states.

Among those respondents living in the states of the Old Confederacy (Model 2), one of the most socially conservative regions of the country, the results are quite similar, except that the effect of attitudes toward abortion no longer reaches standard levels of statistical significance. The relationship between gay marriage and a vote for Bush is somewhat stronger among Southerners than for the nation as a whole, but the effect does not rival the impact of the Iraq war or the economy.

We find that among Independents (Model 3), respondents in battleground states (Model 4), and respondents in states with an anti-gay marriage initiative on the ballot (Model 5), that abortion attitudes and attitudes toward gay marriage had no significant effect on presi-

dential vote choice when party identification, ideology, and demographics are taken into account. In contrast, the effect of the Iraq war, the economy, and terrorism remain critically important to voter decision making among all of these groups.

To better illustrate and compare the substantive effects of these various issues, we estimate the change in the predicted probability of voting for Bush across the range of issue preferences.[22] Given the similarities of the various estimates across the models, we provide graphs for just three groups: all voters, Southerners, and Independents.

Figure 3 illustrates the predicted probability of voting for Bush across issue preferences for all voters, holding all other variables at their means and indicator variables to zero.[23] Not surprisingly, respondents expressing pro-administration positions on the five issues studied in this

Figure 3 • Predicted Probabilities for All Voters

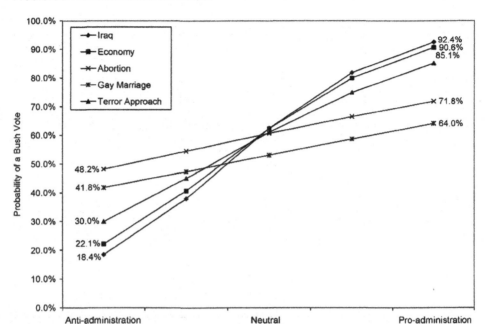

investigation were significantly more likely to vote for Bush, while respondents holding anti-administration positions on these issues were more likely to vote for Kerry, even controlling for party identification, ideology, and demographics. Although all of the issues are related to presidential vote choice, the relationship is much stronger (i.e., the line is steeper) for the war in Iraq, support for a multilateral approach to terrorism, and evaluations of the economy than for either gay marriage or abortion. The first difference, or change in predicted probability, between those with the most anti-administration views compared to those with the most pro-administration views was a whopping 74% points on the issue of Iraq (92.4% minus 18.4%), 68.5% points on evaluations of the economy and 55.1% points on support for a multilateral approach to terrorism, compared to just 23.6% points on the issue of abortion and 22.2% points on the issue of gay marriage.

Although these findings suggest that Bush did not benefit nearly as much from moral issues as initially suspected,

it is interesting to note that Bush generally found support among those with neutral positions on the various issues. Looking at the predictions for those without strong beliefs one way or the other on the issues, we find that they were always predicted to vote for Bush even if they took a moderate position on the issue. The only exception is gay marriage, with those who were neutral on the issue of gay marriage more likely to support Kerry.[24] It appears that when a voter was ambiguous or in doubt about an issue, they ultimately put their support behind the incumbent. In other words, those torn on an issue appeared to revert to the status quo. Consequently, it may be time to modify interpretations of the election outcome: rather than concluding that Bush received a moral mandate, we should instead recognize that Bush simply received a second chance among those who were not ideologically polarized on the prominent issues of the campaign.

Graphing the predicted probabilities for Model 2, we find a similar pattern as indicated in Figure 4. Even in the conservative South, the issues of the war in Iraq, the

Figure 4 • Predicted Probabilities for Southern Voters

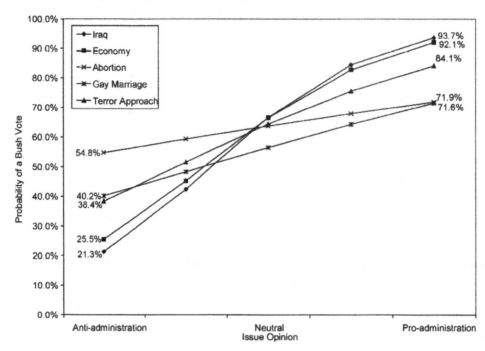

economy, and terrorism did a better job of differentiating vote choice than did gay marriage or abortion preferences. Our model predicts that respondents with the most pro-administration positions on the issue of the Iraq war had a 93.7% chance of voting for Bush, compared to a 21.3% chance among those with the most anti-administration viewpoints—a difference of 72.4% points. That difference was 66.6% points for evaluations of the economy, 45.7% points on support for a multilateral approach to terrorism, and 31.4% points on the issue of gay marriage (the difference was not statistically different from zero for the issue of abortion). Overall, then, the influence of moral issues pale in comparison to the decisive influence of the Iraq war, the economy, and terrorism even in the area of the country thought to be the most receptive to the moral values campaign messages.

Finally, in Figure 5, we graph the predicted probability of voting for Bush across the range of issue preferences for Independents. It might be hypothesized that Inde-

pendents weigh the issues of the campaign more heavily in their decision making since they are likely to be less loyal to a particular party candidate. The relative impact of the various issues is particularly dramatic among Independents, with the graph illustrating a clean separation of values and non-values issues. As in the previous figures, respondents' attitudes regarding the war in Iraq, the economy, and terrorism have much steeper slopes than the issues of abortion and gay marriage (which did not reach statistical significance). Overall, those who held anti-administration positions on the issues of the Iraq war, the economy, and terrorism were almost sure bets to vote for Kerry, while those holding pro-administration positions on these issues were almost sure bets to vote for Bush. The effects of the so called value issues of abortion and gay marriage show little change across the range of responses to these issues. Put simply, to correctly predict who an Independent voted for in the 2004 presidential election, we need to know their evaluation of the Iraq war, not their

Figure 5 • Predicted Probabilities for Independents

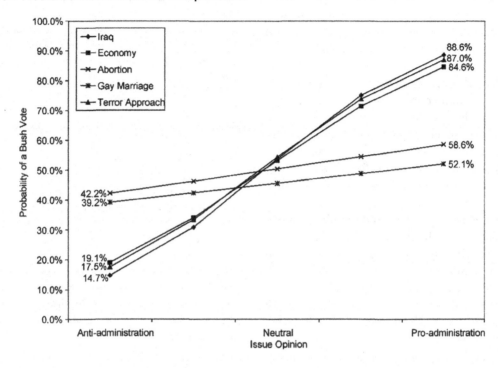

opinions about abortion or gay marriage. To the extent that moral values played a role in 2004, it was to reinforce support among partisans not to attract most Americans to a particular candidate.

Conclusions

In an individual-level analysis of presidential vote choice in the 2004 election, we find only isolated support for the values voters explanation. The effects of respondents' attitudes toward abortion and gay marriage were inconsistent, and even in those cases where they reached statistical significance the effects were substantially smaller than respondents' evaluations of the Iraq war, terrorism, and the national economy. Surprisingly, in the 2004 presidential election, the effects of the Iraq war were at least as strong, if not stronger, than the effects of party identification.

We should note that it is somewhat difficult to differentiate fully the effect of the Iraq war from the war on

terrorism because the two attitudes are so closely related with one another—no doubt in part a consequence of the explicit efforts of the Bush camp to link these issues during the campaign. The correlation between respondents' evaluations of Iraq and opinions about a multilateral approach to terrorism is .556. Similarly, the correlation between respondents' evaluations of the war in Iraq and the personal salience of terrorism as a political issue is .649. Consequently, there is likely an overlap between our measure of evaluations of the war in Iraq and approaches to solving terrorism. Regardless, the importance of these foreign policy concerns for predicting vote choice in the 2004 presidential election remain much greater than the importance of attitudes toward either abortion or gay marriage.

Notably, in this investigation we have focused on presidential vote choice, but have ignored voter turnout. It could be argued that voters may have cast a ballot based upon foreign policy once they entered the voting booth, as our analysis indicates, but the salience of gay marriage and/or abortion sparked interest in individuals who were otherwise unlikely to vote on Election Day. After all, Karl Rove's electoral strategy appeared to focus on mobilizing conservative Christian voters rather than attracting swing voters. Although we do not address the influence of moral values on voter turnout in this analysis, initial research casts doubt on that hypothesis. Burden (2004) reports that rates of turnout among religious voters did not change between 2000 and 2004; nor did rates of turnout in the Bible Belt or Midwest states. Regardless of what brought voters to the polls during the 2004 presidential election, once there the issues of gay marriage and abortion were not strongly related to how they cast their ballot—whether the respondent was an Independent, living in a state with a gay marriage initiative, or living in one of the much talked about battleground states.

Ultimately, the values voters explanation appears to be only a very minor part of citizens' voting calculus in the 2004 presidential election. More important to vote choice in the 2004 election was party identification, ideology, attitudes toward the Iraq war, terrorism, and the economy. Among the most decisive groups—Independents and respondents in battleground states—gay marriage and abortion had no impact on individual vote choice once other factors were controlled. Only in the South did the values issue of gay marriage have an independent effect on vote choice; yet few ever doubted the strength of the GOP, nor Bush's electoral lead, in the South. Even here, the importance of other issues dwarfed the impact of attitudes toward gay marriage and abortion. It appears that values-based appeals only served to reinforce Bush's support among those already planning to vote for him, but failed to persuade new voters. In other words, the moral values issues of gay marriage and abortion matter most where the campaign mattered least. ■

Notes

We would like to acknowledge the generous support of the Diane D. Blair Center for Southern Politics and Society.

1. Dick Meyer, "The Anatomy of a Myth: How Did One Exit Poll Answer Become the Story of How Bush Won?" *Washington Post,* December 5, 2004, B01. Reprinted at www.washingtonpost.com.

2. The exit polls were sponsored by the National Election Pool, a consortium of major television networks and the *Associated Press,* and conducted by Edison Media Research and Mitofsky International.

3. The states with gay marriage ban ballot initiatives include Arkansas, Georgia, Kentucky, Michigan, Mississippi, Missouri, North Dakota, Ohio, Oklahoma, Oregon, and Utah.

4. The amendments in many of these states also banned civil unions between homosexual couples.

5. See for example, www.voteforgod.com or www.st-thomascamas.org/votegod2004/worthiness.htm.

6. See for example, www.st-thomascamas.org/votegod2004/worthiness.htm.

7. See for example, www.jrn.columbia.edu/studentwork/election/2004/catholic_vote.asp.

8. Fiorina (2004) reports that "other post-election polls that explicitly separated out those issues [gay marriage and abortion] found fewer than 1 in 6 voters viewing them as overriding."

9. See http://www.hhh.umn.edu/centers/csp/elections/moral_values.html.

10. Existing analysis risks problems of ecological inference in drawing conclusions about individual behavior from aggregate-level data.

11. "Evangelicals to Bush: Payback Time: Christian Conservatives Say They Gave Bush 'Moral Mandate'; Call on Him to Act on Their Behalf." *ABC News Original Report,* November 28, 2004.

12. Independent comparison studies have found the KN sample representative of U.S. Census averages (Krosnick and Chang 2001; Viscusi et al. 2004). Krosnick and Chang (2001) commissioned a set of side-by-side surveys using a single questionnaire regarding the 2000 U.S. election from national samples of American adults. They find the KN survey is comparable to the RDD telephone survey and representative of the U.S. population.

13. Detailed information on the KN methodology can be found on their web site at http://www.knowledgenetworks.com/ganp/index.html. Research using the KN panel has been published in a number of academic journals including *American Political Science Review, American Journal of Political Science,* and *Journal of Politics,* to name a few.

14. For more elaborate comparison of probability versus volunteer Internet samples see Pineau and Slotwiner (2003).

15. Although polls find widespread support for civil unions, voters did not have an opportunity to vote for civil unions on the ballot; they simply had the option of voting for or against gay marriage bans. For this reason, our survey question asks only about support for gay marriage.

16. See for example, Scott Keeter, "Reading the Polls on Gay Marriage and the Constitution." The Pew Research Center for the People and the Press. July 24, 2004. http://people-press.org/commentary/pdf/92.pdf.

17. Including a measure of church attendance or attitudes toward the Bible does not change results. Adding presidential approval to the model did not change the gay marriage or Iraq effect, but swamped the economy effect.

18. Models have also been estimated, with no change in results, including measures of education, age, and Hispanic ethnicity; none reach statistical significance.

19. Defined here as the 11 states of the Old Confederacy.

20. Independents include those leaning towards one party or the other. Battleground states were defined as those states in which the 2000 two-party vote difference was smaller than five percentage points. These states included New Hampshire, Pennsylvania, Ohio, Wisconsin, Minnesota, Iowa, Missouri, Florida, Tennessee, New Mexico, Nevada, and Oregon.

21. Non-voters and minor party voters are omitted from the analysis, and all variables are rescaled to range from 0–1.

22. For comparability on the x-axis, we have generically re-labeled the five point issue responses as pro-administration or anti-administration. The actual survey response and survey questions are reported in the Appendix.

23. In other words, the probabilities are computed for an average Independent white male.

24. This may reflect the distribution of this variable. Since the majority of respondents were on the Republican side of this issue, those not explicitly opposed to gay marriage were actually more liberal than the average respondent

References

Abramowitz, Alan. 1995. "It's Abortion Stupid: Policy Voting in the 1992 Presidential Election." *Journal of Politics* 57:176–86.

Bartels, Larry. 2000. "Partisanship and Voting Behavior, 1952–1996." *American Journal of Political Science* 44:35–50.

Burden, Barry C. 2004. "An Alternative Account of the 2004 Presidential Election." *The Forum* (4): http://www.bepress.com/forum.

Campbell, Angus, Philip Converse, Warren Miller, and Donald Stokes. 1960. *The American Voter.* New York: John Wiley.

Fiorina, Morris P. 2004. " 'Holy War' Over Moral Values or Contempt for Opinion?" *San Francisco Chronicle,* November 21, B-5. http://sfgate.com/cgi-bin/article.cgi?file=/chronicle/archive/2004/11/21/EDG549TD5K1.DTL.

Hillygus, D. Sunshine, and Simon Jackman. 2003. "Voter Decision Making in Election 2000." *American Journal of Political Science* 47:583–96.

Jacobs, Lawrence. 2004. "Moral Values Takes Back Seat to Partisanship and the Economy in the 2004 Presidential Election." www.hhh.umn.edu/centers/csp/elections/moral_values.html.

Krosnick, Jon A., and Lin Chiat Chang. 2001. "A Comparison of the Random Digit Dialing Telephone Survey Methodology with Internet Survey Methodology as Implemented by Knowledge Networks and Harris Interactive." Stanford University. http://communication.stanford.edu/faculty/krosnick.html.

Lambro, Donald. 2004. "In Search of New Faces." *Washington Times Special Report,* http://washingtontimes.com/special-report/20041107-123932-3944r.htm.

Meyer, Dick. 2004. "The Anatomy of a Myth: How Did One Exit Poll Answer Become the Story of How Bush Won?" *Washington Post,* December 5, B01. Reprinted at www.washingtonpost.com.

Pineau, Vicki, and Daniel Slotwiner. 2003. "Probability Samples vs. Volunteer Respondents in Internet Research: Defining Potential Effects on Data and Decision-Making in Marketing Applications." White Paper. http://www.knowledgenetworks.com/info/main/studies.html.

Viscusi, W. Kip, Joel Huber, and Jason Bell. 2004. "The Value of Regional Water Quality Improvements." Discussion Paper No. 477. The Harvard John M. Olin Discussion Paper Series: http://www.law.harvard.edu/programs/olin_center/.

Appendix: Question Wording

Variable	Question	Possible Answers
Economy	Would you say that over the past year the nation's economy has generally gotten better, or has it stayed the same or generally gotten worse?	Much better, Somewhat better, Stayed about the same, Somewhat worse, Much worse
Gay Marriage	Would you *favor* or oppose an amendment to the U.S. Constitution that would define marriage as being between a man and a woman, thus barring marriages between gay or lesbian couples?	Completely Favor, Somewhat Favor, Neither Favor Nor Oppose, Somewhat Oppose, Completely Oppose
Abortion	Which of the following opinions comes closer to your view about abortion?	It should never be permitted; it should only be permitted when the woman's life is in danger; it should only be permitted if the woman's health or life is in danger; by law, a woman should always be able to obtain an abortion as a matter of personal choice
Party identification	Generally speaking, do you usually think of yourself as a Republican, a Democrat, an Independent, or what? (Followed by strength of identification for Democrats and Republicans and leaning questions for independents)	Strong Democrat, Democrat, Independent/ leaning Democrat, Independent, Independent/ leaning Republican, Republican, strong Republican
Ideology	How about your political views? Do you consider yourself generally liberal, moderate, or conservative?	extremely liberal, liberal, somewhat liberal, moderate/middle of the road, somewhat conservative, conservative, extremely conservative
Iraq	Taking everything into account, do you agree or disagree that the war in Iraq has been worth the cost?	Completely agree, somewhat agree, neither agree nor disagree, somewhat disagree, completely disagree
Terrorism/ International Problems	People have different views on the best way to solve problems such as terrorism and the environment that are of a more international nature. Some people think it is better for the U.S. to work with other countries through international institutions. Other people think that international institutions are slow and bureaucratic, so the U.S. should be prepared to solve such problems on our own. Still others have opinions somewhere in between these two. Where would you place yourself on the scale below?	Scale ranges from 1. U.S. should work through international institutions to 7. U.S. must go it alone.
Issue Importance	Regardless of where you stand on the following political issues, please indicate *how important* each issue or policy is *to you personally* (issues were presented to respondents in random order).	Extremely important, very important, moderately important, slightly important, not at all important.

Why Was This Research Needed?

1. What were the major values issues discussed during the 2004 presidential campaign?

2. In addition to the exit poll results, what aspects of the campaign run by President Bush and his supporters encouraged a "values voters" explanation of the outcome?

3. Who was asked the exit poll question about the most important issue in their vote for president? What were the results? Why were these results misleading?

4. Why do aggregate data limit researchers' understanding of the way that individuals make their voting decisions?

How Was the Topic Studied?

1. What set of issues, moral and other, do the authors consider in their analysis of individual voting decisions?

2. What is the source of the data for this study? Describe the main features of the survey—sample size, sampling method, and so on. What are the potential problems with this type of survey? What steps were taken in this survey to reduce potential response biases?

3. How is it helpful to have the actual wording of survey questions used in a study provided in an appendix? Would you say the questions and response options in this study represent appropriate measures for the issues under examination? Explain.

What Are the Findings?

1. How do the bar graph findings in Figure 1 contradict claims that gay marriage was one of the most important issues considered by voters?

2. How does Figure 2 make use of party identification as a control variable in analyzing the relationship between the Bush vote and voters' issue preferences? What are the main findings of this data breakdown?

3. To the extent that voters did vote against their own party's presidential candidate in 2004, what issue disagreements were most associated with these defections? Pick one of these issues and discuss the percentage comparison that documents the extent of defection.

4. Diagram the multivariate model of vote choice that is analyzed in the final part of this reading. What control variables were incorporated in the equation? How were they selected? What other control variables were omitted because they did not prove to be significant?

5. The authors estimate the effects of their model five times, focusing on different populations of interest. Explain the rationale behind this procedure. How does this introduce another kind of control into the analysis?

6. Logit is a statistical approach for using multiple regression with discrete dependent variables. In this case, the dependent variable is the dichotomous measure of voting for Bush or for Kerry. How do you interpret the regression coefficients produced by this model (shown in Table 2)? What is the overall measure of the success of each of the five models?

7. Figures 3, 4, and 5 present predicted probabilities of voting for Bush, arrayed against anti-administration, neutral, and pro-administration issue positions; the three population groups examined, in turn, are all voters, southern voters, and Independents. Explain the meaning of these predicted probabilities. How does this analysis (and the crossing of lines on the graph) demonstrate which issues were more important than others in influencing voters?

What Do the Results Mean?

1. In their conclusion, Hillygus and Shields write that "the moral values issues of gay marriage and

abortion matter most where the campaign mattered least." What is the evidence for this statement?

2. What lessons for the next presidential campaign might each party draw from the findings of this study?

3. Do you feel this research convincingly demonstrates the advantages of political science quantitative methodology as compared to journalistic interpretations of voting results? Explain your answer. How might the political science perspective be incorporated to a greater extent in journalistic practice, without ignoring differences in the missions and functioning of the two professions?

Afterword from Todd Shields and Sunshine Hillygus

Cutting-edge research in political science can directly engage, shape, and refine public debate over important current events and has the potential to improve public understanding of "real-world" politics. Many aspects of the 2004 presidential election captivated the attention of the media and the public. In this study, we use statistical analysis to challenge the widespread conclusion that President Bush's reelection campaign was successful because of his stance on "moral issues." Using a multivariate analysis of a national political survey, we find that the economy, Iraq, and terrorism were considerably more important issues to the electorate in 2004 than either gay marriage or abortion. Although the basic analytic tools used in journalistic accounts, such as frequency tables and descriptive statistics, are fundamental aspects of any research process, this study highlights the importance of using rigorous social science methods to understand complex political processes.

This study is also notable because it takes advantage of Web-based survey technology. With the proliferation of cellular phones, answering machines, and caller identification, as well as the generally hectic schedules of the American public, survey researchers are increasingly looking for new technologies to address the growing difficulty of collecting a representative sample of survey respondents. Web-based surveys hold a number of advantages over telephone surveys: they can be answered at the respondent's convenience, they can include innovative visual or audio components, and they are typically less expensive than either telephone or in-person surveys. Most Internet surveys, however, are not representative of the U.S. population because they omit the sizable portion of the population that does not have Internet access. Although the survey for this study was collected over the Internet, the sample is representative of the U.S. population because the survey firm, Knowledge Networks, uses probability sampling to randomly select respondent households, and then installs a WebTV unit in homes without an Internet connection.

Cooperation Through Threats: The Northern Ireland Case

Steven J. Brams and Jeffrey M. Togman

When the Irish Republican Army (IRA) announced in the summer of 2005 that it was abandoning its campaign of violence against the British presence in Northern Ireland, British prime minister Tony Blair called the development "a step of unparalleled magnitude" (DePasquale 2005). The IRA began its paramilitary operations against Great Britain in the late 1960s. Since that time, it has reportedly been involved in scores of killings, robberies, and other crimes in Northern Ireland, England, and, to a lesser extent, the Republic of Ireland. Although the IRA had declared cease-fires and a limited disarmament on earlier occasions, what distinguished this latest announcement was the seemingly unambiguous message that the group was turning away from armed conflict in favor of political engagement to achieve its aims.

If all that the IRA leadership has promised comes to pass, it could indeed represent a decisive moment in the Northern Ireland situation. It is the kind of sudden transformative step whose motivations and likely consequences defy easy explanation by even well-informed observers.

The following reading by Steven J. Brams and Jeffrey M. Togman puts forward a means of thinking about such a quandary. The foundation of their framework is an intellectual approach called game theory that assesses the decision-making alternatives faced by mutually dependent political actors who have divergent goals (Myerson 1991). Brams and Togman propose their own "theory of moves" to examine how the "players" in a political game plot their actions, and anticipate counteractions, well into the future. The case study for their analysis is the Northern Ireland conflict during the eventful period of the late 1990s.

The numbers in this reading are not "statistical" in the same sense as in other readings where the purpose was describing distributions and testing for relationships between variables. Instead, this quantitative methodology uses numbers to identify and to order the different political interactions that can arise in situations of bilateral conflict and cooperation.

References

DePasquale, Ron. 2005. "IRA Says Its Armed Fight Over." *Los Angeles Times,* July 29, 1.

Myerson, Roger B. 1991. *Game Theory: Analysis of Conflict.* Cambridge, Mass.: Harvard University Press.

On February 9, 1996, after a seventeen-month cease-fire, the Irish Republican Army (IRA) set off a bomb in East London. Less than a week later, the London police found and destroyed a bomb that the IRA had left in a telephone booth in the West End. A few days later, another IRA bomb went off on a double-decker bus. The British government, under the leadership of John Major, asserted that it would have no official contact with Sinn Féin, the political arm of the IRA, until the paramilitary activities stopped. The government also deployed 500 additional troops in Northern Ireland. In October 1996, the IRA detonated two bombs at the British Army's headquarters in Lisburn, bringing the violent conflict back to Northern Ireland for the first time since the cease-fire.

On May 1, 1997, Tony Blair was elected Great Britain's prime minister. His election brought a renewed sense of optimism and good will to the conflict in Northern Ireland. Responding to Blair's overtures, including his warning that "the settlement train is leaving, with or without them" (Hoge 1997a, A7), the IRA announced on July 19, 1997, that they had "ordered the unequivocal restoration of the cease-fire" (Clarity 1997c, 1). Soon thereafter, Sinn Féin was invited to participate in the peace talks, which reconvened on September 15, 1997.

These are some of the recent developments in the conflict over British rule in Northern Ireland. The conflict between the British government and the IRA is part of a larger struggle between Catholic Republicans, including Sinn Féin and IRA members, who demand that Northern Ireland become part of an all-Ireland nation-state, and Protestant Unionists, who insist that Northern Ireland remain part of the United Kingdom.

While the British government has tried to portray itself at times as a neutral party, in most instances it seems more accurate to view it as a pro-Union force. Former Prime Minister John Major, speaking about his Conservative party in 1994, asserted, "We are a Unionist Party. We should fight for the Union" (Aughey 1994, 143). Since his election, Tony Blair has not been as blunt about his position, but he has given no indication that he would be willing to let Northern Ireland leave the union. Indeed, Blair stated that it was unlikely that the world would "see Northern Ireland as anything but a part of the United Kingdom" (Clarity 1997a, 5).

The violent nature of the so-called Troubles in Northern Ireland poses life-and-death questions. Is the conflict intractable, or is there any possibility for compromise and an enduring peace? If so, how can the two sides help to expedite a durable settlement? And, finally, why would the IRA change strategies so frequently—first declaring a cease-fire, then resuming paramilitary actions, only to restore the cease-fire?

We address these questions by examining the strategic situation between the IRA and the British government, especially during the period when the IRA first suspended and then resumed its paramilitary actions. Utilizing a dynamic approach to game theory called the "theory of moves" (see Brams 1994), we construct a deductive model of the conflict, based on a 2×2 game, to demonstrate why certain steps were taken by each side. Next, we use this game to analyze how political leaders might find a path toward peace. Finally, we indicate in Appendix A how this game is related to the well-known games of Chicken and Prisoners' Dilemma, based on both standard game theory and theory of moves.

A Centuries-Old Conflict

The present conflict must be seen in the context of the centuries-old Anglo-Irish antagonism. Republicans point to the first Norman invasions of Ireland in 1169 as the start of the conflict, whereas Unionists, who favor British rule, focus on the arrival of Scottish and English settlers, beginning in 1609. The arrival of these settlers in the north, often called the "plantation of Ulster," is the source of Northern Ireland's Protestant, mostly Unionist, majority (57% today).

Republicans have continually fought against British rule, most fiercely at the end of the nineteenth and the beginning of the twentieth centuries. The war of independence, from 1919 to 1921, led to the Anglo-Irish Treaty of 1921, negotiated by the British government and Sinn Féin. The treaty granted independence to the 26 southern counties of Ireland, which became the Republic of Ireland, but it gave Great Britain control over Northern Ireland. Assurances the treaty offered Sinn Féin that the dispute over Northern Ireland would be resolved came to naught.

After 1921 Northern Ireland remained under British control, although the Stormont regime set up by the British did enjoy a certain degree of autonomy. Until the late 1960s, the armed Republican movement in Northern Ireland met with little support or success (O'Leary and McGarry 1993, 161). Then, in the late 1960s, Catholics in Northern Ireland began a series of civil rights marches to protest, among other things, discrimination in voting, employment, and housing. The marchers appealed to the British government to protect their rights as British citizens, but they were attacked by Unionist extremists, including some in the security forces (Rose 1971, 156). Subsequently, violence spread rapidly.

In 1969 the British government sent troops to Northern Ireland in an attempt to quell the unrest. Although Britain desired to maintain the quasi-independence of Northern Ireland, the conflict spiraled out of control; in 1972 the Stormont regime was suspended and replaced by direct rule from London. Attempts by the British government to control the violence during the 1970s and 1980s failed miserably. Since 1969 more than 3,200 people have been killed in sectarian fighting in Northern Ireland (Chepesiuk 1997, 10). Furthermore, 20,000 people have been injured, with economic costs to the British government running well over $1 billion a year (Ruane and Todd 1996, 1–2).

The Conflict from a Strategic Perspective

By 1994 Northern Ireland had experienced a quarter-century of widespread sectarian violence. In this section we present a game-theoretic view of the conflict between Sinn Féin/IRA, treated as one player, and the British government in the 1990s. There are, to be sure, other important actors in the conflict, including the Republic of Ireland, Unionists in Northern Ireland, and Republicans who are not associated with Sinn Féin/IRA. However, by focusing on the struggle between the British government and Sinn Féin/IRA, we highlight the central conflict, whose dynamics we will analyze in the next section.

We consider two basic strategic stances the two sides can take. One is a hard-line stance, denoted by H. For Great Britain, this entails a refusal to negotiate with Sinn Féin/IRA, as well as the maintenance of British rule by force. For Sinn Féin/IRA, it means a refusal to accept any resolution short of complete independence, taking whatever paramilitary actions are necessary to undermine British rule.

Each side, as an alternative strategy, can take a conciliatory stance, denoted by C. For Great Britain, such a stance would mean a willingness to negotiate a compromise solution to the conflict, including a demilitarization of its position. For Sinn Féin/IRA, C would indicate a similar willingness to compromise, including halting its paramilitary activities, at least temporarily.

The choice of C or H by each side leads to four possible outcomes, or states, that can be summarized as follows:

1. **C - C.** Compromise, resulting in a peaceful settlement.
2. **H - H.** Violent conflict, resulting in the continuation of the Troubles.
3. **H (Sinn Féin/IRA) - C (Great Britain).** Capitulation by Great Britain, which unilaterally withdraws its forces.
4. **C (Sinn Féin/IRA) - H (Great Britain).** Capitulation by Sinn Féin/IRA, which unilaterally stops its armed resistance.

We next rank these four states for both sides as follows: 4 = best; 3 = next best; 2 = next worst; 1 = worst. Thus, the higher the number, the greater the payoff to a player. These numbers, however, do not signify any numerical value or utility a player attaches to a state.

Rather, they indicate only that each player prefers a higher-ranked state over a lower-ranked one.

In the payoff matrix shown in Figure 1, these ranks are given by the ordered pair (x, y), where x is the ranking of the row player (Sinn Féin/IRA) and y is the ranking of the column player (Great Britain). We offer the following brief justification of these rankings for each player, starting with the upper-left state and moving clockwise around the matrix:

Compromise: (3,3). This is the next-best state for both players, involving a compromise on the issue of sovereignty.[1] For both Great Britain and Sinn Féin/IRA, the benefits of this state include an end to the violence and the possibility of long-term peace in Northern Ireland.

IRA Capitulates: (2,4). This is the best state for Great Britain, because it has all the benefits of a compromise without having to make any concessions. It is the next-worst state for Sinn Féin/IRA because, while life in Northern Ireland achieves some level of normalcy, British rule remains in place.

Violent Conflict: (1,2). This is the next-worst state for Great Britain because, although it maintains control over Northern Ireland, paramilitary attacks continue; in addition, Britain faces pressure from the Republic of Ireland, the United States, and the European Union to bring an end to the violence. It is the worst state for Sinn Féin/IRA, because both British rule and the violence continue.

Britain Capitulates: (4,1). This is the worst state for Great Britain, which loses all control over Northern Ireland by withdrawing its forces; Britain is also seen as caving in to terrorism. By contrast, Sinn Féin/IRA achieves its best state by gaining independence without the need to compromise its hard-line position.

The ostensible solution to this game is the (3,3) compromise, but this is not the solution that standard game theory prescribes. The reason is that Great Britain has a *dominant strategy* of H: it is a better strategy than C whatever strategy Sinn Féin/IRA chooses. Thus, if Sinn Féin/IRA chooses C, then (2,4) is better for Britain than (3,3); if Sinn Féin/IRA chooses H, (1,2) is better for Britain than (4,1).

Presuming that Britain chooses H because it is unconditionally better than C, what will Sinn Féin/IRA do? Observe that Sinn Féin/IRA does not have a dominant strategy: H is better if Britain chooses C, giving (4,1) rather than (3,3), but C is better if Britain chooses H, giving (2,4) rather than (1,2).

We assume, in a game in which all parties have complete information, that Sinn Féin/IRA can anticipate that Britain will choose its dominant strategy of H. Accordingly, its best response would be to choose C, obtaining its next-worst state of (2,4) rather than its worst state of (1,2).

The strategies that yield (2,4), or capitulation by Sinn Féin/IRA, are what game theorists call a *Nash equilibrium,* because if either player departed unilaterally from its strategy associated with this state (C for Sinn Féin/IRA, H for Britain), it would do worse: by changing its strategy from C to H, Sinn Féin/IRA would move the situation to (1,2), or violent conflict; by changing its strategy from H to C, Great Britain would move the situation to (3,3), or compromise. By contrast, if the players both chose C, leading to compromise, each would have an incentive to depart from C to try to achieve its best state—(2,4) for Great Britain and (4,1) for Sinn Féin/IRA.

The states of (4,1) and (1,2) are also unstable in the sense that at least one player would have an incentive unilaterally to change its strategy. Hence, (2,4) is the unique stable state in this game.

The dominance of H for Great Britain helps to explain that party's refusal to negotiate with Sinn Féin, even during the 1994–1996 ceasefire. However, the actions of the IRA—commencing paramilitary activities, suspending them, resuming them, suspending them once again—belie the supposed stability of (2,4). Within the confines of classical game theory, at least, any use of force by the IRA would seem to be irrational.

In order to account for the changes in strategy by Sinn Féin and the IRA, we next turn to the theory of moves (TOM), which allows for strategy shifts by players as they attempt to implement desired outcomes. It also allows for the exercise of threats by a party that has the power and will to carry them out if the response it seeks from the threatened party is not forthcoming.

Figure 1 • Payoff Matrix of the Northern Ireland Conflict

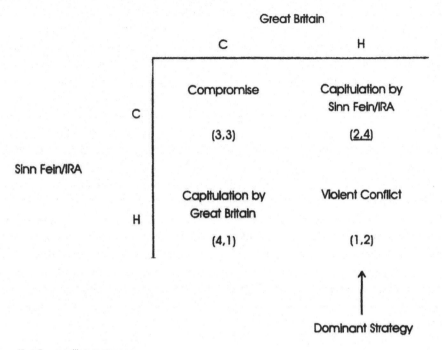

Key: C = conciliatory stance
H = hard-line stance
(*x*, *y*) = (payoff to Sinn Féin/IRA, payoff to Great Britain)
4 = best; 3 = next best; 2 = next worst; 1 = worst
Outcome associated with Nash equilibrium strategies underscored

TOM and Threats

Game theory, as developed initially by von Neumann and Morgenstern, is an approach that is, in their own words, "thoroughly static" (von Neumann and Morgenstern 1953, 44). Classical game theory has little to say about the dynamic process by which players' choices unfold to produce outcomes, at least in so-called normal-form or strategic-form games that are defined by payoff matrices, like that shown in Figure 1. By contrast, the theory of moves adds a dynamic dimension by assuming that players look ahead before making a move, switching strategies in anticipation of the possible countermoves of an opponent.

A key concept of TOM, and one which is very helpful in analyzing the conflict in Northern Ireland, is the notion of "threat power." A player has *threat power* when it can better endure an inefficient state than can an opponent. An *inefficient state* is one that is worse for both players than some other state. Thus, in the Figure 1 game, (1,2) is an inefficient state because it is worse for both players than either (2,4) or (3,3).

Consider the situation in Northern Ireland, as depicted in Figure 1, and how the two sides have attempted to assert their threat power. During most of the post-1970 conflict, the IRA used its paramilitary forces to try to establish its threat power by signaling its willingness to endure the mutually harmful (i.e., inefficient) state of (1,2). Observe that by choosing H, Sinn Féin/IRA ensures that Great Britain is faced with its two worst states, (4,1) and (1,2); presented with this choice, Britain would presumably select (1,2) over (4,1) by choosing H as well.

By asserting its threat power, Sinn Féin/IRA took a hard-line stance—but *not* because it preferred the conflict at (1,2) to capitulation at (2,4). Instead, it hoped to force the British to take a conciliatory stance. As Gerry Adams, the president of Sinn Féin/IRA, put it, "The course I take involves the use of physical force; but only if I achieve the situation where my people prosper can my course of action be seen, by me, to have been justified" (Clark 1994, 79).

Recall that Great Britain has a dominant strategy of maintaining its own hard-line position (H), which is better for it whatever Sinn Féin/IRA does. But when Great Britain implements its dominant strategy at the same time that Sinn Féin/IRA threatens Britain's two worst states with its choice of H, the result is violent conflict. This state held throughout most of the 1970s and 1980s.

One way out of this situation is for both sides to agree to move to the mutually beneficial compromise state. In the early and mid-1990s, there were talks to try to arrive at such a settlement. The British position was that the IRA would have to renounce its use of paramilitary activities before formal negotiations for a resolution of the Northern Ireland conflict could begin. In essence, Great Britain was insisting that Sinn Féin/IRA move from H to C first, shifting the game from (1,2) to (2,4).

On the other hand, if Great Britain moved first to C, the situation would shift from (1,2) to (4,1), at least temporarily. Then Sinn Féin/IRA could move to C, resulting in the (3,3) compromise state. But this sequence of moves could be interpreted as Great Britain's giving in to terrorism at (4,1), which was unacceptable to the British government and also entailed the risk that Sinn Féin/IRA would not subsequently move on to (3,3). Hence, Britain insisted that Sinn Féin/IRA make the first conciliatory move.

Sinn Féin/IRA agreed to these conditions in September of 1994 by declaring a "total cease-fire." This can be seen as a move by Sinn Féin/IRA from (1,2) to (2,4), which is better for both players, yielding an efficient if lopsided state. In return, Sinn Féin/IRA hoped that Britain would also switch strategies to a conciliatory stance by entering negotiations to resolve the conflict, leading to a final settlement at (3,3).

After Sinn Féin/IRA halted its paramilitary activities, and the situation stood at (2,4), Great Britain was not responsive: it did not enter negotiations with Sinn Féin, nor did it make any significant concessions. While (2,4) is Great Britain's best outcome, from which it would have no motivation to move, Sinn Féin/IRA still possessed the threat power to move back to (1,2). In short, the threat was that if the British government did not move to a conciliatory stance, leading to (3,3), the IRA would return to a hard-line stance, reinstating the inefficient state of (1,2).

Great Britain, under the leadership of John Major, was not willing to open negotiations with Sinn Féin unless the IRA first surrendered its weapons. Thus, the situation stood at (2,4) after the IRA declared a cease-fire in 1994. The British, by demanding that the IRA go one step further and disarm itself, sought to eliminate its adversary's threat power—that is, its power to revert to H and, once again, to inflict on Britain one of its two worst outcomes. If Sinn Féin/IRA did return to H, Great Britain would continue to implement its own hard-line stance (because it preferred [1,2] to [4,1]), which would mean a return to violent conflict at (1,2).

By refusing to move from (2,4) to (3,3) by entering negotiations with Sinn Féin during the 1994–1996 cease-fire, Great Britain may have passed up an important opportunity to achieve a lasting peace. After the cease-fire, as the expression goes, the ball was in Britain's court. Yet Britain did little. The Prime Minister of the Republic of Ireland, John Bruton, claimed that "Britain had shown less courage, generosity and decisiveness since the paramilitary cease-fires last year than had many people in Ireland" ("Northern Ireland's Peace Process" 1995, 62). To most observers, Bruton seemed to be saying that Major had not been able to reciprocate the bold action taken by Gerry Adams in declaring a cease-fire and sustaining it for nearly a year and a half.

The IRA refused to disarm, prior to any settlement, for a very good reason: disarming would deprive it of the only leverage it had and would be "tantamount to surrender" (Clarity 1997e, A4). In the absence of a Republican threat, and the resolve and wherewithal to carry it out, Great Britain would have had no incentive to move away from its best state of (2,4).

The international commission that has been chaired by former U.S. Senator George Mitchell implicitly recognized this dynamic by recommending that all-party negotiations be conducted before the "decommissioning" of paramilitary arms. But Major rejected this suggestion and refused to enter ministerial-level talks with Sinn Féin.

In terms of our analysis, Great Britain was unwilling to move from (2,4) to (3,3). While Britain's stay-put strategy is rational in the short run because it enjoys its best state at (2,4), it is irrational if Sinn Féin/IRA is capable of reverting to (1,2), as proved to be the case. Indeed, Kevin Toolis argues that the IRA did not restart their bombing campaign "on a whim" (1996, A19). It believed, instead, that the British government betrayed promises, made in secret negotiations between 1990 and 1993, that it would be forthcoming if the IRA demonstrated good faith by renouncing violence and maintaining a cease-fire.

It was, unquestionably, Major's decision not to negotiate that persuaded Sinn Féin/IRA leaders to resume the use of violence in February 1996 (Holland 1996). Thus, after a cease-fire which lasted nearly a year and a half, the IRA resumed its paramilitary activities by commencing a bombing campaign in London, and later by extending the violent conflict to Northern Ireland, thereby returning the situation to the destructive (1,2) state.

It is always difficult for adversaries to move from hard-line positions to conciliatory ones. When, after years of struggle, leaders of two hostile groups are able to find the will and develop the trust to make such moves, an historic peace can be achieved. Such was the case in South Africa, where Nelson Mandela and F. W. de Klerk found a path to peace in 1990–1991. A similar reconciliation occurred in the Middle East in 1993, when Yasir Arafat, Yitzhak Rabin, and Shimon Peres negotiated a settlement—admittedly shaky today—between the PLO and Israel.

In both cases, the use of threats by the ANC and the PLO were decisive in pushing the process toward a compromise. Moreover, the leaders of the South African and Israeli governments were farsighted enough to see that there was a way out of a seemingly intractable conflict.

Perhaps we should call the game we have explicated the "Nobel Peace Prize Game," because Mandela, de Klerk, Arafat, Rabin, and Peres all were given that award for the courage, generosity, and decisiveness they had shown. If the situation is indeed analogous to the Middle East and South Africa, John Major may have missed an historic opportunity during the cease-fire to forge a peaceful settlement out of the conflict in Northern Ireland.[2]

A Path Toward Peace?

The IRA's restoration of its ceasefire in July 1997 offers hope that a peaceful resolution to the conflict in Northern Ireland might yet be within reach. In what follows, we apply our game-theoretic model to current attempts to attenuate the conflict, highlighting some of the obstacles that surely will be encountered along the way.[3]

Even before Tony Blair's election, it had become clear that a Sinn Féin/IRA cease-fire would have to precede any substantial conciliatory moves on the part of the British government. Like John Major before him, Blair insisted on this conciliatory move.

In theory, the game we present in Figure 1 can be moved from conflict at (1,2) to compromise at (3,3) via two paths. One path to compromise would involve Great Britain's changing from a hard-line to a conciliatory stance first, followed by an analogous change of strategy on the part of Sinn Féin/IRA. As a result, the situation would initially move from (1,2) to (4,1), and subsequently from (4,1) to (3,3). In fact, Gerry Adams tried to see if Blair might be willing to make some concessions before an IRA cease-fire by showing up uninvited at peace talks on June 3, 1997, declaring that Sinn Féin had a mandate to participate regardless of an IRA cease-fire (Clarity 1997b, A8).

But, as we have already noted, Great Britain could easily be seen as having caved in to terrorism if such a path were followed. Not surprisingly, Adams was not allowed to participate in the talks.

The second possible path toward peace requires that Sinn Féin/IRA change from a hard-line to a conciliatory stance first, followed by a reciprocal change on the part of Great Britain. In this scenario, the situation would initially move from (1,2) to (2,4), and subsequently from (2,4) to (3,3). While the outcome would be the same, the British government, under the leadership of both Major and Blair, has been insistent in its demand that *this* path be followed.

With the restoration of the ceasefire, Sinn Féin/IRA has in effect made the first move, shifting the situation to (2,4). This, we believe, is a necessary condition for a peaceful resolution to be reached. But, as the breaking of the cease-fire in February 1996 proved, it is not sufficient.

Sinn Féin/IRA declared a second cease-fire in July 1997 only after it became convinced that Great Britain would respond with significant concessions that would facilitate a lasting resolution to the conflict. In terms of our model, this means that Sinn Féin/IRA was willing to move the situation from (1,2) to (2,4)—temporarily giving Great Britain its best outcome—only because it believed that Great Britain would reciprocate by taking a conciliatory stance as well, thereby moving the situation from (2,4) to compromise at (3,3).

In some respects, Great Britain's unwillingness to make such concessions during the first cease-fire made declaring a second cease-fire a more daunting prospect. Suspicious of any new British promises of accommodation, Sinn Féin/IRA, nevertheless, chose to try again.

This second attempt, we believe, is largely due to the efforts of both Republican and British leaders. For his part, Gerry Adams seems to have personalized past failures, blaming John Major for the fact that Great Britain did not reciprocate Sinn Féin/IRA's last conciliatory move. Adams did this, at least in part, because he needed to convince his fellow Republicans, especially Sinn Féin and IRA leaders, that Blair could be trusted—and that the new British leadership should not be tainted by Major's past acts. In short, the message was that Blair, unlike Major, could be trusted to move from (2,4) to (3,3).

Blair also acted quickly to assure Sinn Féin/IRA that they were now dealing with a leader who had the political will—and a majority in Parliament not beholden to Northern Ireland Unionists ("The IRA Cease-Fire" 1997)—to reciprocate a ceasefire and to push toward a resolution. Within weeks of his election, Blair went to Belfast to explain his position on Northern Ireland. If Republican groups were willing to take a conciliatory stance, he promised, "I will not be slow in my response" (Clarity 1997a, 5).

The disarmament of the IRA is no longer a precondition to peace talks, though it will almost surely have to be part of a final agreement. As was true in the case of the first ceasefire, it seems implausible to expect Sinn Féin/IRA to forfeit the threat of paramilitary activities until a satisfactory settlement is reached.

John Major's insistence during the 1994–1996 cease-fire that the IRA give up its arms before participating in formal negotiations derailed any hope of a compromise at that time. Blair, it seems, has come to office far more cognizant of the fact that Sinn Féin/IRA will refuse to disarm before a settlement is reached; he has also proven himself sensitive to Sinn Féin/IRA's view that one of the most important functions of its weapons is the defense of the Catholic population from Protestant attacks. Blair's peace initiative of June 1997 stipulated that disarmament would *not* be a precondition to talks, that disarmament talks should be held *simultaneously* with peace negotiations, and that *both* Protestant and Catholic groups would, eventually, have to surrender their arms (Hoge 1997a, A7).

The issue of disarmament is shaping up to be one of the most difficult obstacles to overcome. The Reverend Ian Paisley, head of the hardline Democratic Unionist Party, complained that Sinn Féin was being offered a chance to join the peace talks without relinquishing "one weapon" (Hoge 1997a, A7). Some consider Sinn Féin/IRA to have "bombed its way to the negotiating table" (Clarity 1997d, 1, 6). But for the reasons spelled out earlier, no one should expect Sinn Féin/IRA or the Unionists to disarm completely before a final settlement, though it is possible that both Republican and Unionist groups might reduce their arsenals during the talks. At this stage, the participants have committed only to "consider and discuss" the issue of disarmament (Hoge 1997c).

For leaders on both sides, the window of opportunity will be open for a limited period of time. Blair's election, and his stance on Northern Ireland so far, have elicited both good will and some concrete actions. Should the negotiations drag on or terrorism flare up, however, momentum will surely be lost.

The path toward peace that we have laid out here is certainly laden with pitfalls at several junctures. In order for a peaceful settlement to be reached, the Sinn Féin/IRA cease-fire must hold, Great Britain must assure Sinn Féin/IRA that the cease-fire will be reciprocated with significant concessions, and complete disarmament of Sinn Féin/IRA must not be made a precondition to negotiations. Then, even with all these necessary conditions met, the details of a final compromise agreement must be worked out. To add to the difficulties, all this and more must be accomplished within a short period of time—the peace talks are projected to conclude in May 1998 (Hoge 1997b).

Still, it was not that long ago that peace in Northern Ireland seemed impossible, rather than difficult, to achieve. Much rests on what transpires in the near future. If Blair, Adams, and other leaders involved in Northern Ireland—especially David Trimble, the moderate head of Northern Ireland's largest Protestant party, the Ulster Unionists, who has joined the peace talks—can find a path toward peace, their efforts will be worthy of Nobel consideration. Then it may be said that the exercise of threats brought these efforts to fruition. ∎

Notes

This is a substantially revised and expanded version of Brams and Togman (1996). Steven J. Brams gratefully acknowledges the support of the C. V. Starr Center for Applied Economics at New York University.

1. Various compromises that have been proposed include partitioning Northern Ireland between Great Britain and the Republic of Ireland and rule by a joint Anglo-Irish authority. To facilitate reaching a compromise, the simultaneous surrender of weapons by the IRA and Unionist paramilitary groups has been proposed by former U.S. Senator George Mitchell, who has chaired an international commission overseeing peace talks.

2. In fact, the Nobel Peace Prize was given in 1976 to Betty Williams and Mairead Corrigan, founders of the Northern Ireland Peace Movement, which was later renamed Community of Peace People.

3. While the 2 × 2 game we postulate, and the rational play of it based on TOM, seem to us to illustrate how a compromise could be forged, an alternative formal analysis of this conflict is given in Miall (1996) using "drama theory." In contrast to our treatment, Miall contends that there must be *preference* changes, which drama theory allows for, on the part of a number of parties in order to achieve a peaceful settlement. As we see it, however, changes in *strategies* by the players would be sufficient to resolve the conflict, given that Sinn Féin/IRA has threat power. Furthermore, strategy changes, we believe, are more empirically plausible and theoretically parsimonious than preference changes.

References

Aughey, Arthur. 1994. "Conservative Party Policy and Northern Ireland." In *The Northern Ireland Question: Perspectives and Policies,* ed. Brian Barton and Patrick J. Roche. Aldershot, UK: Avebury.

Brams, Steven J. 1994. *Theory of Moves.* Cambridge: Cambridge University Press.

Brams, Steven J., and Jeffrey M. Togman. 1996. "The Dynamics of the Northern Ireland Conflict." *Oxford International Review* 7 (2): 50–4.

Chepesiuk, Ron. 1997. "The Weight of History: Ulster's Troubling Standoff." *New Leader* 80 (4): 10–11.

Clarity, James F. 1997a. "Blair Makes Offer to Renew Contact With I.R.A. Wing." *New York Times,* May 17, 1, 5.

———. 1997b. "Ulster Talks Resume With Warning That Violence Can End Them." *New York Times,* June 4, A8.

———. 1997c. "I.R.A. Announces A New Cease-Fire Beginning Today." *New York Times,* July 20, 1, 9.

———. 1997d. "Sinn Féin Is Invited by Britain to Join Peace Talks." *New York Times,* August 30, 1, 6.

———. 1997e. "I.R.A. Offers Support (of a Sort) for Nonviolence." *New York Times,* September 12, A4.

Clark, Liam. 1994. "Contemporary Republican Politics." In *The Northern Ireland Question: Perspectives and Policies,* ed. Brian Barton and Patrick J. Roche. Aldershot, UK: Avebury.

Hoge, Warren, 1997a. "Blair Offers New Ulster Deal; Key Is Disarming Both Sides." *New York Times,* June 26, A1, A7.

———. 1997b. "Sinn Féin Leader Says He Expects I.R.A. Cease-Fire." *New York Times,* July 19, 1, 5.

———. 1997c. "New Truce, New Questions." *New York Times,* July 22, A8.

Holland, Jack. 1996. "October Surprise!" *Irish Echo,* February 21–27, 1, 39.

"The I.R.A. Cease-Fire" (Editorial). 1997. *New York Times,* July 21, A16.

Miall, Hugh. 1996. "Drama Theory and the Northern Ireland Peace Process." Department of Politics and International Relations. Lancaster University, UK. Preprint.

"Northern Ireland's Peace Process: The Nitty Gritty." 1995. *The Economist,* November 18, 62–63.

O'Leary, Brendan, and John McGarry. 1993. *The Politics of Antagonism.* London: Athlone Press.

Rose, Richard. 1971. *Governing Without Consensus: An Irish Perspective.* Boston: Beacon Press.

Ruane, Joseph, and Jennifer Todd. 1996. *The Dynamics of the Conflict in Northern Ireland.* Cambridge: Cambridge University Press.

Toolis, Kevin. 1996. "Why the I.R.A. Stopped Talking." *New York Times,* February 21, A19.

von Neumann, John, and Oskar Morgenstern. 1953. *Theory of Games and Economic Behavior.* 3rd ed. Princeton University Press.

Appendix A: Comparison with Chicken and Prisoners' Dilemma

The 2 × 2 game we used to model the Northern Ireland conflict combines certain properties of the well-known games of Chicken and Prisoners' Dilemma. In the game depicted in Figure 1, the row player (Sinn Féin/IRA) has the same preferences as those found in the game of Chicken, while the column player (Great Britain) has Prisoners' Dilemma preferences, as can be seen from a comparison of these three games (see Figure 2).

Both Chicken and Prisoners' Dilemma are *symmetrical games:* the players rank the diagonal outcomes the same, and the off-diagonal outcomes are mirror images of each other. In both these games, the row and column players are interchangeable, because they face the same strategic choices: what is rational for one player is also ra-

tional for the other. In the Figure 1 game, by contrast, the row and column players face different strategic choices.

In Chicken, neither player has a dominant strategy and, as a result, it is impossible to predict which of the two pure-strategy Nash equilibrium outcomes, (4,2) or (2,4), will be selected (if either). In Prisoners' Dilemma, on the other hand, both the row and column players have dominant strategies (their second strategies), yielding the unique Nash equilibrium outcome of (2,2). This Nash equilibrium, however, is inefficient, because (2,2) is worse for both players than (3,3).

In the game depicted in Figure 1, the players are in a different predicament from that posed by Chicken or Prisoners' Dilemma. Only the column player has a dominant strategy (its second strategy). According to classical game theory, the row player will anticipate this choice and choose its own first strategy, resulting in the Nash equilibrium outcome of (2,4) that is underscored.

In none of these three games does the compromise outcome of (3,3) constitute a Nash equilibrium. In Prisoners' Dilemma, the outcome that classical game theory predicts, (2,2), is worse for both players than (3,3), and in Chicken the two predicted outcomes, (4,2) and (2,4), lead to a best outcome for one player but a next-worst outcome for the other. The Figure 1 game gives a similar lopsided result, (2,4), but one that favors only the column player.

According to TOM, however, the compromise outcome of (3,3) in all three games can be achieved through the use of threats. Each player can threaten to choose its second strategy, associated with its opponent's two worst outcomes (1 and 2), if its opponent does not choose its first strategy when the threatener does. If this threat it credible, both players will choose their first strategies, producing the (3,3) outcome, which is clearly better for the players than a 1 or 2 outcome.

As we pointed out earlier, Sinn Féin/IRA made such a threat but failed to induce (3,3) during the 1994–1996 cease-fire because Great Britain refused to heed that threat. Sinn Féin/IRA then carried out its threat and resumed paramilitary activities, resulting once again in conflict at (1,2).

Figure 2 • Payoff Matrices of Three Games

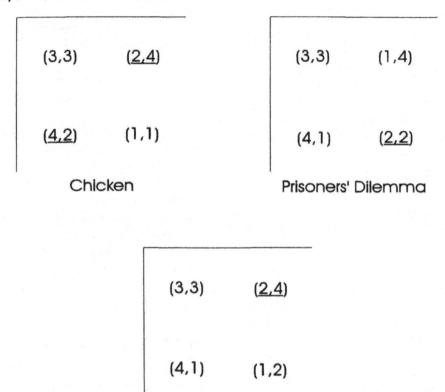

Chicken

Prisoners' Dilemma

Figure 1 Game

Key: (*x, y*) = (payoff to row player, payoff to column player)
4 = best; 3 = next best; 2 = next worst; 1 = worst
Outcomes associated with Nash equilibrium strategies underscored

The deterrent threat that induces (3,3) in the Figure 1 game can be undermined by a compellent threat (Brams 1994, chap. 5). Specifically, the column player, by sticking with its second (dominant) strategy, can compel the row player to choose between the inefficient (1,2) and the efficient (2,4). If the column player has threat power, the row player can thereby induce the choice of (2,4), which is also the unique Nash equilibrium outcome. Similarly in Chicken, if the row player has threat power, it can induce (4,2), whereas if the column player has threat power, it can induce (2,4).

Neither player has a compellent threat in Prisoners' Dilemma, so there is nothing to undermine a deterrent threat, on the part of either player, that can induce (3,3). While it is true that compellent threats might interfere with the choice of (3,3) in both the game depicted in Figure 1 and Chicken, a deterrent threat can, in principle, work to induce (3,3) in these games. In the Northern Ireland conflict, time will tell whether the IRA deterrent threat, after its failure under John Major, will succeed in inducing Tony Blair to choose C, yielding the compromise (3,3) outcome.

Why Was This Research Needed?

1. What is the background of the political conflict in Northern Ireland? Explain the positions of the principal groups involved—Great Britain, Sinn Féin/IRA, and the Protestant Unionists.
2. What ups and downs in the peace process occurred in Northern Ireland in the 1990s?
3. What "life-and-death questions" posed by the violence in the Northern Ireland situation do Brams and Togman seek to address in their analysis?

How Was the Topic Studied?

1. What particular interval of time is of interest in Brams and Togman's strategic analysis?
2. How would you summarize the "theory of moves" presented in the reading? The authors describe it as a "deductive model." Explain the difference between a deductive analysis and an inductive analysis.
3. How do the authors make use of a 2 × 2 table (see Figure 1) in identifying the strategic alternatives available to Great Britain and Sinn Féin/IRA? What is the conceptual variable that defines the table?
4. What do the numbers in the "payoff matrix" in Figure 1 mean? What makes the authors' 1–4 payoff scale ordinal in nature?

What Are the Findings?

1. Although political compromise might seem to be an obvious solution to the Northern Ireland conflict, how do the numerical rankings of this model explain why compromise is not the most appealing strategic option for either of the two major players?
2. According to the authors, why does state (2,4) qualify as a "Nash equilibrium" in game theory terminology? Why are all of the remaining states—(3,3), (4,1), and (1,2)—unstable positions? How does this analysis justify the British government's past refusal to negotiate with Sinn Féin?
3. In what way does the theory of moves introduce a dynamic dimension into game theory analysis?
4. What is the concept of "threat power"? How does adding this variable to the model help explain movements within the payoff matrix? Why might short-term rationality and long-term rationality differ when threat power is taken into consideration?
5. What two pathways to peace does this model suggest from state (1,2) to state (3,3) in Figure 1? Why do the authors maintain that setting the IRA's disarmament as a precondition to talks could be detrimental to a negotiated peace agreement in Northern Ireland?

What Do the Results Mean?

1. Abstract theoretical models sometimes are criticized for oversimplifying reality. If you believe such a criticism applies to the theory of moves, what additional factor(s) would you recommend bringing into the analysis of strategic options and incentives in the Northern Ireland conflict?
2. How would you assess the IRA's July 2005 announcement of its disarmament, according to the game theory application in this reading? Explain how the announcement supports or contradicts the theory of moves. What would the model predict must happen next if this disarmament is to lead to a lasting peace in Northern Ireland?
3. For what other kinds of conflicts between nations, institutions, or individuals could the theory of moves be a useful analytical approach?
4. Give an example of a research hypothesis you can derive from the theory of moves that could be tested through statistical analysis of empirical data.

Afterword from Steve Brams and Jeffrey Togman

Our main argument in this article was that threats could stabilize cooperation in certain conflicts as long as the threats were viewed as credible. That situation came about in Northern Ireland in 1998. Since then, the delicate peace between Catholics and Protestants has mostly held, largely because the threat of new violence remains real if agreements are broken. In addition, the economy of Northern Ireland has prospered with the return of peace, which makes a reversion to conflict even less appealing.

Threats not backed up by force led to futile efforts to bring peace to the former Yugoslavia throughout most of the 1990s; only in 1999 was force finally used to terminate the civil war in that troubled region. Recently, threats against violators of international standards have become more credible through the prosecution of war criminals by an international court of justice in The Hague. But when threats are viewed as empty, which has been sadly true in several African countries and a few other countries (e.g., Haiti), getting warring parties to cooperate has proved far more difficult, which is exactly what the theory of moves predicts.

Putting It All Together

The social learning theory concept of "communities of practice" describes groups of people who have a shared interest and who "value their collective competence and learn from each other" (Wenger n.d.). Communities of practice are devoted to both the development and the application of knowledge. The types of problems addressed, as well as the methods employed, define the community's practice domain. Although the classroom setting can be important for introducing a student to a community of practice, mature participation in the community is achieved only through practical engagement beyond the classroom with work that links the novice to fellow engaged practitioners at varying levels of expertise.

Political science students completing their first course in quantitative methods have taken a big step toward becoming part of a distinctive community of practice within their discipline. Training in statistics and related quantitative methodologies provides them with a means for understanding the conversation that is taking place among empirical researchers who use these techniques in preparing journal articles, books, reports, and other publications that add to the profession's knowledge base. Such training also equips students for data gathering and analysis of their own. While the pathways they follow from projects of modest difficulty to more challenging investigations may differ, depending on the academic or employment situation in which their applied practice takes place, the logic underlying this process of learning remains the same. Competency demands to be used and will grow with use; competency neglected soon will be lost.

Students who have read—and have carefully answered questions about—the twenty *PS* selections reprinted in this book have worked to understand the applications of an extensive collection of quantitative techniques. It is now time for a final, broader view of this subject. Toward this end, this conclusion identifies major conceptual themes that span the readings while offering commonsense advice for keeping an eye on the big picture in quantitative analysis.

It's All about Variation

In an article published in *Discover* in 1985, celebrated Harvard scientist Stephen Jay Gould discussed how the concept of statistical variation came to be of life-affirming importance for him (Gould 1985). Some years earlier, Gould had been diagnosed with mesothelioma, a deadly form of cancer. The bad news was compounded when Gould found published research indicating that patients with mesothelioma survived for a median period of only eight months. Instead of viewing this information as a death sentence, however, the quantitative expert applied his knowledge of variation to reach two conclusions: first, a much longer survival time for some patients was not inconsistent with the eight-month median mortality figure, and second, he possessed all of the characteristics likely to put him among the longest survivors of this illness. This insight was of tremendous value in boosting Gould's spirits as he prepared to battle his affliction. In fact, Gould did not pass away until 2002, and his death was related to a different form of cancer.

Gould (1985) characterized variation "as the hard reality" of biological life; the observation is true of social life as well. If everyone participating in a public opinion poll were to give the same response to one of the questions, the circumstance might be noteworthy because it is so rare. Researchers would be likely, however, to conclude that a larger and more diverse sample or a more sensitive survey instrument was needed. Constant values, like this uniform response to a poll question, leave little room for analysis, whereas variables invite description and exploration. This is why variation lies at the core of the statistical enterprise and is the topic that supports all subsequent learning in a first course on statistics (Moore 1990).

Variation persists as the central construct throughout the quantitative research process. As Pfannkuch (2005) writes, "Consideration of the effects of variation influences all thinking and reasoning through every stage of the empirical enquiry cycle—problem, plan, data, analysis, and conclusion" (83). A focus on proper discussion of variation will prevent a view of statistics as mere mechanical calculations (Makar and Confrey 2005). Describing variation in data distributions is a nuanced skill that requires attention to central tendency as well as dispersion, as Gould recognized, and a way of seeing the whole simultaneous with the parts. Similarly, the distinction between explained and unexplained variation is key to assessing the success of bivariate and multivariate analysis.

By means of answering just a few direct questions about variation, it is possible to fashion a concise but quite inclusive template for examining all of the research readings in this volume: What variable quantity was of principal interest? How was it analyzed? What interpretation was given to the source and/or the impact of this variation?

Level of Measurement as the Master Key

Every statistics textbook contains multiple chapters presenting myriad techniques of analysis, each with its own formulas for calculation and rules of interpretation. How can a student know which method is relevant for the problem at hand? If only there were a master key to help answer this question according to a simple logical principle.

Such a master key does exist, and it is found in the level of measurement of variables in the analysis. The distinction between nominal, ordinal, and interval variables (or, in abbreviated form, between categorical and numerical variables) is basic but of profound importance in the proper use of quantitative methods. Further, a variable's level of measurement has major implications for the conceptual underpinning of analysis because it reflects assumptions about the character of the variation being studied and the precision with which that variation can be gauged. In general, researchers prefer variables to be at the highest level of measurement possible because the associated quantitative techniques are more powerful and informative. But a variable's level of measurement should not be driven simply by the kind of statistics the researcher hopes to exploit.

Students should not be dismayed to find that this seemingly straightforward topic of measurement possesses surprising complexities. Some researchers are not as clear as they could be in explaining how or why their variables are measured as they are. Certain techniques, such as multiple regression, accommodate variables at different levels of measurement by adjustments in the way findings are interpreted. Variables can also sometimes be transformed from one level of measurement to another depending on the investigator's purpose. By paying close attention to these issues, when reading the studies of others or designing their own projects, students will begin to demystify the interrelationship of method and meaning that underlies all empirical research.

Nature, Significance, and Strength

When the time comes for interpreting the outcome of statistical computations in bivariate and multivariate analysis, students often struggle to organize their thoughts and express them clearly. They are uncertain about which facets of the results have greater and lesser importance. They wonder how little is too little to say about the numbers on the page, and how much is too much. In addition, the objective of translating numbers into sentences calls for a relatively standard means of discussing issues that recur across all analytical situations, rather than inventing new verbal formulations at every turn. The triad of concepts that makes order of this seeming chaos comprises nature, significance, and strength.

The *nature* of a relationship describes the type of connection that exists between variables in a sample of data. It addresses whether there are signs of a pattern of covariation between variables and, depending on the level of measurement, the direction of that relationship, positive or negative. Making observations about these phenomena is part (but only part) of evaluating the accuracy of the hypothesis linking independent and dependent variables that frames a study.

Discussion of the *significance* of a relationship moves from talking about a sample to talking about a popula-

tion. The chief concern is whether the relationship that was described in a study's sample data can be said to exist in the population from which the sample was taken, factoring in a certain degree of error when reaching this conclusion. Some quantitative techniques permit specification of an interval that converts sample findings to population values, again at a certain level of confidence in producing these results. Findings of significance in a study can be articulated in several ways—by labeling a relationship as significant, by reporting probability values, or by rejecting the null hypothesis of no relationship between variables—and it is necessary to be conversant with all these alternative formulations.

Strength is a third dimension of interpretation that is connected to, but at the same time different from, the nature and significance of a relationship. Significance is directly influenced by the sample size in a study, whereas strength indicates the degree of association between variables. Consequently, relationships can be significant but not strong, strong but not significant, both significant and strong, or neither significant nor strong. Measures of strength sometimes indicate the direction as well as the magnitude of a relationship. Most are standardized to fall within a designated range, which eases the task of interpretation. Some, like the ubiquitous R^2, have concise verbal equivalents in terms of the percentage of variation accounted for, or explained, in a study's dependent variable.

Together, the concepts of nature, significance, and strength give students a reliable and comprehensive guide for interpreting statistical results when analyzing relationships between variables, whether in the context of a two-variable problem or a more complex multivariate model. They also provide a vocabulary, embedded within a strategy of explanation, which will help students combine numbers and words effectively for diverse audiences.

Quantitative Methodology as a Form of Rhetoric

In recent years, the rhetoric of the social sciences has received increasing attention. In *The Rhetoric of Economics,* Deirdre N. McCloskey (1998) underscores the use of science-based writing as a means of both informing and persuading. Practitioners of the craft make use of a common vocabulary, similar narrative forms, and agreed-upon types of evidence. According to this perspective, becoming proficient in a field of study is only partly about acquiring its accumulated knowledge. It is just as important to develop a facility for communication using the style of professionals who share the same topical interests and methods of investigation.

As illustrated throughout this book, empirical political science research involves a distinctive kind of communication. The author of one guidebook on learning to write in political science describes the main elements of political inquiry this way:

> Professional political scientists, as part of a discourse community, engage in a process of political inquiry that involves using research techniques, critical thinking skills, and theory building. In general, political inquiry involves posing a question (a hypothesis), collecting data, analyzing the data, and drawing conclusions about whether the data support the hypothesis. . . . The process functionally relates questions to evidence to conclusions to knowledge. (Schmidt 2005, 4)

It is useful to think about the readings in this book as a textual specimen for examining political inquiry carried out through quantitative analysis. The book's discussion questions encourage students to evaluate authors' success in putting research into context, presenting study methods and outcomes clearly, and explaining the disciplinary and real-world implications of their findings. Sometimes the effectiveness of such a presentation depends on seemingly minor considerations, such as the use of tables and graphs to display data. The point of this emphasis is to instill in students a critical sense toward writing about quantitative research, helping them see which practices are worth imitating and which might be improved upon.

Discussions of the rhetoric of social science sometimes highlight the way standard writing motifs can disguise weak evidence or make automatic appeals to authority (McCloskey 1998). Language can also be used by communities of shared discourse to exclude nonmembers (Shapiro 1984). These are real dangers to be noted by aspiring quantitative researchers in political science. However, as some rhetorical analysts also point out, specialized styles of communication are an inevitable byproduct of increasing sophistication and organization within a field of study. To avoid the pitfalls of any type of rhetoric, it is necessary first to master its forms, but with a self-consciousness about the strengths and weaknesses of the use of professional language.

More Complex Analysis May Not Be Better Analysis

Another kind of danger lurks in this field of increasingly sophisticated quantitative methods: the tendency to use the most advanced technique possible in all situations. A number of possible motivations underlie this practice. One is simply to demonstrate the depth of the researcher's knowledge of statistics. A second is to conform to the kinds of research being produced by colleagues or appearing in a particular journal where the researcher would like to publish the research. A third is the belief that complex analysis necessarily enhances the value of research findings. This "more is better" orientation is problematic because it can lead, in some circumstances, to poorly conceived research design, the application of techniques ill suited to the data in hand, or the use of quantitative techniques that are not fully familiar.

The readings in this volume contain several examples of basic—yet not simplistic—forms of research that rely on very accessible methods of quantitative analysis. They demonstrate the unassuming power of a percentage breakdown, an uncluttered pie chart, or a rudimentary cross tabulation when the technique is sharply focused on answering a well-framed research question. Sometimes more elaborate analysis will be needed to bring clarity to a picture of tangled causal relationships or to build on previously published research. However, there are many situations, particularly in the beginning phases of research on a topic, in which straightforward description and summary make a real contribution.

The lesson for students is always to be sensitive to matching the method to the question being researched.

The test of quality is not sheer intricacy but appropriateness. Any approach that inflexibly favors complexity over simplicity, or the arcane over the everyday, misses the simple truth that, in quantitative analysis, sometimes less can be more.

Statistical versus Practical Significance

There is a longstanding concern among statisticians regarding interpretation of the concept of significance that merits a brief summary here. As already noted, significance is related to sample size; therefore, it is relatively easy to satisfy the standard for rejecting the null hypothesis when dealing with large numbers in a study. However, all this finding establishes is that, at a certain level of confidence, the observed relationship between variables in a sample is not due to chance. It does not indicate whether this relationship is particularly noteworthy or meaningful in terms of the question being analyzed. In other words, as some researchers have explained, there can be a distinction between the *statistical significance* and the *practical significance* of a relationship (Moore and McCabe 2006, 424–428; Weinbach 1989).

This issue has been raised in this volume with regard to research on educational outcomes. Although Jordan and Sanchez in Reading 8 did not find a clear benefit from using videos in the political science classroom, what would it have meant to learn that a certain classroom innovation, like the use of new technology, resulted in significantly higher test performance for an experimental group? Interpreting the practical significance of such a finding requires additional scrutiny of the data to determine the amount of difference in mean test scores between groups. Also relevant is the distribution of scores within the experimental group, since statistical significance might have been produced by a small number of students for whom technology made a very big difference, rather than by a gain shared more evenly by all students. Such issues are paramount for the administrator who must decide how much money, if any, should be allocated in the budget for new classroom technology.

The analogy between this education example and empirical studies focusing on public policy questions should be plain. The challenge is recognizing when the results are "actionable" and worthy of resource commitments. Political values inevitably come into play when making these judgments, even when the numbers are unambiguous in their statistical meaning. In regard to quantitative research undertaken to advance theoretical understanding of a topic, the finding of statistical significance in a relationship does not necessarily mean that a large amount of variance in a dependent variable has been explained. Nor does it promise that accurate predictions in the dependent variable, whatever the behavior or attitude may be, can be made on the basis of this relationship.

Although the debate over remedies gets more complicated, involving such considerations as the "power" of statistical tests (Moore and McCabe 2006, 430–434), a couple of simple steps can go a long way toward enabling quantitative researchers to avoid overinterpreting small differences in a study. One is to adopt appropriately rigorous standards for hypothesis testing when working with large samples. Another is to include measures of the magnitude, or strength, of a relationship when reporting significance. Not only will these conventions help to put significance testing in perspective, they can also indicate when researchers should pay attention to nonsignificant relationships that have evident explanatory influence. Finally, in this as in other aspects of statistical practice, common sense plays a role. Researchers need to assess the importance of their findings in context, taking into account the purpose of a research project, existing research on the topic, and the audience.

All Research Can Be Criticized

There may be good research and bad research, but there is no such thing as research that is beyond criticism. It is difficult even to imagine what the concept of perfection could mean when it comes to quantitative empirical research. Every research project is an assembly of parts. Numerous choices, big and small, must be made about study design, methods of data collection, use of statistics, presentation of findings, and interpretation of outcomes. And, because most political science research takes place in the real world rather than as a mental abstraction, such choices reflect not just the researcher's ability to conceive a project effectively, but also constraints of time, money, and access to needed information. To say that a project cannot be criticized is to assert that no technical improvement is possible in any of the project's elements. Such a statement also presumes that all consumers of the research product—scholars, practitioners, and others—have had their varying perspectives and interests adequately addressed.

Not all criticism, of course, is fair criticism. It is important to judge a research study on its own terms, based on the author's stated objectives. In addition, the value of a study should be gauged by the contribution it makes to existing knowledge, not according to some ideal of potential scholarly gains. Discussion of the twenty readings in this book should have provided students with good practice in research criticism of a constructive nature, if undertaken with awareness of the kinds of theoretical and practical difficulties confronted on a regular basis by political scientists doing quantitative research.

A more positive way, perhaps, of acknowledging the vulnerabilities of quantitative empirical investigation is to say that no research provides the final word on a subject. It is always possible to imagine a next research effort incorporating methodological adjustments to sharpen or to extend the current state of knowledge. This is the way social science progresses—in zigzag fashion rather than in a straight line with a definite ending point. For students who understand this process, the journey has its rewards.

References

Gould, Stephen Jay. 1985. "The Median Isn't the Message." *Discover*, June, 40–42.

Makar, Katie, and Jere Confrey. 2005. " 'Variation Talk': Articulating Meaning in Statistics." *Statistics Education Research Journal* 4 (1): 27–54.

McCloskey, Deirdre N. 1998. *The Rhetoric of Economics.* 2nd ed. Madison: University of Wisconsin Press.

Moore, David S. 1990. "Uncertainty." In *On the Shoulders of Giants: New Approaches to Numeracy,* ed. L. Steen, 95–137. Washington, D.C.: National Academy Press.

Moore, David S., and George P. McCabe. 2006. *Introduction to the Practice of Statistics.* 5th ed. New York: W. H. Freeman.

Pfannkuch, Maxine. 2005. "Thinking Tools and Variation." *Statistics Education Research Journal* 4 (1): 83–91.

Schmidt, Diane E. 2005. *Writing in Political Science.* 3rd ed. New York: Pearson Longman.

Shapiro, Michael, ed. 1984. *Language and Politics.* New York: New York University Press.

Weinbach, Robert W. 1989. "When Is Statistical Significance Meaningful? A Practice Perspective." *Journal of Sociology & Social Welfare* 16 (March): 31–37.

Wenger, Etienne. n.d. "Communities of Practice: A Brief Introduction." www.ewenger.com/theory/index.htm.

Credits

Almond, Gabriel A., with Wolfgang Kraus. 1999. "The Size and Composition of the Anti-Nazi Opposition in Germany." *PS: Political Science & Politics* 32 (September): 563–569. Reprinted with the permission of Cambridge University Press.

Althaus, Scott L., and Devon M. Largio. 2004. "When Osama Became Saddam: Origins and Consequences of the Change in America's Public Enemy #1." *PS: Political Science & Politics* 37 (October): 795–799. Reprinted with the permission of Cambridge University Press.

Brams, Steven J., and Jeffrey M. Togman. 1998. "Cooperation Through Threats: The Northern Ireland Case." *PS: Political Science & Politics* 31 (March): 32–39. Reprinted with the permission of Cambridge University Press.

Butler, Daniel M., and Ray Christensen. 2003. "Mixing and Matching: The Effect on Student Performance of Teaching Assistants of the Same Gender." *PS: Political Science & Politics* 36 (October): 781–786. Reprinted with the permission of Cambridge University Press.

Clarke, Harold D., and Allan Kornberg. 1996. "Choosing Canada? The 1995 Quebec Sovereignty Referendum." *PS: Political Science & Politics* 29 (December): 676–682. Reprinted with the permission of Cambridge University Press.

Clinton, Joshua D., Simon Jackman, and Doug Rivers. 2004. "'The Most Liberal Senator'? Analyzing and Interpreting Congressional Roll Calls." *PS: Political Science & Politics*
37 (October): 805–811. Reprinted with the permission of Cambridge University Press.

Dulio, David A., Donald L. Goff, and James A. Thurber. 1999. "Untangled Web: Internet Use During the 1998 Election." *PS: Political Science & Politics* 32 (March): 53–59. Reprinted with the permission of Cambridge University Press.

Hillygus, D. Sunshine, and Todd G. Shields. 2005. "Moral Issues and Voter Decision Making in the 2004 Presidential Election." *PS: Political Science & Politics* 38 (April): 201–210. Reprinted with the permission of Cambridge University Press.

Hook, Steven W. 2003. "Domestic Obstacles to International Affairs: The State Department Under Fire at Home." *PS: Political Science & Politics* 36 (January): 23–29. Reprinted with the permission of Cambridge University Press.

Jordan, Donald L., and Peter M. Sanchez. 1994. "Traditional Versus Technology-Aided Instruction: The Effects of Visual Stimulus in the Classroom." *PS: Political Science & Politics* 27 (March): 64–67. Reprinted with the permission of Cambridge University Press.

Mackenzie, G. Calvin. 2002. "The Real Invisible Hand: Presidential Appointees in the Administration of George W. Bush." *PS: Political Science & Politics* 35 (March): 27–30. Reprinted with the permission of Cambridge University Press.

Mayer, Jeremy D., and Lee Sigelman. 1998. "Zog for Albania, Edward for Estonia, and Monarchs for All the

Rest? The Royal Road to Prosperity, Democracy, and World Peace." *PS: Political Science & Politics* 31 (December): 771–774. Reprinted with the permission of Cambridge University Press.

Mayer, William G. 2003. "Forecasting Presidential Nominations, or My Model Worked Just Fine, Thank You." *PS: Political Science & Politics* 36 (April): 153–157. Reprinted with the permission of Cambridge University Press.

Putnam, Robert D. 1995. "Tuning in, Tuning Out: The Strange Disappearance of Social Capital in America." *PS: Political Science & Politics* 28 (December): 664–683. Reprinted with the permission of the author and Cambridge University Press.

Rivera, Sharon Werning, Polina M. Kozyreva, and Eduard G. Sarovskii. 2002. "Interviewing Political Elites: Lessons from Russia." *PS: Political Science & Politics* 35 (December): 683–688. Reprinted with the permission of Cambridge University Press.

Russett, Bruce, Thomas Hartley, and Shoon Murray. 1994. "The End of the Cold War, Attitude Change, and the Politics of Defense Spending." *PS: Political Science &*

Politics 27 (March): 17–21. Reprinted with the permission of Cambridge University Press.

Thies, Cameron G., and Robert E. Hogan. 2005. "The State of Undergraduate Research Methods Training in Political Science." *PS: Political Science & Politics* 38 (April): 293–297. Reprinted with the permission of Cambridge University Press. Table 6 was revised by the authors for this book.

Traugott, Michael, Ted Brader, Deborah Coral, et al. 2002. "How Americans Responded: A Study of Public Reactions to 9/11/01." *PS: Political Science & Politics* 35 (September): 511–516. Reprinted with the permission of Cambridge University Press.

Zaller, John R. 1998. "Monica Lewinsky's Contribution to Political Science." *PS: Political Science & Politics* 31 (June): 182–189. Reprinted with the permission of Cambridge University Press.

Zhong, Yang, Jie Chen, and John M. Scheb II. 1997. "Political Views from Below: A Survey of Beijing Residents." *PS: Political Science & Politics* 30 (September): 474–482. Reprinted with the permission of Cambridge University Press.